American Jewry
and the
Civil War

By

Bertram Wallace Korn

Introduction by
Allan Nevins

A *Bellum Edition*
R. Bemis Publishing, Ltd.
Marietta, Georgia 30007
1995

ISBN: 0-89176-087-3

Cover Concept by David Productions
Cover Design and Graphics by
Penstroke Graphics, Atlanta, GA

Printed in the United States of America

First Printing: September, 1995

This edition is published by arrangement with
The Jewish Publication Society
Philadelphia, Pennsylvania

Bellum Editions
is a registered trademark of
R. Bemis Publishing, Ltd.
PO Box 71088
Marietta, GA 30007

DEDICATED

with love and reverence
to the blessed memory of
my grandparents

Rebecca Bergman (1866-1938)
Joseph Bergman (1860-1954)
Ray Folkman Korn (1870-1930)
Charles Korn (1866-1945)

BERTRAM W. KORN

Bertram W (allace) Korn was born in Philadelphia on October 6, 1918. He was educated at the University of Pennsylvania, Cornell, the University of Cincinnati, and at Hebrew Union College, where he was ordained rabbi in 1943 and received his doctorate in Hebrew Letters in 1949. During World War II, Rabbi Korn served as a chaplain in the U.S. Navy, and he has been Senior Rabbi of the Reform Congregation Keneseth Israel in Philadelphia since 1949. Rabbi Korn is the author of numerous articles and of a number of books, among them *Eventful Years and Experiences: Studies in Nineteenth Century American Jewish History*, *The American Reaction to the Mortara Case*, and *Benjamin Levy, New Orleans Printer and Publisher*. He received an honorary doctorate from Temple University in 1957, and served as president of the American Jewish Historical Society from 1959 to 1961.

TABLE OF CONTENTS

TABLE OF CONTENTS

INTRODUCTION

by ALLAN NEVINS

THIS IS A STRIKING STORY which the Reverend Doctor Korn has to tell; and it is safe to say that no student of the Civil War period will fail to be astonished by its scope, color and importance. The Jewish community when the war began was not numerically large—only about 150,000 people. It did not, as Dr. Korn points out, possess any great, dominant leader, such as English Jewry had in Sir Moses Montefiore, hero of the successful movement to gain British Jews full civil and political rights. But circumstances repeatedly made the American Jews the focal point of a significant and far-reaching struggle to establish principles of exact justice and equality and make them triumph over ignorance, prejudice and intolerance.

It is this struggle which gives Dr. Korn's scholarly and interesting book, with its wealth of new detail, its chief importance. He has not permitted himself to become immersed in local or special topics—in the history, for example, of the two Jewish companies which were raised for the Union armies in Chicago and Syracuse, and the two Jewish companies mustered for Confederate service in Georgia, or in the record of Jewish war activities in Cincinnati, New York and other centers. Such matters are not neglected, but they are not emphasized, for he is concerned primarily with the Jewish community as a whole—which, of course, was chiefly a Northern community. And in the record of this community what interests him most is the effort to lift human rights above restrictions based on race or religion; to make sure that in a war for enlarging the boundaries of freedom, minority groups which were doing their full share to gain victory would have their full share of liberty and respect. There are thus inspiring episodes in the story which he tells.

It was a battle for a great principle that Rabbi Fischel of New York led in urging that Jewish clergymen should have their due place in the corps of chaplains. The Congressional Act of July 22, 1861, which provided that all chaplains must be regularly ordained Christian ministers, was perhaps rather an expression of heedlessness than of bigotry; most Americans never thought of the Jews, a tiny group until the immigration of the 1850s. But Rabbi Fischel and his followers, rebuffed by Secretary Cameron, had to fight hard before they obtained the virtual repeal of the discriminatory and oppressive rule. With the detachment of a true historian, Dr. Korn shows that Fischel's brave and self-sacrificing effort was by no means given the complete rabbinical support it should have had. After Lincoln acted, success was slowly won; and on September 18, 1862—a memorable day—Jacob Frankel became the first American rabbi to serve as army chaplain.

Equally striking is the story of the spirited protest of Jewish champions against the shocking General Order No. 11, which General Grant issued on December 17, 1862, for the expulsion of all Jews "as a class" from his army department. That Order is a blot on the fame of one of our greatest generals; and the indifference which some high officials (such as Attorney-General Edward Bates) showed toward the instant movement for its abrogation is a blot on the record of our government. Here, again, a brave fighter arose. Cesar Kaskel of Paducah, one of the chief organizers of the protest, hurried to Washington and held a conversation with President Lincoln of which Dr. Korn gives a delightful account. The result was Halleck's peremptory revocation of The Order on January 4, 1863. All honor to Lincoln!—but the responsibility of Grant himself for this unjust act seems clear, and the historian shows also that not only the crass Ben Butler, but the brilliant and generally enlightened William Tecumseh Sherman, had shared a prejudice based on ignorance of the facts. It is good to note that Grant never again manifested any feeling against the Jewish community and was, indeed, a warm friend of some of its members. Cesar Kaskel's gallant captaincy of the campaign against this display of intolerance deserves to be remembered by all lovers of American liberty and fraternity.

Other parts of Rabbi Korn's book, based as it is on original and often previously unused sources, will instruct every student of the Civil War period. He tells us far more than we knew before about Lincoln's friendship for the talented British Jew, Abraham Jonas of Quincy, Illinois, and for that other interesting British-born figure, the chiropodist-peaceplanner Isachar Zacharie. Having Jewish contacts in the South, Zacharie felt able to carry on consultations with Southern leaders in which Lincoln (but not the Cabinet) took a keen interest. It was with good reason that the Jewish community took a fervent share in the national mourning on Lincoln's death. He had been a warm and constant friend of that community. But it was primarily because of their own determined energy that the Jewish group emerged from the war with their rights and immunities fortified and acknowledged; and in battling for their own due place in the American democracy, they had performed an important service to all Americans.

AUTHOR'S PREFACE

THIS VOLUME is an effort in group biography. Its subject is the American Jewish community and its experiences during that most fascinating of all eras in the American drama, the four years of Civil War.

It does not attempt to offer a full-scale portrait of American Jews—as individuals—in this period, but rather a portrait of American Jewry—as an organized, articulate, self-conscious community of Jews who expressed their sense of togetherness or distinctiveness in a concrete manner: religious, cultural, philanthropic, social or political. Our concern is not with individuals, Americans who happened to be Jews, but with the community *qua* community, with group experience rather than personal experience.

Severe limitations are inherent in this approach. It excludes such areas as the individual participation of Jews in the army, as well as their personal political affiliation and economic activity, except as these have some direct bearing upon religious or other communal problems.

It is with the area of consciously-lived Jewish experience that we are here concerned: the support which Jews, acting together as Jews, gave to the war efforts of the Union and the Confederacy; the expressed attitudes of their recognized leaders—rabbinic, lay and journalistic, speaking as Jews—towards slavery and abolitionism, Union and secession, war and peace; the problems of equal treatment before the law which confronted Jews as Jews in connection with the war; the prejudice against Jews as Jews which was stimulated by wartime tension; the attitude towards Jews which was expressed in the life and words of the Civil War President; the influence of war experiences upon the developing American Jewish community.

Comparison with more recent experience is unavoidable. The reader will instinctively draw his own parallels. . . There has never been a duplication of the Grant order of expulsion of Jews from the Department of the Tennessee, yet World War II saw as serious a rise in anti-Jewish prejudice as did the Civil War. Confederate Congressman Henry S. Foote has long since been forgotten, yet violent bigotry like his was again heard in Congress during World War II. Over three hundred Jewish chaplains served in the Army, Navy and Air Corps during the years 1941–1946, but thousands of isolated Jewish servicemen were still without benefit of a Jewish chaplain's ministrations. Early in World War I, American Jewish organizations centralized their welfare work for servicemen by the creation of the National Jewish Welfare Board, a step which

Civil War Jewry was too weak to make; yet Jews were still as unwilling as their grandfathers had been to accept the idea of segregated Jewish participation in other war-related welfare activities. More accurate records of the numbers and honors of Jewish servicemen were compiled during the two World Wars than during the Civil War, but their major purpose was still to refute the canards of the prejudiced. 1945 saw as sincere an expression of grief over the loss of a martyred war president as 1865, another president who demonstrated firm friendship for the Jews in a time of stress. . . .

Has the nature of the American Jewish experience changed drastically since 1860–1865? Let us see.

B.W.K.

Philadelphia, Pa.
August 5, 1950

AUTHOR'S PREFACE TO THE
PAPERBOUND EDITION (1961)

This book was originally written ten years ago without thought of the Civil War Centennial commemorations which are now focusing popular attention on every aspect of the most fascinating period in American history. Current interest prompts this republication in convenient paperback form, although I should have preferred to prepare a more thorough revision at this time. But in view of the flood of new Civil War source materials now appearing in ever-increasing numbers, it would be wiser, I am told, to defer a complete rewriting of the book, embodying the results of my continuing research during these years since 1951, until the Civil War Centennial has been concluded. I accede to this counsel, although I suspect that in the future as in the past, Civil War materials may well continue to outweigh those relating to any other event in our nation's history. Indeed, it seems quite unlikely that any volume on the Civil War, no matter how narrow its compass, will ever be "definitive" or "complete."

I cannot hope, in this brief preface, to present very much of the additional data which I have accumulated during these intervening years; but it may be instructive to add some references to and examples of new material, as indications of the rich and varied detail yet to be gleaned from the documents and publications of a century ago.

It should be stated, however, that none of the major contours or conclusions of any chapter or theme has been controverted as a result of my own researches or those of historian colleagues. Indeed, I have been heartened by the verification of my conclusions which has been provided by other students of the period.

The one general work of great significance which the interested reader should consult is Jacob Rader Marcus' three-volume *Memoirs of American Jews, 1776–1865* (Philadelphia, 1954–5). This splendid compilation includes a goodly proportion of informative Civil War reminiscences and autobiographical fragments which present the war from the vantage-point of many varied individuals.

There is little to add to the first chapter, other than to refer the reader to Barbara Miller Solomon's *Pioneers in Service, The History of the Associated Jewish Philanthropies of Boston* (Boston, 1956), for the history of one community's charitable organizations, an example of local historical research which has unfortunately not been followed by other

Jewish federations; and to the writer's *The American Reaction to the Mortara Case, 1858–1859* (Cincinnati, 1957), for an account of the maturing of American congregations and leaders under the pressure of that notable case, together with an examination of the attitudes towards Jews expressed by Catholics, Protestants, the secular press, and government officials.

Two works provide additional material on the subject of the attitudes of Jews towards slavery. The writer's paper on "Jews and Negro Slavery in the Old South, 1789–1865," in *Publications of the American Jewish Historical Society*, Vol. 50 (1961), pp. 151–201, offers a detailed examination of the following subjects: Jews as planters, and as owners of slaves; the treatment of slaves by Jews; the emancipation of slaves by Jews; Jews as harsh taskmasters; business dealings of Jews with slaves and free Negroes; Jews as slave dealers; cases of miscegenation involving Jews and Negroes; and opinions of Jews about the slave system. Morris U. Schappes (in his *Documentary History of the Jews of the United States* [New York, 1950], pp. 405ff. and 682ff.) has presented some interesting facts about the circumstances surrounding the second oral delivery and subsequent publication of Rabbi Morris J. Raphall's crucial sermon on slavery. The presentation of the sermon was originally requested by non-Jews associated with the American Society for Promoting National Unity, which was composed of Northerners and Southerners who were strongly opposed to abolitionism and the Republican Party, and who wished to promote American unity even at the cost of supporting slavery. The sermon was then repeated at a public meeting called by the Society, at which an appeal was made for funds for its publication. Raphall was not the only rabbi listed as a supporter of the Society's program and thesis; George Jacobs of Richmond, James K. Gutheim of New Orleans, and J. Blumenthal of Montgomery joined a number of Jewish laymen in giving public commendation to the Society.

A further interesting note needs to be added to the material on the experiences of the rabbis as narrated in the third chapter. Charles M. Segal has published an important new letter from Isachar Zacharie to President Lincoln in his article, "Isachar Zacharie: Lincoln's Chiropodist," in *Publications of the American Jewish Historical Society*, Vol. 44 (1954), pp. 112–13, which relates, in part, to Rabbi Gutheim:

St. Charles Hotel
New Orleans, May 8th, 1863

To his
    Excellency A Lincoln
    President of the United States
      Washington D C
        Dear Sir
        An intense excitement has pervaded this city for the past few days. First the issuing of General Banks' order notifying "regestered [*sic*] enemies" to leave this Department by the 15th inst. Then the arrival of the invincible

Illinois Cavalry at Baton Rouge, having performed the most brilliant feats of the War. Again the news of Porter joining Farraguet [*sic*]. You can form no idea of the joy which overcomes the hearts of all loyal people.

As for the rebels, I can see their despondency, not only for themselves but their cause. Were it not for the female portion of their families who I fear have become perfect monomaniacs, they would in many instances take the oath.

Revd Doctor Gutheime [*sic*] Minister of the Portagees [*sic*] Israelite Congregation of this city—registered enemy—called yesterday to see me & spoke most feelingly. In his heart he wishes the Union restored—for he says under its Government the Israelite has lived and prospered—Why then should he leave? It is his wife who influences him. Another thing he took the oath of allegiance to the Confederacy & could not satisfy his own conscience to take it now to the Government, but as I said before at heart he's for the Union & I believe his going out will do good.

Col Gardner Commanding the Illinois Cavalry is now here on a few days furlough. he is one of the most modest unassuming gentlemen I have ever seen[.] You should make him a General as he possesses the true mettle.

A friend with Schooner left here yesterday on mission to Pemberton. I look for him back in ten or fifteen days when I expect to go over. Please inform Mr Seward of this fact. While writing Commodore Farraguet has arrived from above Port Hudson, Porter took possession of Alexandria on the morning of the 6th that evening the advance Column of General Banks reached them. Thus the work goes bravely on.

Very respectfully
Your Most Obt Sert
I Zacharie M D.

Zacharie wrote a similar description of Gutheim's feelings to General Banks, which Segal quotes in *Publications of the American Jewish Historical Society*, Vol. 43 (1953), pp. 97–8. Segal takes Zacharie's report as evidence that Gutheim was a pure and simple opportunist. But I question this conclusion. Gutheim was probably a Unionist at heart, as were many if not most Southerners before Secession; but there is no evidence of disloyalty to the Confederacy on his part either before or after his journey into exile. At no time during his years in Montgomery after the writing of Zacharie's letter, so far as we know, did he attempt to influence people against the Confederacy, even in the darkest days of 1865. His friends in New Orleans and elsewhere continued to think of him as a patriotic Southerner. Had he actually felt as Zacharie reported, would he have gone into exile, would he have ministered to Southerners with such devotion, would he have returned to New Orleans, and would he later have refused to remain in the North as he did when he left the Temple Emanu-El pulpit in New York? Perhaps Zacharie's report was only wishful thinking; perhaps the chiropodist was trying to impress

Lincoln and Banks with his influence on a Jewish leader. The diary of Major Isaac Scherck (in the possession of his grandson, Henry J. Scherck of St. Louis), contains notations referring to Rabbi Gutheim's friendly ministrations to Confederate military personnel in the Montgomery area; this day-by-day loyalty can hardly be squared with Zacharie's report. If a choice has to be made between the chiropodist-spy and the gentle rabbi, I prefer to believe Gutheim, not Zacharie.

The chapter on the Jewish chaplaincy can be expanded with the addition of a number of further items. My suggestion, on page 57, that the Confederate Congress was more liberal than its Federal counterpart has caused a few eyebrows to be raised fairly high. One critic asserted that this thought could not be sustained with factual evidence. The simple truth is, of course, that there is no evidence whatever to the contrary; no rabbi is known to have applied for a commission as chaplain, nor did anyone in the government indicate that such an application would have been fruitless. But I have now turned up an interesting piece of ancillary evidence, which ought to satisfy all but the most rabid anti-Confederate historians. On September 4, 1862, a bill was introduced into the Confederate Senate, known as the Exemption Bill, which listed all of the categories of persons who would be exempt from conscription. The phrase which referred to the clergy was originally worded in this form: "every minister of the Gospel, licensed to preach according to the rules of his sect, and in the regular discharge of ministerial duties." This section was discussed in the Senate on September 16; an anti-clerical Senator moved to strike it out altogether, but his effort was defeated. On the following day, the word "licensed" was changed to "authorized," and an additional exemption which applied to all members of the Quaker and Dunkard sects was introduced. At that session, no one questioned the omission of rabbis from the list. On the following day, September 18, however, the *Richmond Dispatch* featured an editorial discussion of the issue, referring to the discrimination against rabbis and urging the further emendation of the bill. "Whilst this is a Christian country," said the editorial writer, "the principles of religious liberty are opposed to any such discrimination as is implied. . . . The Jewish ministers are entitled to exemption on the principles of the Constitution as much as any others. . . ." There are no verbatim minutes of the Confederate Congress' sessions nor of the meetings of its committees; fortunately, the Richmond newspapers reported these sessions quite fully, and their reports have been assembled and published in the *Southern Historical Society Papers.* But these reports do not record any discussion of the question. When the bill was passed on September 20, 1862, the phrase had been changed from "every minister of the Gospel" to "every minister of religion." Obviously what had happened in the meantime was that some legislators had read the *Dispatch's* comments and were disturbed by the implication of the original wording of the bill. Without any public debate or comment on the issue, then, they changed the bill so that Southern rabbis would also be exempted. These details are taken from *SHSP*, VIII (1928), pp. 29–30, 158, 168–9, 192–3. This swift remedy must be compared with the experience in the Union, as narrated in the text, where a Congressman actually did call attention to the question but was ignored, and where a whole year's worth of protests, petitions, conferences, and intercessions were necessary before the Federal law was changed. There was quite enough wrong with the Confederate Government without anyone's imputing to it a lack of consideration for Jewish citizens for which there is no evidence.

Although no Confederate rabbi was commissioned as a chaplain, two Confederate privates, who had previously acted as volunteer rabbis in their communities, may actually have officiated as chaplains. These men were Uriah Feibelman of Petersburg, Virginia, who later "produced proof of his ordination as a minister of the gospel in the Hebrew Church [*sic*] and of his being in regular communion with the said church and . . . [was] authorized to solemnize the rites of matrimony"; and B. Nordlinger of Macon, Georgia, who served as spiritual leader of Temple Beth Israel for a time during 1862. Feibelman was a private in the Petersburg Grays, Company C, of the 12th Regiment of Volunteer Virginia Infantry, and Nordlinger was a bugler in the Macon German Artillery. Louis Ginsberg refers to Feibelman in his *History of the Jews of Petersburg, 1789–1950* (Petersburg, 1954), pp. 42–5, and Nordlinger appears in Dr. Newton J. Friedman's manuscript *History of the Jews of Macon*, p. 32. There is, however, no contemporary documentary evidence of these men's services; only family traditions attest to their activity as leaders of Jewish worship in the Confederate forces.

Chaplain Jacob Frankel's monthly reports to the Office of the Surgeon General, recently located in the National Archives in Washington, indicate his responsibility for all of the Jewish patients in six military hospitals in the Philadelphia area. In view of the transportation problems, he could not visit more than one hospital a day, but the Chief Medical Officer of one complained to Washington that he had never been there at all; Frankel retorted by way of a letter that he had indeed served regularly at the institution, and had consistently reported his presence to the Executive Officer. That personage probably never bothered so to inform his superior.

Chaplain B. H. Gotthelf bore a heavier duty; he attempted to serve eighteen army hospitals, traveling as far as New Albany and Jeffersonville, Indiana. Since there were only two other (Christian) chaplains visiting these institutions, Gotthelf did not restrict his ministrations to Jews, as he informed his superiors in his monthly reports. In one of these, dated April 1, 1865, Gotthelf reported that he had thus far "succeeded in procuring about one thousand volumes of good German books for the hospitals," in his campaign to establish German libraries for both Jewish and non-Jewish German-speaking soldiers, which is discussed in the text.

An interesting problem which Rabbi M. Michelbacher of Richmond faced in his career as a volunteer civilian chaplain for the Confederacy concerns the court-martial of Private Isaac Arnold, of Company D of the Eighth Alabama Regiment, who was sentenced to execution by a firing-squad for cowardice and absence without leave in the presence of the enemy. Michelbacher appealed to General Robert E. Lee for mercy, and submitted a petition signed by a number of distinguished non-Jews, including Confederate Congressmen from Mississippi and Alabama. Michelbacher urged consideration for this young immigrant because, said the rabbi, he had not been aware of the seriousness of his offenses; and he also suggested that anti-Jewish prejudice had played some part in the court-martial:

> From what we have heard, we fear that the fact of being an Israelite and of foreign birth, has had an injurious tendency towards the decision of his deplorable fate—we hope for the sake of the common humanity of our race, that this report may be untrue. You, we feel assured, would not hesitate, were it necessary, to testify to the courage and soldier-like abilities of the Israelites in those legions of our beloved Confederacy that have aided in giving an heroic name to the army....

It has not been possible to ascertain any further information about Arnold's fate beyond Lee's reply to another letter from Michelbacher, which stated that "the sentence in the case of Isaac Arnold has been suspended, until the decision of the President shall be known." (The petition, dated March 18, 1863, is in the possession of Mrs. Harry Fivel of Norfolk, and was brought to my attention by Rabbi Malcolm Stern of that city; Lee's letter, dated April 2, 1863, is in J. William Jones, *Personal Reminiscences of Gen. Robert E. Lee* [New York, 1875], p. 443.)

Rabbi Michelbacher's requests to General Robert E. Lee for leave for Jewish soldiers so that they might attend services on Holy Days were more successful than I had originally thought. The London *Jewish Chronicle* (Dec. 16, 1864), in an undated reprint from a Richmond newspaper which relates the story of the death of Captain Madison Marcus at the defense of Fort Gilmer, states that Marcus had "asked no leave, considering that in performing his duty to his country he worshipped his God in an acceptable manner," "although a number of his people who were in the army were granted leave of absence to attend upon the ceremonies of the 'Feast of Atonement,' which is a season of release from all labor." Private Eugene Henry Levy of Company C, Dreux's Louisiana Battery, wrote in his diary on October 1, 1864, "as Mr. Michelbacher had appealed to Gen'l Lee on the subject of granting furloughs to Israelites, I attended his synagogue to testify my appreciation of his conduct." (Marcus, *Memoirs of American Jews, 1775–1865*, III, pp. 305–7.) We have discovered no record of such consistent activity on the part of any rabbi in the Union.

There is a heart-warming epilogue to Joseph A. Joel's description of the *Seder* in the mountains of West Virginia on Passover, 1862, as related on pp. 90–2. Subsequent to the original publication of this book, I discovered a letter from Joel's commanding officer which referred to the Jewish soldier:

> I got a letter from Joel tonight. He is the Jew who got eight bullet holes in his person and lives. He says he thinks he can stand service in a couple of months. He dont want to be discharged.

This commanding officer was a future President of the United States: Rutherford B. Hayes; the letter, dated "Log Cabin Camp, Dec. 21, 1862," and addressed to Hayes' wife, is in the Hayes Memorial Library, Fremont, Ohio, which also has files of a fascinating correspondence between Hayes and Joel indicating a long friendship and great mutual regard.

As local Jewish historical research continues, more data will be made available on the participation of Jews as individuals and as members of synagogal groups in war efforts on the home front. Newton J. Friedman's previously mentioned dissertation on the Jews of Macon refers to Mrs. S. Dessau's role as a founder and directress of the Macon "Ladies' Soldier Relief Society" (p. 30); Irving I. Katz's *The Beth El Story* (Detroit, 1955), p. 75, describes the participation of a number of Jewish ladies, representing their synagogue, at the organizational meeting of the Detroit Soldiers' Aid Society. Kate Cumming, in her *Kate: The Journal of a Confederate Nurse*, ed. by Richard B. Harwell (Baton Rouge, 1959), pp. 85, 152, refers to gifts to her hospital unit of money and food delicacies by the Hebrew Military Aid Society of Mobile. The Jews of New Orleans gave notable support to their city's Free Market, which was established for the benefit of the families of soldiers away on duty. Henry Florance, a noted Jewish leader, was a member of the executive committee of the Free Market, while B. DaSilva and B. Cohen held other committee posts. Lists of contributions sent to the Market by individual Jews include such varying items as a bundle of tape, boxes and barrels of fish, one live sheep, and four sacks of meal. Two New Orleans congregations made cash contributions, and the proceeds of a Hebrew Charity Ball were also presented to the committee. These facts are gleaned from *The Report of the Committee of the Free Market of New Orleans Established for the Benefit of the Families of Our Absent Volunteers* (New Orleans, 1862), pp. 2, 58, 60, 61.

Further investigation of the reports of Jewish companies at West Point and Macon, Georgia, has failed to establish their authenticity. The diary of Louis Merz of West Point, indicates that all of the Jewish young men of the community tried to enlist in the West Point Guards, but two were rejected because of poor eyesight; only five, including himself, were accepted. In view of this eyewitness account of Jewish participation in the Guards, which ultimately became Company D of the Fourth Georgia Regiment, it is unlikely that an all-Jewish Company existed. (*Pioneer Members and History of Temple Beth-El, 1859–1959; Diary of Private Louis Merz, C.S.A. of West Point Guards 1862*, [Chattahoochee Valley Historical Society Bulletin 4, West Point, 1959], pp. 10–11, 46–7.) Rabbi Newton J. Friedman searched the Macon records for information about a Jewish company, but he reports, as did Simon Wolf, (in *The American Jew as Patriot, Soldier and Citizen*, p. 135), that while more than thirteen Jews enlisted in the Macon German Artillery, references to an exclusively Jewish company cannot be found.

No further data has been published which might cast additional light on the circumstances surrounding the issuance of Grant's Order Number 11. But a slight flurry of excitement has been created over the detail of the numbering of the order, by Nathan Reingold's "Resources on American Jewish History in the National Archives," *PAJHS*, Vol. 47 (1958), p. 193. Originally labeled "Order Number 12," the heading of the edict expelling civilian Jews was changed by the government's editors when the total compilation of army orders was published in *The War of the Rebellion: Official Records.* The facts are clearly explained by Kenneth P. Williams, in *Lincoln Finds a General* (New York, 1956), Vol. IV, p. 512: General Order Number 9, which was drawn up at La Grange, Mississippi, on November 25, 1862, was never issued. The headquarters records carry the notation, "Recalled—will not be issued." But it was too late to change the numerical sequence of later orders. To avoid confusion now, however, it would seem to be wise for all concerned to accept the Federal editorial decision, and to continue to utilize the emended number rather than insist puristically that the original number be cited.

I find myself unable to permit Louis Ruchames' contentions in "The Abolitionists and the Jews," *PAJHS*, Vol. 42 (1952), pp. 131–56, to remain unanswered. Though the abolitionist movement was not *per se* anti-Semitic, some of its leaders did have anti-Jewish leanings. At the very least it can be asserted that the abolitionists were *not* interested in defending the civil rights of Jews; their reactions to the Mortara case, as outlined in the writer's volume on the subject, make that clear. Despite Ruchames' advocacy, it is certain that if they and other Republican Congressional leaders had been friendly to Jewish interests, they would have had *something* to say about the Grant order. As we have indicated, the Democrats utilized the Grant affair for political purposes; but Republicans should not be applauded for doing the same thing. Ruchames insists that "no question of constitutional rights was involved." Does he really believe that the banishment of members of a specific religious group, without trial, and without any evidence of grave conspiracy or danger, was not a violation of constitutional rights? Ruchames says further, in defense of the refusal of the Republicans to criticize Grant, that the real responsibility for denouncing the Grant order was Lincoln's, and that if the President did not see fit to do so, the Republican Senators and Congressmen certainly should not be expected to have done his job. But Lincoln's revocation of Grant's anti-Semitic order was highly publicized! Newspapers throughout the land carried reports far and wide that "the President instructed Gen. Halleck to countermand the order imperatively"—those were the words of the Washington correspondent of the *New York Tribune;* and the *New York Times* said, "The immediate and peremptory abrogation of Grant's order by the President saved the Government from a blot, and redeemed us from the disgrace of a military assault upon a people whose equal rights and immunities are as sacred under the Constitution as those of any other sect, class or race" (*Baltimore Sun,* Jan. 9, 1863; *New York Times,* Jan. 18, 1863). Dr. Ruchames has presented a useful corrective to Isaac Mayer Wise's prejudices against the abolitionists; but he has gone to the other extreme of rationalizing everything relating to the Jews that the abolitionists did or said. Perhaps reformers always need to be single-minded. I would not want to imply that the abolitionists were wrong in opposing slavery; I do suggest that their humanitarian concerns were quite limited if they could not interest themselves in the problems which Jews also faced.

The *American Jewish Archives,* Vol. IX (1957), pp. 83–125, has published a fascinating document about the life and activities of Jews in Memphis during the period of the Grant order, entitled "Kronikals of the Times," a composition in mock-Biblical style by Abraham Ephraim Frankland, president of the Memphis congregation. A fanatical supporter of the Confederacy, Frankland insists that he himself never took part in any of the speculative excesses of the time, and that he was innocent of wrong-doing, even on the one occasion when he himself was arrested, during services, at the synagogue. But, despising both the Northern Jews who came South after the Federal occupation, and the local Jews who took the oath of allegiance to the Union, he bitterly criticizes most of his co-religionists. He tells one story after another: of Rabbi Tuska's preaching to the congregation, warning the people against malefaction, and being denounced to the military authorities by Northern worshippers; of Northern Jews being driven out of town by Southern Jewish boycott; of cotton smuggling by Jews whom he calls by name; of the arrest of certain Jews for the sale of contraband; of Jewish prisoners bribing their way out of jail; of deals which Jews consummated with high-ranking (Gentile) officers. It makes for enthralling reading:

this spiteful, self-righteous man's denunciation of his co-religionists. But it is especially important because even Frankland, with all his disdain for so many of his fellow-Jews, was shocked at the widespread corruption of detectives, civil officials, and military officers.

The chapter on anti-Semitism might well be expanded to twice its present length. Much additional material has appeared in newly published diaries, reminiscences, and letter collections, revealing a serious amount of anti-Jewish prejudice both North and South. Yet when I describe it as "serious," I should not want to be misunderstood. All of the anti-Semitism of the war period put together, including the Grant order, was only a minor social malady in the total outpouring of hatred, fear, anger, privation, suffering, propaganda, tragedy, and grief which made the war so cruel an experience for the American people. Yet, in terms of the Jewish experience in America, with which we are here concerned, this outbreak of prejudice loomed large. It was far greater in articulation, repetition, frequency, and in action too, than had ever before been directed against Jews in America.

There is no need here for further illustrations of this prejudice, since I hope to be able to publish a fresh study of the subject within the next several years. But some indication of the shock of the all-pervasive mood of recrimination against Jews on a sensitive young Jewish boy's mind might be gathered from a letter which Gratz Cohen, a student at the University of Virginia at Charlottesville, wrote to his distinguished father, the Honorable Solomon Cohen of Savannah, on January 9, 1864, now preserved in the Miriam Gratz Cohen Papers at the Southern Historical Collection of the University of North Carolina:

> It is a mournful fact that in these troubled times when intolerance & prejudice cast their baneful seed throughout the land, which from one quarter of it to another rings with abuse of God's people, that we have done nothing for our religion & are so blind to our own interests. Jewish wealth, rapidly gained has been scattered in all directions & for every body's benefit, but their own—private charities, public charities, sectarian charities have been enriched by their bounties, yet the newspapers of the country lift up their lying tongues against them & no defending voice has been heard. . . . Why have we no Jewish newspaper to justify us before the world & explain to us our position, to remind Israel, that it is not a race of shopkeepers, but a peculiar people set apart by *Jehovah* for His service & glorification. Indeed! there should be a paper devoted to Jewish interests, established at Columbia or some other safe inland town, with Mr. [George] Jacobs or some other such man as editor & those Jews, who have given their thousands to Gentile charities should contribute their mite to its support. . . .

The journal was never established; before the war came to its inevitable end, Gratz Cohen had been drafted from his studies and killed in battle. Despite his resentment at the anti-Semitic propaganda so characteristic of the time, Gratz Cohen did not withhold from the Confederacy the greatest service in his power to offer—his life.

My reading of anti-Semitism in general and in particular has been challenged by Dr. Oscar Handlin in *Commentary*, XII (1951), pp. 287–9. He calls special attention to certain articles in *Harper's Weekly* by the commentator who signed himself "the Lounger," and suggests that they were really "a long argument *against* anti-Semitism." Without taking up too much space, I will ask the reader to judge from this excerpt from *Harper's* of August 1, 1863, whether its author was encouraging anti-Semitism or arguing against it:

AN OPEN LETTER
My Dear Friend:

You are a German and a Jew, and you have come to make your living in a foreign land, of which Christianity is the professed religion. You have no native, no political, no religious sympathy with this country. You are here solely to make money, and your only wish is to make money as fast as possible. You neither know our history nor understand our Government; but, believing that all men are selfish and mean, nothing is absurder to your mind than the American doctrine of popular government based upon equal rights.

This being the case with you and thousands like you, you are inevitably a Secessionist, a Copperhead, and a Rebel. But why deceive yourself since you deceive nobody else? Your opinion is of no value, because you neither know nor care anything about the subjects upon which you pronounce. If things can be kept quiet by agreeing to dissolve the Union and to destroy the Government, you are for that course. And you are the enemy of all who will risk war to save the nation. If things can be kept still by slaughtering Irishmen, you cheerfully agree. . . . You want money. . . . If you can have a fine house, and horses, and servants, and fifty thousand dollars a year, you have what you want, and all the rest is moonshine. . . . And whatever in this country is despotic, mean and repugnant to the great and fundamental doctrines of equal rights before the law, receives your hearty sympathy and support. The country you left did not regret your coming away; the country in which you trade will not mourn your departure.

Yours, with all the respect possible,
THE LOUNGER

Handlin conveniently forgets to mention that this writer of "a long argument *against* anti-Semitism" (his italics) was silent at the time of the Grant order, when he really had an opportunity to declare himself in favor of the "great and fundamental doctrines of equal rights before the law" over which he so piously pontificated.

Charles M. Segal has added to our knowledge of Isachar Zacharie's war-time career in two articles already cited; Zacharie will probably continue to attract interest as one of the most unusual personalities in the entire constellation of Lincoln's Washington. Yet another Lincoln-

Zacharie letter needs to be added to the Appendix in order to complete the record of that peculiar relationship. The letter, the only extant one which Lincoln wrote to Zacharie, is in the Robert T. Lincoln Papers in the Library of Congress in draft form:

Executive Mansion,
Washington, Sep. 19, 1864.

Dr. Zacharie
  Dear Sir

I thank you again for the deep interest you have constantly taken in the Union cause. The personal matter on behalf of your friend, which you mention, shall be fully and fairly considered when presented.

Yours truly
A. Lincoln

The writer has given additional consideration to Lincoln's relationship to the Jews, with particular reference to his "About Jews" letter of January 25, 1865, in "Lincoln and the Jews," *Journal of the Illinois State Historical Society*, XLVIII (1955), pp. 181–90. This paper also furnished the writer with the opportunity to publish and discuss a newly discovered Lincoln letter (in the writer's collection of Jewish Americana), only the third known letter in which the Civil War President referred to a Jew as such:

Executive Mansion,
Washington, Nov. 4, 1862.

Hon. Sec. of War.
  Sir

I believe we have not yet appointed a Hebrew—As Cherie M. Levy, is well vouched, as a capable and faithful man, let him be appointed as Assistant Quarter-Master, with the rank of Captain.

Yours truly
A. Lincoln

Much more research into Civil War Jewish history remains to be done. The whole story of Jewish military participation needs to be told; hundreds upon hundreds of regimental histories will have to be searched before that can be done. The remarkable story of Jewish economic development in the North, particularly in the clothing industry, has yet to be written. Hardly any community's local experiences during the Civil War, with the notable exception of Memphis, Tennessee, have been transcribed in detail. If this book can serve an additional purpose beyond informing and enlightening the casual reader and the serious student, it will be to encourage some of those in the latter category to make it possible for all of us to learn more about Jewish experiences during that crucial period, 1861–1865.

B.W.K.

Wyncote, Pa.
March 2, 1961

I AMERICAN JEWRY IN 1860

ALTHOUGH JEWS had lived in the New World since 1654, when twenty-four unwanted refugees had insisted on remaining in New Amsterdam over the objections of Peter Stuyvesant, the American Jewish community as a nationally organized community was still in the process of birth in 1860. There had simply been too few Jews previously to establish anything more complex than a localized communal life in various cities and towns. At the time of the first census, in 1790, it is estimated, there were, at the most, two thousand Jews in a population of four million. By 1850, when the nation had passed boldly through a period of tremendous territorial expansion and numbered over twenty-three million inhabitants, there were about fifty thousand Jews.[1]

During the decade 1850–1860, however, when a little less than two million immigrants flooded into the United States from Ireland, England, and Central Europe, the number of Jews almost tripled. It was American Jewry's greatest period of expansion prior to the 1880s. Severe economic depression, the failure of the revolutionary movements which swept through Europe in 1848–9, and America's gradual growth in stature in the mind of the downtrodden peoples of Europe, combined to propel ever more Jews as well as non-Jews across the Atlantic. Exact statistics are unavailable, but we cannot be very far from the mark in estimating that at least two-thirds of the approximately one hundred and fifty thousand American Jews in 1860 were immigrants. Sizable Jewish communities had already been established in the metropolitan areas of New York, Philadelphia, Cincinnati, Baltimore, and Louisville by 1850, with a sprinkling of individuals and family groups in every other section of the country. There were, then, about fifty Jewish congregations in the country, with fifteen concentrated in New York City alone. New York City's Jewish community had already become the leading one in the country, with a population of eleven or twelve thousand souls, over twenty percent of all the Jews in the United States. The following decade saw the formation of fifteen more congregations in that metropolis, and one hundred and thirty-five others spread far and wide across the nation.[2]

By 1860, cities whose Jewish population had been insignificant in 1850 had become Jewish centers: St. Louis, San Francisco, Boston, Cleveland, New Orleans, Newark, Milwaukee, Detroit, Pittsburgh, and Chicago. Immigrant Jews came to those cities because they were growing commercial and manufacturing centers; Jews followed general population

1

trends. Altogether, those ten cities, and the five mentioned above which had large Jewish communities prior to 1850, contained about two-thirds of all the Jews in 1860. The urban tendency of American Jews had already become fixed as a norm: European despots had prohibited them from owning land through too many centuries for many to think of tilling the soil; as a religio-cultural minority they were naturally inclined to dwell together in order to preserve their religious practices and worship.

These hundred thousand immigrants of the pre-Civil War era were faced with the necessity of adjusting themselves to a strange new civilization. Practically all of them came from lands where the life of the Jew was hemmed in by mediæval restrictions. Not only were the rights of citizenship denied them, but freedom of residence, of travel, of education, of occupation, of religious expression—all these facets of life were subject to discriminatory regulations. Jews suffered all of the disabilities of their neighbors and many others designed especially for them. Large numbers of those who came to America had fled from Europe not only for materialistic reasons, although they were human enough to hope for a good livelihood, but even more because they despaired of achieving any kind of equality with their neighbors under the rotting political systems of a reactionary Europe. Practically all of the immigrant Jews came to the United States to taste the nectar of the freedom which was denied them in their native lands.

The story of their individual adjustment to this new, free life is a fascinating story, but too long for telling here. It should be told: how they learned the new language and manners and attitudes, how they earned a living, how they adjusted themselves to their neighbors, how they reacted to the freedom they sought, and how they contributed of their talents and imagination to the country in which they built their home.

Our concern, however, is with the other adjustment which the Jews were forced to make: the group adjustment. What, if any, kind of Jewish life should they establish in the new land? Their forebears had for centuries preserved and nurtured a separatistic, autonomous religion-culture, set up walls against the stratagems and onslaughts of a hostile environment. There had not yet been time or circumstance to effect a gradual realignment of Jewish life in a modern, liberal environment. In most of Europe the problem was still primarily theoretical; in America it was immediate and urgent. How much of the Jewish religion-culture should or could be maintained in a democratic society? What intra-mural relationship between Jews should or could be contrived to replace the old European patterns?

It was both an individual and a communal problem. Individual Jews could and did decide to abandon their Jewish affiliation, not as in Europe where public conversion was necessary to obtain what Heine called the "passport" to participation in European culture, but by default. Many of the colonial Jewish pioneers had chosen not to maintain their Jewish loyalties; practically every Jew who settled in Connecticut prior to the Revolution intermarried with his neighbors and reared his children as Christians.[3] Sometimes the process took two generations or even three, but eventually the majority of the descendants of colonial Jews disappeared into the non-Jewish environment. Many Jews who attained prominence in American life—men like August Belmont, the banker and leader of the Democratic Party; Judah P. Benjamin, the senator from Louisiana and active Confederate statesman; and David (Levy) Yulee, the Florida politician and senator—intermarried with Christians and abandoned Jewish life. Untold numbers of immigrants in every generation made the same choice.

For those Jews who were determined to remain faithful, however, a vague, amorphous pattern of American-Jewish life, centered in the synagogue, had already been established. During the colonial age, wherever a sufficiently numerous and stable Jewish community existed, a Jewish congregation was founded. By the time of the Revolution, congregations had been organized in New York, Newport, Philadelphia, Charleston, and Savannah. These synagogues were not merely houses of worship. They were Jewish communal centers; educational, philanthropic, and social activities were carried on within their precincts. This pattern became fixed during the following decades. In an average town, like Mobile or Easton, parochial schools, charitable and philanthropic societies, and fraternal organizations were all part of the synagogue complex in 1860. In larger cities, however, where the population was numerous enough to support a number of synagogues, Jewish life had already begun to expand beyond the boundaries of the synagogue, and the gregarious German Jew organized clubs and societies of every character and description.

The inpouring of poor immigrants had always taxed the ingenuity of established communities. So long as the rooted population outnumbered the newcomers, the synagogue could serve as a centralized relief agency. When immigrants came in such overwhelming numbers as they did during the 1850s, however, the synagogues were unable to cope with the need for assistance. A large number of extra-synagogal philanthropic societies sprang up in all of the metropolitan areas, cutting across synagogue lines and attracting membership from affiliated and unaffiliated alike. Their leadership was substantially the same as that of the synagogues, but it had already been discovered that denominational divisions hindered effective action. In 1860 there were thirty-five permanently organized charitable societies in New York City, and twenty-three in Philadelphia. Generally they selected one specific aspect of need and concentrated upon it: fuel, clothing, loans, assistance to widows and orphans, burial, visitation of the sick, mutual benefit among immigrants themselves, collections for the poor in Palestine, employment, food, hospitalization, education of poor children, and the distribution of Passover *Matzot* (unleavened bread) to the poor.[4]

Philanthropy had become a major activity of the Jewish community, although it was completely disorganized and anarchic. Charity balls and carnivals and benefit banquets, which had previously been infrequent and unusual, were commonplace in the large cities during the 1850s. Some leaders realized that complete chaos would result if the multiplication of charitable activities continued, so they bent their efforts towards the establishment of *institutions*, rather than *organizations*. The first steps towards centralized, unified Jewish philanthropy were taken during this decade: Jewish Foster Homes for orphans were organized in New Orleans (1854), Philadelphia (1855), and New York (1860), and the first Jewish Hospitals were created in Cincinnati (1850) and New York (1856).[5] It would take another half-century, however, before the logical instrumentality for Jewish charity, a city-wide federation of all activities, was first tested in Boston in 1895.

Organized social activities had also been separated from the synagogue by 1860. Jewish fraternal orders were already an accepted expression of the Jewish community. The Independent Order of B'nai B'rith (Sons of the Covenant), the first in the United States, had been created in New York in 1843 by a group of German Jews who proposed to undertake a varied program of cultural, philanthropic, and mutual-aid activities. By 1855 the Order had expanded to twenty lodges in various sections of the country. German had been abandoned as the official language of lodge meetings, thus paving the way for a completely Americanized membership and program. By 1860, the Order was organizing District Grand Lodges to supervise and centralize the activities of its more than fifty local chapters, and its annual conventions were beginning to attract nation-wide attention. Other organizations followed the B'nai B'rith pattern and attempted to duplicate its success. By 1860, four more fraternal orders had been founded: the Independent Order Free Sons of Israel, the Order of B'nai Abraham (Sons of Abraham), the Order of B'nai Mosche (Sons of Moses), and the Order Kesher shel Barzel (Chain of Iron).[6]

Even more fashionable and numerous during the 1850s were Jewish young men's literary societies and associations. Ignoring the secret ritual appeal of the fraternal orders, they concentrated on cultural programs. In reading rooms which they established for the exclusive use of their members, debates, poetry-readings, plays, and German songfests were regular features. These societies, the forerunners of the Young Men's Hebrew Associations, also had an elaborate social phase consisting of dress balls and parties. Their membership was almost exclusively Jewish, but their programs were practically void of Jewish content. An unacknowledged purpose of these literary associations, perhaps even an unconscious one, was the Americanization of young immigrant lads. Other than these groups, which were organized in all of the major Jewish communities during the 1850s, there was no formal Americanization activity by Jews—a decided contrast to the 1890s and 1900s when the native-born bent every effort to "Americanize" the Eastern European Jewish immigrants.[7]

Although philanthropic and social activities had by 1860 very largely been separated from the synagogue, educational functions still remained within its purview. Practically every congregation had some kind of school. Parochial schools, which met on weekdays and included general as well as Jewish subjects, were maintained by the synagogues in all of the larger and many of the smaller communities. Many had adopted the Jewish Sunday School idea which was first propounded by Rebecca Gratz in 1838. But if there was any constant complaint throughout the ranks of American Jewry, it was in reference to education: rabbis as well as laymen bewailed the lack of trained teachers, the lack of satisfactory textbooks, the indifference of the children.

There were a few pedantic, dull textbooks translated from the German or written by local rabbis, but the complaints were fully justified. Some parents turned to private Jewish schools, but these were hardly more satisfactory. All in all, the state of American Jewish education was depressing, if not frightening; but the manifest concern of congregational leaders and their willingness to experiment with varying techniques were healthy signs which pointed towards a more satisfying future. Basically, however, the whole dilemma of American Jewry was and continued to be symbolized by its failure to construct an adequate program of religious education.[8]

Jewish leadership was divided, on the local scene, between well-intentioned laymen, who frequently tended to be autocratic, and earnest, conscientious (but too often ill-trained and inept) spiritual leaders. The laymen worked hard to mould their communities into self-respecting, active, and productive entities. Apparently, however, they were men of little imagination and forcefulness, for no single lay leader of the pre-Civil War era achieved national prominence. There was no American counterpart to Sir Moses Montefiore of Britain. Judah Touro of New Orleans, for all his wealth and philanthropic virtue, was a shy and colorless person. Major Mordecai M. Noah, the Grand Sachem of Tammany, had come upon the scene too early, and his schemes for Jewish colonization in the Niagara River smacked too much of the visionary. Leading Jews there were—senators like Benjamin and Yulee, and a sizable number of congressmen and military officers—but no single one of them threw his weight of mind and energy into the arena of Jewish life. If American Jewry lacked a single essential element, it was national leadership by laymen possessed of vision and ability.

Fortunately, national leadership was not entirely lacking. Although the rabbis were in many cases dominated by the petty jealousies and struggles of their local lay leaders, some of them were strong and inspired enough to direct their energies beyond the local scene. They were the leaders who attempted to lift American Jewry up by its bootstraps. Every major step towards unity and harmony in American Jewish life prior to the Civil War was initiated by a rabbi.

There have been, from time to time, complaints about the domination of Jewish life in America by the rabbinate. Those who are jealous of the role of the rabbis should not forget that the entire future and structure of American Jewry at one time depended solely on the talents, imagination, and perseverance of clergymen. There would be today hardly a trace of Jewish life had it not been for the devotion of these consecrated leaders—men like Isaac Leeser, Samuel M. Isaacs, Isaac M. Wise and David Einhorn. Most of them, incidentally, were not actually ordained rabbis. Some were only cantors or teachers who assumed the functions of spiritual leaders because they were the only available personnel to fill the vital role of full-time congregational leadership. For the sake of convenience, we shall call all of them "rabbi," although many did not have the technical requirements for the title and some of them conscientiously insisted that they could only be regarded as "ministers," a term previously unknown in Jewish religious life.

Isaac Leeser was the earliest to offer the kind of leadership which American Jewry required so desperately. Born in Westphalia in 1806, he had come to Richmond at the age of eighteen to enter his uncle's mercantile establishment. He had been given a modicum of Jewish education in Germany, and continued studying on his own in Richmond, where he voluntarily assumed such tasks as conducting services and teaching the youngsters of the local congregation. Several articles in defense of Judaism, which he wrote for the *Richmond Whig* when he was only twenty-two years old, attracted nation-wide attention. The following year (1829) Mikveh Israel Congregation of Philadelphia invited him to become its *hazzan*. For thirty-nine years Leeser served Philadelphia and American Jewry with love and devotion and energy. He was responsible for so many "firsts" in American Jewish history that it is difficult to list them all: the introduction of regular preaching in English in the synagogue; the organization of an American Jewish Publication Society; the publication of an English translation of the Bible in keeping with the traditions of Jewish scholarship; the publication of a monthly Jewish journal (*The Occident*); the successful organization of a Jewish school; the founding of an American institution for higher Jewish learning (Maimonides College). Many of his ideas were so new and revolutionary that they failed for want of popular support. He was a difficult and eccentric man; his sermons and writings were so long-winded and pedantic as to exasperate the most patient. Despite all his faults and troubles, however, he was one of the heroes of American Jewish communal development: traditional (called conservative today) Judaism might never have survived without his leadership.[9]

Ten years after Leeser was called to Philadelphia, Samuel M. Isaacs, who in many ways was his counterpart and partner, was invited to come to New York from England. Born in Holland in 1804, he was taken to London at an early age and educated in the family's rabbinical tradition. Before coming to the United States he acted as principal of the Jewish Orphan Home in London. Like Leeser, Isaacs was highly conscious of the wilderness that was Jewish life in America, and was unremitting in his efforts to create some sensible pattern out of the chaos. He did not have Leeser's imagination, but he was unassuming enough to assist his Philadelphia friend as a kind of New York agent. He was, in addition, active in every Jewish institution and organization of any significance in that city, and frequently held embattled elements together by the persuasiveness of his peace-making. His weekly periodical, *The Jewish Messenger,* was a strong unifying force in New York, where unity was most difficult to achieve even on a local scale. To Isaacs goes the credit for initiating the first successful nation-wide Jewish organization, which we shall discuss later. Less original than Leeser, Isaacs had the more difficult assignment: his achievements in New York were possibly greater than Leeser's in Philadelphia simply because the Empire City's Jewish community was already the phantasmagoria which makes it simultaneously the greatest and the most chaotic Jewish community in history.[10]

Isaacs and Leeser were the stalwarts of the traditionalist movement. Leading the agitation for Reform was Isaac M. Wise, destined to make his great contributions long after the period under discussion: the founding of the Union of American Hebrew Congregations (1873), the Hebrew Union College (1875), and the Central Conference of American Rabbis (1889). Born in Bohemia in 1819, Wise had emigrated to New York in 1846 after his rabbinical activities in Radnitz had been interfered with by the governmental authorities. Even during his early years of service in Albany, from 1846 to 1854, he demonstrated those qualities which were to make him a storm-center all his life. He attracted nation-wide attention as a fighting Reformer in theological articles in Leeser's *Occident* and Robert Lyon's *Asmonean.* Attempts to organize American Jewry into a religious union, which we shall trace later in this chapter, pointed to him as a determined practical idealist. After his departure from Albany to Cincinnati in 1854, Wise became the most active rabbi in the mid-West and the acknowledged leader of the Reform movement everywhere but in the East. His *Israelite,* founded in 1854, and *Die Deborah,* its German-language counterpart which was first published in 1855, were his personal sounding boards: they bound Jews all over the country to him and were an important factor in the later success of his organizational proposals.[11]

A second great leader of the Reform wing was David Einhorn, the last of the great Civil War rabbis to come to the United States. Born in Bavaria in 1809, he was an outspoken liberal from his early youth. After studying at the rabbinical academy in Fürth and at the Universities of Würzburg and Munich, he entered the active rabbinate, arousing opposition to his radical Reform ideas wherever he served. He played an energetic role in the Reform rabbinical conferences in Germany during the 1840s and was widely attacked and acclaimed by the respective parties of the era. When the Austrian government ordered the Reform temple in Budapest to be closed because Einhorn had been selected as its rabbi, he turned his eyes to the west. He was the first of the great leaders of the German Reform movement to come to America. Arriving in Baltimore in 1855 as the rabbi of Har Sinai Congregation, he immediately became the focal point of religious conflict. His sermons and writings were attacked unmercifully by moderate Reformers as well as traditionalists all over the country. He in turn founded a monthly organ, *Sinai*, in 1856, for the dissemination of his radical ideas, and published his own prayer book, *Olath Tamid*, in 1858, by far the most extreme prayer book to appear in America in this period. In 1860 there was still no sign on the horizon that Einhorn's version of Reform would win out over Wise's in the long run, but because of the bitter criticism by his opponents, he was probably better known than most of his colleagues.[12]

These, then, were a few of the outstanding leaders of the Jews in 1860, men who fought among themselves over details of theology and ritual but who were simultaneously waging war against Jewish ignorance and apathy. Theirs was no easy task. They had to revise the institution of the rabbinate before they could succeed, for the traditional European rabbi had been a learned judge who rendered verdicts on questions of ritual but preached infrequently. The Jewish immigrants had little use for such a rabbi; very soon after their arrival most of them sloughed off ritualistic scruples, and they were far too busy earning a living to engage in leisurely Jewish scholarship. A new kind of rabbinate and a new kind of congregational life, the first faint glimmerings of an American Judaism, were gradually being created by the rabbis who jumped into the fray, determined that Judaism should take root in America. They instituted regular preaching in the vernacular (German as well as English) to combat religious ignorance; they wrote and preached and organized new institutions in the effort to perpetuate that kind of Judaism which they believed to be true.[13]

One of the agencies which the rabbis adopted in the attempt to transmit their attitudes to a wider public was the periodical press. With three exceptions[14] all of the periodicals published for the Jewish reading public prior to the Civil War were edited by rabbis. Leeser's *Occident* (1843), Wise's *Israelite* (1854) and *Deborah* (1855), Einhorn's *Sinai* (1856), Isaacs' *Messenger* (1857) and Julius Eckman's San Francisco *Gleaner* (1858) were the sounding-boards for a virile, positive Jewish life in America.

These papers fulfilled a multitude of functions. Those which appeared in English became a tool in the process of Americanization, while the German papers and magazines sustained the interest of those who had not yet learned the vernacular. Serious articles and essays brought a knowledge of Judaism to the untaught; short stories and serialized novels transmitted the facts and atmosphere of Jewish history. News of Jewish personages and events in all parts of the United States and Europe welded bonds of brotherhood which counteracted the isolation of Jews in small towns and rural areas. They publicized the success of Jewish ventures in one locality and thereby stimulated similar projects in many other cities. Funds were raised for overseas relief through appeals printed in their columns; rabbis were secured through advertisements; decisions of European rabbis on ritual problems were printed for the information of readers. The battle between the Reformers and traditionalists was fought with ink and type, Leeser and Isaacs speaking in behalf of traditionalism, Wise and Einhorn for the cause of Reform. Both sides strengthened their forces through the periodicals by offering the reading public an opportunity to come to its own decision. Communication between Jews in those days when transportation was slow and uncertain was almost completely dependent upon the periodicals: they thereby became a tangible step in the building of a united American Jewish community. All of the positive forces in American Jewish life were represented in the newspapers and magazines and for a few dollars a year the Jews of Summit, Mississippi, and Keokuk, Iowa, could read the sermons of the great rabbis, take part in the debates of the times by writing letters to the editors, and feel as though they were participants in the unfolding story of American Jewry.

Rabbinic leadership had initiated every attempt at the formation of an American Jewish union. Leeser had earned himself another "first" in 1841 when he and another Philadelphia minister had issued the first call for a congregational union. They persuaded five Philadelphia laymen to sign with them an appeal which was sent to every Jewish congregation then in existence. Their purpose was threefold: to raise the standards of the ministry and of *shehitah* (ritual slaughter); to organize a system of Jewish schools throughout the country; and to facilitate unity of action, whenever necessary, by the various Jewish communities. There is no record of the answers to these proposals, but they must have been disappointing. No action was taken.[15]

Leeser joined forces with Isaac M. Wise in 1848–9 in another attempt to convoke a national meeting of congregational leaders. Only eight synagogues responded to the appeal, however, and the two rabbis were forced to admit failure. Six years later they tried a different tack: a rabbinical conference. Cleveland was the scene of this first American Jewish ecclesiastical gathering. It opened auspiciously: both Reformers and traditionalists appeared willing to compromise on certain theological issues for the sake of harmony. Unfortunately, however, after Leeser left for Philadelphia and while the conference was still in session, the Reformers decided that they had compromised enough, and passed some resolutions which utterly alienated the Orthodox camp. No further meeting of the group was ever held, but the personal hostility engendered between Wise and Leeser predetermined the ultimate failure of the next and most promising attempt at Union: the Board of Delegates of American Israelites, founded in 1859 at the behest of Samuel M. Isaacs.[16]

The immediate cause of Isaacs' appeal was the Mortara case. On June 23, 1858, Edgar Mortara, an Italian Jewish child of six years, was seized by the Papal guard on the grounds that, during an illness some years before, he had been secretly baptized by his Catholic nurse. All efforts to restore him to his family were fruitless. News of the incident reached Jewish communities all over the world; a fever-pitch of indignation was the natural result. Had mediæval experiences come back again to plague the harried Jews? Liberal governments instructed their envoys to the Papal States to intercede, but to no avail; Sir Moses Montefiore, the leading British Jew, made a personal trip to Rome, but for the first time since he began traveling in defense of his people his efforts were fruitless.[17] In this emergency, when Jews all over the world were united in the effort to defend the most elementary of human rights, the integrity of the family, many American Jews became aware of and felt impelled to correct the anarchy which prevailed in American Jewish life. Isaacs argued that a union of American Jewry could no longer be postponed; nine New York congregations responded to his call in the *Messenger* and thirteen congregations outside New York agreed to send representatives to the organizational meeting of the Board. The delegates were enthusiastic; a constitution. was drawn up, officers were elected, and the first representative, nation-wide body of American Jews was in existence.[18]

But the Board was doomed to a slow death. None of the radical Eastern Reformers was willing to participate in it; they would not even consider joining an organization partly composed of traditionalists.[19] Snobbery and insecurity were equally involved in their objections. The Board might have survived none the less had Wise been willing to rise above his personal animosity and cooperate with Leeser. He, after all, controlled the policies of numerous congregations in the mid-West and South; their adherence would have strengthened the Board so greatly that Einhorn and his fellow radicals could not have remained outside the fold. But Wise was stubborn and declared his opposition from the first. The traditionalists, for their part, could not counteract the opposition of both radical and moderate Reformers. Although it survived for a number of years, the Board of Delegates thus never had a fair opportunity to develop its program and demonstrate its effectiveness. Wise's hostility to rivals and his fear of domination by New York Jewry postponed by seventeen years the realization of his own vision of an American union of Jewish congregations.

The factors militating against the success of all these union projects are an interesting indication of the state of American Jewry in 1860. Religious disunity obviously played a major role. The rabbis were the only leaders convinced of the desirability of a single, all-encompassing, representative Jewish organization, and yet they were least likely to succeed because they were so deeply committed to one religious position or another. Powerful and influential lay leaders, free of religious prejudices, would have been able to achieve the goal which the rabbis failed to reach, but the day of Schiff and Straus was many decades in the future.

The Reform movement had been initiated in the United States with the secession of a group of liberals from the congregation in Charleston, S.C., in 1824. Strongly influenced by echoes of German Jewish Reform ideas, the new congregation might have endured had it not been for the premature death of its most ardent leader, Isaac Harby, one of the most famous dramatic critics and essayists of the day. Its members returned to the parent congregation in 1833, but continued to agitate for Reform and eventually, in the 1840s, successfully captured the congregational offices. Meanwhile, a liberal congregation was organized in Baltimore in 1842, and Temple Emanu-El of New York, still one of the leading Reform congregations of the country, followed in 1845. During these years, also, rabbis who were liberal or potentially liberal had begun to arrive in the United States from Germany and Austria.[20]

Motivated by a desire to modernize Judaism through the use of the vernacular, to harmonize traditional ideas and practices with nineteenth-century rationalism, and to supplement the ancient ritual with attractive innovations such as the Confirmation ceremony, the Reformers found a favorable climate in the free and fluid American civilization. American democracy seemed to invite the development of Judaism into a more modern and Westernized faith. Conditions of living seemed to demand the abandonment of practices which were difficult to fulfill in a non-Jewish environment. Although laymen, in the final analysis, were responsible for the acceptance of change, Reform would never have made the rapid progress it did in America without the leadership of rabbis like Wise and Einhorn.[21]

That the agitation for change did not proceed without opposition goes without saying. The traditionalist congregations were firmly entrenched in the United States and were gifted with splendid leadership. Leeser and Isaacs and their colleagues were no mean opponents for the Reformers, and they had the advantage of numbers. Their logic was concise and pointed: simple changes in ritual cannot be made without endangering the entire structure of Judaism; challenge the divine sanction for one law or practice or idea, and all laws and practices and ideas would be bereft of authority; Judaism is all that tradition means it to be, or nothing!

There was bitterness and name-calling on both sides of the conflict. The Reformers felt that the Orthodox were reactionary fanatics, holding back the forces of progress and enlightenment; the traditionalists accused the modernists of being destructive opportunists, radicals, atheists, heretics.

To men of both camps Judaism was a precious heritage; its future in the American environment was a matter of deep personal and spiritual concern to all of them. The occasions were all too infrequent, however, when they understood that they had a common enemy: indifference and, worse, hostility towards any version of Judaism. Neither Reform nor traditionalism would win the day; secularism was already on the march, and the internecine warfare which raged between the two camps paved the way towards the time when the majority of American Jews would belong to no synagogue whatever. Indeed, there were already considerable numbers of German-Jewish secularists and atheists in the large cities. They attacked Judaism as "priestcraft" and "superstition" with the same vehemence with which their non-Jewish German friends denounced Christianity. Since they despised all religion, they did not turn Christian, but their life as Jews was restricted to social contacts, marriage and burial. They, of course, were utterly opposed to any nation-wide organization of Jews on a religious basis.[22]

Added to the incompatibility of Reformers and traditionalists was a further heterogeneity of background which divided the immigrant Jews. Unlike national immigrant groups like the Irish, the Germans, the British, and the Swedes, Jews had come to America from widely separated European areas. They spoke different languages (Yiddish, German, French, Dutch) and represented a wide variety of cultural backgrounds. Even in regard to Jewish culture, there was no unity or harmony. Jewish life, handicapped and cramped though it may have been, had flourished for centuries in Poland, Bohemia, Austria, Hungary, the German states, England, and Holland. The hundreds of rooted Jewish communities in Europe had developed distinctive customs and traditions of their own. Groups of immigrants sought to preserve these local religious usages in the new American milieu by organizing their own synagogues. Indeed, these local traditions were frequently the cause of bitter disagreement in smaller communities. To give up familiar synagogue chants and customs was too much like repudiating one's parents and grandparents. In Zanesville, Ohio, the Jews were unable to organize a congregation because they could not agree on any one of the four rites represented among them.[23] In New York City, in 1860, there were over twenty different German congregations, perpetuating specific local backgrounds and religious modes, in addition to synagogues maintained by French, Polish, Portuguese, English, Russian, Dutch, and Bohemian Jews.[24] If Jews were so divided by linguistic and cultural barriers that they could not unite for synagogue organization on a local scale, is it any wonder that these divisions contributed to the failure of schemes for national unity?

Another factor which worked against the successful accomplishment of Leeser's and Wise's ideas was, strangely enough, the very democracy for which most Jews had come to America. Throughout the centuries, European Jews had been forced to maintain an inner discipline in self-defense. Disaster could sometimes be averted through absolute unity of effort, though frequently even this did not avail. Even in times of prosperity, the government often required representation of the community by plenipotentiary representatives. Frequently, therefore, the community and its institutions were under the control of self-appointed plutocrats and rabbinical dictators.[25] Here in America every organization was a voluntary one, and there were undoubtedly many Jews who saw no need for a national agency, or who actually relished the anarchy in which it was now possible for them to live. Why should they, who had fled from authoritarian governments and sometimes chafed under ecclesiastical tyranny, surrender their new-found freedom and set guardians over their religious life? This fear was, of course, unfounded, but it was, nonetheless, genuine.

Anxiety about prejudice was undoubtedly another strong factor which deterred Jews from supporting the union projects. They were afraid to call attention to themselves, afraid of creating suspicion. They knew the effects of anti-Jewish hatred from personal experience. Disabilities, expulsions, riots—these were the legacy of mediæval bigotry to the Europe which they had left behind. Newcomers, they had not been in America long enough to assess its democratic strength; they could not know how much anti-Jewish prejudice lay latent under the smooth appearance of equality. They were determined, therefore, to avoid offense. Unquestionably, the underlying sense of the preachments of rabbis and editors against a "Jewish vote," and the background of much of the reluctance to support the idea of a national Jewish organization, was this fear: perhaps the Gentiles would misunderstand the purposes of such an organization, regard it as a counterpart of the Catholic hierarchy against which the Know-Nothing crusade was waged, attack it as un-American. The insecurity which Jews brought from their European experience was an unconscious freight which they carried over the ocean. It is still among our possessions.[26]

These were the inner cleavages, tensions and dissensions which prevented the realization of any of the projects of union which the leading rabbis envisaged. *Actually, however, despite the failure of all attempts to create a formal nation-wide Jewish organization, there was already an American Jewish unity in an emotional sense.* An American Jewish community did exist, without specific agencies or instrumentalities. It expressed itself in the sense of community which most American Jews shared.

This sense of comradeship revealed itself in many actions, opinions, feelings and reactions which were characteristic of the overwhelming majority of American Jews. They were, for instance, bitterly opposed to all attempts to convert them from their ancient faith. The implication that they were adherents of an inferior religion was a source of deep and constant resentment.[27] This was a negative aspect of the loyalty which held them faithful to the religion and heritage of their fathers . . . they were still the "stiff-necked" people, even in the pioneer towns of Texas and Kansas. Another characteristic shared by most Jews was their determination to fight for the civil rights which all citizens were accorded by the Constitution. As Jews, they asked for equal treatment with Christians before the law: permission to work on Sunday because it was not the Sabbath which they observed; excision of references to Christianity in public proclamations and documents; repeal of religious tests for office in those few states which still maintained such tests.[28] This willingness, even eagerness, to stand up in America as Jews also expressed itself in their jealous safeguarding of their name. It was not only fear which impelled them to defend themselves against anti-Jewish libels, but pride in their heritage and the high resolve to bring honor to their name in this new land. Yet another area which revealed their unity of purpose was a growing sense of companionship with Jews all over the world. They responded with eagerness to calls for assistance from Sir Moses Montefiore for oppressed Jews in Morocco, in Turkey, in Tripoli. They shared the anguish of their European brethren over the Damascus bloodlibel trials and the Mortara case.[29] Palestinian messengers came in increasing numbers to this frontier of the Western world for contributions to the funds which supported the poor in Jerusalem. These were hints and signs of the relationship between American and world Jewry which was to expand and deepen with the passing years. In all of these ways, there was an unconscious, groping, aspiring American Jewry.

How this American Jewish community acted in and reacted to the holocaust of the Civil War, and what its experiences, activities and status were during the years of fratricidal conflict, form the burden of the following pages.

II THE RABBIS AND THE SLAVERY QUESTION

The Jews of the United States have never taken any steps whatever with regard to the Slavery question. As citizens, they deem it their policy "to have every one choose which ever side he may deem best to promote his own interests and the welfare of his country." They have no organization of an ecclesiastical body to represent their general views; no General Assembly or its equivalent. The American Jews have two newspapers, but they do not interfere in any discussion which is not material to their religion. It cannot be said that the Jews have formed any denominational opinion on the subject of American slavery. Some of the Jews who reside in slave States, have refused to have any property in man, or even to have any slaves about them. They do not believe that anything analogous to slavery, as it exists in this country, ever prevailed among the ancient Israelites . . . The objects of so much mean prejudice and unrighteous oppression as the Jews have been for ages, surely they, it would seem, more than any other denomination, ought to be the enemies of *caste* and the friends of *universal freedom*.[1]

This report by a non-Jew on the relationship of the synagogue to the slavery issue, presented to the 1853 meeting of the American and Foreign Anti-Slavery Society, was substantially correct, and in that regard rather unusual for an age in which so much misinformation about the Jews was broadcast far and wide. The autonomy of the individual congregation, and the freedom of individual rabbis from hierarchical control, precluded any official Jewish pronouncements on the most important single religio-cultural question of the day.

Individual Jews, of course, had participated in the development of the institution of slavery, as well as in the discussion of its merits, from the very first. Jewish merchants of Newport, Rhode Island, had been active, before the Revolution, in the well-known "triangle trade" which brought African slaves to the colonies.[2] Jewish residents of the slave states had bought Negroes for use on their plantations and in their homes, and had even made their living from slave marketing.[3] As the report to the Anti-Slavery Society stated, there were other Jews, in the South as well as in the North, who had, out of personal kindness or in keeping with their general convictions, freed their slaves. The records of the Manumission Society of New York City preserve the names of many Jews who emancipated their Negroes.[4] In the political arena, Jews were to be found

15

on both sides of the question: Mordecai M. Noah's New York news-papers took a strong pro-slavery position,[5] while Moritz Pinner's *Kansas Post* was vehemently pledged to the opposite course.[6] Judah P. Benjamin[7] and David Yulee,[8] the two Jewish senators, were both champions of the slave system, while other Jews who were active in politics, like Isidor Bush[9] of St. Louis and Philip J. Joachimsen[10] of New York, were enlisted in the anti-slavery ranks.

If it were possible to uncover and catalogue the opinions of all the Jews who lived in the United States during the years leading up to the Civil War—slave dealers like J.F. Moses of Lumpkin, Ga., who, "being a regular trader to this market," said that he would "warrant every Negro sold to come up to the bill, squarely and completely";[11] immigrants like Seligman Kakeles of New York who, in the perennial manner of hero-worshippers, named his first-born American child after the abolitionist leader Gerrit Smith;[12] philanthropists like Judah Touro who, living in a slavery environment, disagreed with the system enough to free his own slaves;[13] abolitionists like Michael Heilprin of Philadelphia, who was mobbed by a pro-slavery crowd at a Democratic Party meeting in 1858[14] —we should have to conclude that Jews were represented in all the various shadings of opinion from fanatic abolitionists to fire-eating slavery proponents. The Jews were as thoroughly divided as the American pop-ulation itself. It is possible, however, that we should discover that there were fewer Jews than other Americans, proportionately, at the extreme wings of the controversy, and more in the middle ground, because, as immigrants, the great majority of them would naturally have taken less interest in theoretical and sectional political questions than in the more personal problems of economic and social adjustment.

Since there was no unified expression of Jewish opinion on the sub-ject, Judaism, unlike the various Christian denominations, played no role in the moulding of public sentiment in the crucial years when the battle lines were being drawn. This is not to say, however, that Jewish leaders were silent. The rabbis and publishers spoke *for* no official group of Jews, certainly not for their congregations and readers—but, speaking *to* American Jewry they could hardly avoid exerting the influence of their religious and intellectual leadership. An examination of the opinions voiced by the rabbis during the turmoil over slavery will be interesting for a number of reasons. It will, firstly, demonstrate the extent to which the rabbis participated in the various political currents which eddied through American life, and, secondly, it will indicate how far they were from unanimity.

I

The most highly publicized rabbinical pronouncement on the merits of slavery was made at the very peak of the secession crisis by Dr. Morris J.

Raphall of New York City, one of the most celebrated orators in the American rabbinate of his time. President Buchanan had proclaimed January 4, 1861, as a National Fast Day, in an effort to mobilize national sentiment against the impending break-up of the Union. Jews as well as non-Jews all over the nation gathered for worship and prayer; Rabbi Raphall believed that this was the logical occasion for a discourse on "The Bible View of Slavery."[15]

What he did was to place Judaism squarely in opposition to the philosophy of abolitionism. He denied that any statement or law in the Bible could be interpreted to prohibit slavery, and insisted that, to the contrary, biblical tradition and law guaranteed the right to own slaves. Translating the Hebrew word for servant (*'ebed*) as "slave," he claimed that "the very highest authority" in the Bible, the Ten Commandments, sanctioned human slavery.[16] He accused Henry Ward Beecher and the other abolitionist preachers of rationalistic attempts to pervert the meaning of the biblical text and challenged them to produce factual evidence to back up their contention that biblical law was designed to abolish slavery:

> I would therefore ask the reverend gentleman from Brooklyn and his compeers—How dare you . . . denounce slaveholding as a sin? When you remember that Abraham, Isaac, Jacob, Job—the men with whom the Almighty conversed, with whose names he emphatically connects his own most holy name . . . —that all these men were slaveholders, does it not strike you that you are guilty of something very little short of blasphemy? And if you answer me, "Oh, in their time slaveholding was lawful, but now it has become a sin," I in my turn ask you, "When and by what authority you draw the line? Tell us the precise time when slaveholding ceased to be permitted, and became sinful?"[17]

Raphall made a half-hearted attempt to appear objective by distinguishing biblical slavery from the evils of the Southern system. The Bible, he said, had regarded the slave as "a *person* in whom the dignity of human nature is to be respected," while the Southerners treated the slave as "a *thing*" without rights and privileges. The Bible had safeguarded the slaves against cruelty, mutilation, and abuse; the Bible was humanitarian, and the South would do well to adopt its merciful attitude.[18] But he directed his major attack against the abolitionists for their misrepresentation of the Bible and for their agitation against the legitimate rights of the Southerners who, to his mind, had done no wrong. He claimed that he himself was not an adherent of slavery, but that an objective consideration of the text of the Bible forced him to assume this position.[19]

This sermon aroused more comment and attention than any other sermon ever delivered by an American rabbi. The pro- and anti-slavery forces had for years been arguing about the attitude of the Old Testament to slavery. For Fundamentalist ministers, at least, the testimony of the Bible on slavery was preeminently important. Now, at the very time when propagandists, both North and South, were delivering their final appeals for support, a learned rabbi had finally settled the argument in favor of the proponents of slavery. Printed in its entirety in the daily press,[20] as a separate pamphlet, and in a compilation of similar sermons, "The Bible View of Slavery" was given wide circulation. The *Richmond Daily Dispatch* said that it "receives the praise of the press as the most powerful argument delivered" in the entire religious controversy about slavery.[21] It was used frequently, throughout the Southland, as proof of the sympathy of the Jews for the seceding states. In the Virginia House of Delegates, for instance, when ex-Governor Wyndham Robertson[22] was urging support for his resolution to invite the Richmond rabbis to open the daily sessions of the House with prayer (only Christian clergymen had previously been permitted to do so), the Raphall sermon served as a fine argument:

> .... It is fit, at a time when we are standing on our rights of equality in other respects, we should be careful not to refuse lightly the benefit of that principle to others. Nor perhaps is it inappropriate to remember here a late powerful and eloquent voice that has been raised by a learned Israelite in New York in vindication of that social institution in which our peace and welfare are vitally involved, and in defense of which we are now engaged in a struggle before (I might almost say against) the world.[23]

In Memphis, when the Rev. Simon Tuska wrote a letter to the *Memphis Daily Appeal* defending Jews as loyal citizens, he pointed to the fact that it was not a Christian clergyman, but a rabbi who had delivered "the most forceful arguments in justification of the slavery of the African race, and the most thorough refutation of the rabid, abolition views of Henry Ward Beecher."[24] The *Charleston Mercury* praised Raphall for "defend[ing] us in one of the most powerful arguments put forth north or south."[25]

Abolitionist Jews and non-Jews could not, therefore, permit Raphall's theses to go unanswered, or it would be assumed that he spoke for all Jews, and that his summary of the biblical attitude was the final, definitive one.

The first Jewish answer to Raphall's presentation, published in *The New York Tribune*,[26] was written by Michael Heilprin, a Polish-Jewish intellectual who had taken an active part in the 1848 Revolution in Hungary and was now a member of the editorial staff of Appleton's *New American Cyclopaedia*.[27] He was shocked that a Jewish voice should be raised in support of slavery:

> I had read similar nonsense hundreds of times before; I knew that the Father of Truth and Mercy was daily invoked in hundreds of pulpits in this country for a Divine sanction of falsehood and barbarism; still, being a Jew myself, I felt exceedingly humbled, I may say outraged, by the sacrilegious words of the Rabbi. Have we not had enough of the "reproach of Egypt?" Must

the stigma of Egyptian principles be fastened on the people of Israel by Israelitish lips themselves? . . .[28]

A learned Jew himself, Heilprin proceeded to examine and refute each of Raphall's contentions and interpretations. His invective and scorn of Raphall's scholarship and ideas were unbounded. He did not even try to disguise his feeling that Raphall was either a fool or a knave; he could discover no excuse for the rabbi's misinterpretation of Judaism. Beyond all the details of translation and interpretation, he could not understand how Raphall could ignore the fact that Jewish law is fluid, flexible and organic. The rabbis of the Talmud had "explained away" many "contradictory, unjust, and even barbarous" laws and statements in the Bible, he said—it was nonsense to pretend that everything preserved in the Bible retained a divine sanction.

Several months later, Christian abolitionists began the serial publication of another Jewish analysis of the biblical attitude towards slavery, a treatise on "Slavery Among the Ancient Hebrews" by Dr. Moses Mielziner, then principal of the Jewish school at Copenhagen, later to become the rabbi of Anshi Chesed Congregation of New York City. Written as Mielziner's doctoral dissertation at the University of Giessen, without any reference to the contemporary American agitation, Mielziner's work was a dispassionate, rationalistic study of the scriptural law governing slavery. The Danish rabbi was convinced that the Mosaic law had so thoroughly delimited the practice of slavery as to all but abolish it, and that the enslavement of Hebrews had actually ceased with the destruction of the First Temple. Of course, he had not intended to write a textbook for abolitionist clergymen, but his work so impressed its first American reader, Professor Francis Lieber of Columbia University, as an antidote to Raphall's supposedly authoritative presentation, that its translation and publication were arranged for immediately, first in the *American Theological Review* of New York in April 1861, and again in the *Evangelical Review* of Gettysburg, Pa., in January 1862."[29]

Raphall's sermon was answered even in England. Rabbi Gustav Gottheil, later to become rabbi of Temple Emanu-El of New York City, preached two sermons to his Manchester congregation on the subject:[30]

> We have had to learn, by reports in the public journals, that a Teacher in Israel, a man to whom people would look as having a right to speak with authority; and at a time when any utterance on the Slave Question could not fail to be eagerly listened to, did from his pulpit maintain that *slave-holding is no sin according to the Scriptures* . . . How can we be silent when we find him using [this] . . . as an argument to show that the people of the Republic are wrong in condemning and denouncing the slavery of the south . . .[31]

He, like Heilprin, examined and refuted Raphall's points, one by one, and discussed the relevance of Negro rights to Jewish rights, of Negro freedom to human freedom. For him, slavery found justification neither in the Bible nor in Jewish history.

II

The leading abolitionist propagandist among the rabbis was David Einhorn of Baltimore, who had been writing and preaching against slavery since 1856.[32] He devoted four separate articles in his monthly, *Sinai*, to the Raphall sermon and its arguments.[33] The question, he said, was not whether slavery was mentioned in the Bible, but

> whether Scripture merely *tolerates* this institution as an evil not to be disregarded, and therefore infuses in its legislation a mild spirit gradually to lead to its dissolution, or whether it *favors, approves of* and *justifies* and *sanctions* it in its moral aspect.[34]

Christian clergymen were apologizing for slavery, even in the South, he said; could a *rabbi* sanction it? If a Christian, he continued, had said Judaism was pro-slavery, all Jews, from the extremest Orthodox wing to the most radical Reformers, would have "call[ed] the wrath of heaven and earth upon such falsehoods."[35]

Einhorn had never had any patience with literalists like Raphall. Jews should be concerned with the spirit of the Bible, he felt, not with its letter. Of course, slavery was acknowledged in the Bible: it had been established long before biblical times. Since it could not be eradicated all at once, certain regulations were ordained to prohibit its most serious abuses. But it was always intended that the system would be abolished in its entirety. It was blasphemy, he believed, for the proponents of slavery to identify God and the Bible with the cruelty and heartlessness of slavery:

> . . . Is it anything else but a deed of Amalek, rebellion against God, to enslave human beings created in His image, and to degrade them to a state of beasts having no will of their own? Is it anything else but an act of ruthless and wicked violence, to reduce defenseless human beings to a condition of merchandise, and relentlessly to tear them away from the hearts of husbands, wives, parents, and children . . . ?
>
> It has ever been a strategy of the advocate of a bad cause to take refuge from the spirit of the Bible to its letter, as criminals among the ancient heathen nations would seek protection near the altars of their gods. Can *that* Book hallow the enslavement of any race, which sets out with the principles, that Adam was created in the image of God, and that all men have descended from *one* human pair? Can *that* Book mean to raise the whip and forge chains, which proclaims, with flaming words, in the name of God: "break the bonds of oppression, let the oppressed go free and tear every yoke!" Can *that* Book justify the violent separation of a child from its human mother, which,

when speaking of birds' nests, with admirable humanity commands charitable regard for the feelings even of an animal mother? . . .[36]

Arguing religious sanctions for human bondage on the basis of ancient practice made as much sense to Einhorn as urging the reestablishment of polygamy, blood vengeance, or royalty, because they were conventional in biblical times. As to the historic right to enslave others, could custom ever justify evil? "Does a disease, perchance, cease to be an evil on account of its long duration?" Would mankind ever progress if improvements were thwarted out of consideration for the past? Would the United States ever have been created if the national founders had been moved by regard for "historic right?" "If such principles were true, could it ever have been possible to cease burning heretics and witches, aye! even to sacrifice the blood of one's own children?" Did God himself show any regard for "historic right" when he emancipated the Hebrew slaves from Egyptian slavery? Religious principles of freedom and righteousness, Einhorn maintained, must ultimately triumph over "ancient prejudices, over usurped titles and privileges, over hallowed atrocities."[37]

Like Heilprin and Dr. Gottheil, Einhorn perceived a fundamental relationship between the rights of the Jew and the rights of the Negro. He saw no possibility of freedom for minorities in an atmosphere which condoned the enslavement of any people. The philosophy of exclusionism would inevitably set more and more people outside the bounds of equality, unless it were repudiated completely. For him, slavery and the Know-Nothing agitation against aliens were of a piece; as it was intended to enslave the Negro forever, so foreigners were to be degraded into second class citizens. The extension of democratic rights to the Negro would safeguard the status of all other groups. Even more important, it would also enable America to forge to the forefront of leadership in the movement for world-wide democracy.[38]

The Rabbi of Har Sinai Temple in Baltimore was not merely preaching. Maryland was a festering sore of sectional strife; it would in all probability have joined the Confederacy after the outbreak of hostilities, had it not been for the prompt action of the government in arresting secessionist ring-leaders and declaring martial law in order to safeguard the passage of Northern troops through to the national capital. Anti-slavery declarations were not idle talk in such an atmosphere. Einhorn had been warned many times before, by both friends and enemies, to discontinue his public crusade. His articles against Raphall, printed in New York papers and in separate pamphlet form, were the last straw; open threats were made against him, and Baltimore Jews who belonged to other congregations were forced to state in the public press that they did not accept his leadership.

Open rioting between Baltimore Unionists and Confederate sympathizers broke out on April 19, 1861. Abolitionists and many innocent persons who were merely suspected of sharing their ideas were molested; some were beaten and killed. Printing presses, including those which printed Einhorn's *Sinai*, were destroyed; homes were set afire. His friends urged the rabbi to flee north, but he refused to show the white feather. Soldiers came to him with proof that his name was listed among those proscribed by the secessionist instigators of the riots. Still he refused to leave. A group of young men of his congregation, armed for guard duty, set up a cordon around his home to protect him and his family. Finally, on the fourth day of the rioting, he consented to leave, for his family's sake, proposing to return as soon as law and order were restored in Baltimore.[39]

He never did return. His congregation was itself so riddled by political differences, and many members were so thoroughly frightened by the violence of the rioters, that the only condition on which they would consent to their rabbi's return was that he promise to refrain from political controversy. On May 13, the Board of Trustees directed that he be written to as follows: "it would be very desirable—for your own safety, as well as out of consideration for the members of your congregation—if in the future there would be no comment in the pulpit on the excitable issues of the time."[40]

Such a condition was utterly unacceptable to David Einhorn. If he had been interested in conciliating the secessionists he would never have undertaken to write and preach against slavery in the first place. He could not and would not compromise one of his most fundamental principles for the sake of expediency.

It was painful to part with his first American congregation without a word of personal farewell; Baltimore had been the scene of his initiation into America and American-Jewish life. There he had first flexed his muscles against American Orthodox and Conservative Judaism in the battle for Reform. He had made many enemies, with his ruthless logic, and his outspoken criticism of reaction in religion and politics; but he had found close friends and supporters in Baltimore, men and women who upheld his hands in controversy, and with whom he still longed to sit and talk.[41]

But a warm welcome had been given him in Philadelphia. Keneseth Israel Congregation promptly invited him to occupy its pulpit; there he could speak his mind and his heart without hindrance. The problems of the war continued to be a major subject of his preaching and writing, but the *Sinai* lasted only another year and a half. Its transfer to Philadelphia was healthier for its editor, but completely unprofitable. Even in the North, Jews were not prepared to identify their religious thinking with the anti-slavery movement. Einhorn wrote in the final number of the journal that "Sinai . . . dies in the battle against slavery."[42]

The only other abolitionist among the rabbis was the Rev. Bernhard Felsenthal of Chicago, who had, while occupying the pulpit in Madison,

Ind., taken an active role in the Fremont presidential campaign in 1856,[43] and later refused to apply for the rabbinical position in Mobile, Ala., because he felt that he could not live at peace with himself in a slave environment.[44] As the rabbi of Sinai Temple in Chicago, and then of the newly organized Zion Congregation, he is said to have delivered many anti-slavery sermons and speeches during the war.[45] In his only sermon to be preserved in print, a Thanksgiving Day message of 1865,[46] he rejoiced over the successful termination of the war and the final death-blow to slavery. God had freed America from the bondage of Egypt, he said; the nation was now rid of "an ugly and hateful institution" which had shamed her before the entire world:

> Four millions of men, children of the same heavenly Father, descendants of the same Adam, were held in—slavery! And now they were freed, and now they will be free . . . And should the nation not rejoice? Still many more millions of white people languished in slavery. They were fettered by the shackles of prejudices. Were not those who spoke for universal freedom and acted for universal justice in a small, small minority? And was not the name *Abolitionist* a name of disgrace? And now this name has become a name of honor, and three-fourths or seven-eighths of the nation glory in this name. The fetters of prejudices are broken. The white people have become emancipated just as well as the black people. The Abolitionists were the true statesmen of the nation. . . .

Unlike Einhorn, who believed that "any Jew who lifts his hand against the Union, is as a Jew to be considered equal to a parricide,"[47] Felsenthal apologized for but did not condemn Jews who approved of slavery and supported the Confederacy.[48] They were in the small minority, he said; American Jews by and large were "heart and soul, dedicated to the anti-slavery movement." He agreed that "if anyone, it is the Jew above all others who should have the most burning and irreconcilable hatred for the 'peculiar institution of the South,'" but he was still unwilling to disown them for their mistaken ideas.

III

Indicative of the mood of large segments of the Jewish population of the North were the comments of Isaacs' *Jewish Messenger* on Einhorn's flight from Baltimore:

> It seems that he has been mistaking his vocation, and making the pulpit the vehicle for political invective. The citizens of Baltimore, not regarding this as part of the Dr's duty, politely informed him, that 12 hours' safe residence was about all that they could guarantee him, in *that* place. Accordingly, taking the hint, the political Rabbi left, and at last accounts, was in the neighborhood of Philadelphia. We wonder whether our Baltimore co-religionists grieve over his departure? At the same time, we commend his fate

to others, who feel inclined to take a similar course. A Minister has enough to do, if he devotes himself to the welfare of his flock; he can afford to leave politics to others. Let Dr. E's fate be a warning.[49]

Samuel M. Isaacs nursed his own private grudge against the Baltimore rabbi for his refusal to co-operate in the establishment of the Board of Delegates of American Israelites. This accounted in part for his gloating over the Baltimore experience. But Isaacs did honestly seek to avoid controversy over national politics unless a Jewish issue was involved. When letters about the Raphall sermon poured into the *Messenger's* office, he refused to print any of them. "We are determined not to engage in a controversy, and have made up our mind to admit in our columns *no* articles on the subject, either for or against slavery."[50]

Later, when inflammatory discussions of slavery were no longer so common, the *Messenger* was willing to commit itself by reprinting parts of a learned German treatise which maintained that slavery did not have divine sanction.[51] Still later, it gave its support to the passage of the Thirteenth Amendment, but cautioned that equality would have to be earned by the Negro, rather than legislated for him.[52]

Although his Virginia background undoubtedly gave a pro-slavery bent to his thinking, Isaac Leeser never published his personal views in *The Occident*. Like the *Messenger's* editors, he said he was profoundly opposed to any Jewish discussion of general political questions. Judaism, so far as he was concerned, had nothing specific to say about slavery and abolitionism, about the North and the South. So he chose not to preach on the National Fast Day on January 4, 1861, because "we could not have avoided political allusions had we spoken"; instead he gave a brief prayer for peace and harmony. He regretted that Dr. Raphall had decided to speak on slavery, although he admitted that he agreed with most of the New York rabbi's conclusions.[53]

The closest that Leeser ever came to discussing slavery was an editorial in which he cautioned Jewish merchants in the South against disobeying local regulations concerning commerce with Negro slaves. In late 1860 he wrote, "we have been shown a notice from a committee of vigilance addressed to a Hebrew in a town of Georgia, ordering him 'and his brethren' to quit the place by the 15th of November, alleging as a reason, that they had offended the public sense of propriety by their traffic . . ." If Jews disagreed with regulations against commercial intercourse with Negroes, said Leeser, let them move North rather than stir up trouble.[54]

IV

Isaac Mayer Wise[55] was another rabbi-editor who objected to political discussions from a Jewish viewpoint, from any religious viewpoint, in fact. He carried his attack against the Protestant abolitionists so far, however, that he actually did take a political position without admitting that he did so. He considered the abolitionists to be "fanatics," "demagogues," "red republicans and habitual revolutionaries, who feed on excitement and delight in civil wars, German athei[sts] coupled with American puritan[s] who know of no limits to their fanaticism, visionary philanthropists and wicked preachers who have that religion which is most suitable to their congregations," and "demons of hatred and destruction." It was the Protestant preachers, in the final analysis, who were responsible for the outbreak of the civil war, Wise was convinced:

> Who in the world could act worse, more extravagant and reckless in this crisis than Protestant priests did? From the very start of the unfortunate difficulties the consequences of which we now suffer so severely, the Protestant priests threw the firebrand of abolitionism into the very heart of this country . . . There was not a Protestant paper in existence that had not weekly an abolitionist tirade. There was scarcely a sermon preached without a touch at least of the "existing evil." You know who made Jefferson Davis and the rebellion? The priests did, and their whiners and howlers in the press. The whole host of priests would rather see this country crushed and crippled than discard their fanaticism or give up their political influence.[56]

Never did the editor of *The Israelite* write on an issue connected with the war without pausing to attack abolitionism. But he was not a proponent of slavery, although he would have been quite willing to see the perpetuation of slavery guaranteed forever, in order to avoid civil bloodshed.[57] From a moral and ethical viewpoint he was moderately anti-slavery. Far from approving Raphall's stand, as has been charged, Wise was one of those who found many flaws in Raphall's analysis of the biblical text.[58] When the controversial discussions of slavery in the Bible died down, he published a series of articles in which he concluded that Moses had attempted to abolish slavery "by indirect-direct laws which rendered its existence impossible."[59] Agreeing with Einhorn to a surprising extent, he said:

> It is evident that Moses was opposed to slavery from the facts: 1. He prohibited to enslave a Hebrew, male or female, adult or child. 2. He legislated to a people just emerging from bondage and slavery. 3. He legislated for an agricultural community with whom labor was honorable. 4. He legislated not only to humanize the condition of the alien laborers, but to render the acquisition and retention of bondmen contrary to their will a matter of impossibility.[60]

Taking a totally unrealistic view of the situation in the South, however, he said that:

> We are not prepared, nobody is, to maintain it is absolutely unjust to purchase savages, or rather their labor, place them under the protection of the law, and secure them the benefit of civilized society and their sustenance for

their labor. Man in a savage state is not free; the alien servant under the Mosaic law was a free man, excepting only the fruits of his labor. The abstract idea of liberty is more applicable to the alien laborer of the Mosaic system than to the savage, and savages only will sell themselves or their offspring.[61]

For all his theoretical objections to the inhumanity of slavery he was more hostile to the war-mongers in the North than to the evils of slavery, and became, in effect, a defender of the South.[62]

In thorough agreement with Wise on the question of abolitionism was the Rev. Judah Wechsler of Portsmouth, Ohio. He, too, believed that the abolitionist preachers were responsible for the war.

> Under the pretext of philanthropy [he said], the everlasting slavery question has been made the text point of almost every sermon. This more than anything else has been instrumental in [bringing on] this war . . . Had the clergymen excluded politics entirely from the pulpit . . . I for one believe we should not have experienced this war.[63]

Wechsler's ideas on the subject were well known to the Indianapolis Hebrew Congregation, whose rabbi he had been in 1858–1860; when he applied for the position again in 1863, the Board of the congregation resolved that he be not permitted even to conduct services on trial because of his "disloyal" political ideas.[64]

Another rabbi who agreed with Wise was Einhorn's Orthodox colleague in Baltimore, the Rev. Bernard Illowy, who denounced the abolitionists as "ambitious aspirants and selfish politicians, who, under the color of religion and in the disguise of philanthropy, have thrown the country into a general state of confusion." Illowy preached the same kind of message as Raphall on the National Fast Day on January 4, 1861, but it did not attract the same amount of attention from the public as Raphall's; it must have been partially responsible, however, for Einhorn's violent outbursts against pro-slavery rabbis. Illowy asked:

> Why did not Moses, who, as it is to be seen from his code, was not in favor of slavery, command the judges in Israel to . . . take forcibly away a slave from a master? . . . Why did Abraham, Ezra, etc., not free slaves? . . . All these are irrefutable proofs that we have no right to exercise violence against . . . institutions even if religious feelings and philanthropic sentiments bid us disapprove of them. It proves, furthermore, that the authors of the many dangers, which threaten our country with ruin and devastation, are not what they pretend to be, the agents of Religion and Philanthropy . . .[65]

One of Wise's major objections to the abolitionists was his suspicion that they were not actually humanitarians who were interested in the progress of mankind, but politicians bent on securing power. He believed that their religious fanaticism would fasten upon the Jews as their next victims, after the conquest of the South. As evidence of this he cited the 1859 Massachusetts law which denied the right to vote and hold office to the foreign-born until they could certify a residence of seven years in the United States. "Do you think," he asked, "the Israelites of the South must be your white slaves, as you in your naturalization laws treat the foreigner, placing him below the Negro?" The preachers who were so incensed about the treatment of the Negro, Wise claimed, turned a deaf ear to the Jew's claim for equality.[66]

The Jewish Record of New York seconded Wise's opposition to the abolitionist forces on the grounds of their attitude towards the Jews. They were only scheming fanatics who were determined to seize hold of the government and then destroy every free institution, smother every group, with which they disagreed. After the Confederacy was quelled, said the *Record*, the New England radicals would set themselves to the task of disfranchising the Jews.[67]

It is interesting to compare the diametrically opposed views of the *Record* with Einhorn's *Sinai* in reference to the Negroes. For Einhorn, Jewish rights would not be safe until Negro rights were secure. His humanitarianism made him the friend of the oppressed Negro. The *Record*, however, became a vicious spokesman of anti-Negro prejudice:

> We know not how to speak in the same breath of the Negro and the Israelite. The very names have startlingly opposite sounds—one representing all that is debased and inferior in the hopeless barbarity and heathenism of six thousand years; the other, the days when Jehovah conferred on our fathers the glorious equality which led the Eternal to converse with them, and allow them to enjoy the communion of angels. Thus the abandoned fanatics insult the choice of God himself, in endeavoring to reverse the inferiority which he stamped on the African, to make him the compeer, even in bondage, of His chosen people.
>
> There is no parallel between such races. Humanity from pole to pole would scout such a comparison. The Hebrew was *originally* free; and the charter of his liberty was inspired by his Creator. The Negro was never free; and his bondage in Africa was simply duplicated in a milder form when he was imported here . . . The judicious in all the earth agree that to proclaim the African equal to the surrounding races, would be a farce which would lead the civilized conservatism of the world to denounce the outrage . . .
>
> Alas, that the holy name and fame of the Prophet Moses should be desecrated by a comparison with the quixotic achievements of President Lincoln![68]

The *Record*, in typical Democratic fashion, revealed no sympathy with the Administration's program of emancipation or with its hopes for the Negro. Lincoln might just as well have abolished the institution of monarchy throughout Europe, it said, as proclaim the emancipation of slaves in the very parts of the South which were not under Union control.[69]

It objected to every step taken for the welfare of the Negro with sarcastic comments to the effect that whites would soon have to disguise themselves as colored men to obtain favors from the government.[70] The *Record* had no faith in the ability of the Negro to take his place in the ranks of the civilized. Those who said that he would do as well as the Jew were blind to the facts. Compare the achievements of Jews in the arts and sciences even under the most oppressive regimes of Europe with the failure of freed Negroes in the North to demonstrate any potentialities whatever, said the *Record*, and it would be clear that the Negro did not deserve freedom.[71]

At the very beginning of the slavery agitation, one of the most respected rabbis in America, Max Lilienthal of Cincinnati, had agreed with most of his colleagues that the abolitionists were incendiary radicals who were bringing the nation to the brink of disaster. However much he believed that slavery was an immoral institution, he was willing to defend the right of the Southern states to determine their own economic system. But once the war broke out, he threw all his strength on the side of Lincoln and the Union cause, confident that it was right and just to drive back "the surging waves of the ocean of rebellion" for the sake of the Union.[72]

Lithographs of Lilienthal, a very popular rabbi, had been sold all over the country. One of these was returned to him, shortly after his declaration of allegiance to the Union, with a message scrawled across its face:

> Sir:
> Since you have discarded the Lord and taken up the Sword in defense of a Negro government, your picture that has occupied a place in our Southern home, we return herewith, that you may present it to your *Black Friends,* as it will not be permitted in our dwelling. Your veneration for the Star Spangled Banner is, I presume, in your pocket, like all other demagogues who left their country for their country's good. I shall be engaged actively in the field and should be happy to rid Israel of the disgrace of your life. Be assured that we have memories; our friends we shall not forget. Should you ever desire to cultivate any acquaintance with me, I affix my name and residence, and you may find someone in your place who can inform you who I am.
>
> Jacob A. Cohen,
> New Orleans, La., C.S.A.[73]

How wrong Jacob Cohen was to regard Lilienthal as an abolitionist was demonstrated in his Victory Sermon, delivered on April 14, 1865, in which he publicly apologized for not having been anti-slavery until Lincoln issued the Emancipation Proclamation! He confessed his shame that he had been willing to defend the slave property of the Southern states, and that he had been wanting in the moral courage to denounce "the scourge of slavery." He realized now, he said, that the abolitionists were the heroes of the age: "Right must be right, whatever may be the consequences." All the credit for having "freed [the country] from the everlasting blemish of slavery" was due to the abolitionists who had risked reputation, honor, and security, for a moral principle.

V

If the rabbis of the North were in such thorough disagreement about the Jewish approach to slavery and abolitionism, it is not surprising to find that their Southern colleagues gave complete support to the slave system. At least one of them, George Jacobs of Richmond, employed slaves in his own home without feeling that he was acting contrary to the dictates of Judaism. He was no Simon Legree, of course; in fact, long after the Negroes had been freed, a former slave woman continued to cling to his family, following them to Philadelphia where the Rev. Jacobs accepted a pulpit. She continued to serve them until old age forced her retirement.[74]

The Rev. J. M. Michelbacher of Richmond appears to have been completely convinced of the justice of Negro slavery, judging from his only war-time sermon to be preserved. In a lengthy prayer summoning God to the assistance of the Confederacy in an hour of danger, he revealed his belief that slavery was ordained of God:

> The man servants and maid servants Thou has given unto us, that we may be merciful to them in righteousness and bear rule over them, the enemy are attempting to seduce, that they, too, may turn against us, whom Thou has appointed over them as instructors in Thy wise dispensation . . . Behold, O God, [our enemies] invite our man-servants to insurrection, and they place weapons of death and the fire of desolation in their hands that we may become an easy prey unto them; they beguile them from the path of duty that they may waylay their masters, to assassinate and to slay the men, women and children of the people that trust only in Thee. In this wicked thought, let them be frustrated, and cause them to fall into the pit of destruction, which in the abomination of their evil intents they digged out for us, our brothers and sisters, our wives and our children.[75]

Michelbacher was voicing the fears of most Southerners in this prayer, unjustified fears that the Union would inspire the slaves to savage destruction.

VI

It is important to note that, with the exception of the activities of the two abolitionist rabbis, David Einhorn and Bernhard Felsenthal, and of a few isolated editorials on abolitionism and the Fugitive Slave Law in *The*

Asmonean[76] in 1850–51, the discussion of slavery among the rabbis did not begin until late 1860, when the fate of the nation had already been fixed, and public opinion, by and large, already formulated.[77] This would indicate that the rabbis, with the exceptions already noted, were followers, rather than leaders, in political thought, and that they were not prepared to discuss the most burning issue of the day until it was already tearing the Union apart. As immigrants new to the nation's problems and as spiritual leaders of a minority faith, then, they were, for the most part, wary of political activity.

Once they felt it essential to commit themselves, however, they adopted no single political formula, but, to the contrary, all the varieties of political thought then current on the national scene. Personal background and environment, rather than Jewish teachings, determined their views; their version of Judaism was cut to fit the pattern of the conclusions which they reached independently. As with the Christian denominations, so with Judaism; religious ideals and principles were interpreted in widely disparate ways when a crucial issue faced the entire nation.

Yet another observation is necessary. The division of the United States into two warring fragments had been foreshadowed long before 1861 by the violent sectional strife in Christian denominational conventions, conferences and assemblies. As early as 1845, the Southern Baptists had seceded from their national convention over the issue of slavery. In 1854, after eleven days of heated debate, the Annual Methodist General Conference ordered a slave-holding Methodist bishop to dispose of his slaves; the Southerners left the Methodist fold the following year. Schism along sectional lines took another form in the Presbyterian ranks when the New School group, including most of the abolitionists, withdrew from the national synod in 1857. The inability of Southerners and Northerners to adjust their differences within a religious framework concretized and perhaps even deepened the nation's dilemma.[78]

Such a split did not occur among the Jews. There *were* national Jewish bodies, although they were not in the least comparable to the Protestant denominational organizations. The Independent Order of B'nai B'rith and other fraternal groups appear to have ignored the South-North turmoil in the pre-war years, tolerated the enforced separation of the war years, and continued as before once the war had been ended; indeed, in 1866, the Memphis Lodge of B'nai B'rith urged that the annual district convention be held in that Southern city because "it would tend greatly to the extension of our beloved Order in the South."[79] The Board of Delegates of American Israelites discussed only Jewish subjects during its few pre-war years, and hardly even met during the period of the war. It was a weak, incomplete organization, altogether, but its leaders were moderates who would not for an instant have injected politics into its proceedings. Einhorn and Felsenthal might have attempted to do so, but they were among its more forceful opponents. There was actually, then, no attempt to divide the few nation-wide organizations along sectional lines on the basis of the slave question, nor on the issue of war either, although, as we shall see, certain rabbis did take an active political role when the military phase of the Civil War followed hard upon the heels of the propaganda phase.

III THE RABBIS TAKE SIDES

I

ORGANIZED RELIGION serves one of its most obvious purposes in moments of crisis in the life of an individual or of a community. During the Civil War, the churches of the Union and Confederacy zealously fulfilled their religious role as sources of inspiration, comfort, and strength; they were significant factors in the reinforcement of that spirit which the twentieth century has labeled "civilian morale." Several times during every year of the conflict, Lincoln and Davis called upon their people to attend special church services on Days of Humiliation and Prayer and on Thanksgiving Days, to seek divine blessing for their respective armies. It is impossible to calculate in statistical terms the benefit which accrued to both sides, the number of men who enlisted in the armed forces, the number of war bonds purchased, the number of hours devoted to war work, as a result of the hymns sung, the prayers spoken, and the sermons preached at religious services during the war. But it is probably no exaggeration to say that neither the Union nor the Confederacy could long have maintained the war effort without the active participation of the churches.

The synagogues of both sections cooperated fully in this religio-patriotic activity. Wherever there were Jewish congregations—in Peoria,[1] New Haven,[2] Syracuse,[3] Rochester,[4] Easton,[5] Memphis,[6] Richmond,[7] to name only a few—the Jews gathered together to pray for the success of the cause and the end of hostilities. Special penitential prayers were chanted, and inspirational sermons were delivered by the rabbis. The periodicals published the proclamations of the President and urged the attendance of their people. Afterwards, the sermons were printed so as to reach those Jews who had not themselves participated.

Typical of the editorial comment on the Days of Prayer was that of *The Jewish Messenger*, which said:

> By no class of people will this recommendation of the President be more faithfully acceded to, than by those whom we are particularly addressing. To no body of citizens has the Union been more prolific of good, of blessings untold, than to us; and by none is its present afflicted condition more deeply, earnestly deplored than by the Israelites of America. It is but natural, then, that a day set apart for national prayer should be observed with a due sense of its import, and that thereon should ascend to the God of Abraham, Isaac

FORM OF SERVICE

FOR

Thursday, 13th June, 1861.
(5th Tamuz 5621.)

Being a day of Humiliation and Prayer appointed by the President of the C. S. A.

————:o:————

AFTERNOON SERVICE.

————

(The Ark is opened and the Sepharim taken to the Tebah.)

————:o:————

ROMAMOO.

Prayer for the Government.

————

Psalm LXVII. Lamnatsayach Bingenoth.

————

LACHOO VENASHOOBA.
ELOHAYNOO VELOHAY ABOTAYNOO.
Psalm XCI. Yoshabe Basayter.

YIMLOCH ADONAY.

Psalm XXIX. Mizmor L'David.

(The Sepharim are returned to the Ark.)

————

AYN KAYLOHAYNOO.

—

ALAYNOO.

—

SERMON.

—

ADON NGOLAM.

Facsimile of the program of a Patriotic Confederate Service at Beth Shalome Synagogue, Richmond and Jacob, fervent aspirations for the deliverance of this hitherto most favored land from the evils surrounding it, and its speedy restoration to its wonted tranquility and prosperity . . .

We should be as ready as the heroic men of the Revolution, to pledge even our lives for the maintenance of the national honor. But we desire to see a speedy termination to this war, for we feel it a blot on our escutcheon, that there should be found among citizens of America, any who would calmly contrive her downfall, who would deliberately plot her ruin . . . Our satisfaction with a vigorous prosecution of what is conceived to be a necessary resort to force, is not at all inconsistent with the earnest desire we at the same time experience, that the "swords may soon again be beaten into plowshares." For a successful issue to the nation's efforts for the reestablishment of law and order, as well as for the early enjoyment of the blessings of peace, right heartily do we pray to Heaven. . . .[8]

In addition to these special services held in response to presidential request, prayers for the welfare of the government and the success of the armed forces were read in many synagogues at weekly Sabbath services and on Jewish holidays.[9] At least one synagogue held a special service one day every week during the entire four-year war period.[10] The raising of the national emblem over synagogues in New York City,[11] Cleveland,[12] and Easton,[13] to name those which were recorded, was celebrated by special prayers; the departure of large numbers of members of the congregation for military duty was also utilized as the occasion for patriotic religious devotions.[14]

Non-Jewish clergymen and military officers occasionally came to the synagogues to participate in patriotic demonstrations.[15] One interesting example of this was recorded by *The Jewish Messenger*. When Major Anderson of Fort Sumter fame returned to New York, some of his Jewish friends escorted him to Sabbath services at Temple Emanu-El where, naturally, his presence created a sensation. Raphael de Cordova, the lecturer-humorist who was employed to deliver English sermons at Emanu-El, hastily revised his address of the morning and paid tribute to the guest of the congregation, urging his congregants to tender their complete support to the Union cause. At the conclusion of the service, the organ played the national anthem while those in attendance milled around the national war hero and overwhelmed him with congratulations.[16]

A list of the sermons and prayers on patriotic subjects which were delivered by the rabbis is printed as an appendix to this volume. Every preacher and minister had his own individual attitude towards specific aspects of the war; but there was a common denominator, which transcended the differences of opinion between abolitionists, moderates and pro-slavery men, which transcended even the diametrically opposed views of Unionists and Confederates. They were, after all, rabbis, dedicated to a religious interpretation of life. There was an almost uniform quality of sadness, compassion, and piety in their religious pronouncements. Whether they supported or opposed the Administration in the North, whether they bespoke God's blessing on the Federal or Confederate cause, human suffering and need concerned all of them: the horrors of war on the battlefield, the snuffing out of young lives, the misery of poverty-stricken families on the home front, the destructive passions and hatreds engendered by the war.

Beyond this common denominator of interest were specific aspirations and personal loyalties. We are limited, of course, to the records preserved in synagogue minute-books, periodicals and personal manuscripts. Five rabbis emerge from the faded print and yellowing paper of the 1860s more clearly than their colleagues: They were men whom personal conviction and fate conspired to set in the path of the excitement and anxiety of the war years.

II

Of those rabbis who spoke out most forthrightly in favor of the Union cause—Max Lilienthal of Cincinnati, Liebman Adler and Bernhard Felsenthal of Chicago, David Einhorn of Philadelphia, S. M. Isaacs of New York —Sabato Morais of Philadelphia was perhaps the most dynamic.

Unlike Einhorn and Felsenthal, he was not an abolitionist. His profound loyalty to the Union and his unswerving support of the Lincoln administration derived rather from his conviction that the future of republicanism all over the world would be severely threatened by America's failure to preserve its constitutional integrity. If the United States were unable to quell internal dissension, democracy would be ridiculed everywhere as too weak to live up to its promise. He recognized the evils of slavery, but he could not side with the abolitionists who were willing to sacrifice all of the cherished achievements of four generations of American life rather than live with slavery. It goes without saying that he was equally opposed to the Southerners who would, in defense of slavery, "cast away as worthless the precious legacy of their fathers." When the South did seek to destroy his beloved Union, he could do naught else but support the war effort:

> When dearly bought freedom is in jeopardy; when the angry billows of a political sea impede the march of civilization, and the adversaries of human brotherhood are skilfully marshalled for the onslaught, deeds of self-denial, more than psalmody, will sanctify the life of man . . . Let him, therefore, who values his country's honor speed on, let him trustingly follow the path which leads to national deliverance, and when the happy goal shall have been attained, raise the anthem which will be reverberated from sea to sea, even from the Atlantic to the Pacific Ocean . . .[17]

Peace was as dear to him as to any other American, but the integrity of the Union was even more precious. "We *must* have peace," he exclaimed, "but not at the cost of our national existence." Only a peace of unity which would "render America what its illustrious founders had made it, the pattern of freedom and the haven of the oppressed," was worth accepting.[18]

Much as he urged his people to take part in the struggle for the Union, Morais could not find it in his heart to stir up their hatred against the people of the South. They were invaders, it was true, enemies who had erected a "citadel of Rebellion" against the nation which had nourished them. But they were still brothers, for all their rebelliousness and treachery. He prayed for the defeat of the military forces of the Confederacy, but he also asked God to speak to the hearts of his "misguided . . . disaffected children," and to renew within them the loyalty which they had once felt for the United States. He applauded Lincoln's conciliatory policy towards the slave states and hoped that they would return to the Union of their own free will, without having to be conquered.[19]

Morais had a deeper affection for Lincoln than any other rabbi. He responded almost instinctively to those qualities of Lincoln's mind and soul which served the nation in its most serious crisis. He, like millions of others, shared in Lincoln's most intimate personal problems. After the death of Lincoln's little son, Willie, Morais prayed in this wise:

> . . . Direct the hands into which the temporal welfare of this people is entrusted. Sustain them, that their strength may never flag. Bless the President of the United States; bless him for his sterling honesty, bless him for his firmness and moderation. Rekindle with joy his domestic hearth; pour on him the balm of divine consolation. Grant that the issues of his momentous obligations be a united and prosperous country. Grant that the end of his career be the maintenance of this Government, unimpaired and unsullied as bequeathed by our illustrious ancestors . . .[20]

Copies of this prayer and the sermon which preceded it were sent to the President by Abraham Hart, the *Parnas* of Morais' congregation.[21] Lincoln acknowledged its receipt with hearty thanks "for your expressions of kindness and confidence."[22] Hart also sent the President a copy of his rabbi's Thanksgiving Sermon of 1863 in which he had suggested, in keeping with Lincoln's national message proclaiming Thanksgiving Day, that the major task of those who remained at home was to stretch out the hand of sympathy to the widows and orphans of the soldiers who had given their lives in battle.[23]

Like many of his colleagues, Morais criticized those who placed personal safety and profit above the national welfare while men were dying for the cause. He could not honestly ask God's blessing, he felt, while selfishness and materialism were rife on the home front. Why should God help the country, when the people themselves were not bending every effort to win the war? Pernicious politicians, greedy men of commerce,

Executive Mansion,

Washington, May 13 , 1862

My Dear Sir

Permit me to acknowledge the receipt of your communication of April 23ᵈ containing a copy of a Prayer recently delivered at your Synagogue, and to thank you heartily for your expressions of kindness and confidence

Have the honor to be
Your Ob't Serv't

A. Lincoln

A. Hart Esq
Pres't Cong'n Hope of Israel
Phila

Facsimile of Lincoln's letter to A. Hart, President of Mikveh Israel congregation, Philadelphia.

and dishonest military officers, he said, must be exposed and stripped of power before the nation would be worthy of God's favor upon its struggle for life:

> Dare we, with hands polluted with bribe, with minds engrossed in the pursuit of ill-gotten wealth, with hearts of stone that will sacrifice the dearest interests of mankind, aye the lives of myriads, too, in order to obtain some ephemeral power; dare we invoke in our favor the assistance of the God of Justice and Truth? . . . Like the inflexible Joshua, we must destroy the impious Achans with their plunder . . .[24]

If America would repent herself of "vice and pride . . . fraud, perjury and rebellion" against God, then, in truth, God would bless the Union with victory and peace.[25]

Morais preached pro-Union sermons on every possible occasion, National Fast Days, Thanksgiving, Jewish holidays, and on the Fourth of July. One he delivered at the express request of the Philadelphia Union League, of which he was an honorary member.[26] He offered his services to the government as a chaplain, and was responsible for the organization of a women's group in his synagogue which cooperated with the United States Sanitary Commission. More of his sermons were printed in the daily press than any other American rabbi's.[27] Short of giving his life in battle, Dr. Morais could hardly have done more for the cause to which he was so sincerely devoted.

It was inevitable that there should be complaints against his undisguised Republican sympathies by those members of the congregation who were Democrats. The *Parnas* (president), Abraham Hart, seems to have defended him against such criticism during his term of office. In late 1864, however, Hart was succeeded by L. J. Lieberman, one of those who resented Dr. Morais' frequent political allusions and activities. A struggle immediately commenced between the rabbi and the *Adjunta* (Board of Trustees) over the freedom of the pulpit.

Shortly after Thanksgiving, 1864, when Morais had delivered one of his customary pro-Union addresses, Lieberman was able to persuade a majority of the Board to pass a resolution which declared that "henceforth all English Lectures or Discourses shall be dispensed with, *except by particular request of the Parnas, made in writing. . . .*"[28] This denial of Morais' right to express his personal political philosophy in the pulpit was a radical action considering the fact that the minutes of the *Adjunta* contain no record of previous discussion of the problem. It indicates, however, how hostile the new regime was to Morais' Republican declarations.

The rabbi was not content to accept the Board's verdict, but inspired a campaign among his friends for a reversal of the Board's action. To the *Parnas* he wrote, not by way of apology, but in explanation, that the paragraphs of the Thanksgiving Sermon which were regarded as objectionable had not been intended to gloat over the re-election of Lincoln and the defeat of the Democratic Party's nominees, but merely to express "the gratification, which every honest man must have felt, at the absence of sedition and violence in our midst."[29] Unfortunately, no copy of the sermon has survived, and we are therefore unable to judge for ourselves. But, at any rate, this explanation appears to have been unacceptable to Lieberman. Meanwhile, Morais' supporters were circulating a petition among the members of the congregation, demanding a revision of the Board's policy.

On February 5, 1865, this petition was presented to the Board; it insisted that Morais be permitted to speak at least once a month and on all holidays. So many members and seat-holders had signed the document that the Board could not reject the demand, but it emphasized in its new declaration of policy that all sermons would have to be "religious Discourse[s]" and that they could only be delivered at the discretion of the *Parnas*.[30]

This was a victory, but only a partial one. On April 7, 1865, therefore, Morais again petitioned the Board for permission "to address the Congregation, whenever I deem fit."[31] It was decided to air the entire matter at a congregational meeting two days later. The voting demonstrated how loyal the rank and file membership was to the rabbi. Every effort to secure approval for the Board's action was defeated, and a final motion, passed by a large majority, empowered Morais to preach on "moral and religious subjects" whenever he chose to do so, and "on the subjects of the day . . . whenever the Synagogue may be opened by order of the *Parnas*."[32] Just a few days later, Morais preached his first sermon on a "subject of the day"—a moving eulogy in memory of the martyred President. Never again was his freedom to preach disputed. In 1866 he was elected to life-time occupancy of the Mikveh Israel pulpit.

Why should the fate of America have been so close to the heart of this immigrant rabbi that he was willing to risk the displeasure of his congregation and, even more, to forfeit the fulfillment of his professional duties? He explained the reason for his passion, indirectly, in many of his sermons. He had been born and educated in Italy. His father had been imprisoned for republican activities. Mazzini and other Italian revolutionaries were his personal friends. He knew at first hand the effects of political strife and disunity, the evils of autocratic regimes. He knew how difficult it was to regain freedom once it was lost. He knew, also, how profoundly the example of democratic America had inspired irredentist and revolutionary movements all over Europe. How could he remain silent when the great shining beacon of freedom was threatened with extinction? Risk displeasure, indeed, he would have said; his father had risked his freedom! He felt he had good reason to lecture his congregation on the value of democracy.[33]

III

Isaac Mayer Wise was in many ways the direct antithesis of Sabato Morais. Peace was more important to him than the Union. He believed that once the South had seceded, the North had no right to resort to arms, "Force will not hold together this Union," he said; "it was cemented by liberty and can stand only by the affections of the people."[34] With the outbreak of war he lapsed into a resentful silence:

> What can we say now? Shall we lament and weep like Jeremiah over a state of things too sad and too threatening to be looked upon with indifference? We would only be laughed at in this state of excitement and passionate agitation, or probably abused for discouraging the sentiment. Or should we choose sides with one of the parties? We can not, not only because we abhor the idea of war, but also we have dear friends and near relations, beloved brethren and kinsmen in either section of the country, that our heart bleeds on thinking of their distress, of the misery that might befall them . . .[35]

Wise abided by this declaration of neutrality. He rarely commented upon the war or its problems when there was no specific Jewish aspect which required his attention; he made no profession of loyalty to the Union nor did he urge his readers to support the war effort. Rather than blame Southern Jewry for its advocacy of the Confederacy as Einhorn did, or apologize as Felsenthal did, Wise defended its right to do so:

> If the largest proportion of the Jewish population of Richmond, Charleston and New Orleans give "aid and comfort to rebellion," as our opponents maintain, they do exactly as others do in the same localities . . . You abolitionists with the grandiloquent and bombastic declamations of philanthropy, freedom and attachment to the government, why do you not go down South and expound your doctrines to the community; and if you dare not do it, why do you expect the Jews there to stand in opposition to the masses of people?[36]

Always eager to keep abreast of Jewish news from the South during the war, Wise questioned every Southerner who reached Cincinnati and published as much information as he was able to obtain. In 1862, for instance, he took pleasure in telling his readers that all was well with the congregations in Jackson and Summit, Miss., Atlanta and Columbus, Ga., Montgomery and Mobile, Ala., and that "our informant tells us wonders of the material prosperity of our friends in the far South."[37] Wise did consider the Southerners to be friends, not enemies, and after the war he preached vigorously for an end to the bitterness against the ex-Confederacy.

Feeling as strongly as he did against the abolitionists, Wise had little sympathy for Lincoln and the Republican Administration. When Lincoln stopped in Cincinnati on his way to his Inauguration, Wise wrote:

> Poor old Abe Lincoln, who had the quiet life of a country lawyer, having been elected President of this country, and now going to be inaugurated in his office, the Philistines from all corners of the land congregate around their Dagon and worship him . . . Why all this noise? . . . Wait until he has done something . . . Some of our friends might like to know how the president looks, and we can tell them; he looks . . . "like a country squire for the first time in the city." He wept on leaving Springfield and invited his friends to pray for him; that is exactly the picture of his looks. We have no doubt he is an honest man, and, as much as we can learn, also quite an intelligent man; but he will look queer in the white house, with his primitive manner.[38]

After Lincoln, in his first Inaugural Address, referred to Christianity as a mainstay for the country in its hour of crisis, Wise wrote:

> We have only to say for Mr. Lincoln, that his style of writing is so careless and without any successful attempt at either correctness or elegance that he must not be criticized in using this or that word to express an idea. He takes domestic words, as used in Springfield and vicinity to express familiar ideas. In Springfield religion is called Christianity, because people there do not think of any other form of worship, hence Mr. Lincoln uses the same word to express the same sentiment. We do not believe there is a German infidel, American eccentric, spiritual rapper or atheist in the northern states who did not vote for Mr. Lincoln. Let us see how much benefit he will derive from their Christianity, or how he will settle the political troubles with such piety . . .[39]

Editing a Jewish newspaper in war time was no easy matter. Like *The Occident* and the *Messenger*, Wise's *Israelite* lost large numbers of its subscribers when the war broke out: over half, he said, had been Southerners. The cost of paper and printing rose steadily and money was so scarce that some of his Northern readers cancelled their subscriptions.[40] Some refused on principle to continue reading his "Secessionist sheet" as it was called by some non-Jewish Cincinnatians.[41] But that was not the worst of his troubles.

For all his theoretical objections to mixing politics and religion, Wise was a loyal member of the Democratic Party and derived many of his political sympathies from that affiliation.[42] On September 5, 1863, he was nominated for the office of State Senator by the Democratic State Convention at Carthage, Ohio, on the first ballot. Since the meeting was held on the Sabbath, Wise himself could not be there, but his friend Israel Brown apologized for his absence "and informed the convention that the Doctor would accept the nomination." "Cheers," followed this announcement, according to the *Cincinnati Daily Enquirer*, a Democratic paper, which said that "Dr. Wise . . . a gentleman of learning and accomplishment . . . well known as an estimable Hebrew Rabbi of this city . . . would make an excellent Senator."[43] The *Cincinnati Daily Gazette*, a Republican organ, had some sarcastic things to say about ministers and politics, and made a ribald statement about the possible relationship of circumcision to the biblical attitude towards slavery.[44]

Both the *Gazette* and the *Enquirer* understood that Wise had accepted the nomination. But no one seems to have taken the feelings of his Board of Trustees into consideration. Two days after the nominating convention, the Board held a meeting, discussed the matter, and decided to instruct the rabbi to decline:

> The Board feels greatly honored by this demonstration of confidence bestowed upon you; they are also well aware of your sincere attachment to our common country; nevertheless, as it is an established law with us that our minister should be present in the synagogue whenever divine service is held, and also, your services otherwise being indispensably necessary in our congregation, as well as in the scholastic department, you are hereby politely, but most emphatically requested to decline said nomination at once . . .[45]

The Board of the Talmud Yelodim Institute, the congregation's parochial school, passed resolutions to the same effect and forwarded them to the rabbi.[46]

Wise could have argued with his Boards. There had never been any objections to his extensive travels all over the country to preach at temple cornerstone laying and dedication ceremonies. No one had ever before invoked a congregational ruling about his attendance at all services. But he knew very well that the Boards were inventing excuses and hiding the real reason for their "emphatic" order. Most of them were Republicans and they were shocked to think that their own rabbi might attract votes to the Democratic Party in so crucial an election. The Democratic gubernatorial candidate was Clement L. Vallandigham, now returned from political exile in Canada, leader of the anti-Lincoln Copperheads; he was a hateful symbol to all Republicans, and those who controlled the Jewish community in Cincinnati were willing to go to any length to prevent their rabbi's helping to elect Vallandigham. The pressure they brought to bear was more intense than their communications indicated. The alternative which they offered was dismissal from the pulpit. On the surface all was politeness and respect, but underneath there was agitated resentment on both sides, as reports in the Cincinnati dailies indicated.[47] Wise actually had no choice:

> As you maintain you cannot dispense with my humble services for the time I might be obliged to spend at the Capital of the State, and the law of the congregation especially ordains it so, I certainly feel obliged to decline a nomination so honorably tendered, notwithstanding my private opinion, that

I might tender some services to my country, not altogether unessential, especially as those who nominated me know well my sincere attachment to this country and government. God will save the Union and the Constitution; liberty and justice for all, without my active cooperation, being, after all, without any political aspirations—only an humble individual . . .[48]

The fact that he wrote nothing about the episode in *The Israelite* and published only the correspondence, might indicate that for once in his life he was intimidated. But actually we do not know what he thought about the political tactics of the Republican Jews of Cincinnati. The *Cincinnati Daily Enquirer* was not so silent as the rabbi himself:

The Rev. Dr. Wise has been forced, by outside pressure, to decline the Democratic nomination for State Senator. Had his name been on the other ticket, the Shoddy contractors who have been so busy in pulling the wires to produce this result, would have been contented to let it remain. The names of these Shoddy contractors do not appear on the record, but they are known nevertheless.[49]

He was never intimidated, however, into withdrawing from the position which he took in *The Israelite*. A year later he was still inveighing against the materialism, demagoguery, and fanaticism which had brought on the war, and was still refusing to take either side in the struggle:

Either [a man] must rejoice over the defeat of our armies and pray for their destruction, or he must blindly admire the blunders of our military leaders and shout Hosannah to Abe Lincoln and his thousand and one demonstrations of imbecility, in order to gratify one or the other faction. Either one must believe the Negro was created to be a beast of burden to others or you must say he is just as good as you are . . .[50]

The other Jewish papers, with the exception of the *Record*, had nothing to say about Wise's nomination. The *Messenger* and *The Occident* tried to ignore him as much as possible; otherwise they would have devoted most of their editorials to attacks upon him. The *Record* was not interested in his politics or religious creed, but felt that the stand taken by the Cincinnati Jews was completely unpatriotic: "while the country is in danger, everybody must put his shoulder to the wheel, and do his utmost to save it." The *Record* said that Wise was a "bright ornament . . . among the wilderness of stupidity and ignorance out West," that he would have brought honor to Jewry and America in the sordid game of politics, and that the Cincinnati Jews had performed a grave disservice to the nation and to American Jewry by refusing to permit him to run for the office.[51]

What is so interesting, of course, is that whenever a rabbi took an outspoken political position, the right of every American citizen, those who controlled his congregation used every means to silence him. The Democrats refused to permit Morais to preach; the Confederate sympathizers in Baltimore made it impossible for Einhorn to return to his congregation; the Republicans in Cincinnati forced Wise to withdraw from the 1863 election. It was not a question of the rabbi's *brand* of politics; powerful Board members objected to *all* politics. They interpreted Judaism in a narrow, ritualistic sense; they preferred a religion which was withdrawn to a safe distance from all of the controversial problems of the day. It was to take another generation before the American rabbinate defied the laity and declared itself firmly in favor of Jewish pronouncements on questions of social justice.[52]

IV

Isaac Leeser was a natural bridge between the rabbis of the North and those of the Confederacy. If anyone tried with desperate sincerity to occupy the unhappy, sad position of neutrality during the entire war period, it was the bachelor rabbi of Philadelphia. Five years of young manhood spent in Richmond and close ties of blood and friendship with many people throughout the Southland could not be erased by thirty years of devoted ministry in the North. But he was too much a part of the life of the Union to lean towards the South either. Actually, he understood and sympathized with both sides of the conflict so sincerely that he was unable to divorce himself from one or the other. He gave his thoughts and his prayers to both the Union *and* the Confederacy, as though he were living far, far away from Philadelphia.

Sincerely and wholeheartedly believing that all politics (not merely those he disagreed with) should be eschewed by the Jewish preacher and editor, Leeser consistently avoided discussions of a political nature in his *Occident*, except when Jews and Judaism were directly involved. He believed that Jews should participate in the political life of the nation, as individuals, not as Jews. As he had refused to discuss the slavery issue, so he would not present his personal opinions on other differences between the North and South.[53]

But he did write a few incidental words in criticism of the demagogues and agitators on both sides who were pushing the nation towards disaster, "the ruthless spirit of intermeddling in matters which concern them not on the part of the inhabitants of the North,"[54] and "the partisan leaders of the opposite section" who, if they "would but *think* . . . could not be so ready to subvert the government, and would rather put up with some grievances, and forego even some rights, sooner than run the risk of establishing a military despotism. . . ."[55] Leeser thought that it was the responsibility of Jews to act as peacemakers, to attempt to placate the people on both sides. In his own prayers and writings, he spoke only for "conciliation and truth . . . moderation . . . peace and brotherly love."[56]

It was agony for Leeser to think of civil war, of Jews lifting up their hands to slay those "with whom they were but lately on terms of friendship," of all America divided into two warring camps.[57] This was not verbiage. With his vivid imagination, Leeser was dramatizing his own feelings. If he had been young enough to serve in the Army, he would not have been able to fight for the North against his Southern friends any more than he could have fought for the Confederacy against the Union. This was not fence-straddling; it was the dilemma of a man of divided loyalties in a day which required undivided allegiance.

All through the war, Leeser wrote from a neutral point of vantage, with equal regard for both sides. He hoped that the contest would be brief and that peace and plenty would bless the land again,[58] but the protracted war did not change his sentiments. He was proud that Jews in both sections were loyal to their neighbors, and asked Jews in the South as well as in the North to

> turn to the God of their fathers for support in the direful calamity which now sweeps over this once peaceful country, and brings sorrow and mourning to many a bereaved heart. Now is the time for the soul to be touched with contrition when the Lord makes it manifest to all on what a broken prop they lean when they trust in human strength, and a mortal's wisdom . . . Let us be humble when we contemplate the extent of the evil which no human forethought or knowledge was able to avert.[59]

After the cessation of hostilities, Leeser made several trips to the South. On a visit to Richmond, where he installed two new Lodges of the Independent Order of B'nai B'rith, he noted with pleasure that the congregations and charitable organizations of the city had survived the havoc of war, although their members had endured much suffering and were now in very narrow straits. He was delighted to see his old rabbinical friends again, and hoped that "the intercourse now resumed between the sections may be productive of harmony and concert of action, among the Israelites especially. . . ."[60] From Chattanooga, Tenn., he wrote feelingly of the battlefields "literally trodden down by the steps of marching armies making roads, or tracks, rather, in every direction, obliterating forests, houses, fields, and the natural growth of the soil. . . ." He was pleased that war-time enmity had not been perpetuated in the Jewish soldiers' cemetery there, that "those who were not personal enemies, but merely driven to slaughter each other by the folly and madness of rulers, will sleep side by side in undisturbed rest, awaiting the resurrection."[61]

The impression that Leeser was pro-Confederate seems to have been rather wide-spread. It was not easy for the partisan to understand a genuine and sincere neutrality. After Leeser's death, for instance, Congregation Beth Elohim of Charleston, S. C., paid tribute to his supposed Confederate sympathies in a memorial resolution:

... As Southerners, we grieve over the loss of a bold defender of our rights; a true and consistent friend to constitutional liberty, who, through great personal peril, remained unshaken in our vindication, undismayed by our reverses, unconquered by our defeat . . .[62]

The Charleston Jews did not grasp the fact that Leeser's friendship for and interest in the South did not preclude an equal interest in and friendship for the North.

Moses A. Dropsie, a prominent Jewish lawyer in Philadelphia, one of the organizers of the Republican Party,[63] who later bequeathed to the community the funds with which the Dropsie College for Hebrew and Cognate Learning was established, was also unable to understand Leeser's attitude. On May 7, 1861, Dropsie gave a resounding patriotic address when the flag was raised atop the school house of the Hebrew Education Society. In his next issue of *The Occident* Leeser wrote an article on the event, deploring as always the outbreak of the war, but congratulating the Southern Jews for being as loyal to the Confederacy as Northern Jews were to the Union.[64] Dropsie sought out the rabbi and gave him a verbal whipping. After a long denunciation of Leeser's supposed Secessionist proclivities, Dropsie said: "You better take care what you say; you are already on the suspected list, and you may be compelled to quit the city before long!"[65]

Poor Leeser could not contain his anxiety. He immediately wrote a letter to Mayor Alexander Henry informing him of Dropsie's threat and asking for an official statement on the matter:

... I know nothing of a *legal* or illegal suspected list of the inhabitants of this city, nor am I conscious of any offense against the laws of this corporation, or the constitution, or the laws of the State or the Union, why I should be suspected of anything, much less why I should be ordered by anyone to quit Philadelphia. You will therefore greatly oblige an old resident who knew your grandfather thirty years ago, whether such a suspected list is in existence, and if so, for what cause my name was placed thereon; and if so whether I shall be liable to a summary expulsion from this place; so that I may make in time the necessary preparations, to go back to a country less free than this, but where the people at least have the assurance, that they are not liable to be molested by anyone who, in time of trouble, may endeavor to denounce them to an irresponsible power which being unknown to the law places the law and common sense at defiance.[66]

It is quite interesting to note that Leeser thought of being deported back to Germany, not of being transported across the Confederate lines. It is also noteworthy that he appeared willing to accept the fate of an exile if necessary, rather than give up his neutral position.

Mayor Henry put Leeser's spirit at rest. Not only was there no list of the proscribed, to his knowledge, but he had no idea "why the language of which you complain should have been used by Mr. M. A. Dropsie."

And to reassure the rabbi completely, he concluded his letter with the statement that "your loyalty has never been impugned, so far as I am aware."[67]

This was the only "peril" on record which Leeser had to endure during the war years, so the Charleston congregation's eulogy was something of an exaggeration. But the forty-eight hours which elapsed between Moses Dropsie's threat and the Mayor's reply were time enough for Isaac Leeser to contemplate, with sadness, the necessity of leaving the little comforts of his rooms, the homes of his friends, accustomed haunts, and the strong odor of printer's ink.

V

One of the leading rabbis of the South, the Rev. James K. Gutheim, who had inaugurated his rabbinical career at the Nefutzoth Jehudah Congregation in New Orleans, after a few years in business in New York and teaching in Cincinnati, agreed with his Northern colleagues that it was not "the province of the pulpit, to discuss the political questions of the day and to point out the course, which should be pursued."[68] His sermons over a long and fruitful ministry lived up to his declaration. Religion, for him, was not intended to be mixed with specific political considerations.[69]

Even during the excitement of secession talk after Lincoln's election, Gutheim would not depart from his policy. The farthest he would go was to counsel his people to be deliberate and objective:

> Whatever the cause or the result of the present agitation may be, every good citizen ought . . . with moderation and wisdom espouse the cause of right and justice, be ready for all sacrifices, and, discarding all prejudice and self-interest, exhibit a true and pure patriotism. Actuated by such a spirit we may at all times assuredly count on the protection of Providence, and look with a cheerful countenance into the immediate Future . . .[70]

What Gutheim meant by "the cause of right and justice," and how sincerely he intended his congregants to "be ready for all sacrifices" became abundantly clear in May 1863.

The Union's military policy in New Orleans required that each citizen take an oath of allegiance to the United States, or be transported into the Confederacy. Innumerable men took the course of least resistance and pronounced the words of the oath, rather than give up their homes, livelihoods, and personal belongings; they did not really think they were committing a sin; it was the enemy of their people whom they were deceiving. But Gutheim was a rabbi; he could not take a false oath to God, nor could he betray "the cause of right and justice" which was, to him, the cause of the South. So he prepared to go into exile. The day before his departure for Mobile, Ala., he wrote to his friend in Philadelphia, Isaac Leeser, who, he knew, would not think of him as an enemy:[71]

New Orleans
May 8th 1863.

Rev. I. Leeser -
My dear friend -

Day after tomorrow I shall leave N[ew] O[rleans] by order of the military authorities. All those who have refused to take the oath of allegiance to the Dictator of Washington are ordered beyond the lines—that is, into Dixie. I am of that number. Nearly the whole of my congregation are similarly situated.[72] We can now realize what a [deportation] means. Nothing but my wearing apparel and provisions for ten days are permitted. My heart feels sick. Amidst the general distress I forget my own. I am so far lucky, that I have an asylum for my wife and child—at La Grange Geo. where the family of Mr. Jones [Mrs. Gutheim's father] now resides. What I shall do in [the] future, I cannot say. I trust to God, to guide my steps. If possible I shall write you from the Confederacy. You must excuse my brevity. I am too busy in preparing for my departure. You are well! May God bless you and grant you length of days and happiness!

Yours truly,
James K. Gutheim

Please acquaint Dr. [Jonas] Bondi [of New York] of my condition, and remember me kindly to him.

From another friend in New Orleans, Leeser gained further details of Gutheim's departure:

The Sabbath before he left, the Synagogue was crowded, as many persons besides his own congregation wanted to hear him once more in the place which will know him no longer under the present condition of things . . . When about to sail with his banished members and their families from their late home, he offered up a touching prayer to the throne of the Most Merciful, which moved the hearts of his hearers . . .[73]

Even in this case, Leeser was cautious, quoting word for word from the letter which he had received from New Orleans, and offering no opinions of his own besides the hope that Gutheim would find security and safety somewhere in the Confederacy, and that a swift end to the war would soon permit him and his members to return home.

Neither Leeser nor Gutheim need have had any fears about his future. Jews all over the South knew and respected him as one of the most eloquent and learned of the Southern rabbis. His reputation, indeed, was enhanced by his heroic decision to remain true to the Confederacy. On May 21, 1863, the Mobile congregation met and paid tribute to his courage:

WHEREAS, We have learned with deep regret that the Rev. James R. [sic] Gutheim is among the numerous victims of tyranny now exercised in New Orleans, and has nobly preferred the martyrdom of his principles and sacrifice of worldly goods to a degrading submission . . .
RESOLVED, That the members of the Congregation "Shangarai Shamayim"

will be proud of the presence of that worthy and learned defender of Judaism in their midst, and most cordially tender him the hospitality of this Congregation.

RESOLVED, That they desire him to consider himself entirely at home among them, and they will endeavor, by showing him that love and respect which he so highly deserves, to sink all his past troubles into a state of oblivion . . .[74]

But Mobile already had a rabbi, so Gutheim looked elsewhere for a position. He had no difficulty in obtaining one; in fact he obtained two positions, and occupied both! The Kahl Montgomery Congregation, whose new Temple he had dedicated a year previously, voted to engage him as their preacher on June 23, 1863,[75] little over a month after he left New Orleans, although the congregational treasury was so depleted that his salary had to be raised by private subscription. A month later the B'nai Israel Congregation in Columbus, Ga., which had been disappointed when he declined the invitation to occupy its pulpit, requested the Montgomery congregation to permit Gutheim to circuit-ride to Columbus every sixth Sabbath.[76] For the duration of the war, Gutheim and his family resided in Montgomery, while he served his two congregations. Even after milder treatment of the New Orleans population made it possible for many exiles to return to their homes, Gutheim preferred to remain in the Confederacy.

His passionate loyalty to the Southern cause is revealed in a prayer which he delivered in Montgomery:[77]

Regard, O Father, in Thine abundant favor and benevolence, our beloved country, the Confederate States of America. May our young Republic increase in strength, prosperity and renown; may the helm of state be piloted with judgement; may wisdom resound in the halls of legislation, and harmony, obedience to the law, fortitude in trials and a self-sacrificing devotion prevail among the people. Endow, O God, the chosen Executive and his advisers with the spirit of wisdom, of knowledge and of strength, so as to be able to devise and to execute the best measures for the defense of our liberties and the protection of our homes and our lives. Behold, O God, and judge between us and our enemies, who have forced upon us this unholy and unnatural war—who hurl against us their poisoned arrows steeped in ambition and revenge. May they soon discover the error of their ways, relinquish their cruel designs of subjugation, their lust of gain and dominion, and yield a ready and willing ear to the dictates of humanity, of justice and of right. Bless, O Father, our efforts in a cause which we conceive to be just; the defense of our liberties and rights and independence, under just and equitable laws. May harmony of sentiment and purity of motive, unfaltering courage, immovable trust in our leaders, both in national council and in the field, animate all the people of our beloved Confederate States, so as to be equal to all emergencies—ready for every sacrifice, until our cause be vindicated as the light of day.

And we pray Thee, O God, to bless and protect the armed hosts, that now stand forth in the defense of our sacred cause.—Vain are the exertions of man without Thy aid. Behold, O Father, and cover with the shield of Thy heavenly Guardianship our sons, our brothers and our friends—the flower and the hope of the land. Endow their hearts with courage—nerve their arms with strength in the hour of combat. May the breaches lately made in our lines soon be repaired, a series of glorious victories blot out our recent reverses, and the unrighteous invaders be repulsed on every side, abashed, confounded and discomfited. Thou, O Lord, who makest peace in the highest heavens, mayest Thou bless us with a speedy and honorable peace, so that safety, confidence and happiness again smile upon the land, and our independence be recognized by all families of the earth . . .

On July 9, 1865, the New Orleans congregation invited their rabbi to return to his ministry in their midst. The war had ended; the "chivalrous" cause had been lost; there was no longer any point in suffering exile. Kahl Montgomery knew that they were too small to retain his services. The fluctuations of Confederacy currency had made it extremely difficult to raise even his small salary. But they were grateful that his Confederate loyalties had enabled them to be served by him for two years. On his departure the Montgomery Board of Trustees presented him with a set of engrossed resolutions which hailed him as "a shining light in Israel." He had been that to them in the crushing last months of the Confederacy.[78]

News of Dr. Gutheim's return to New Orleans was greeted with pleasure by his Northern friends. Dr. Bondi, who had recently assumed the editorship of *The Jewish Record* (renamed *The Hebrew Leader*) wished him "joy most cordially, and expect[ed] soon to receive favorable news from him . . ."[79] Isaac Leeser recorded the event with typical reserve, but anticipated that a spiritual revival would be under way in New Orleans now that Gutheim would be preaching there again.[80]

Gutheim did not give up his devotion to the South with the end of the war. In 1868 he accepted the call to occupy the pulpit of Temple Emanu-El of New York, but four years away from New Orleans was as much as he could bear. In 1872 he asked Emanu-El to release him from his contract so that he could return home and become the rabbi of the newly-organized Temple Sinai.[81] In 1875 he joined with Catholic and Protestant spokesmen in public declarations which denied General Sherman's charges that the people of Louisiana were still rebellious against Federal authority.[82] He was an active member of the Southern Historical Society, that thinly disguised attempt to perpetuate Confederate loyalties, and spoke at its New Orleans meeting in 1882.[83] Mrs. Gutheim was one of the founders of the Ladies' Confederate Memorial Association of New Orleans, and is said to have collected a larger amount of money for the erection of their Confederate monument than any other member.[84]

Who can look deeply enough into the heart of a man to search for the roots of loyalties? Why should a German immigrant rabbi, who had been in New Orleans only eleven years when Louisiana seceded, have been so devoted to Southern interests that he would face the hardship of exile in preference to taking an oath of loyalty to the United States? Perhaps part of the answer is to be found in Mrs. Gutheim, the young and vivacious daughter of a proud and wealthy Mobile family. Perhaps she was partly responsible for instilling in her husband a love for the South. Actually, however, we know so little about his experiences in New Orleans during the pre-war years, and so little about his inner life, despite a plethora of manuscript sermons, that we are ill-fitted for any real explanation of his personal devotion to the Confederacy. All we know is that he and the large majority of his congregants were so fiercely opposed to the Union that they went into voluntary exile.[85]

VI

The Jewish Messenger of New York City, edited by the conservative Rev. S.M. Isaacs, avoided political discussions as it would a plague.[86] But when secession began to take its course among the slave states, it seemed to Isaacs to be no longer a political question: "We are not citizens of the North or of the South, we are not republicans or democrats, but loyal citizens of that great republic, which has ever extended a welcome to the oppressed and has ever protected Israel."[87] The *Messenger*, therefore, could not but proclaim its loyalty to the Union and to the maintenance of the Constitution:

... The Union—which binds together, by so many sacred ties, millions of freemen—which extends its hearty invitation to the oppressed of all nations, to come and be sheltered beneath its protecting wings—shall it be severed, destroyed, or even impaired? Shall those, whom we once called our brethren, be permitted to overthrow the fabric reared by the noble patriots of the revolution, and cemented with their blood?

And the Constitution—guaranteeing to all, the free exercise of their religious opinions—extending to all, liberty, justice, and equality—the pride of Americans, the admiration of the world—shall that Constitution be subverted, and anarchy usurp the place of a sound, safe, and stable government, deriving its authority from the consent of the American people?

... Then stand by the flag! ... Whether native or foreign born, Christian or Israelite, stand by it, and you are doing your duty, and acting well your part on the side of liberty and justice.[88]

From the moment that editorial was published, name-calling letters from Southern readers began to pour into the *Messenger's* offices.[89] Unfortunately for us, Isaacs did not choose to publish them, but one communication amused him so much that he could not forebear passing it on to his readers. It was a series of resolutions which was passed by the congregation in Shreveport, La.:[90]

WHEREAS, we received the "Jewish Messenger" of the 26th of April, a paper published in New York in which an appeal has been made to all, whether native or foreign born, Christian or Israelite. An article headed "Stand by the Flag!" in which the editor makes an appeal to support the stars and stripes, and to rally as one man for the Union and the Constitution. Therefore be it

RESOLVED, That we, the Hebrew congregation of Shreveport, scorn and repel your advice, although we might be called Southern rebels; still, as law-abiding citizens, we solemnly pledge ourselves to stand by, protect, and honor the flag, with its stars and stripes, the Union and Constitution of the Southern Confederacy with our lives, liberty, and all that is dear to us.

RESOLVED, That we, the members of said congregation, bind ourselves to discontinue the subscription of the "Jewish Messenger," and all Northern papers opposed to our holy cause, and also to use all honorable means in having said paper banished from our beloved country.

RESOLVED, That while we mistook your paper for a religious one, which ought to be strictly neutral in politics, we shall from this [hour] treat it with scorn as a black republican paper, and not worthy of Southern patronage; and that, according to our understanding, church and politics ought never to be mingled, as it has been the ruination of any country captivated by the enticing words of preachers.

RESOLVED, That we, the members of said congregation, have lost all confidence and regard to the Rev. S. M. Isaacs, Editor and Proprietor of the "Jewish Messenger," and see in him an enemy to our interest and welfare, and believe it to be more unjust for one who preaches the Word of God, and to advise us to act as traitors and renegades to our adopted country, and raise hatred and dissatisfaction in our midst, and assisting to start a bloody civil war amongst us.

RESOLVED, That we believe like the Druids of old, the duties of those who preach the Holy Word to be first in the line of battle, and to cheer up those fighting for liberty against their oppressors, in place of those who are proclaiming now from their pulpits, words to encourage an excited people, and praying for bloody vengeance against us. Brutus, while kissing Caesar, plunged the dagger to his heart.

RESOLVED That a copy of these resolutions be sent to the editor of the "Jewish Messenger."

RESOLVED, That papers friendly to the Southern cause, are politely requested to publish the foregoing resolutions.

M. Baer, President.

Ed. Eberstadt, Secretary, pro tem.

What amused the Rev. Isaacs so much was that there was only one subscriber to the *Messenger* in Shreveport, and he had not paid his bill for two years!

Another one of those who wrote in anger to the Rev. Isaacs was Henry S. Jacobs, the rabbi of Congregation Shearith Israel of Charleston, S.C. Jacobs said later that "at the breaking out of the War, [Isaacs] became so political and violent in his crusade against the South that I abandoned the agency of the paper and even my continuance as a subscriber."[91] Jacobs' own deep political convictions are revealed by his interpretation of Isaacs' moderate expression as "violent."

When Charleston was shelled in 1863, as many of the civilian residents as could departed for safer places. Some, including Penina Moise, the gentle poetess, went to Sumter, S.C.[92] Most of the Jews, however, moved to Columbia, among them the Rev. Jacobs, who officiated in the Tree of Life Synagogue[93] there until the city was captured and set aflame by General Sherman's army. Jacobs wrote later of this experience:

> I will not now recall the horrors of that Sabbath Eve, (the 17th of February), when I and my family were driven forth from our home to a park in the suburbs, where wrapped in blankets we passed Friday night, and nearly the whole [Sabbath]. Save a change or two of raiment and my [phylacteries], I lost everything in the world—clothing, furniture, books, manuscripts, provisions, even my canonicals and [prayer shawls]—everything except hope and confidence in our Heavenly Father. He indeed helped me, for I have found warm friends here in Augusta [Ga.], whence wagons were sent for my family as soon as intelligence reached of our sad condition . . . I have accepted the ministry here for one year certain, and, if my field of labor is not very large, still I hope to be useful, and to accomplish some good to the God of Israel."[94]

Henry Jacobs did not write then about the hours he had spent searching through the smoking ruins of the Columbia synagogue, hoping that some of the eight Torah scrolls and other religious objects might have escaped damage, and how at last he found one partially burned Torah and a single Torah bell, which were returned to Charleston "as Sacred Relic[s]."[95] Nor did he write of his sorrow that he himself could not return to Charleston, before the war the most distinguished Jewish community of the South, where two virile congregations had vied with each other for the spiritual leadership. Now there were so few Jews left in Charleston, and they so poor and broken in spirit, that even the single congregation which resulted from the amalgamation of Beth Elohim and Shearith Israel was not able to maintain a rabbi.[96]

On Thanksgiving Day, 1865, this rabbi, who had suffered fear and flight and personal danger and loss, delivered one of the most touching Jewish sermons of the war.[97] "What cause have the people of the South for thanksgiving on an occasion like this, which celebrates the conclusion of a war which has been one of disaster to them?" he asked. Here they were, nursing their wounds, mourning their dead, rebuilding broken homes and lives, enduring the trials of life under a military government, witnessing the upheaval of old social customs and conventions—should they, indeed, offer thanks to God?

He found at least one reason for thanksgiving:

that after four years of bloody strife the sword at length is sheathed; the canon's deafening roar no longer vibrates on the ear; the desolating march of armies no more spreads misery, want, and ruin through the land.

Peace had come, forestalling yet greater misery. Were the people unconvinced that peace was a blessing, even if coupled with defeat, let them look around them at the effects of war:

A soil returned almost to primal wilderness, and charred, blackened, and prostrate homesteads . . . troops of childless mothers, widowed wives, and orphaned children, whose poverty forbids the "customary suits of solemn black" . . . the robust man, the support of many dear ones who looked up to him for bread, the tenderly nurtured stripling the hope and pride of the parental home . . . alike sunk before the leaden messengers of death . . .

He reminded his listeners that *all* had not been taken away. There were many loved ones who yet survived and they still had life and health, food and clothing, and the future stretching before them with its infinite possibilities for achievement and accomplishment. "Life," he said, "is still before us with its peaceful victories to be achieved by perseverance, energy, and industry."

And even as supporters of the Confederacy, they had cause for gratitude. "With the close of the war, which terminated so disastrously to the South, it might have been expected that, flushed with success, the mailed hand of power would have closed over us with a crushing and resistless grasp; that a merciless tyranny would have consigned us to the worst fate which could be inflicted on a subjugated people." But no— President Johnson had "no thirst for blood, no appetite for plunder." His Reconstruction policies were generous and merciful. "By his adoption of a mild and conciliatory policy, he had achieved the greatest, because the noblest victory of all, in winning the *hearts* of the people lately in open and armed defiance of the Central Government." With their allegiance reaffirmed, through appreciation rather than force, they might now look forward to a future "of safety, of peace and restored prosperity," even "though the bark which was launched a few years ago amid such joyous acclamations, which was freighted with such precious hopes, which was wafted with such earnest prayers, has suffered shipwreck." Yes, the rabbi of Augusta thanked God that the policies of Reconstruction were guided by a friendly, compassionate man. (How poignant it is to read those words and realize that they were spoken too soon, that the "mailed hand of power" was actually to fall upon the Southland.)

And finally the Rev. Jacobs found cause for thanksgiving in the strength which the people of the South had found in religion all during the years of agony.

How great soever was the anguish of our souls, we rebelled not against our Maker; for even during the times of our gravest trials, even when homeless and helpless, we sought His countenance as the strength of our hearts and our portion forever. Oh! let us be thankful that religion thus supported us, . . . that its spirit revived us, that it became indeed a tree of life to us, under whose umbrageous boughs we found shelter, peace, and security.

From another than Henry S. Jacobs these sentiments might sound like formal, meaningless words, whistling in the dark, unrealistic religiosity. From him they come as the reflection of a deeply pious and spiritual personality, clinging to his faith in God and in himself despite the shattering of his personal fortunes and the disappointment of his hopes for the success of the Confederacy.

* * *

Morais, Wise, Leeser, Gutheim, and Henry S. Jacobs had, during the war, unusual experiences which distinguished them from their colleagues and which have required special narration at this point. As we shall see, however, all of the leading rabbis of the time had something important to say or do in connection with various aspects of the war. They were clergymen who took seriously the responsibility of guiding the thoughts and ideals of their people into constructive channels.

IV A QUESTION OF EQUALITY: THE CHAPLAINCY CONTROVERSY

I

THE AMERICAN TRADITION of the military chaplaincy is as old as the United States itself. Clergymen served with the armies of the individual colonies almost from the first battle of the Revolution, and provisions for the payment of chaplains were enacted by the Continental Congress as early as 1775. The first regular army chaplain was commissioned in 1781, immediately following due authorization by Congress in its legislation for a second regiment to supplement the small national military establishment. From then on, post and brigade chaplains were an accepted feature of the army table of organization.

These chaplains were all Protestants, though of varying denominations. The possible service of Roman Catholic chaplains received no official attention until the time of the Mexican War, when President Polk held several conferences on the subject with members of the American church hierarchy. Polk's suggestion that the bishops appoint two priests to serve with the army in a *civilian* capacity was adopted, but he apparently had no intention of recommending them for military appointments. During the 1850s Catholic priests served several military posts in the capacity of chaplain, but their official status is open to question. It was actually not until the Civil War that Catholic priests were explicitly granted the right to serve as army chaplains.[1]

There is no evidence that the legal status of Jewish chaplains was ever discussed prior to the Civil War. But once the conflict had begun, with thousands of Jews enlisting in the Armies of both the Union and Confederacy,[2] it was inevitable that these members of a minority faith would press for their right to be served by clergymen who could truly minister to their spiritual needs. The personal liberties and civil rights of members of all religious minorities had been safeguarded by a Constitution which carefully separated church from nation, although North Carolina and New Hampshire lagged far behind in their application of this principle to their internal politics. The chaplaincy was, however, another realistic test of the equality which the Federal government theoretically accorded to all American citizens.

In the Confederacy, this equality was apparently recognized immediately upon the outbreak of hostilities. The acts providing for the appointment of chaplains in the Confederate military establishment merely stipulated that they should be "clergymen," with no denominational specifications.[3] There was probably not a sufficient number of Jews in any one Confederate regiment to warrant the appointment of a Jewish chaplain, but at least there was no *legal* barrier to such an appointment.

In this instance the Confederate Congress was more liberal and tolerant than its Washington counterpart, and it was in the North that the storm broke over the right of Jewish soldiers to chaplains of their own faith. The original Volunteer Bill, as reported to the floor of the House, required that regimental chaplains, who were to be "appointed by the regimental commander on the vote of the field officers and company commanders present," be "regularly ordained minister[s] of some Christian denomination."[4] On July 12, 1861, in a discussion of this proviso, an Ohio Congressman moved an amendment which would substitute the phrase "religious society" for the words "Christian denomination." The Congressman was Clement L. Vallandigham who was later to become notorious for his leadership of the Copperhead movement and who was eventually arrested by military order and exiled across the Confederate border. Apparently on his own initiative and without any Jewish prompting he spoke out clearly in defense of Jewish rights. "There is a large body of men in this country, and one growing continually, of the Hebrew faith," he said, "whose rabbis and priests are men of great learning and piety, and whose adherents are as good citizens and as true patriots as any in this country." He denounced the underlying implication of the bill that the United States is a Christian country, in the political sense, and branded the law as entirely unjust and completely "without constitutional warrant."[5] Vallandigham's appeal failed to move his fellow members of the House, or perhaps they paid no attention to his comments. At any rate, they rejected his amendment and passed the bill with its discriminatory clause intact.

This brief episode attracted very little notice. But perhaps because he also was an Ohioan and a member of the Democratic Party, Rabbi Isaac Mayer Wise did grasp its significance. He labeled the qualification clause an "unjust violation of our constitutional rights" and applauded Mr. Vallandigham for his staunch advocacy of the American conception of equality. But Wise was more furious than imaginative and had no constructive suggestion to offer to remedy the situation. His fear of dictatorship and of militarism ran away with his confidence in democratic action, and he could only urge his readers to remember this deliberate act of injustice and to hold their indignation in check until the end of the war, when surely they would be free to "square accounts."[6]

For all that Vallandigham, Wise and the few others who were interested, knew, the question of the Jewish chaplaincy would remain a theoretical one. Wise himself had no inclination for personal military service, since he was totally antagonistic to the purposes of the war. Fortunately for America and the Jew, however, the question did not remain a theoretical one and was not permitted to die for lack of excitement and interest.

In September 1861, less than three months after the House had refused to sanction the service of Jewish chaplains, a YMCA worker happened to visit the military camp in Virginia where the 65th Regiment of the 5th Pennsylvania Cavalry, popularly known as "Cameron's Dragoons," was temporarily stationed. He was horrified to discover that a Jew, one Michael Allen of Philadelphia, was serving as the regimental chaplain, and promptly began such an agitation in the public press that ultimately the Assistant Adjutant General of the Army, George D. Ruggles, was forced to state in writing his official warning that "any person mustered into service as a chaplain, who is not a regularly ordained clergyman of a Christian denomination, will be at once discharged without pay or allowance."[7] Allen felt so humiliated that he resigned his commission on the excuse of ill health rather than suffer the dishonor of dismissal from the service; but the clamor raised by the zealous YMCA worker brought the issue before the public once again.[8]

Obviously, Allen had been elected without any deliberate intention on the part of his regiment's colonel and officers to disobey the law. They were probably ignorant of the Congressional bill which forbade them to designate a Jewish chaplain for their regiment even though the Commanding Officer, Colonel Max Friedman, and a large proportion of his officers and 1,200 men were Jewish.[9] Allen, moreover, had been a very fitting choice for the office. Born in Philadelphia on November 24, 1830, he was, from childhood, a pupil of the Rev. Isaac Leeser, and for a time he undertook to follow, under his rabbi's guidance, a regular course of study for the Jewish ministry. In 1850–1, he took a formal course of study in *Shulhan Aruch* with Rabbi Max Lilienthal in New York, and was granted a certificate as *Haber* (Fellow in Jewish Studies) by him on March 22, 1851.[10] Even after he abandoned this ambition, he remained close to Jewish affairs and preserved his relationship with Leeser. He taught classes for the Philadelphia Hebrew Education Society, and substituted for Leeser as *Hazan* (Cantor) in the conduct of services, when that frequent traveler was out of town. The Rev. Samuel M. Isaacs, editor of *The Jewish Messenger*, wrote a few years later that Allen was "the only gentleman not actually a minister, accustomed and able to read the entire ritual according to the *Portuguese minhag* [rite]. He really deserves credit for the alacrity with which he has always responded to . . . calls [to act as *Hazan*], having frequently officiated at the *Franklin* street and *Seventh* street Synagogues of Philadelphia, and occasionally at the 19th street Synagogue of N.Y."[11] As a layman, Allen took a further leading role in Jewish communal affairs, and served as secretary to both the United Hebrew Beneficial Society and the Hebrew Education Society.[12]

Surely there was no one in the entire regiment better equipped by training as well as inclination to serve as its chaplain. During the two months of his service, Allen was not a Jewish chaplain, but the regimental chaplain for men of all faiths. On the New Year, the Day of Atonement, and the Feast of Tabernacles, as well as on the Jewish Sabbath, he went to Washington or Philadelphia to attend services. But on Sundays, he held non-denominational services, consisting of brief Scriptural readings and a hymn or two, as well as a sermon. An entry in his diary for Sunday, September 8, 1861, reads:

> Arose at 5½ am. Very cool, pleasant and invigorating. "Fast of Gedaliah." Did not fast, not feeling able to do so. Had service at 8 o'clock. Lectured on "Peace and Harmony." All the officers and companies were present under command of Lieut. Col. Becker, and they all in their uniform looked very well.[13]

On that Jewish holiday, filled with remembrances of the pain of exile and the destruction of Jewish statehood, the chaplain preached a message about friendship and consideration to his men, without a single indication of the meaning of the day in his own religious thinking!

Indeed, one who reads the manuscript copies of his sermons, preserved by his family, would never know they were written by a devout Jew. Of course, there is no reference to Christianity or its central figure, but neither is there any reference to the most pivotal of Jewish concepts. Theologically, his sermons approached the various aspects of religion—immortality, ethics, faith—from a general and common Judaeo-Christian background. They were realistic, practical, down-to-earth talks, designed to touch the most basic problems of men stationed only a few miles from the battle-front: fear, restlessness, doubt, and homesickness. Chaplain Allen spoke of faith in God, "our shield and our buckler . . . in the hour of battle, of danger, and of tribulation." He urged them to prepare for the strife by learning the arts of the soldier as conscientiously as they could, because theirs was a "good and just cause . . . to save our country from the hands of the spoiler;" but he also pleaded for a spiritual preparation for the death that surely faced some of them. Never discussing political issues as such, he nevertheless took care that they came to have some understanding of his conviction that the Union was in danger, that the Confederacy was a rebellion against the Constitution, and that their erstwhile fellow-Americans were now their deadly foes. He never avoided the most difficult subjects: desertion, sex, obedience to superiors, the evils of camp life; but he tried as best he could to impart a reasonable, loyal, and high ethical attitude to his men. Reverence for the Deity and love of

Scripture infused every sermon with a warmth and humanity which must truly have "endeared him to all." Those were words used by his friend, Alfred T. Jones, who gave an address when the regimental colors were presented to Col. Friedman by a group of Philadelphia Jews in a formal ceremony on September 10. Jones said further, in the ornate fashion of his day, that Allen "taught the Word of God with pure unadulterated piety; he breathed into the ears of his hearers no sectarian hatred toward others, but labored zealously for their moral and spiritual welfare."[14]

In a passage of one sermon, Allen presented his own conception of some of the duties of the chaplain:

> I [must be] as one of you ... I must share with you, the pleasures and privations of a soldier's life, and I trust that I shall be able to gain the esteem and confidence of each and every one of you ... [Since] there are many of you who are good and loyal *adopted* citizens of this our country, and as there are amongst you those not very well conversant with the English language, I wish you to consider me as your Teacher, and during your leisure hours in camp, should you wish to perfect yourself in the vernacular language of this country, I will be glad and willing to impart all the necessary information which my time and abilities will permit.

To teach, to inspire, in his own humble way—this was Allen's purpose in serving as substitute rabbi, and as military chaplain. The "Cameron's Dragoons" were deprived of a sincere and superior religious mentor when Michael Mitchell Allen was forced to resign his office.

On the other hand, we must not overlook the fact that Allen was disqualified from serving as chaplain for two reasons: he was not a Christian, it is true, but neither was he a "regularly ordained clergyman." Even under the revised provisions of the following year which permitted rabbis to enter the military service, Allen would still have been ineligible. An unknown Philadelphian, writing a "letter to the editor" in an effort to clarify the issue which he felt had been unjustly confounded by accusations of intolerance, insisted that Allen's appointment had been called into question not because of his faith but because he was "a liquor dealer ... doubtless a very worthy man, but no clergyman."[15]

This editorial correspondent was not attempting to whitewash the War Department. Great as their excitement about Allen had been, the original letter from the YMCA had not complained about him but about "a number of Chaplains in our Pennsylvania regiments [who] are entirely disqualified ... for the high and important position to which they have been raised;"[16] and Ruggles' letter nowhere specified the Allen case, although it undoubtedly included it. Indeed, the election of non-clergymen to the office of chaplain plagued War Department officials and thoughtful Protestant leaders all during the war. It was a subject which obtained recognition and reference in many investigation reports and exposés. The

Paymaster General of the Army, for instance, wrote to Senator Henry Wilson of Massachusetts on December 5, 1861, that:

> I regret to say that very many holding this position [of chaplain] are utterly unworthy . . . I think none should be appointed who did not come recommended by the highest ecclesiastical authority . . . It is said one regiment employs a French cook, and musters him as chaplain to meet the expense . . .[17]

It was probably not the same cook, but Henry Blake told the story of a colonel who threatened his regimental cook-chaplain with the strongest kind of punishment:

> "If you don't cook a better dinner than this tomorrow, I will have you tied to the flag-staff next Sunday, and make you preach two hours to the regiment . . ."[18]

Rabbi Isaac Mayer Wise took great delight in quoting the assertion of a Presbyterian journal that "two thirds of the chaplains in the army are unfit for their place,"[19] and offered his own personal testimony that at least two professed atheists of his acquaintance were serving as chaplains.[20] One of Lincoln's private secretaries, W.O. Stoddard, charged that military chaplains were, for the most part, "broken down 'reverends', long since out of the ministry for incompetency or other causes, men who could not induce any respectable church to place itself under their charge," and quoted Lincoln's angry comment that "I do believe that our army chaplains, take them as a class, are the worst men we have in the service."[21]

Colonel Friedman and his officers were undoubtedly distressed by this valid legal objection which complicated their determination to be served by a Jewish chaplain. They now realized that Allen would have had no right to serve as chaplain even if the law could be stretched to permit Jews to be elected to that position. So they resolved to try again. This time they would elect an ordained rabbi, but they would also take the precaution of electing a civilian who would not so easily be frightened into resigning and who would have to apply directly to the Secretary of War for a commission. This would indeed be a test case which would determine whether discriminatory legislation against the Jews was to be enforced with the full knowledge and consent of the government and the people! Colonel Friedman lost no time in selecting the Rev. Arnold Fischel, the Dutch-born lecturer at Shearith Israel Synagogue of New York and one of the earliest students of American Jewish history,[22] as the regiment's chaplain-designate. This was Fischel's introduction to the cause célèbre in which he participated for many months. His service in the Potomac area as a civilian chaplain, and his lobbying activities in the nation's capital as the representative of the Board of Delegates of American Israelites, have been known for a long time, but the motivation behind his application for a commission has never been fully understood.[23]

The simple truth is that he sought the commission, after his election by the officers of the regiment, in order to test the law and to secure a public statement about Jewish rights in the matter. His application was denied, of course, and ironically, the letter of rejection (warm and friendly as it was) was signed by the very same Simon Cameron, Secretary of War, in whose honor the "Cameron's Dragoons" was recruited and named.[24] To be fair to Cameron, we must understand that he had not dictated the law and that he had no choice about obeying it—but now there was no possible doubt of the interpretation of the law, and American Jewry had to recognize it.

These, then, were the circumstances which led up to the Jewish chaplaincy protest movement: the illegal election of Allen; the exposé by the YMCA; Allen's chagrined resignation; the election of Fischel as a test case; and, finally, the rejection of his application on the basis of the discriminatory clause. This was the chain of events which confronted American Jewry in late 1861 with the first instance of outright discrimination and legal inequity in a Congressional enactment. Would the Jewish community of America be able to convince Congressional leadership that the requirements for chaplaincy service should be amended?

II

The release of the Cameron-Fischel correspondence to the press proved to be a stimulant to public notice—a stimulant which had been lacking five months previously when Isaac Mayer Wise had been a solitary voice. Now there began a three-pronged campaign, participated in by all manner of organized Jewish groups, to effect a change in the law.

The first feature of the campaign was publicity. All of the Jewish periodicals recognized the importance of the issue, carried voluminous news and editorial articles on the question, analyzed its legal and ethical aspects, and prompted various courses of action.

Wise, of course, continued to blast away at the Republican Party, blaming it for intentional discrimination against American Jewry. He believed that this was a deliberate effort to penalize rabbis because they had not supported the abolitionist movement as wholeheartedly as the Protestant clergymen had. The entire chaplaincy system was, to his mind, a violation of the American principle of the separation of church and state; no clergyman should be employed and paid by the American government. He charged that the government, moreover, was utilizing the chaplaincy as a means of rewarding those ministers who had helped bring on the war by their agitation against the South and slavery. If there were to be *any* chaplains in the military service, American ideals of democracy required that an opportunity be extended to ministers of all faiths to serve their co-religionists. Jews pay taxes, he said, serve in the military forces, die in battle if such be their destiny; why then should rabbis who might apply for military commissions be discriminated against?[25]

Isaac Leeser shared none of Wise's strongly partisan opinions on political matters, but he was equally outspoken in behalf of the rights of the Jewish minority in America. He said that he had never been one of those who took pride in the election of Jews to public office, nor did he take offense when a Jew was defeated in a fair election. He was not interested in chaplaincy appointments merely because they were government offices, but he was fearful for the future of the American democratic structure if Jews could be excluded, by law, from appointment to any office. Leeser, always sincerely and deeply moved by human need, could not avoid thinking about the suffering of wounded and dying soldiers. A chaplain could comfort such men, and it was the right of a Jew to have a rabbi by his side at such times, just as it was the right of a Christian to have his minister or priest near at hand to offer the consolations of his religion. Leeser was primarily interested in the humanitarian aspect of the question: caring for the needs of "our brothers who expose themselves daily to all the horrors of war."[26]

The father and son editorial team, Samuel M. and Myer S. Isaacs, who directed the policies of *The Jewish Messenger*, was generally inclined to be cautious and conservative in editorial opinions. Sometimes they buried their heads in the sand, albeit with dignity, and ignored the most obvious facts. In the instance of the chaplaincy question they tended to be overindulgent and to excuse Congress of intentional malice. They denied that the discriminatory clause was the result of a deliberate decision to exclude rabbis, and predicted that as soon as Congress recognized the error a revision would be voted—almost as though Vallandigham had never spoken of the matter of Jewish rights, had never offered his corrective amendment, and as though the House had never voted it down. The *Messenger*, nevertheless, favored a forthright and united campaign on the part of American Jewry to bring their case to the attention of the politicians in Washington—for, as the Isaacs' editorials correctly pointed out, the chaplaincy provision had far-reaching implications: it made Christianity the only officially recognized American religion, and reduced Judaism to the status of a second-class, inferior faith. Repudiating Wise's "partisan considerations" at a time when the future of the nation was at stake, the *Messenger* advised a supra-political approach, eschewing any reference to political party or principle, but concentrating on constitutional arguments.[27]

The Jewish editors, in this publicity phase of the Jewish protest movement, agreed on several points. Firstly, they did not feel that they were asking the government to grant them a special favor; it was equal treatment before the law which they sought, neither more nor less than was accorded to all other citizens. Secondly, they realized that a principle was at stake—the treatment of minorities. It was the Jews now, but the discrimination against Judaism might provide a precedent for the "oppression of other religious societies" at some later date. And thirdly, they were aware that the Cameron's Dragoons was an exceptional case and that there would be few, if any, regiments which would elect Jewish chaplains. It was not the commissions they were interested in, but the right to apply for such commissions. If any religion was to receive official recognition, they were determined that Judaism should have equal status with all others.[28]

It was exactly this point which aroused the opposition of some fundamentalist Protestant groups—the recognition of the equality of the Jewish religion before the law. *The Presbyter*, published in Cincinnati, expressed its misgivings on this subject in very outspoken terms:

> . . . Our government has already gone a great length in this respect in appointing Roman Catholic and Universalist Chaplains to the army; but here is a proposal immeasurably beyond anything it has yet done. These denominations at least call themselves Christians, and profess to honor the Lord Jesus, however much they may really dishonor Him, (and of this the Government may, with show of reason, be unwilling to judge.) But Jews regard Jesus of Nazareth as an impostor, a deceiver, and one worthy of every term of reproach. And yet, (should this bill become a law, which God forbid that it should,) the government would, in effect, say that one might despise and reject the Savior of men, and thus trample under foot the son of God; and this, too, not inferentially or by implication, but formally and professedly, and yet be a fit minister of religion!

The author of the article said he had a profound interest in the spiritual welfare of the Jews, but he saw no reason why the government itself should "foster their prejudices" and "harden them in unbelief." The principle that all religious groups in America are equal before the law was "as broad and universal, as it is wicked and pernicious," to *The Presbyter*. Imagine the effect of granting the privilege of chaplaincy service to "Jewish rabbis, Mormon debauchees, Chinese priests, and Indian conjurors!" Democracy had its limits—and to permit non-Christian clergymen to serve the military in the office of chaplain overstepped those limits, said *The Presbyter*.[29]

Various Christian religious groups, in concert with the YMCA, were meeting in Washington in December 1861 to discuss the imperfections of the chaplaincy system. They were worried about the inferior caliber of many clergymen who had received chaplaincy appointments, about the spiritual welfare of regiments which had gone for months without any religious services whatever, and about the low state of morality in the army as a whole. They were asked by certain Congressmen for their reaction to a change in the law regarding chaplaincy appointments.

These congressmen quoted them as saying that they would protest even if 100% Jewish regiments were organized were this to be used as an excuse to appoint rabbis as chaplains. They would not consent, under any circumstances, to the commissioning of rabbis as army chaplains.[30]

This narrow, sectarian view was not characteristic of the American secular press, however; the metropolitan dailies gave significant assistance to the Jews in their publicity campaign. A *New York Tribune* editorial reprinted Cameron's letter to Fischel, expressed the belief that it was altogether proper that Jews in uniform should be granted the right to be served by ministers of their own faith, and demanded that "the unconstitutional and unwise provisions" of the act be rescinded immediately.[31] The *New York Journal of Commerce* admitted that it would be a shock to some Christians to think of non-Christian chaplains, but argued that since Jews had volunteered for military service "with alacrity," and there had been no objection to their joining the army, no one had a logical right to object to their request for the ministrations of rabbis.[32] The *Philadelphia Sunday Dispatch*, in which a great deal of the public discussion about Chaplain Allen had taken place, went deeply into the constitutional and legal background of the matter and concluded that "so soon as it becomes a settled point that a *native born American* is disqualified, by his peculiar religious belief, from filling any position under government, we need boast no longer of our vaunted liberty, freedom, and equality."[33] The *Baltimore Clipper* took a strongly pro-Jewish position, and urged all Christians, in the name of democracy, to participate in the protest movement against the offending legal clause. Its editor reminded his readers that Congress itself, but a year and a half previously, had invited a rabbi to open a House session with prayer. Was it logical for Congress to deny Jewish soldiers the right to share the prayers of a clergyman of that faith?[34]

The next phase of the protest movement was first suggested by Rabbi Wise in *The Israelite* and eagerly adopted by the other Jewish editors, as well as by the editor of the *Baltimore Clipper*. Wise believed that no technique could be used so effectively as the petition, and he urged his readers to flood Washington with petitions:

> Petition that body from all parts of the United States. Wherever Israelites live draw up a petition to abolish that unconstitutional law, have it signed by every neighbor you find disposed to do so, and send it to your representative or senator in congress. Let the petition be written by one who understands the business, have it printed and circulate it as much as possible, do not spare your time or save a few cents, it is your duty to protect your rights. This is the only way to remedy the evil; do not neglect it . . . [35]

Six times, in one issue of *The Israelite* alone, he printed the line, "Forget not to attend to the petition to the Congress of the United States."[36] His energetic editorial prodding was the backbone of the petition phase of the campaign.

There is no record of the exact number of petitions which were received in Washington. Some senators and congressmen took formal action, presented the petitions on the floor of the House they served and saw that they were referred to the proper committees. Others merely acknowledged their receipt and regarded them as informal guides for the formulation of their own position. The *Congressional Globe* registered seven such petitions which were presented by senators and representatives from Pennsylvania, Massachusetts and Illinois.[37] The Jewish periodicals recorded dozens more, dispatched from every section of the country and, in most cases, signed by Christians as well as Jews.

The largest petition on record was prepared by F. Friedenreich of Baltimore, who secured the signatures of seven hundred Christians. A Mr. Warner, member of the Maryland legislature from Baltimore, was joined by thirty-seven of his fellow representatives in a memorial to Congressman C.L. Leary.[38] Although there were only three Jewish residents in Bangor, Me., Leopold Kind obtained two hundred endorsements for a petition which he passed around the town.[39] In such small towns as Columbus, Iowa,[40] and Edinburgh, Ind.,[41] Jews were assisted by sizable numbers of their fellow citizens. Almost no record was kept of the petitions sent in from the metropolitan areas, New York, Philadelphia, and Cincinnati, where individuals as well as congregations and other Jewish organizations were active in the movement; but judging by letters of acknowledgment from senators and other indirect references we may safely say that they were very numerous.[42]

The moderate tone and cautious wording of these petitions are typified by one which was directed to Washington by the Board of Delegates:[43]

MEMORIAL

To the Honorable, the Senate and House of Representatives, of the United States of America.

The Subscribers, your memorailists [*sic*], respectfully show: That they are the President and Secretary of the "Board of Delegates of American Israelites," and that they are duly empowered to submit to your honorable body the facts therein set forth, and to crave at your hands, that attention to the subject, which its importance to American citizens professing the Jewish religion, demands.

Your Memorailists respectfully show, that by the 9th Section of the Act of Congress, approved July 22, 1861, is provided that "the Chaplain appointed by the vote of the field officers and company commanders, must be a regular ordained minister of the Christian denomination," and that, as appears by the following letter from the War Department, to which your memorailists beg to refer, the said Sections have been interpreted to exclude from the office of Chaplain in the service of the United States, "regular ordained Ministers" of the *Jewish* faith:—

War Department,
October 23, 1861.

"Rev. A. Fischel, Rabbi, Jewish Synagogue
New York.

"Sir,—Your communication of the 17th inst . . . has been received.

"In reply, you are respectfully informed that by the 9th Section of the Act of Congress, approved July 22, 1861, it is provided that the Chaplains appointed by 'the vote of the field officers and company commanders, must be a regular ordained minister of some Christian denomination.' A like provision, also, is made in the 7th Section of the Act of Congress, approved August 3, 1861. Were it not for the impediments thus directly created by the provisions of these two Acts, the Department would have taken your application into its favorable consideration.

I have the honor to be,
Very Respectfully,
SIMEON CAMERON,
Secretary of War."

Your memorailists respectfully submit that the body of citizens of the United States, whom your memorailists represent, numbering not less than two hundred thousand, are unexcelled by any other class of citizens in loyalty and devotion to the Union; that thousands of them have volunteered into the Army of the United States, and are, by the provision of the Acts hereinbefore mentioned, excluded from the advantages of spiritual advice and consolation provided by Congress for their fellow citizens professing Christianity:—

That the said Acts are oppressive, inasmuch as they establish a prejudicial discrimination against a particular class of citizens, on account of their religious belief, and further

That the said Acts, inasmuch as they establish "a religious test as a qualification for an office under the United States," are manifestly in contravention of Section 3, Article VI of the Constitution and Article I of Amendments thereto.

Your memorailists, therefore, respectfully pray that your honorable body will take this, their memorial into favorable consideration, and that you will in your wisdom cause the acts of Congress approved July 22nd and August 3d, 1861, respectively, to be formally amended, so that there shall be no discrimination as against professors of the Jewish faith, in the several laws affecting the appointment of Chaplains in the service of the United States. And your memorailists will ever pray, &c.

(Signed)
HENRY I. HART, President

MYER S. ISAACS, Secretary.
New York, December 6th, 1861
Tabeth 3d, 5622.

Many thoughts were omitted from the petitions, many sentiments were unexpressed: the shock, the pain, the fear, of the average American Jew who had always believed that his rights were secure in the hands of the people's representatives, and who was now subjected to the sharp realization that civil liberties are not always secure, but must be defended and safeguarded in every generation.

The petitions were undoubtedly an effective weapon. They attracted the attention of the national legislators to an inexcusable breach of the principle of democratic equality, and forced them to reconsider an action which might ultimately have been declared unconstitutional by the Supreme Court. The pressure of lists of constituents' names, Jewish and non-Jewish, is not to be discounted, either, in evaluating the worth of the petition phase of the campaign.

The Board of Delegates of American Israelites was responsible for the third phase of the campaign for redress. Not content to limit its activities to documents and petitions, the Board resolved to send an envoy to Washington, a representative who would be empowered to press the issue in personal interviews with political leaders in the nation's capital. Anything might happen to deter Congress from amending the law, and much time might be consumed if matters were permitted to take their course. A lobbyist on the spot would be in a position to shepherd the Jewish case through the confusion and bickering of representative government in a nation at war.

On December 4, therefore, the Board invited the Rev. Arnold Fischel to assume this challenging mission, and also to act as a civilian chaplain in the Washington area until such time as the successful accomplishment of his task would make possible the official appointment of a Jewish Army chaplain.[44] Fischel immediately accepted the invitation—he regarded it as a privilege of inestimable worth to be selected to render such a service in behalf of American Jewry. It was understood that his expenses were to be paid by the Board, but he would receive no salary. He was to report to headquarters in New York by letter as often as developments required, but he was to have a free hand in determining upon a course of action. To assist him in his task the Board provided him with personal credentials and with letters of introduction to important political figures in Washington.

The next day Fischel set out for Washington,[45] taking time off only to stop over in Philadelphia to confer with the Rev. Leeser and other local dignitaries. They provided him with additional letters of introduction, made various suggestions about political tactics, and assured him that they would redouble their efforts to supplement his work with as many petitions as they could possibly assemble. Arrived in Washington, Fischel immediately set about securing an interview with the President. Although he was assured by many prominent persons, including John Nicolay, one of the White House secretaries, that Mr. Lincoln would not even have the time to read his documents, let alone to discuss the matter with him, Fischel was confident that his contacts would obtain a hearing for his case.

He had been furnished with a letter from Moses Grinnell, the millionaire merchant-prince of New York, a powerful supporter of the Republican Party, who wrote the President that this was important enough a matter to disturb the Presidential routine, and that "Dr. Fischel is of high literary abilities and greatly esteemed by distinguished men of all religious denominations." Another letter of introduction which Fischel used to good advantage had been given him by the U.S. District Attorney for New York, E. Delafield Smith, who explained the legal nature of Fischel's mission, and praised the rabbi as "a gentleman of great worth and intelligence."[46]

Fischel never actually explained who transmitted these letters to Lincoln and thereby arranged for an appointment at the White House, but he had obviously learned some of the secrets of political handicraft at Washington—secrets which were to be useful in his work in Washington during the coming months.

On December 11, Fischel appeared at the White House, armed with his credentials and documents. He wrote later of the "hundreds of people [who] were anxiously waiting for admission, some of whom told me that they had been for three days waiting their turn." The President received him with a cordial smile and his usual quizzical look, invited him to take a seat, and then listened to his explanation that he did not come as an office-seeker, but to "contend for the principle of religious liberty, for the constitutional rights of the Jewish community and for the welfare of the Jewish volunteers." The President examined his documents, read them thoroughly, and then "questioned me on various matters connected with this subject." Lincoln "fully admitted the justice of my remarks, [told me] that he believed the exclusion of Jewish chaplains to have been altogether unintentional on the part of Congress, and agreed that something ought to be done to meet this case." Fischel suggested that the President might well appoint some Jewish chaplains on his own initiative, as he had done previously in the case of hospital chaplains, and then ask Congress to confirm the appointments. But Mr. Lincoln demurred, explaining that the action in connection with hospital chaplains had been taken at a time when Congress was adjourned, but that he did not feel he could take the responsibility upon himself while Congress was in session, as was then the case. At all accounts, something would be done—"he told me that it was the first time this subject had been brought under his notice, that it was altogether new to him, that he would take the subject into serious consideration, that I should call again tomorrow morning and if he has five minutes to spare he would receive me and let me know his views."[47]

December of '61: the Trent affair was raising the image of a possible war with Britain; McClellan's army was still growing, but going nowhere; the Union was still in the doldrums over previous military defeats. Would Lincoln have time, any time, to consider the infinitesimally small matter of a few Jewish chaplains—or did he understand that democracy was also at stake in the Rev. Fischel's cause? Next day the President was too busy with Cabinet meetings to see the rabbi, but sent him a note that "he is not forgetting my case and will lay it before the Cabinet today."[48] There is no record of the discussions. We have no idea of what Seward, Bates, Chase, Welles, Cameron, Smith, Blair, had to say, if anything. Were they interested, impressed? Did Lincoln spend much time on the question? Did he joke? Or did he merely tell them what he wrote the Rev. Fischel the following day, that he would bring the question before the proper Congressional committee:[49]

Executive Mansion
Dec. 13, 1861

Rev. Dr. A. Fischel
My dear Sir:
    I find there are several particulars in which the present law in regard to Chaplains is supposed to be deficient, all which I now design presenting to the appropriate Committee of Congress. I shall try to have a new law broad enough to cover what is desired by you in behalf of the Israelites.

Yours truly,
A. Lincoln

According to Fischel's subsequent reports to New York, the President fulfilled his pledge and submitted to the Committee on Military Affairs of the House of Representatives a long list of suggestions covering a wide gamut of military matters, including various aspects of the chaplaincy law. Meanwhile, Fischel had been interviewing Congressmen and Senators, particularly those who were members of the Military Committees of either house.

So there was no element of surprise when on December 20, Congressman Holman of Indiana, who had already received several petitions from his constituents, introduced a resolution in the House instructing the Committee on Military Affairs "to report a bill so amending the act of the last session of Congress authorizing the appointment of chaplains in the Army as not to exclude from appointment as chaplain a minister, regularly ordained, of any religious society in the United States. . . ." Holman explained that his resolution was specifically designed to include rabbis. "Whether they be appointed or not," he said, was not the question, for he had been told by Fischel that it was unlikely that there could be many Jewish chaplains, but "it is certainly proper . . . that they should not be excluded by law." Congressman Vallandigham could not resist this opportunity of reminding his Republican colleagues that at the last session his resolution on the same subject had been defeated by an overwhelming majority. But the Jewish petition campaign, and Fischel's representations in Washington, had since corrected the situation; the Holman resolution was passed with only minor disagreements about its wording, none about its substance.[50]

This was, however, not the end of Fischel's lobbying activities. There now began an interminable series of committee meetings, at which he had to present his proposals and suggestions for the exact wording of the clause in the new bill, and discuss the various aspects of the question with committee members. There were no objections voiced to the principle of equalizing the status of Judaism before the law, but the Congressmen and Senators were acutely conscious of a dilemma which they had set up for themselves. Once having provided for "Christian" chaplains, it was impossible to repeal the provision, for that would appear to be a repudiation of Christianity. Their constituents would never stand for that! The YMCA delegates had already indicated as much. Even the Congressional chaplains were mentioning the "sacrilege" in the prayers with which they opened the daily sessions. It was an extremely delicate matter.

When Senator Henry Wilson of Massachusetts first introduced his Bill S.139 on January 8, 1862, as Chairman of the Senate Military Committee, the question of wording had still not been resolved. The paragraph provided:

> That so much of section nine, approved July twenty-two, eighteen hundred and sixty-one and of section seven, chapter forty-two, approved August three, eighteen hundred and sixty-one, as requires Army chaplains to be of some 'Christian denomination,' be, and they are hereby repealed . . . [51]

It was apparent, however, that this language would never pass the Senate or House, and a compromise was reached whereby the original clause would be interpreted away, rather than be repealed outright. This revised wording did not mention Christianity and thereby avoided the pitfall of attracting too much attention from fundamentalist Protestants:

> That so much of Section ix. of the Act approved July 22d, 1861, and of Section vii. of the 'Act providing,' &c., &c., approved August 3d, 1861, as defines the qualifications of chaplains in the army and volunteers, shall hereafter be construed to read as follows: 'That no person shall be appointed a chaplain in the United States Army that is not a regularly ordained minister of some religious denomination.'[52]

Shades of talmudic dialectics! The Senate "construed" "some *Christian* denomination" to mean "some *religious* denomination."

But even after the matter had been settled, it took more time before the Bill finally became law. There were so many other details of the Bill to be argued about that the Senate did not pass it until March 12, 1862. It took even longer in the House. On January 20, Philip Johnson, Representative from Pennsylvania, introduced a resolution to instruct the Committee on Military Affairs "to inquire into the expediency of changing the existing law as to the employment of chaplains in the Army so as to authorize the appointment of brigade chaplains, one or more of which shall be of the Catholic, Protestant, and Jewish religions. . . ."[53] A Bill embodying the revision was finally presented to the House in March, and it became law on July 17. One addition had been made to the chaplaincy section by then—the further stipulation:

> . . . and who does not present testimonials of his present good standing as such minister, with a recommendation for his appointment as an army chaplain from some authorized ecclesiastical body, with not less than five accredited ministers belonging to said religious denomination.[54]

And so, on July 17, 1862, just over a year after Vallandigham had first broached the subject, rabbis might, with the proper recommendations and qualifications, seek appointments as chaplains in the United States Army. A Dutch immigrant, the Rev. Arnold Fischel, had represented American Jewry in the negotiations which successfully achieved this change. His patience and persistence, his unselfishness and consecration, had accomplished the mission for which he was sent to Washington—he won for American Jewry the first major victory of a specifically Jewish nature, to the writer's knowledge, in a matter touching the Federal government. But, actually, it was more than a Jewish question, as Fischel recognized, and certainly more than the acknowledgment of a Congressional blunder and the erasure of a mistake. Because there were Jews in the land who cherished the equality granted them in the Constitution, the practice of that equality was assured, not only for Jews, but for all minority religious groups.

III

The successful completion of Fischel's political mission was in no wise due to the united support of American Jewry. Antagonism and indifference on the part of large sectors of American Jewry, and especially the Reform rabbis and congregations, hampered his representations in Washington. The Israelite and Sinai both carried editorials deriding his mission. More serious was a protest which six rabbis, five of whom were Reform leaders, issued to the public press in early January 1862. Published in newspapers in Washington, Philadelphia, and New York, the protest denied the representative character of the Board of Delegates and thus aimed to render its activities ineffectual:

PROTEST[55]

The undersigned, Rabbis of various Congregations have learned that several gentlemen of the city of New York and elsewhere, styling themselves a "Board of Delegates of American Israelites," and claiming to represent all the Israelites in the United States, have, in the name and in behalf of all citizens of the United States professing Judaism, petitioned Congress for the repeal of a clause concerning Chaplains.

While the undersigned, in behalf of their congregations and themselves, and in the name of freedom of conscience, pray Congress to repeal the clause (or clauses) of a bill (or bills) by which regularly ordained ministers of our persuasion are denied their constitutional right to officiate as Chaplains in the Army or Navy of the United States, they consider it their duty in behalf of truth to protest against the assumption of titles and functions by the so-called "Board of Delegates," and to state that, to the best of their knowledge, neither their congregations, nor any of those presided over by regularly ordained Rabbis, have ever delegated men or powers to that body, or otherwise recognized it. Justice to the Hebrew community demands the announcement that, as a religious organization, it is represented by no particular body of men in this country or elsewhere.

> Dr. M. Lilienthal,
> Rabbi Cong. Bene Israel, Cincinnati
>
> Dr. Isaac M. Wise,
> Rabbi Cong. Bene Jeschurun,
> Editor of the Israelite, Cin.
>
> Dr. S. Adler,
> Rabbi Cong. Emanu-El, New York
>
> Henry Hochheimer,
> Rabbi Cong. Oheb Israel, Baltimore
>
> B. Felsenthal,
> Rabbi Cong. Sinai, Chicago.
>
> Dr. David Einhorn,
> Rabbi Cong. Kneseth Israel, Phila.

It was not news that these rabbis refused to cooperate in the efforts of the Board of Delegates to create a democratically elected and effectively operative American Jewish organization, or that they objected to its maintenance. Anyone who knew anything at all about American Jewish life knew that the Board represented only those congregations which desired to participate in it, and that those were mainly of a conservative religious character. The protest was not issued to inform Jews of the opposition of the six rabbis; it was a deliberate attempt to sabotage the campaign being waged in Washington by Fischel for the revision of the chaplaincy clause, and was published with an eye to the national lawmakers. Fischel was relieved to be informed by a member of the Military Affairs Committee "that it made no impression on them, that it excited ridicule rather than otherwise and that they had resolved to adopt my suggestion."[56] But if any Congressmen had been looking for an excuse to withdraw their support from Fischel's proposals, the "Protest Rabbis" had handed them an excellent one. No possible benefit could have accrued from the publication of the protest; much harm might have come to the cause which the "Protest Rabbis" admitted was a valid and just one. But so bitter was their hostility to the leaders of the New York and Philadelphia Jewish communities that they were willing to air their grievances in the public press in order to bring shame upon the Board and the Rev. Fischel.

It would have been eminently more fitting and constructive if these rabbis had, for the time being, shelved their personal and religious differences with the leaders of the Board, and had aided in the support of Fischel's devoted labors in Washington. Their lack of support had an important bearing upon the outcome of the second phase of the Board's assignment to their Washington representative.

The second task which had been entrusted to Fischel by the Board of Delegates, it will be remembered, was the fulfillment of the duties of a civilian chaplain in the Potomac area. He undertook this religious phase of his mission with as much enthusiasm and efficiency as he did the political phase, and rendered a service which could not have been more admirable even if he had been in uniform.

Almost immediately upon his arrival in Washington, he secured passes of admission, as a religious worker, into the various camps and hospitals in the Department of the Potomac and began a systematic series of trips which eventually included every military establishment in the Department. Needless to say, being the first rabbi to seek out the Jewish soldiers, he was heartily welcomed wherever he went—sometimes he spent many hours on trains or on horseback traveling to the distant encampments in Maryland and Virginia. New York men, in particular, some of whom were members of his last congregation, were delighted to see his familiar face. They plied him with questions; asked him to write letters home for them; complained that they had no idea which of their comrades were Jewish until he gathered them all together; and requested copies of the Jewish prayer book, and of the Book of Psalms. He always left his address so that, in case of emergency, he could be notified, and invited the men to visit him if duty or furlough should bring them through Washington.

Soldiers confined in the hospitals were especially grateful for his visits. His prayers at their bedside and his conversation were a relief, they said, after the "torture of religious controversy" to which Christian chaplains were wont to subject them. Whether their cases were critical or not, they begged him to promise that they would be buried in Jewish cemeteries—they seemed to have a horror of resting among strangers. When one of his patients died, a young Pennsylvania boy named Marcus Dreyfus, Fischel kept his promise, telegraphed the soldier's family, and arranged for the body to be held pending their arrival to take their son home again.[57] After he had visited all the camps and hospitals, the Rev. Fischel realized that he would never be able to cover the entire area as thoroughly as he might like, and that he had spread his visits to the hospitals so far apart that he was unlikely to fulfill his duty to the sick and wounded men who, after all, were his first responsibility. So he made the unavoidable choice, notified the men in camps that he could not visit them except in cases of emergency, and, for the duration of his stay in Washington, limited his further pastoral work to patients in the hospitals.

The only exception to this general rule was a long trip into Virginia which he undertook in March. He hoped to be with the army when it captured Richmond:

> I am off, where to I don't know, but I am with the left wing. Altho' the army left this morning, yet as they march slowly, I shall be able to overtake them on horseback with greatest ease. They have bridges to build and roads to cut, and as there will be no fight this week, I don't lose anything. I will send Mr. Hart a brief report from Richmond . . .[58]

In one of his reports, Fischel recorded a group of suggestions for the guidance of his successor, if a Jewish chaplain should eventually be assigned to the Potomac area. This advice is especially interesting because it foreshadowed the activities of Jewish chaplains in World Wars I and II, many of whom were assigned to areas, rather than to specific units:

> I would advise the following "modus operandi": [First] that he be required to visit the Hospitals daily. [Secondly] that he visit each division of the army once a week, and [thirdly] that a card be extensively circulated in the camps to the effect that Jewish soldiers in camps and hospitals who are in need of personal assistance send in a written request to Dr. ———, ——— St., etc. Every Jewish soldier would then have the opportunity of enjoying the Chaplain's services at any time he may wish.[59]

When Dr. Fischel undertook his mission in December, the Board of Delegates had promised to defray his expenses at the rate of $20 a week. For this purpose, the sum of $250 was borrowed from a fund for the relief of the Jews of Morocco which had been raised by the Board. An appeal was then composed and circulated among congregations and individuals all over the country, informing them of Dr. Fischel's tasks and soliciting their financial contributions for the support of his work.[60] In addition to the printed circular, personal letters were also sent to leaders in various communities, asking for their help, and suggesting that other rabbis might well be appointed to perform civilian chaplaincy duties in areas other than Washington.[61]

Meanwhile, Dr. Fischel came to the realization that $20 would not suffice to meet his expenses. He had to pay $35 for a hotel room his first two weeks, and his first trip to Frederick, Md., cost $20. At this rate, he was spending as much of his own money as the Board's. But he was nevertheless willing to abide by his agreement, although he was profoundly disturbed by the Board's apparent inability to raise the necessary funds. He even suggested the names of wealthy men who might be interested in contributing funds for what he felt was a laudable purpose.

Fischel would have been even more disturbed if he had known, in December, how few responses would be received by April. A total of *four* congregations forwarded their contributions: B'nai Jeshurun, Providence, R.I.; the congregation in New Bedford, Mass.; B'nai Jeshurun and Shaaray Tefila, New York.[62] A token donation of $5 was also received from the children of the Pittsburgh Hebrew School.[63] Editorials designed to stimulate the campaign for funds were published in the *Messenger* and *The Occident*, but they proved to be even less successful than the Board's solicitation. At the end of the guaranteed period, Dr. Fischel was recalled from Washington, despite the fact that there was still no legal provision for the appointment of a Jewish chaplain, for the simple reason that the money had run out and there was no indication that more would ever be forthcoming. So poorly rewarded were the patriotic efforts of this unselfish rabbi that American Jewry did not even defray his complete expenses, let alone offer him any remuneration for the time which he had devoted to a significant cause.[64]

No wonder that one of the anonymous contributors to the columns of the *Messenger* bewailed what he called "A National Disgrace:"

> . . . I cannot avoid a pang of humiliation and sorrow at the disgrace I conceive to have been inflicted on the Jewish national name by the lethargic indifference with which American Israelites have contemplated the spiritual interests of their co-religionists now fighting under the "stars and stripes."
> . . . poor fellows—they have risked all—even their lives, to assist in restoring peace and concord to our distracted country. They have displayed bravery worthy of the Maccabaeans, endurance and courage befitting heroes—but their brethren have forgotten them, have neglected their silent but powerful appeal—and they are left to die among strangers, their last moments agonized by the attention of ministers and "Sisters of Mercy" . . . They are left to be buried near the field of battle, "unwept, unhallowed and unsung," their graves unmarked—whereas, they should be interred in consecrated ground, where rest the bones of their ancestors, and co-religionists should be with them when on their beds of sickness, to administer consolation, and soothe their dying moments . . .
>
> It is all very well to say "Congress should provide for Jewish soldiers as well as Christian." I admit it; but because Congress is dilatory and slow to do justice, is that any reason why *we* should fail in our duty to our brethren? The action of Congress is not to be palliated—but shall the Jewish soldiers therefore be debarred of all religious consolation? . . .
>
> I . . . know of a young man killed at the recent battle at Williamsburgh—whose parents, in England, are looking forward to the day when their sight may be blessed by his return to the home of his childhood—who can picture their grief, their agony, when it shall be told to them, that their boy died on the field of battle—no one near him to say the *Shemang*, no preparation made to have his body interred in holy ground—when it shall be told to them, that

the Israelites of America felt no interest in the spiritual welfare of Jewish soldiers? . . .[65]

This was no idle exhortation, nor mere exhibition of eloquence. As the *Messenger* correctly stated, one thousand dollars would have sufficed to see Dr. Fischel's mission through to the end, but the antagonism of the Reform group and the indifference of the large masses of the Jewish population to any causes but their own synagogues and local charitable organizations militated against the Board's endeavors.[66] This was a tragic and disillusioning conclusion to the notable and noble service which the Board of Delegates and Dr. Fischel had rendered to American Jewry and to America.

IV

In July of 1862, then, it was permissible for rabbis to apply for commissions in either of two categories: as regimental chaplains, or as members of the newly-organized hospital chaplaincy. And, as might be predicted, it was not long before President Lincoln received a communication in this regard—a month later, to be explicit. It was a petition from the Board of Ministers of the Hebrew Congregations of Philadelphia requesting the appointment of a Jewish hospital chaplain for the Philadelphia area. This representative body had met on August 19, the letter said, and discussed the hospital problem. Two soldiers of the Jewish faith had already died without the consolation of prayers by a Jewish clergyman, and, since Philadelphia was increasingly becoming "a central depository for sick and wounded soldiers," more and more Jewish men would be sent to those hospitals. Although the Board had been in touch with the hospital officials and were assured that their Secretary, the Rev. Isaac Leeser, would be notified of the admission of Jewish wounded, they nevertheless believed it advisable that a Jewish chaplain be officially appointed, and they suggested further that he be assigned not only to the Philadelphia hospitals but also to those located in "York, Harrisburg, Chester, and other towns at not too great a distance."[67]

John Hay, Secretary to Mr. Lincoln, wrote Leeser, on September 6, that the President "recognizes the propriety of your suggestion, and will appoint a chaplain of your faith if the Board will designate a proper person for the purpose." The Board of Ministers was called to conference again, and after deliberating on the relative merits of their membership, selected the Rev. Jacob Frankel, minister of Rodeph Shalom Congregation of Philadelphia, then fifty-four years old, as their nominee for the commission. The President was informed of this action, and Frankel's commission arrived a few days later, duly signed by the President, together with all the requisite papers and directions.[68] Thus, on September 18, 1862, Jacob Frankel became the first American rabbi to be appointed a military chaplain.

The Rev. Frankel was a native of Grünstadt, Bavaria, where he was born on July 5, 1808. His family was one with a long musical tradition, and, at an early age, he set out on his first concert tour, through the Alsace-Lorraine district, with two brothers. His first position as cantor was in his native town. He next went to Mainz, where he remained for a number of years. In 1848, he applied for, and was elected to, the position of Minister of Rodeph Shalom Congregation of Philadelphia. A pleasant and popular man, blessed with a stirring voice and a kindly disposition, the Rev. Frankel was greatly beloved by his congregation and served it well until his retirement from the active ministry a year before his death on January 12, 1887. Contemporary descriptions of his gentle character and mild manner render it easy to understand why his fellow rabbis selected him from among their number to be honored with the chaplaincy assignment. Further evidence of his popularity can be discovered in the results of a good-humored election, in 1866, for the most popular rabbi in Philadelphia, incidental to a raffle to raise money for the new Jewish hospital. The Rev. Frankel's friends bought so many tickets that he had more votes than all the other ministers combined.[69]

Frankel's service as chaplain continued for almost three years, until July 1, 1865, when the war had ended.[70] It was, of course, only a part-time activity, and his fellow rabbis assisted him in visiting the various military hospitals.[71] A small fund was placed at his disposal for purchasing inexpensive gifts and necessities for the men he visited; but the men were most grateful for the gift of his voice. Frequent were the occasions when they asked him to sing during his rounds in the hospitals; and many were the men, wounded and well, who came to his synagogue whenever they could to hear his inspired chanting of the service. Chaplain Frankel arranged, as best he could, for religious furloughs for ambulatory cases during the High Holy Days and at the Passover. In his typical summarizing style, Leeser wrote, after Frankel was mustered out, that the latter had "faithfully discharged the duties incident to the office, and the Jewish soldiers in the hospitals in this vicinity were properly cared for under his supervision."[72] Frankel so cherished this war-time experience that he framed his commission, signed by Lincoln and Stanton, and had it hung on the wall of his home, where it remained until his death. It has been a treasured possession of his family ever since.

Frankel and the other Jewish hospital chaplain who served during the Civil War have been all but ignored by writers who have somehow assumed that, because it was different, the hospital chaplaincy was inferior to the regimental chaplaincy. This is an historical error completely unwarranted by the facts. Both hospital and field chaplains were enrolled in the volunteer army and were appointed to office on temporary commissions. Indeed, all hospital chaplains were commissioned by the President and the War Department, whereas many regimental chaplains were appointed by governors and other state officials. Equal remuneration was

Department of the Susquehanna,

MEDICAL DIRECTOR'S OFFICE,

1103 Girard Street.

Philadelphia, Mar. 30th 1864

Surgeons in Charge of
US Genl Hosp. Dept
of the Susquehanna.

You will please admit
into your respective Hospitals at any
time, if not injurious to the sick and
wounded. The Rev Isaac Leeser for
the purpose of administering to the
spiritual wants of the sick of his
persuasion.

Very Respectfully
Your Obdt Servant

John Campbell
Surg & Med. Director

Facsimile of the Rev. Isaac Leeser's pass for visiting military hospitals provided for both types of service by Congressional law—the pay of a cavalry captain—but neither was responsible for the military duties of that rank. The same uniform regulations were applied to the chaplain in the field and the chaplain in the hospital: neither wore a military uniform; they were both instructed to wear their customary civilian garb.[73] Hospital chaplains were subject to the same type of military discipline as regimental chaplains, and were equally responsible to their military superiors. For purposes of centralized efficiency, all hospital chaplains were subordinate to the Surgeon General of the Army and assigned by him to hospitals in the cities of their residence, where, in turn, they were supervised by the surgeons in charge.[74] Regimental chaplains, on the other hand, were subject to the orders of their colonels. It was a fortunate decision to place all hospital chaplains under a single authority, for they could never have successfully fulfilled their essential role within the complicated and often contradictory structure of state and national military authority.

Much of the confusion regarding the two types of appointment has resulted from the history of the hospital chaplaincy itself: it was new for the entire country as well as for the American-Jewish community. No such office had existed prior to the Civil War, and Congress alone might never have created it even then. The urging of various Protestant ministers and of Archbishop John Hughes of New York[75] was necessary to convince President Lincoln of the desirability of such a new departure. When convinced, he did not wait for Congressional action; instead he requested certain clergymen to act as hospital chaplains and pledged that at the first opportunity he would press Congress to legalize their appointments. He fulfilled his promise in his Annual Message to Congress on December 3, 1861, and such a bill was finally enacted in May 1862 (without any denominational provisions), a short time before the bill was passed which revised the regimental chaplaincy qualifications.[76]

V

In his report to the readers of *The Occident* informing them of the steps taken to secure a commission for the Rev. Frankel, Isaac Leeser had urged his colleagues in New York, Baltimore, St. Louis, and Cincinnati, to organize themselves as the Philadelphia rabbis had, and to apply in a similar fashion for Jewish chaplaincy appointments for the benefit of the Jewish soldiers in their areas.[77] This suggestion was never adopted, but the Board of Delegates of American Israelites, through its president, Henry I. Hart, petitioned the President on October 6, 1862, for an appointment as hospital chaplain for the Rev. Fischel, who richly deserved such official recognition for his noteworthy and unique activities. His work had come to a halt only because the member congregations of the Board failed to contribute adequate funds to pay his expenses. But now that chaplaincy appointments were obtainable due to his own personal activities in Washington more than any other factor, it was more than fitting that the Board should recommend him to Mr. Lincoln and ask that he be assigned to the hospitals in Washington and vicinity with which he was already so familiar. This letter of application was endorsed by John Hay, Lincoln's secretary, in these words:

> The President directs me to refer the enclosed to the notice of the Surgeon General and to inquire whether a Jewish chaplain is needed here.[78]

The Surgeon General's Office did, indeed, investigate the matter. According to a report addressed personally to the President, on October 27, by the Medical Inspector General of the Army and countersigned by the Surgeon General, a survey was made of the hospitals in the Washington area: 13 hospitals with a total bed capacity of over 5,000 reported the presence of only seven Jewish patients. "I have therefore no hesitation," concluded the communication, "in expressing an opinion that it is inexpedient to appoint a chaplain of that faith. There would not be over 25 soldiers, to whom he could administer and they so scattered, that it would be impracticable for a clergyman to find and attend to them."

It is not possible to determine the relative accuracy of the Surgeon General's survey; we do know that hospital records carried no listing of a soldier's faith and that "dog-tags" had not yet been invented; we also know from the testimony of Leeser and other rabbis that some Jewish men in uniform were reluctant to identify themselves as Jews out of fear of anti-Semitism. Nevertheless, Fischel must have known approximately how many Jewish men would be patients in the hospitals in and around Washington; if the number was small it was certainly an unwise tactic to have the Board request appointment for him as a hospital chaplain. Perhaps an application for a commission as chaplain for camps and forts as well as hospitals in the area would have had a better chance of success.

At any rate, Fischel never received a commission and never served as a military chaplain. The noteworthy service he performed was as a civilian. Our knowledge of his later career is extremely hazy, but it is reported that he returned to Holland shortly after this episode, although the date is uncertain.[79] This was a disappointing conclusion to the war career of a rabbi who, by virtue of his interest in, and efforts in behalf of, the Jewish soldiers of the Union Army, should have been privileged ultimately to serve as an officer of that Army.

Still another chaplaincy application was rejected—that of the Rev. Isidore Kalisch of Indianapolis, who was sponsored by Adolph Dessar, a close friend of John P. Usher, Secretary of the Interior. Usher wrote Dessar on October 16, 1863, that he had spoken to Lincoln in Kalisch's behalf, but that no further commissions as post chaplains were being issued, and that Kalisch's name would be held on file, however, in the event of future need. It is quite strange that Kalisch should have applied for an appointment as post chaplain, rather than as hospital chaplain; there was probably no army post in the country whose personnel contained more than a handful of Jews.[80]

There were not enough rabbis in Louisville, Ky., to form a Board of Ministers, but the entire Jewish community of Louisville was conscious enough of the Jewish war wounded in Kentucky hospitals to initiate a public movement to secure the appointment of a Jewish chaplain for that area. Prominent non-Jewish citizens joined with Jews, and urged Robert Mallory, a Kentucky member of the House of Representatives from 1859 to 1865, to seek a commission for the Rev. Bernhard Henry Gotthelf, the rabbi of Adath Israel Congregation of Louisville. This public movement coincided with the furor over General Grant's anti-Jewish General Order No. 11, which had so many repercussions in the state of Kentucky—indirect evidence that the majority of non-Jews in this area where Jews were accused of disloyalty did not share the suspicions of Grant's staff officers. The petition met with success and the Rev. Gotthelf received his appointment on May 6, 1863, although the commission dated his rank from February 16.[81]

The Rev. Gotthelf, born in Bavaria on February 5, 1819, had come to the United States at the age of twenty-one, and served several congregations in the East, including Keneseth Israel of Philadelphia, of which he was the first cantor and preacher, prior to his call to Louisville in 1851. After the Civil War he moved to Vicksburg, Miss., where he ministered to Anshe Chesed Congregation until his death in 1878, a victim of the yellow fever epidemic which swept the whole Southland that year. The inscription on his tombstone records his life and character in these laudatory terms: "a wise teacher, a faithful minister, a tender husband, a devoted father, a good man."[82]

So successful had been the campaign to convince the American public of the right of rabbis to serve as military chaplains, that the news of Mr. Gotthelf's appointment was noted in the public press, although chaplaincy appointments (for Christians, at least) were by that date quite commonplace. The editor of the *Louisville Journal* celebrated the occasion in these words:[83]

An Excellent Appointment.—We are gratified to announce that President Lincoln has appointed the Rev. B. Gotthelf, the minister of the German Jewish Congregation of this city, as Hospital Chaplain, to be stationed here. The fact that a very respectable number of Jewish soldiers have been and still are receiving medical treatment at our hospitals having been brought to the notice of the Hon. Robert Mallory, he made an application for the appointment of Mr. Gotthelf, which we took pleasure, with other citizens, in endorsing. These invalids can now enjoy the instruction and consolation of a minister of their own faith, and we are, therefore, convinced that the appointment was as timely as it is well merited.

A careful search for family papers and examination of contemporary periodicals has disclosed only one interesting detail of the Rev. Gotthelf's twenty-eight months of chaplaincy service (he was mustered out of the Army on August 26, 1865). Since the responsibility of the Civil War chaplain to his men included the provision of various items of comfort and entertainment, the Rev. Gotthelf was eager to obtain reading matter for his men, most of whom were German-Jewish immigrants. During January and February of the final year of the war, he made a tour of the larger Jewish communities of the midwest to secure donations in cash, and in books, to establish German language libraries in the various military hospitals under his jurisdiction. An editorial in *The Israelite* endorsing the purposes of this trip conveyed the information that "there are almost always from 2,000 to 3,000 sick and wounded German soldiers in [the Louisville] hospitals, among them from 200 to 300 Israelites."[84] Undoubtedly the libraries were to be assembled for the use of all German-speaking patients, non-Jews as well as Jews. This was perhaps the first example of that type of non-denominational service which Jewish chaplains and war service agencies rendered so frequently during the subsequent wars of the United States.

In Cincinnati, at least, Rabbi Wise's assurance that "Mr. G., well known to our readers, will find the encouragement this matter deserves," was not disappointed. Beth El Lodge of B'nai B'rith appointed a special committee to assist Mr. Gotthelf in the project, as did other Jewish lodges in the community. There is no record of the other cities which Gotthelf visited, or of the general success of his tour,[85] but the whispered word of criticism, which seems to make the lives of so many rabbis miserable, pursued even this meritorious mission of beneficence. A certain William Kriegshaber of Louisville was compelled later to send a public letter of retraction to *The Israelite*, apologizing for some bitter reflections on the character of the Rev. Gotthelf and of his mission which he had written to friends in Cincinnati.[86] This episode marks the sum total of the information available concerning Gotthelf's military career. It was unfortunately typical of Jewish interests during the Civil War that once Jewish chaplains were appointed, their work was all but ignored by the Jewish press, and the more glamorous military exploits of individual Jews received the greater amount of publicity.

VI

So incomplete has been our knowledge of the Civil War chaplaincy that no notice has been taken of the one rabbi who did serve as a regimental chaplain. On April 10, 1863, the Rev. Ferdinand Sarner enlisted in the army at Brooks Station, Va., for three years, and was immediately elected chaplain of the 54th New York Volunteer Infantry.[87] On the same day, he sent notes to the editors of *The Israelite* and *The Occident* telling them of his appointment and change of address. They lost no time in passing on the news to their readers.[88]

Who was Ferdinand Leopold Sarner—this rabbi who achieved, without any great influence, that appointment over which all American Jewry had been aroused only a year before? Mrs. Martha Sarner Levy of Bradford, Pa., his daughter, has generously contributed various documents and reminiscences which help to outline the course of his life.

Ferdinand Sarner was born in Lissa, Posen, on February 8, 1820,[89] the son of a humble tanner. Bent on securing a modern academic training, he first studied at the *Gymnasium* in Hamburg. In July 1851, he entered the Royal Friedrich Wilhelm University in Berlin. There he remained for three years, undertaking a difficult course of studies, particularly in the field of philosophy. In 1854 he went on to the University of Hesse where he studied for four more years, finally passing the examinations in 1858 and achieving the coveted Doctor of Philosophy degree. Meanwhile, in 1856, he had been elected rabbi of the congregation of Battenfeld, and was therefore concurrently student and spiritual leader for two years. He retained this position for a very short time thereafter, and was ready to leave for America by January 1859, with the blessings of the mayor of the town inscribed on his travel permit in formal documentary language, and his diplomas and certificates packed securely in his luggage. This was, however, not the first time he had planned a trip to the United States. In 1850, he had secured a passport marked for Pittsburgh, Pa., but evidently changed his mind and decided to remain in Europe until he had taken advantage of German academic opportunities.

Almost immediately upon his arrival in the United States, he secured the position as rabbi of Brith Kodesh Congregation in Rochester, N.Y., where he served ably for about a year. Upon his resignation from that post in July 1860, two formal resolutions were presented to him: one by the officers and members of the congregation, the other by the Board of Trustees. Both paid high tribute to his ministrations. He had conducted himself "in the most virtuous and exemplary fashion," the congregation testified, adding that "his beautiful lectures have been full of instruction and never failed to inspire his hearers with a true sense of our holy religion." No doubt in order to preclude any suspicion that he had been dismissed by the congregation, it was explicitly stated that he had "voluntarily resigned his office as our Rabbi, thereby causing his numerous friends and admirers great sorrow." The Trustees' resolutions recorded these same sentiments in other words, but they also added their recommendation of Dr. Sarner "to every Congregation in this Country," expressing their belief that he was "an excellent scholar, an eloquent lecturer, and a good, truly religious man, for whom we shall ever bear the kindest feelings."

Virtually nothing is known of Sarner's activities between 1860 and 1863, beyond the fact that his application for the position of rabbi of the Anshi Chesed Congregation of New York City was tabled by its Board of Trustees on June 2, 1861.[90] But perhaps he had taken to haunting the government agencies in Washington, for a traveler's report to *The Israelite* mentioned a meeting with him in mid-1861 in the Capitol building. The reporter commented that Sarner was not only a "learned" man, but that he was also "the author of several plays."[91]

At any rate, Sarner was elected to the chaplaincy of the 54th N.Y. Volunteer Regiment, also known as the "Hiram Barney Rifles" and the "Schwarze Yaeger," on April 10, 1863. The meeting of regimental officers required by law was held on that day, and the assembled officers certified his election.[92] Strangely enough, of the thirteen officers who signed the document, only three could possibly have been Jewish. An examination of the muster-rolls of enlisted men, company by company, reveals the fact that Jews were a small minority in the entire regiment.[93] Why they should have preferred a Jewish chaplain is a question which it is impossible to answer with any categorical certainty. Perhaps, since the regiment was composed almost exclusively of German immigrants, the officers deemed the language their chaplain used in his sermons, and his educational background, more important than the faith he professed. Indeed, one of the documents which he had presented when first interviewed by the officers was a letter from the Prussian Ambassador in Washington, certifying to his German academic attainments; and when he was examined by a board of chaplains on May 15, his colleagues seem to have been impressed by the evidence he presented that he was a graduate of "two of the German Universities."[94] This emphasis might indicate that the regimental officers were more concerned to secure the services of a cultured German than of a chaplain of a particular denomination.

The 54th Infantry had an active combat career. During the year and a half of Sarner's service, the regiment saw action at Chancellorsville and Gettysburg, and in the invasion of South Carolina. Of all the details of his chaplaincy experience during days of battle and weeks of rest and then intensified preparation, we know only that he himself was wounded at Gettysburg. A single line to that effect was printed in *The Jewish Record* of New York on January 15, 1864, with the hypothetical guess that "Dr. Sarner is probably the first Rabbi who voluntarily took a part in a fight since Rabbi Akiba." A more elaborate report of the incident appeared in the French-Jewish monthly, *Archives Israelites*,[95] stating that during the battle, Sarner's "horse was killed under him, and he himself received a dangerous wound, from which he subsequently recovered; this was the result of the very courageous manner in which he conducted himself during that terrible battle." Although he would undoubtedly have served out his period of enlistment, or at least have seen the end of the war with his regiment, the wound apparently did not heal for a long time, and he was ultimately discharged on October 3, 1864, to date from July 31, for physical disability.[96] But we have not yet finished with the wound, although it is the only single shred of detail which has been ascertained about Sarner's military career.

After his discharge, the ex-chaplain returned to New York City and delivered guest lectures in various pulpits. It was not long, however, before he was engaged in a new venture. Jointly with the Rev. Jacob Levi, rabbi of the Adath Jeshurun Congregation of Syracuse, he undertook to edit and publish a new German-Jewish monthly, *The Rebecca*, and to travel in its behalf for funds and subscriptions. Leeser, in his review of the first number of this periodical, noted that part of a drama was included in its contents, that it was obviously more of a literary journal than a religious one, and that what there was of a religious nature smacked too much of religious liberalism to suit his taste.[97] Another contemporary went into the more practical details of its publication, affording us a valuable insight into its problems which we would otherwise not possess, since no copy of *The Rebecca* has survived the neglect of the intervening years:

> . . . Notwithstanding the attractive features of the paper, however, and the ability with which it seems to be edited, still there seems to be some difficulty in the way of its continuation. For, in the second number the publisher informs us that the appearance of the third number of "The Rebecca" is postponed until Dr. Sarner returns from a journey, which he is about to make in search of subscribers. He says that each number of the paper costs the sum of $92, and that it will be useless to continue its publication unless the subscription lists are increased. This is but another example of the difficulties that await those who attempt to publish Jewish periodicals in America. For it is an undeniable fact that, however generous the Israelites may be in other matters, they always seem loth to encourage the establishment of Jewish newspapers.[98]

It was during this trip which might mean life or death for *The Rebecca* (and which did mean its demise, since no further issues are recorded), that Dr. Sarner's war-wound became the subject of a scandalous accusation. In Cleveland, where he attempted to secure new subscribers, he apparently secured a few especially vicious enemies instead. One of them, B. Dettelbach, Secretary of the Board of Trustees of the Anshe Chesed Congregation, wrote an open letter to *The Israelite*, denouncing the traveling rabbi-editor as a liar and a slanderer. Part of the evidence concerned the Gettysburg wound:

> On his last visit to our city, being requested to state the cause of his lameness, he [Sarner] very piously remarked, to have been wounded in a battle in the

service of the United States. Unseen by him, though, he has been observed walking as erect as an arrow! Why this deception? Why this denial of truth? . . . Does he think that such malicious expressions of falsehood will either benefit him or his sheet?[99]

Undoubtedly Dettelbach's comments were the malicious, slanderous ones; a few weeks later another Anshe Chesed Trustee, Abraham Bloch, wrote that the meeting out of which the letter (signed "by order of the Trustees") had proceeded was an illegal one, and that, if there was any quarrel, it was only between Rabbi G.M. Cohen (of the congregation), Mr. Dettelbach, and Sarner, and, futhermore, purely of a private nature.[100]

The further details of Sarner's post-war career are not altogether in order. His daughter remembers that he taught languages at various schools in New York, and there are indications that he continued preaching from time to time in various synagogues.[101] He became rabbi of the Beth-El Emeth Congregation in Memphis, Tenn., sometime late in 1872, and ministered there until his death on August 18, 1878, when he fell victim to the same yellow fever epidemic which took the life of B.H. Gotthelf.

Little remains of Rabbi Sarner's career: some faded documents; the memories of a loving daughter; typical rabbinical souvenirs of the period: a silver butter dish, a gold-headed cane and a large water service, presented to him on special occasions and engraved in his honor. But the hundreds of rabbis who served with United States combat units during World War II may remember with pride their predecessor—the first of a long and honorable line who have served their nation and their faith with courage and blood—Chaplain Ferdinand Leopold Sarner.

VII

Although none of the explicit details of the Rev. Sarner's chaplaincy service have been preserved, he probably followed the same procedure as Chaplain Allen: non-denominational worship and ministrations with, perhaps, occasional Jewish services. Sarner served only one regiment; what of the thousands of Jewish men scattered throughout the other regiments and stationed in the widely separated areas over which the fury of war swept? Did they resign themselves to a moratorium on Judaism "for the duration," or did they create distinctive religious patterns of their own, without benefit of clergy?

Judaism, as a religion, is so constructed as to permit of emergency adjustments and readjustments. Services may be held anywhere, in a synagogue or in a home or in a field; any layman who is well acquainted with the ritual may conduct a service; ritual paraphernalia are altogether dispensible. Although the age-old emphasis of the Jewish tradition upon the education of laymen in Hebrew liturgy and literature was not successfully transplanted to the American scene, at least some American Jewish laymen were equipped to lead their brethren in prayer. The obligation of working out their religious problems, therefore, rested securely upon the soldiers themselves—the character of Judaism made it possible for them to be independent of rabbinical guidance.

They accepted the responsibility. It was not unusual for Jewish men to seek out each other and to gather together in formal religious worship. One soldier who wrote a number of highly interesting sketches on the military life for *The Jewish Messenger* told his readers, with obvious pleasure, that it was customary for the Jewish men in his outfit to meet regularly for Sabbath worship in some secluded spot on the outskirts of the camp. To walk through the Virginia forests and hear the echoes of the chanted Hebrew prayers was a rare and thrilling experience, he said. He was reminded of Joshua's army, and the men who followed the young David; of the Hebrew soldiers who fought against Assyria and Babylonia and Egypt; of the Maccabees. There was an historic quality about Jews in the uniform of the Union, away from home to defend the principles of American democracy, gathering together to say the prayers of the Hebrew liturgy. And, he said, the religious life of his comrades was quite characteristic of Jewish soldiers in many other outfits.[102]

The men of the 13th Ohio Volunteer Cavalry Regiment organized themselves along more formal lines. They held meetings and discussed their mutual problems. When any of their comrades was killed in battle they arranged for a traditional Jewish burial, attempting to carry out as many of the minute prescriptions of Jewish law as possible, and read the Hebrew funeral services themselves. They visited their fellow-Jews in the hospitals and gave them all the attention they could. Farrier Henry M. Auerbach, their chairman, told all this to Isaac M. Wise in a letter requesting assistance in obtaining a supply of prayer-books, phylacteries, and ritual prayer-shawls. He also asked that *The Israelite* be sent regularly to their camp near Petersburg, Va.; they were "tired,' said Auerbach, "of reading the Evangelist and others."[103]

Meanwhile, in the Confederacy, where there was not even one Jewish chaplain, the Rev. M.J. Michelbacher, rabbi of Beth Ahabah Congregation in Richmond, had been giving much thought to the religious needs of the isolated Jewish soldier and came upon an idea which seems not to have occurred to any rabbi in the North. He composed a prayer for Confederate soldiers, had it printed, and distributed it to as many men as he could reach. Reading this prayer, he believed, would give Jewish soldiers a feeling of closeness to their people and help bridge the long periods when they were unable to attend Jewish worship services:[104]

Shemang Yisroel, Adonoy Elohainoo, Adonoy Achod!

O God of the Universe! Although unworthy through my manifestold transgressions, I approach the seat of thy mercy, to crave thy favor, and to seek thy protection. I supplicate thy forgiveness, O most merciful Father, for the many transgressions and the oft repeated disobedience, which cause Thee to command destruction over me. Behold me now, O my Father, supplicating Thy protection! Thou who art near when all other aid faileth! O spare me, guard me from the evil that is impending!

This once happy country is inflamed by the fury of war; a menacing enemy is arrayed against the rights, liberties and freedom of this, our Confederacy; the ambition of this enemy has dissolved fraternal love, and the hand of fraternity has been broken asunder by the hands of those, who sit now in council and meditate our chastisement, with the chastisement of scorpions. Our firesides are threatened; the foe is before us, with the declared intention to desecrate our soil, to murder our people, and to deprive us of the glorious inheritance which was left to us by the immortal fathers of this once great Republic.

Here I stand now with many thousands of the sons of the sunny South, to face the foe, to drive him back, and to defend our natural rights. O Lord, God of Israel, be with me in the hot season of the contending strife; protect and bless me with health and courage to bear cheerfully the hardships of war.

O Lord, Ruler of Nations, destroy the power of our enemies! "Grant not the longings of the wicked; suffer not his wicked device to succeed, lest they exalt themselves. Selah. As for the heads of those that encompass me about, let the mischief of their own lips cover them. Let burning coals be cast upon them; let them be thrown into the fire, into deep pits, that they rise not up again" (Psalm 140). Be unto the Army of this Confederacy, as thou were of old, unto us, thy chosen people– Inspire them with patriotism! Give them when marching to meet, or, overtake the enemy, the wings of the eagle—in the camp be Thou their watch and ward—and in the battle, strike for them, O Almighty God of Israel, as thou didst strike for thy people on the plains of Canaan—guide them O Lord of Battles, into the paths of victory, guard them from the shaft and missile of the enemy. Grant that they may ever advance to wage battle, and battle in thy name to win! Grant that not a standard be ever lowered among them! O Lord, God, Father, be thou with us!

Give unto the officers of the Army and of the Navy of the Confederate States, enterprise, fortitude and undaunted courage; teach them the ways of war and the winning of victory. Guard and preserve, O Lord, the President of the Confederate States and all officers, who have the welfare of the country truly at heart. Bless all my fellow-citizens, and guard them against sickness and famine! May they prosper and increase!

Hear me further, O Lord, when I pray to Thee for those on earth, dearest to my heart. O bless my father, mother, brothers and sisters. (if married: my wife and children.) O bless them all with earthly and heavenly good! May they always look up to Thee, and may they find in Thee their trust and strength.

O Lord, be with me always. Show me the way I have to go, to be prepared to meet Thee here and hereafter.

My hope, my faith, my strength are in Thee, O Lord, my God, forever— in Thee is my trust. "For thy salvation do I hope, O Lord! I hope for

Thy salvation, O Lord! O Lord, for Thy salvation do I hope!" Amen! Amen!

> Shemang Yisroel, Adonoy Elohainoo, Adonoy Achod!

Satisfactory though it might be for soldiers to meet in the woods for the reading of prayers on the Sabbath, or to meditate over words written in their behalf by the rabbi of Richmond, when the important festivals and holy day seasons approached, they longed to be home again. There must have been hundreds who felt like Edwin Kursheedt, when he wrote to his sweetheart:

> . . . I have not been able to see the Chanucka lights this year. Last year I was with my aunt and officiated in reading the service as I always did at home, for in addition to lighting the lamps in Synagogue we always did so at home. That was our Christmas, as children and we always rec'd presents & enjoyed ourselves—but those times have passed and I only expect to see them again when I shall have a family of my own to hand down these ceremonies to. Don't you say so too my Pet? . . . After I shall have been with you in February not many weeks will elapse ere Pesach . . .[105]

Some were not so prone as Kursheedt to postpone more complete observance of the holidays of the Jewish year until the return of peace; they attempted to find the best available substitute for being at home.

In 1862, J.A. Joel and twenty of his Jewish comrades in the 23rd Ohio Volunteer Regiment found themselves in winter headquarters at Fayette, W.Va., with Passover near at hand. After talking the matter over among themselves, they presented a request to their commanding officer for permission to absent themselves from duty for several days in order to observe the holiday. Their request granted, they set about organizing a *Seder* (Passover ritual dinner). The camp sutler, a Jew who was going back home to celebrate the festival with his family in Cincinnati, readily agreed to send some *Matzot* to them as soon as he reached his destination. The day before Passover, therefore, a supply train unloaded seven barrels of *Matzot* at the camp. Although they had not thought of asking for Passover prayer-books, the sutler had sent some of those along, too.

> We were now able to keep the *Seder* nights [wrote Joel in his lively narrative of the experience] if we could only obtain the other requisites for that occasion. We held a consultation and decided to send parties to forage in the country while a party stayed to build a log hut for the services. About the middle of the afternoon the foragers arrived, having been quite successful. We obtained two kegs of cider, a lamb, several chickens and some eggs. Horse radish or parsley we could not obtain, but in lieu we found a weed, whose bitterness, I apprehend, exceeded anything our forefathers "enjoyed." We were still in a great quandary; we were like the men who drew the

elephant in the lottery. We had the lamb, but did not know what part was to represent it at the table; but Yankee ingenuity prevailed, and it was decided to cook the whole and put it on the table, then we could dine off it, and be sure we had the right part. The necessaries for the *choroutzes* we could not obtain, so we got a brick which, rather hard to digest, reminded us, by looking at it, for what purpose it was intended.

So the make-shift *Seder* was prepared, with the assistance of "Yankee ingenuity!" Substitutes and symbols-upon-symbols were contrived to fulfill the elaborate Passover prescriptions. It was as though the Passover tradition were being recast in a new mould. Cider served as the symbol of rejoicing, instead of wine; a whole lamb replaced a lamb-bone as the representation of the Paschal sacrifice; the agony of the servitude in Egypt was recalled by bitter weeds instead of the usual horse-radish; in lieu of the delicious *haroset* (an edible mortar concocted of chopped apple, nuts, and wine) a brick symbolized the brick-building of the Hebrew in Egypt. *Matzot*, eggs, and chicken were the only conventional items. But still it was a *Seder*, and the very originality of the religious symbols was an index to the devotion and piety with which these soldiers, far away from home, were determined to commemorate the exodus from Egypt.

Joel himself took the role of the leader of the service, and chanted the blessings ordained by centuries-old practice. It must have been quite a sight: these twenty men gathered together in a crude and hastily-built log hut, their weapons at their side, prepared as in Egypt-land for all manner of danger, singing the words of praise and faith in the ancient language of Israel.

Everything was solemn and decorous (Passover dinners always are at the outset, until the wine stimulates some fun). But let Mr. Joel continue with his version of an unexpected development:

The ceremonies were passing off very nicely, until we arrived at the part where the bitter herb was to be taken. We all had a large portion of the herb ready to eat at the moment I said the blessing; each [ate] his portion, when horrors! what a scene ensued in our little congregation, it is impossible for my pen to describe. The herb was very bitter and very fiery like Cayenne pepper, and excited our thirst to such a degree, that we forgot the law authorizing us to drink only four cups, and the consequence was we drank up all the cider. Those that drank the more freely became excited and one thought he was Moses, another Aaron, and one had the audacity to call himself a Pharaoh. The consequence was a skirmish, with nobody hurt, only Moses, Aaron, and Pharaoh, had to be carried to the camp, and there left in the arms of Morpheus.

After this debacle, the survivors nonchalantly continued with the prayers, then partook of their dinner, and completed the service with the traditional blessings and hymns.

> There [wrote Joel] in the wild woods of West Virginia, away from home and friends, we consecrated and offered up to the ever-loving God of Israel our prayers and sacrifice . . . there is no occasion in my life that gives me more pleasure and satisfaction than when I remember the celebration of Passover of 1862.[106]

Other soldiers were closer to large cities where, at the very least, if they could not obtain furlough from military duties, they were able to purchase the necessary unleavened bread. But there must have been many cases where the soldiers were unaware of the exact dates of holidays, as in Isaac J. Levy's account of his Passover celebration at Adam's Run, S.C., narrated in a letter to his sister Leonora:

> No doubt you were much surprised on receiving a letter from me addressed to our dear parents dated on the 21st inst. [of April, 1864] which was the first day of [Passover]. We were all under the impression in camp that the first day of the festival was the 22d and if my memory serves me right I think that Ma wrote me that [Passover] was on the 22d inst. Zeke was somewhat astonished on arriving in Charleston on Wednesday afternoon, to learn that that was the first [*Seder*] night. He purchased [*Matzot*] sufficient to last us for the week. The cost is somewhat less than in Richmond, being but two dollars per pound. We are observing the festival in a truly orthodox style. On the first day we had a fine vegetable soup. It was made of a bunch of vegetables which Zeke brought from Charleston containing new onions, parsley, carrots turnips and a young cauliflower, also a pound and a half of fresh beef, the latter article sells for four dollars per pound in Charleston. Zeke did not bring us any meat from home. He brought some of his own, smoked meat, which he is having with us, he says that he supposes that Pa forgot to deliver it to him . . .[107]

So Isaac J. Levy and his friends and many others like him celebrated the holidays as best they could. More fortunate, however, were those soldiers who were stationed in cities or at camps so close to them that they could celebrate holidays with their civilian co-religionists. After the capture of Memphis, for instance, Jewish men with the Union army were delighted to learn that there were two synagogues in the city, where they could attend services on the Sabbath and on festivals.[108]

When his parents heard that Lieutenant Simon S. Brucker of the 39th Illinois Volunteer Regiment was to supervise the building of fortifications near Suffolk, Va., during the High Holy Days of 1862, they wrote and suggested that he try to get time off to attend services in Norfolk where, they remembered, there had been an active Jewish community before the war. He took their advice, made the short trip, and found the synagogue without much trouble. Services for the New Year had already begun, but he no sooner heard the familiar chanting of the minister than —"Oh! it made me feel as though I were at home among friends once more." They were not exactly friends, of course: "All the Yehudin in Norfolk are embittered against the northern soldiers. I had several little arguments with some of them and find most of them pretty reasonable excepting the young *ladies, they* can outargue the smartest statesman in the world according to their own way." But, despite the bitterness, they all treated him with courtesy, and he mentioned that the Nathan Baums, the Barney Kaytons, and the Samuel Franks had been particularly friendly to him. But those young ladies![109]

Another Union soldier, Myer Levy of Philadelphia, had an even more humorous experience. Around Passover time, one year, he was strolling through the streets of a Virginia town captured by the Federals, and noticed a little boy sitting on the steps of a house, eating *Matza*. When he asked the boy for a piece, the child fled indoors, shouting at the top of his lungs, "Mother! There's a 'damnyankee' Jew ouside!" The boy's mother came out immediately and invited him to return for a Passover dinner that night. One presumes that the family's heir became friendlier at dinner time.[110]

It was close to the New Year when Henry Frank and Isaac Lowenberg, two soldiers with the commissary department of the invading Union army, happened to drop into John Mayer's store in Vicksburg, Miss. They identified themselves as Jews and inquired about religious services. They had come to the right man. Mayer was the president of the small Vicksburg congregation, Anshe Chesed, which was not then large enough to afford its own synagogue building or to hold regular services. But *Rosh Hashanah* and *Yom Kippur* were holidays which the congregation would not neglect to celebrate; so Mayer invited Frank and Lowenberg to attend services with the local folk on the second floor of the engine house on North Union Street. The boys came to the Mayer home frequently thereafter and friendship ripened into something more. By the end of the war Isaac Lowenberg had convinced Mayer's daughter, Ophelia, to marry him despite her strong prejudices against the Yankee *Yehudim*.[111]

The Rev. Michelbacher was not content with sending his prayer to the Confederate Jewish soldiers; in anticipation of the Passover Festival and the High Holy Days, year after year, he asked the commanding generals to grant furloughs to Jewish men in the Virginia area in order to enable them to attend services in Richmond. Generals Lee and Beauregard answered, reluctantly, that military movements were always imminent, and that a whole class of soldiers could not therefore be spared from duty at one time.[112] General Lee's first letter is typical of the others:

Hd Qrs: Valley Mt:
29 Aug 1861

Rabbi M. J. Michelbacher,
Preacher Hebrew Congregation,
"House of Love" Richmond, Va:
Revd Sir

I have just re[ceive]d your letter of the 23d inst: requesting that a fur-lough from the 2nd to the 15th Sept. be granted to the soldiers of the Jewish persuasion in the C.S. Army, that they may participate in the approaching holy services of the Synagogue.

It would give me great pleasure to comply with a request so earnestly urged by you, & which I know would be so highly appreciated by that class of our soldiers. But the necessities of war admit of no relaxation of the efforts requisite for its success, nor can it be known on what day the presence of every man may be required. I feel assured that neither you or any member of the Jewish congregation would wish to jeopardize a cause you have so much at heart by the withdrawal even for a season of a portion of its de-fenders. I cannot therefore grant the general furlough you desire, but must leave to individuals to make their own applications to their Several Com-manders, in the hope that many will be able to enjoy the privilege you seek for them. Should any be deprived of the opportunity of offering up their prayers according to the rites of their Church [I trust] their penitence may nevertheless be accepted by the Most High, & their petitions answered.

That your prayers for the success & welfare of our Cause may be granted by the Great Ruler of the universe is my ardent wish.

I have the honor to be, with high esteem,
Your obt' Servt.
R.E. LEE,
Gen'l Commd.

Jewish men attached to units in the Baltimore area were more fortunate than their enemies down in Virginia. Rabbi Szold requested furloughs for them from General Tyler and his request was granted. According to a report in *The Israelite*, "all Hebrew soldiers in [the] department . . . received furloughs for the holidays." The men were taken home for festive dinners on *Rosh Hashanah* and after the *Yom Kippur* fast by mem-bers of the various Baltimore congregations.[113]

Undoubtedly, however, many soldiers both North and South were un-lucky enough to be on duty or in battle on the High Holy Days. One pious young man was on the line of battle near Harper's Ferry on *Yom Kippur* of '61. Fight he must, but he did not have to violate the com-mandment to fast from sundown to sundown; and so he observed the Holy Day by fasting while fighting; and when the enemy retreated in the late afternoon, he betook himself to the woods, where he remained reading his prayers until the sunset signalized the end of the Day of Atonement.[114]

Holiday or no holiday, contacts between Jewish soldiers and civilians

H[d]. Qrs: Valley Mt[s]:
29 Aug 1861

Rabbi M. I. Michelbacher,
Preacher Hebrew Congregation
"House of Love" Richmond Va:

Rev[d] Sir

I have just rec[d] your letter of the 23rd
Inst: requesting that a furlough from the 2nd to the
15th Sept: be granted to the soldiers of the Jewish persua
-sion in the C. S. Army, that they may participate in
the approaching holy services of the Synagogue

It would give me great pleasure to comply with
a request so earnestly urged by you, & which I know
would be so highly appreciated by that class of our
Soldiers. But the necessities of war admit of no re
laxation of the efforts requisite for its success, Nor can it
be known on what day the presence of every man may
not be required. I feel assured that neither you or
any member of the Jewish Congregation would wish
to jeopardize a cause you have so much at heart by
the withdrawal even for a season of a portion of its de
-fenders. I cannot therefore grant the general furlough
you desire, but must leave to individuals to make their
own application to their several Commanders, in the
hope that many will be able to enjoy the privilege you
seek for them, & should any be deprived of the oppor
tunity of offering up their prayers according to the
rites of their Church, that their penitence may be
accepted by the Most High, & their petitions answered

That your prayers for the success & welfare of our Cause
may be granted by the great ruler of the universe is
my ardent wish.

I have the honour to be with high esteem
your obt. Servt
R E Lee
Genl Comdg

were eagerly sought after. When Dr. D. Mayer, Assistant Surgeon of the 5th Virginia Regiment, found himself in Cincinnati for a few days, he and his companions took advantage of the opportunity to pay calls on the local rabbis. Both Isaac M. Wise and Max Lilienthal showed them the finest hospitality, and Lilienthal urged the military surgeon to write him if the sick and wounded men in his regiment should be in need of the little comforts and luxuries which make hospitalization bearable. The rabbi promised that he would do his utmost to collect a shipment of such articles.[115]

Dr. Mayer's men were well off in comparison with the Jewish wounded who were sent to the Baptist College Hospital in Washington. One of the physicians at that hospital was a proselyte to Christianity who devoted himself to conversionist activities among the Jewish men placed under his care. It was a continual source of annoyance to be pestered with proselytizing books and pamphlets and exhortations, while one was trying to recover from painful wounds sustained at the Battle of Manassas. So wrote the brother of a soldier hospitalized there, in a letter of complaint to *The Israelite*.[116]

One soldier thought it better for Jews, wounded or well, to be circumspect about mentioning their religious background, because

> it would at once involve them in an intricate controversial disquisition with the Christian Chaplains, for which they do not always feel themselves qualified, and which, of course, can, under no circumstances, afford them anything but annoyance.[117]

Isaac Leeser, who did volunteer chaplaincy work in the military hospitals in Philadelphia, had something to say on this same problem.

> To some [soldiers] [he said] we were welcome, while others would scarcely confess their Jewish origin. Some even refused prayer-books when tendered to them, and all had to partake of the hospital foods, and only on holy days we could get permits for them to leave, when one or more again refused to come out. There was, on the whole, a hesitancy to confess our religion, in fear of taint or shame, false indeed, yet powerful enough to act as a check on them . . .[118]

Christian chaplains were not all of the evangelical variety, of course. Many Jewish soldiers who were unable to attend Jewish worship felt that it was better to attend Christian services than none at all, if the particular chaplain was not disposed to utilize the opportunity to attempt to proselytize. Henry Beck, who served with Rode's division of the Confederate Army of Northern Virginia, attended Christian services practically every week, according to Sunday entries in his diary.[119] Solomon Emanuel of Dalton, Ga., wrote to his mother from the field that his chaplain had "preached a very interesting sermon suitable to the times and the occasion" on the Confederate Fast Day, April 8, 1864. He himself fasted for twenty-four hours, he wrote, "and felt but little inconvenience from the effects."[120]

Writing from Corinth, Miss., a Union soldier commented on the general attitude towards his regimental chaplain. Most of the men were thoroughly dissatisfied with his sermons because they felt he "preached too much nigger." But from a Jewish viewpoint, there was no complaint whatever: "Upon religious questions . . . our chaplain is quite circumspect, taking every care to avoid wounding the feelings of those who are not of the same creed as himself."[121]

August Bondi had nothing to say about the religious aspects of his chaplain's service, but he minced no words in regard to his character. Bondi wrote in his diary that Chaplain Fisher was "the most useless person in the regiment"—"as useless as a wagon's fifth wheel"—so lazy that he "would not attend even to the regimental mail." It was unfortunate that Bondi should have been assigned to a regiment which contained only two other Jews—and that both of them denied their background. After the death of one, a Hungarian named Marcus Wittenberg, Bondi found among his remains some letters from his parents, in Yiddish, reminding him of the dates of the Jewish holidays. It was unfortunate that he had no Jewish companionship because he was such a devout and loyal Jew. A veteran of the bloody Kansas battles with John Brown's men in '55 and '56, Bondi insisted on enlisting in '61 because "as a Jehudi I had a duty to perform, to defend the institutions which gave equal rights to all beliefs." He felt keenly, all during the war, until his discharge for disability in late '64, his separation from Jewish activities and synagogue services. The closest he came to satisfying his intense Jewish loyalties was eating a *Rosh Hashanah* dinner with a Jewish family in Pine Bluff, Ark.[122]

Undoubtedly there were hundreds and hundreds of Jewish men and officers in the Union and Confederate armies who, like Bondi's comrades, thought they would avoid trouble by attempting to hide their background, or whose religious interests were so tenuous that they were undisturbed by the absence of formal and organized Jewish activities in the camps.[123] Like their non-Jewish fellow-soldiers, they were much more concerned about battles and skirmishes, military gossip and gripes, entertainment and comforts, safety and health, than they were about Jewish Holy Days and the requirements of the faith. But there was always the "saving remnant" who overcame the obstacles in the way of religious observance and, in the midst of danger and death, not only retained their faith in God, but practiced that faith in ritual and prayer —despite the absence of a spiritual guide.

V ON THE HOME FRONT

THE CIVIL WAR brought immeasurable suffering to the people of America. Few had bethought themselves in April 1861 of battlefields strewn with wounded and dead soldiers, of military and civilian hospitals too small to contain the injured and diseased, of the women who would be widowed, the children orphaned, and the elderly folk whose source of sustenance would be taken away. Those who hastened the "irrepressible conflict" had not paused to consider the pall of tragedy which would hang heavy over millions upon millions of homes in the far stretches of both sections of the sundered nation.

But when death and disease, pain and want, took up a four year abode in America, the nation's great humanitarian heart responded with devout warmth. The stronger the determination of Federals and Confederates to achieve their declared objectives, the more generous was the outpouring of help and assistance to the men who carried the fight to the field, and to their families who remained at home. Few military chapters of the Civil War story can equal in glory and honor the heart-warming narrative of the civilian relief activities which healed the hurts of war, and the spontaneous deeds of mercy performed by millions of individuals in hospitals and in sorrowful homes. From Florida to Maine and from Chicago to New Orleans, church societies and non-sectarian groups alike raised funds for relief measures, collected and produced hospital supplies, distributed clothing, food, and cash to destitute soldiers' families, and carried out the hundreds of other tasks for the well-being and consolation of war sufferers which go unnoticed in the military and political histories. Unpaid volunteers worked long and tedious hours to guide these activities and fulfill essential functions. Only a few, notably those determined women who imposed their conception of nursing upon reluctant government officials, received any acclaim, but all achieved that high sense of satisfaction which comes to those who give of themselves to relieve pain.

Certain Northern leaders who early in the war apprehended the immense proportions of the conflict were responsible for a unique and remarkable development in American society: the organization of relief activities on a national scale. The United States Sanitary Commission coordinated and supervised the raising of funds and the distribution of supplies, as an unofficial adjunct to governmental agencies. It raised millions of dollars in mammoth fairs and festivals in the metropolitan areas, conducted under local auspices, but with the advantages of national publicity and universal approval. Supplementing the inevitably limited work of the military medical services in the hospitals and on the battlefields, the Commission distributed fifteen million dollars worth of bedding, sanitation supplies, medicines, food, and clothing. Equally important were the personal ministrations of the Commission's workers who fulfilled the office of nurse in the hospital and corpsman in the field. Red Cross was a new name when its charter was granted by Congress in 1882, but in terms of objectives, scope, and activities, it had been anticipated by the meritorious role played in the Civil War by the United States Sanitary Commission.[1]

As individual American citizens, many Jews participated in these manifold relief activities. August Belmont, for instance, opened his art collections to the public eye and swelled the coffers of the Sanitary Commission with the proceeds from admission fees.[2] Three Jewish firms in San Francisco contributed $1,000 each to the Commission's California campaign.[3] C.W. Starbuck, President of the Cincinnati Relief Union, collected $2,000 from various Jews in a few hours one June day in 1862, even though he had been reluctant to approach them because the local Jewish charitable groups had just completed their own drive for funds. In his report to the Relief Union, Starbuck made particular reference to his "day among the Israelites," as he called it, and said that the Jews had shown "a manliness and sympathy . . . for the objects of the Relief Union that was highly gratifying to my feelings."[4] Nathan Grossmayer of Washington, D.C., contributed ideas as well as money for relief purposes; he was the first to suggest the establishment of a national veterans' hospital and home. In a letter to Lincoln on November 16, 1864, he called the President's attention to the provisions for disabled veterans made by various European governments and urged that the United States could do no less. Lincoln was assassinated before he could carry out the suggestion, but Grossmayer wrote Andrew Johnson about the idea, enclosed $1,000 as his contribution, and suggested that the home be designated a memorial to Lincoln. Congress adopted the proposal in 1866.[5] M. C. Mordecai of Charleston, S.C., was one of the most generous contributors to the "Free Market of Charleston," which was organized for the support of the families of soldiers, and which, in December 1862, maintained over six hundred families at a monthly expense of $6,000.[6]

Jewish women responded as devotedly as did their neighbors to the spoken and unspoken needs of the time. In Columbus, Ga., fourteen-year-old Isabel Adeline Moses became the youngest member of the Soldiers Aid Society and spent long hours in the Columbus hospital nursing the wounded. When her friends, Dr. and Mrs. F.O. Ticknor, took a dying

Tennessee soldier into their home, young Isabel helped teach him to read and write, hoping he would forget his pain in the concentration of study.[7] Mrs. Rosanna Osterman of Galveston, Texas, contributed large stores of food to the overcrowded hospital in that city and spent an incredible number of hours at the bedsides of convalescing soldiers. When she died, in 1866, the *Galveston News* paid high tribute to her generosity and prophesied that she would never pass from the memory of those soldiers whose suffering she had eased.[8] The Hausman family of Montgomery, Ala., earned a similar encomium for its attentions to the wounded.[9] The wife of a Confederate General remarked, in her diary, on the devotion with which the Jewish ladies of Columbia, S.C., tended wounded men in the military hospitals.[10] In her reminiscences of the Civil War, Mrs. Philip Phillips wrote many detailed pages about her imprisonment for outspoken support of the Confederacy, and only a few about her knitting and sewing and visits to the hospitals—but those words deserve to be recorded as typical of the feelings of the women who participated in the work of mercy:

> We passed our days in doing what we considered to be our duty—giving our all to the poor soldiers—making their garments—and looking to the well being of their poor families—making lint, bandages and as far as in our limited power doing everything to encourage the cause we thought ourselves right in espousing . . . We at last found a home [in La Grange]—devoting our lives and fortunes to the support and clothing of the poor soldiers—nursing the wounded and dying—alleviating in every way the desolation and misery which Civil War surely brings . . .[11]

II

Jewish welfare societies, social organizations, and synagogues, as well as individuals, took an active role in the war relief and patriotic activities. Wherever there were Jewish women's societies, in New York, Philadelphia, Rochester, Pittsburgh, Cincinnati, Charlotte, Mobile[12]—to name only a few—they met regularly in synagogue vestry rooms and private homes, devoting a major portion of their time to the preparation of bandages and lint, the collection of funds for the relief of soldiers' families, the organization of booths and tables at Sanitary Fairs, and other such activities. Many new women's groups were organized specifically to meet war-time needs.

One of these was the Ladies Hebrew Association for the Relief of Sick and Wounded Soldiers, organized in Philadelphia on May 11, 1863, as the result of an interchange of correspondence between the Rev. Sabato Morais of Mikveh Israel Congregation and Mrs. Mary Rose Smith, head of the women's division of the Sanitary Commission branch in Philadelphia. Mrs. Smith hoped the rabbi would designate some Jewish woman to serve on the executive board of her division; the Rev. Morais hoped for even more.[13] A few days after receiving Mrs. Smith's letter, he preached in his synagogue on the necessity of organizing a woman's war relief society:

> While *we* dwell here securely, in the fruition of God's bounty, thousands of our fellow-beings are exposed to dangers and privations. They are the defenders of our Union. But, even on the battlefield, where many lie wounded, and on their couch of sickness, charity—the handmaid of religion—can soften their pangs. More I need not say, in order to strike a sympathetic chord in Jewish hearts. But, as many a generous gift has been wasted, for want of a systematic distribution, I would urge the ladies of my persuasion to join hands with their sisters of a different creed in the discharge of a philanthropic task . . .[14]

The ladies of the congregation met and elected Mrs. Henry M. Cohen as their delegate, then proceeded to organize themselves as a permanent body, with Miss Celia Myers as their presiding officer. Within a month they had obtained two hundred and fifty persons as contributing members—the fee was fifty cents a year. Then they set their hands to their task which, according to the *Philadelphia Public Ledger*, was to provide "sick and wounded soldiers, irrespective to religious creed . . . with delicacies and clothing while they lie in the army hospitals."[15] Some idea of their enthusiastic activities may be gathered from the report which Rebecca Moss, their secretary, read at the second annual meeting, on May 8, 1865.[16] Ten crates of supplies, said Miss Moss, had been sent to the Sanitary Commission during the year, and their total contents were as follows:

82	flannel shirts	58	sponges
38	canton flannel shirts	144	lbs. of smoking tobacco
11	white cotton shirts	23	bundles of lint and linen
133	colored cotton shirts	23	jars of pickles
11	old cotton shirts	7	cans of tomatoes
7	cotton drawers	2	lbs. black tea
222	towels	30	lbs. corn starch
216	pocket handkerchiefs	24	lbs. farina
80	pillow cases	13	lbs. rice flour
2	feather pillows	6	lbs. cocoa
63	pairs of woolen socks	6	lbs. wheaten grits
13	pairs of slippers	16	lbs. barley and oat meal
7	pantaloons	1	lb. biscuits
2	coats	1	peck onions
2	arm slings	6	reams of note and letter paper
24	knitted ear warmers	600	envelopes
16	knitted gloves and cuffs	48	pencils
1	chintz coverlet	1	gross steel pens
12	cakes of fancy soap	24	pen holders

and innumerable needle sets, magazines and books! Immediately after the capture of Savannah, an additional shipment was collected and sent, together with $63 in cash, to the 20th Army Corps Hospital. No wonder that Mrs. Cohen, the Society's delegate to the Sanitary Commission, wrote General Ben Butler an indignant letter in 1864 when he cast public aspersion on the patriotism of Jews![17]

In Pittsburgh, a similar Hebrew Ladies' Soldiers' Aid Society was organized and meetings were held every Thursday during the war to sew garments, wrap bandages, and pack food cartons. On December 9, 1863, the Society held a festive evening for the benefit of the Sanitary Commission. The tables, according to a newspaper report, "literally groaned beneath the weight of luxuries."[18] A band was hired to play for those who wanted to dance, and there were songs by versatile German vocalists for those who preferred to sit. The evening also groaned with speeches by the local rabbis, the mayor, and other dignitaries. Toasts to the nation, to womanhood, and to the President, completed the official program. Professor Josiah Cohen, who had already delivered one speech in praise of Jewish charitableness and generosity, offered this toast:

> The American woman—May the cause which gave rise to the Sanitary Committee be lost amid the more congenial strains of peace; but may the spirit of philanthropy which actuates them, descend to the Daughters of America to unknown generations.[19]

Jacob Affelder was called upon to offer the toast to the Chief Magistrate:

> Abraham Lincoln, President of the United States—The Noble Pilot, called by the voice of the people to the position of danger and responsibility, when traitors' hands had directed the Ship of State toward the breakers of national destruction. Nobly has he buffeted the mad waves of Disunion, until now, with the assistance of Providence and our gallant Army and Navy, he has brought us within sight of our longed for peace. His name will ever be synonymous with Patriotism, Honesty, and Justice.[20]

$700 was cleared from admission fees and the sale of refreshments, and Rabbi Isaac Mayer Wise, who happened to be in Pittsburgh, said it was altogether "one of the most liberal and pleasant entertainments which it has been our good fortune to attend."[21]

Good fellowship was frequently a part of philanthropic activities. The cause was significant—but fun could not be repressed. After a meeting of Pacific Lodge of B'nai B'rith in San Francisco one night, some fifteen members detoured to Salburg and Levy's "Eureka Saloon" for some liquid refreshments. Spirits induced good spirits and before long one of those present rose to his feet and began auctioning off a few stray weeds (dignified by the title "A Sanitary Bouquet") for the benefit of the Sanitary Commission. Fifty-one dollars was raised at the sale, and the purchaser who parted with $25 for the privilege of taking the weeds home, advertised the next day that he would be happy to sell them again for the same cause.[22]

Nine young Philadelphia ladies organized a club they named "Alert!" for the purpose of preparing embroidery and other needle work for eventual sale at a Sanitary Fair. But the eyes become tired and the fingers clumsy after three hours of work, so they worked only from 7 to 10 in the evening. By coincidence their beaux would appear at the latter hour and there was dancing and merrymaking until midnight. One young gentleman was so loyal an attendant that he began referring to himself as the club's secretary, and even wrote to Germany and asked his cousin there to send on a few examples of her artistry to add to the club's stock of merchandise.[23]

Every possible occasion was utilized to raise funds for relief purposes. At the Purim Balls which were held in many cities to celebrate the Feast of Esther, refreshments were frequently sold for the benefit of the Sanitary Commission.[24] Appeals were made from the pulpit on Passover, Shavuot, and other holidays: $200 was collected for the Volunteer Relief Fund of New York at Anshi Chesed Synagogue on Shavuot of 1861;[25] and Temple Emanu-El of the same city raised $500 for the benefit of wounded soldiers on the first day of Passover, 1862.[26] Shearith Israel Congregation of New York raised what was probably the largest sum collected by any congregation, $2,500, for the Sanitary Commission on Purim, 1864.[27] One of Rabbi David Einhorn's patriotic sermons was printed and sold, with the profits ear-marked for the Sanitary Commission.[28] No estimate can be made of the amount of contributions by Jewish groups and organizations to the Sanitary Commission and other societies because no systematic record was kept, but all indications point to the conclusion that the organized American Jewish community strove to the utmost to fulfill its duty in this time of need.[29]

The great Sanitary Fairs offered an unequaled opportunity for Jewish participation on a large scale. In Cincinnati, four stands were maintained by the Jewish community: one each by the Allemania Club, the Phoenix, a group calling themselves the "Independent Ladies," and the Broadway Synagogue. Among the four, a total of $5,402.58 was raised, but an observer guessed that, all in all, Jews had contributed about one third of the entire sum collected at the Fair.[30] At the Washington, D.C., Fair, in 1864, the Washington Hebrew Congregation raised $756.95—a total which was surpassed by only one other group, the Treasury Department![31] Similar records were achieved by Jewish organizations which managed booths at Sanitary Fairs in Philadelphia[32] and Pittsburgh.[33]

The 1864 Sanitary Fair in New York was the largest held anywhere in the country; it raised over a million dollars. Representative Jewish citizens were named to various committees in connection with the Fair, undoubtedly to assure the cooperation of all the Jewish organizations. Mrs.

Benjamin Nathan and Moses Lazrus were appointed to the Executive Committee, and Lewis May and Moses Schloss were members of the General Committee. There were also Jewish representatives on each of the committees charged with the solicitation of particular trade and business groups. May and Schloss wrote a circular which was addressed to the Jews of New York requesting that contributions to the Fair be sent through them, so that they could "hand over to the Treasurer of the Commission such a contribution from our people as will do honor to our faith and race."[34] Unfortunately, Messrs. May and Schloss published no record of the response, and we have no way of knowing how much the Jews of New York contributed. The periodicals inform us that the congregations were active in soliciting their members,[35] however, and that several benefits for the Fair were held by the young men's organizations. The irrepressible R.J. de Cordova delivered at least three readings and lectures, the proceeds of which went to the Commission,[36] and even Dr. Ridskopf's private school pupils (practically all of whom were Jewish) gave a performance of literary declamations and musical renditions at Niblo's Saloon to aid the Fair.[37]

Jewish institutions and periodicals[38] gave unstinting support to all worthy relief activities, but there was a division of opinion concerning the practice of Jewish *group* participation. The Jewish community of Rochester, N.Y., for instance, rebelled against what it considered to be segregation when Mrs. W. Barron Williams, President of the Ladies' Hospital Association, asked the women of Congregation Brith Kodesh to take part in a benefit Bazaar as a group. S. Stettheimer, President of the Congregation, explained his members' objections in a letter to Mrs. Williams: the Jews have no nationality other than American—"the only national character in which they wish to appear would be under the Star Spangled Banner, the glorious flag of the Union—the banner of civil and *religious* liberty." They would therefore have to decline the invitation as a group, but were offering their services individually. In order to preclude any suspicion that they were unwilling to support the Bazaar financially, Mr. Stettheimer enclosed a check for $400 in the name of the Jewish women of Rochester, with the hope that this contribution might "help to relieve the sufferings of our wounded patriotic soldiers, and soon return them to their brave comrades in the field, to give the final blow to that criminal attempt to destroy this Union, in the maintenance of which none are more interested than our Jewish fellow-citizens."[39]

Although it is possible that particular local conditions in Rochester gave rise to these objections, similar sentiments were voiced by two periodicals in New York at the time of the Sanitary Fair in that city. *The Jewish Record* believed that national relief campaigns offered no excuse for "Ghettoes" or "Judenstrassen." Why should "pretty Jewesses" be separated from other women? Were stands set apart for "pretty Catholics," "demure Quakeresses," or "smiling Presbyterians?" Let the Jewish men and women of New York participate as "*citizens* whose sympathies are with the brave men who are fearlessly doing their duty in the dark hour of peril," and not as Jews segregated from their neighbors. The *Record* approved of the Fair wholeheartedly, but not of the practice of labeling Jewish participation as Jewish.[40]

The Jewish Messenger's editors were suspicious of the circular issued by Messrs. May and Schloss.

> Have the several denominations of New York citizens taken measures to be represented by special departments, or are the Israelites to be the only body thus distinguished? . . . We have not noticed in the religious press a disposition to have space set apart in the Fair for denominational "stands" . . . We are disposed to regard as inopportune all attempts to establish a Jewish department while there is no similar arrangement designed, with respect to other religious denominations.

The *Messenger* hoped, however, that the synagogues would be successful in their effort to raise large sums to defray the expenses of the Fair, since churches of many other denominations were engaged in raising funds for this purpose.[41]

These were the only comments made in this connection, however, and neither the *Messenger* nor the *Record* pressed the issue. Perhaps it was better, after all, as Isaac M. Wise felt, that there should be an opportunity for Jews to demonstrate their patriotism, so as to counteract the accusations made against them. If every Jewish criminal brought censure to Jewry, Jewish philanthropists ought also to be identified with their people.[42]

III

By far the most noteworthy non-sectarian relief effort in which Jews participated was the voluntary conversion of several wards of the Jews' Hospital of New York to military purposes. Founded in January 1852, by Sampson Simson, the Rev. S.M. Isaacs, and seven other public-spirited gentlemen, this institution was of first importance in the development of New York Jewry's social service system. The tide of Central European Jewish immigration had reached its peak; incessant appeals were made by the destitute to synagogues and charitable organizations for a hospital in which Jewish practices would be observed and respected, and in which Jews would not be subjected to the conversionist tactics of Christian clergymen. Three years of fund-raising, and a legacy in 1854 from the will of the renowned New Orleans philanthropist, Judah Touro, were required before the Society was able to erect its Hospital on a lot on 28th Street between 7th and 8th Avenues. Many more years were to pass before the Hospital was on a firm financial footing, but now the largest Jewish community in America had its own Hospital, as modern as any other in the country, with a consultative staff of the ablest Jewish and non-Jewish physicians in that city.[43]

Conscious of the acute shortage of hospitals and medical personnel, the Board of Directors of the Hospital lost no time in offering the use of its facilities to the government. On April 20, 1861, a resolution was passed extending this offer in official manner, and forwarded to the governor.[44] Military processes moved at snail's pace, however, and more than a year had passed before Dr. Satterlee, the Army Surgeon in charge of medical operations in the New York area, notified that Board that he was about to assign fifty soldiers for treatment at Jews' Hospital.[45] Forty-eight new beds were ordered immediately, doubling the capacity of the wards, and another twenty-one were purchased four months later. Exact statistics of the number of wounded soldiers cared for in the Hospital throughout the war are not available, but incomplete figures show that military patients outnumbered civilian during many months in late 1862, early 1863, and late 1864.[46] For a six month period in 1862, 117 soldiers were given treatment—no small record for an institution whose original capacity had been limited to forty-eight patients![47]

The Board of Directors had volunteered to provide complete care for these wounded soldiers: beds, medical care, medical supplies, food, and entertainment, and all New York Jewry shared in the fulfillment of this promise. Even the Reform Jews, who had been excluded from membership on the Board of Directors, were now invited to participate: Lewis May and L.M. Morrison were elected to the Board, and Temple Emanu-El contributed a sizable sum for the expenses entailed in the new project.[48] Gifts poured into the Hospital's offices and kitchens: one hundred and thirty-six individuals and ten organizations sent donations of cash and merchandise: bandages and other medical supplies, all manner of clothing, bedding, mattresses, wine, beer, chickens, canned food, ice-cream, eggs, fresh fruit, books.[49] The patients were rarely without visitors: young ladies of the community sat at their bedsides and read to them;[50] the rabbis made regular visitations, and Christian clergymen were invited to pray and converse with non-Jewish patients; wealthy women called for ambulatory cases in their carriages and took them riding through Central Park.[51] A Saturday evening lecture series was organized, with entertainment and patriotic talks by prominent citizens and military officials.[52] No need which the men could possibly have had was overlooked; even new uniforms were presented to them when they were about to return to duty. The *New York Times* commented that the uniforms sewed by the ladies of the community were "far better made than some specimens turned off from the contractors' shelves."[53] No wonder that, as the Rev. Isaacs reported, "the patients . . . express themselves more than gratified with their treatment."[54] There were probably very few hospitals in the country where so much attention was lavished upon so few soldiers.

To be sure, there were motivations for this outpouring of attention beyond the desire to make the patients happy. Only the smallest proportion of the soldiers, one or two out of fifty or more, were Jewish. This was an opportunity to prove to other Americans that Jews were patriotic, generous, and charitable.[55] It was probably also a reflection of New York Jewry's frustrated eagerness to attain full social equality. But whatever the psychological motivations, the war-time service of the six year old Jews' Hospital offered an eloquent index to its value and efficiency.

This experience also had a far-reaching effect on the future of the Hospital. Before the war, the only non-Jewish cases admitted were accident cases; non-emergency cases were directed elsewhere. Now the sectarian policy was permanently shelved. To symbolize this new trend, the name of the institution was changed in 1866 to Mount Sinai Hospital, albeit over the opposition of some who felt that a hospital intended primarily for Jews was still a desideratum.

IV

The support of impoverished families of soldiers away with the army had to be borne by established Jewish communal charitable organizations. Never before had they faced so severe a test. In Baltimore, Chicago, Cincinnati, New York, the relief associations and benevolent societies suddenly found themselves called upon for three and four times the amount of money, food, clothing, and fuel which they had distributed the year before the war.[56]

Typical of the war-time reports of charitable organizations were those of Rebecca Gratz, the acknowledged leader of Jewish women's activities in Philadelphia, and Secretary of the Philadelphia Female Hebrew Benevolent Society. In 1861 she called the Society's attention to the number of "husbands and fathers who have been obliged to seek occupation at a distance, or enlist as soldiers in the service of the country, leaving helpless families unprovided for the coming winter, and wholly dependent on the benevolence of their fellow citizens."[57] In 1862 she cited several heartrending cases which had been referred to the society: one the mother of a wounded soldier who was literally starving to death, and was kept alive only by the desire to see her son again; the other a soldier's wife who died after the Society obtained admission for her to the Pennsylvania Hospital, leaving behind a young child. "Your committee," said Miss Gratz, "was there, attended to the last offices of humanity, and took charge of the little orphan, now placed in the Jewish Foster Home."[58] These acts of mercy must have been repeated many times all over the country.

Emergency meetings of charitable associations were a continuing feature of the war-time Jewish calendar. When funds were exhausted, there was no other way to replenish them. The Hebrew Relief Association of Cincinnati, for instance, the only source of support for eight orphans and seventeen widows, found itself unable to meet its commitments in October 1862. A special meeting was summoned, eloquent appeals were made by the rabbis, and a large number of subscriptions were pledged to permit a continuation of the Association's activities.[59] A similar meeting of the Hebrew Relief Association in Philadelphia had been called a year before. The president lost no time in getting to the point; the treasury, he said, had been completely exhausted, and the organization's work would have to cease until further funds were pledged. Over $3,300 had been spent in a few months, and much more would be needed to finish the year. There was an incalculable need, he admitted, but "charity," he said, "is most needed, when suffering is general."[60]

The Jews of Washington, D.C., were utterly unable to support their charges—the families of local men who had enlisted in military companies before the war, and were called to service as soon as hostilities broke out. One of their number wrote an open letter to *The Jewish Messenger*, asking the Jews of New York for assistance:

> ... The danger to our city was too imminent to be weighed in a scale with mere dollars and cents for the balance, and hence, with pride be it said, *they* at least were not influenced by any sordid motive. Unlike you in New York, we have no fund to support the families of poor soldiers, and the unhappy consequence is, the wives and the children of these poor men are in *abject want* ... The men, like true soldiers, say, they willingly undergo every and any deprivation, but they feel it hard, indeed, as only our people *can* feel, to see those they love, and who have a right to look to them for their support, suffer for the *necessaries of life*.[61]

Because it was one of the smallest and least affluent Jewish communities in the country, Washington Jewry could not meet most of the demands made upon it during the war. Many Jewish men were patients in the Washington hospitals, but except for the period when the Rev. Fischel had acted as their chaplain, no one had the time to visit them. Rabbi Raphall's son-in-law, Captain C.M. Levy, assigned to the Quartermaster Department in the capital, was willing to undertake the task of distributing clothing and food delicacies to them, he told his friends in New York, but they would have to send them; the local Jews could simply not afford to contribute as much as was needed.[62] One task they did perform regularly. They provided a traditional Jewish burial service for every Jewish man who died in a Washington hospital, and for that they earned the heartfelt appreciation of many a bereaved family.[63]

Many other Jewish communities performed this act of faith for Jewish soldiers who died in their midst. There had never been a sufficient number of Jews in Knoxville, Tenn., to warrant the organization of a synagogue; but so many soldiers perished in the area, that the Knoxville

Jews founded a Hebrew Benevolent Association in 1864 to maintain a cemetery for the burial of Jewish soldiers.[64] The Jews of Savannah volunteered their services to the German Artillery of Macon, Ga., when Private A. Nordlinger was killed in battle, and for this kindness to "their deceased friend and comrade in arms" the members of the Artillery passed a resolution of thanks which was published in the Savannah papers.[65] In Cincinnati,[66] Philadelphia,[67] and other cities, lots in Jewish cemeteries were set aside for the interment of Jewish soldiers. Sometimes, when the authorities had Jewish men buried in military cemeteries, with Christian rites, rabbis and communal leaders would secure permission to have the bodies disinterred and then would perform the burial services according to the Jewish ritual.[68]

Twenty-two year old Pvt. George Kuhn of the 118th Pennsylvania Volunteers was one of five substitute deserters who were sentenced to be shot on August 29, 1863. Army authorities had ordered the execution in a desperate effort to discourage desertion; thousands of men were taking the easy way out to avoid the hardship and danger of military service. Kuhn insisted on seeing a rabbi before the execution; since there was none in Washington, the army sent for Rabbi Benjamin Szold of Baltimore. After a conversation with the boy, the rabbi was convinced that there were grounds for clemency in the case and he went to the White House to ask the President to grant a pardon. Lincoln had already received petitions on the matter from some New York people and declined to intercede, but he listened patiently to the rabbi and then sent him with a letter of introduction to General Meade. The General, too, listened patiently to his story and to his biblical quotations, but insisted that the execution had to proceed as planned—only such an example, he said, would stem the tide of desertion.[69]

Rabbi Szold had done all he could, but his task was not ended. He returned to Rappahannock Station, where the regiment was located, and told Kuhn of his failure. The boy asked the rabbi to be with him at the execution and to perform the burial ceremony. On Saturday, the 29th, twenty-five thousand people, including the troops of the regiment, were on hand to witness the execution. The regimental chaplain was talking with the three Protestant boys; a Catholic priest from Washington prayed with the one soldier of his faith; and Rabbi Szold stood by the side of George Kuhn. According to the report of an eyewitness, "the condemned man, much agitated, stood up and recited after the Rabbi a portion of Thillim, Yigdal, and Shimas [Psalms and other prayers]. At the close, the minister, much affected, kissed the accused, who convulsively clung to him." At three o'clock the clergymen were asked to conclude their prayers; the five men stood at attention in front of the graves which had already been dug for them; the order to fire was given and thirty-six muskets discharged their bullets. The five bodies were then placed in the graves and the three clergymen, side by side, read their burial services.

This was probably the first case in American history of an all-denominational funeral.[70]

After the war, monuments in honor of the Jewish war dead were erected in Jewish cemeteries both North and South.[71] The most ambitious project of this nature was that of the Hebrew Ladies' Memorial Association of Richmond, organized in 1866 to care for the Jewish Confederate graves in the Hollywood cemetery on Shockoe Hill. The work of turning the sod was performed by Jewish veterans. A Richmond reporter who went out to the cemetery one day said that "it was a gratifying sight to behold young men of this city, some of them frail of limb, with coats off, wheeling gravel and turf, as the last sad tribute they could pay to departed worth."[72] Because the Richmond Jewish community, impoverished by the war, was unable to defray all the expenses of the plot, a general appeal for financial support was issued by the Association "To the Israelites of the South:"

> While the world yet rings with the narrative of a brave people's struggle for independence, and while the story of the hardships so nobly endured for Liberty's sake is yet a theme but half exhausted, the countless graves of the myriads of heroes who spilled their noble blood in defense of that glorious cause, lie neglected, not alone unmarked by tablet or sculptured urn, but literally vanishing before the relentless finger of Time . . .

> In our own cemetery repose, alas! the sacred remains of many a loved brother, son and husband, to whose relatives, in the far sunny South, it would be a solace to know that the pious duty of preserving from decay the last resting place of their lost ones, although denied to them to perform, is yet sacredly fulfilled by the members of the "Hebrew Ladies' Memorial Association."

> It is our intention to mound and turf each grave, and to place at the head of each a simple stone, inscribed with the name, State, and time and place of death; subsequently, to rear a monument commemorative of their brave deeds.

> In order, however, to successfully accomplish our object, we need some pecuniary assistance. Our scant and somewhat needy community, already so heavily taxed, has done well; but we find "this work is too great for us;" therefore, with a full confidence in the sympathy and co-operation of our people elsewhere, we make this appeal for aid well knowing that as Israelites and true patriots, they will not refuse to assist in rearing a monument which shall serve not only to commemorate the bravery of our dead, but the gratitude and admiration of the living, for those who so nobly perished in what we deemed a just and righteous cause; and while as Israelites we mourn the untimely loss of our loved ones, it will be a grateful reflection that they suffered not their country to call in vain.

List of Soldiers, of the Confederate army buried by George Jacobs - Richmond Va

Names	Regiment &c	Date of interment	Remarks.
Henry Cohen	— S. C	30th June 1862	Killed in Battle
Edwin Sampson	— Texas	16 July 1862	Killed in battle, 27 June.
Jacob A. Cohn	12 Louisiana Rg.t	29 Sept. 1862	" " " 30 Aug
Lewis Lipman	5 " "	2 may 1863	Died of wound - 1 May 1863
Isaac J. Levy	46 Va.	23 aug 1864	Killed in battle 21 Aug 64
Dan.l Levy	— "	9 Feb.y 1866	Died of Disease contracted

Richmond Va, May 17" 1866.

Mrs R. C. Levy.

Cor. Sec Heb. Ladies association &c.

D.r madam,

Above I hand you the list of Soldiers buried by me during the late war, as requested by the association, in your letter of 16th inst

Very respectfully Yours

Geo. Jacobs

Facsimile of a list of Confederate soldiers buried by the Rev. George Jacobs

> In time to come, when our grief shall have become, in a measure, silenced, and when the malicious tongue of slander, ever so ready to assail Israel, shall be raised against us, then, with feeling of mournful pride, will we point to this monument and say: "*There* is our reply."[73]

Pride in their people and grief over the fate of the "lost cause" combined to further this loving project. Rebekah Bettelheim, who came to Richmond in 1868, remarked how the entire Jewish population of Richmond would go out to the cemetery every Confederate Memorial Day, setting wreaths on the headstones, and standing before the monument with tears in their eyes.[74]

The Richmond ladies need not have limited their appeal to Southern Jews as though their brethren to the North had lost all feeling for them. Both Isaac Mayer Wise and Isaac Leeser were deeply grieved at the narrow straits of the once wealthy and proud Richmond Jewish community when they visited the city in 1866.[75] But even during the war, northern Jews had demonstrated their fraternal feelings for Southern Jewry. Rabbi Wise had done all he could in 1863 and 1864 to obtain the release of some Confederate Jewish prisoners at Fort Delaware who had written to him for assistance. Failing in this effort, he appealed to his readers to send foodstuffs to them, published their names so that Northern relatives, if there were any, might take a special interest in their lot: Henry Mass, Julius Braunschweiger, Max Newgas, A. Waterman, Louis Meyersberg, S. Cohen and H. Brasch.[76] Chicago Jews made more than a few trips to Camp Douglas, to visit with Jewish prisoners of war and to secure their release on parole.[77]

There were numerous other instances in which Jews whose loyalty to the Union was unquestionable tried to be of assistance to Confederate brethren captured by Union forces.[78] But perhaps the outstanding example of Jewish fellowship was the enheartening response of Jewish communities all over the North to appeals for assistance by Southern congregations. In February 1865, Savannah Jewry addressed a request to Isaac Leeser and S.M. Isaacs for Passover *Matzot*. "Many of the inhabitants, formerly wealthy, are now in extremely straitened circumstances; and besides [we] have entirely lost the means of baking for the ensuing Passover." Isaacs pointed out in an editorial that the Jews of Savannah had in previous years been most generous and charitable, and urged that all feelings of hostility be shunned now that the city had fallen to the Union. So prompt was the response from congregations and individuals, who sent their contributions to the *Messenger* and *Occident* offices, that 3,000 pounds of the unleavened bread were shipped from New York, and 2,000 more from Philadelphia.[79] The congregations at Columbia[80] and Charleston, S.C.,[81] both hard hit by the war, also addressed appeals for assistance to congregations and periodicals in the North. In each case they were treated with consideration and affection. *The Jewish Record*, after the surrender of the Southern armies, urged the Jews of New York to form a special benevolent association to meet the crying needs of Southern Jewry.

> This is no time to look back upon petty differences that may have arisen between communities. Nor can any one now allude to political discussions or angry passions, quenched by an all-potent and universal yearning for peace and prosperity. Let all of us join in tendering to our brethren a part of that wealth with which the God of Israel has blessed us. The poorest of all may thus feel that he has practically aided the suffering of his own race, and bound up the wounds of those who are almost his next of kin. Responding to the call made upon us, the Israelites of New York should assemble at once and devise means by which to relieve the most pressing wants of our unfortunate Southern brethren . . .[82]

Such an organization was never formed, but for three or four years after the war, ex-Confederate Jews continued to send letters and representatives to the North, seeking financial assistance.[83]

V

The *Record's* proposal of a unified welfare organization to centralize contributions to Southern Jewry at the end of the war was not the first public appeal for a coordination of Jewish relief activities. The earliest battles had no sooner been fought than some Jews were already urging the establishment of a central Jewish Military Hospital in Washington. One of the frequent contributors to the pages of the *Messenger*, writing under the pseudonym "Semi-Occasional," was the first to offer a detailed plan.[84] He had inspected the military hospitals in the national capital and was shocked at the insensitive treatment of wounded men and the unsanitary conditions of the wards. Even if the hospitals were immeasurably improved, he believed, Jewish men who risked their lives for the preservation of the nation's unity should still be nursed in a hospital maintained by their own people, in which the Jewish dietary laws would be observed and a rabbi would minister to their spiritual needs. The cost would not be prohibitive.

He had already consulted Miss Dorothea Dix, who was supervising the organization of hospitals for the War Department. She had not only given her complete approval to the proposal, but had gone to the trouble of preparing detailed directions for the establishment of such a hospital. If the Jewish community would secure the services of competent nurses and physicians, and provide a house which could be converted into a hospital, she would undertake to supply linens, bandages, and clothing. The government, she said, had a plan under consideration whereby military hospitals under private auspices would be permitted to draw upon the Quartermaster for all equipment and rations which were supplied to military hospitals—and if this program were adopted, the cost of maintaining a Jewish Soldiers' Hospital would be very small. But since, for the time being, all such items would have to be obtained from private sources, "Semi-Occasional" presented a complete list of furniture, surgical and medical supplies, clothing, and food which would be required to set such an institution in operation. If the hospital were to be organized, he suggested, the names of all Jewish soldiers should be collected by local congregations and forwarded to a central office, from which circulars would be sent to the men, notifying them of the provision made for their care in case of need. Whatever the defects of his plan, and the writer knew there were many, they could be ironed out as time went on; but "at all events, let a *beginning* be made and if only *one* valuable life be saved, it will amply repay all the trouble and outlay."

The *Messenger's* editors eagerly applauded the scheme:

> We heartily endorse the recommendations of our correspondent, and await, with confidence, the response that they will receive. We shall be happy, likewise, to open a book at our office, for the immediate reception of donations in aid of the object.[85]

The next week, in a long editorial entitled "Our Present Duty," the editors again reviewed the need for the establishment of a Jewish Military Hospital, defended the proposal against those who regarded it as "sectarian and selfish," and saluted Dr. Simon Abrahams and Dr. Levy J. Henry, two New York physicians who had volunteered to serve as house physicians of the hospital at their own expense. Now, said the editorial, nurses and contributions in money were needed. "[We] shall indeed be ashamed of our co-religionists, if six or seven noble hearted Jewesses could not ultimately be found, who would be willing to volunteer their services in attending on the sick and wounded of their people." As to the finances, "probably, before our next number is published, a sufficient amount to establish and maintain the proposed Hospital, will have been subscribed."[86]

But the next week came and went, and the *Messenger* published no list of contributions, only a hopeful note to the effect that, apparently, more time was necessary for the public to accept the reasonableness of the proposal.[87] But those who objected to the idea for its "sectarianism and inexpediency," not to say their own apathy and lack of interest, disappointed all of the *Messenger's* expectations. It was more than a year before the idea was mentioned again.

In September 1862, *The Jewish Record* called for the establishment of a "Jewish Sanitary Commission," in connection with a letter which it had received from a Jewish soldier stationed with Couch's Division:

> Do not forget to send me the "Record" wherever I am to be found, it will no doubt be a welcome visitor to many Jewish soldiers in the army, now

almost neglected by the wealthy congregations of your and other cities, who do not even make the least attempt to alleviate the sufferings of their brave co-religionists who are lying in the various U.S. hospitals at the seat of war. It is our fervent prayer, Messrs. Editors, that "The Record" will endeavor to plead our cause in its columns, and forcibly advocate our claims upon those stay-at-home gentlemen who no doubt are always ready to criticize, but mighty slow to nurse the wounded and alleviate the sufferings of the dying Jews. Why have we not a committee exclusively Jewish, who will make it their business, like so many other societies are doing, to attend to their wants?[88]

This letter revealed the bitterness of many volunteers who, with or without justification, resented the comfortable life of the men on the home front—but it also revealed the Jewish soldier's yearning for contact with his people, intensified by isolation in a non-Jewish environment. This plea, also, went unanswered.

Several weeks later, "Semi-Occasional" was again championing the soldiers' cause. No grandiose scheme for a hospital this time; he had learned his lesson. All he suggested now was the establishment of a "Jewish Soldiers' Sanitary and Relief Fund," to be administered by the officers of the Jews' Hospital of New York. Its activities, directed by Dr. Fischel or some other rabbi, would include visiting "the sick and wounded Israelites in the hospital, and if necessary, upon the battlefield; supplying them with such necessities and comforts as they may lack; advising and communicating with relatives and friends, and imparting that spiritual comfort which those who may lie ill among strangers know so well how to appreciate." The writer enclosed his own contribution of twenty-five dollars to initiate the drive, and urged that collections be taken up in all the synagogues on the approaching Holy Days. "Semi-Occasional" indicated why he was so interested in the welfare of the wounded soldiers:

It has been my privilege to pass some time among these co-religionists, both among our own troops and among the rebel prisoners in hospitals, and if my pen enabled me to convey to the reader one tithe of what I have witnessed, I am sure this feeble appeal for assistance [would] be responded to with a will and alacrity worthy of the well known instincts of our people and the cause of our common country.[89]

Again the *Messenger* gave its hearty editorial approval to the plan, tracing the history of previous efforts to establish an organization for the benefit of wounded Jewish soldiers. The reasons were as compelling as ever, said the editors; of course the government nursed the men in its hospitals, but what of their spiritual welfare? And there was no intention to impugn the generosity of Jews: "We acknowledge that the Israelites of New York have manifested a commendable liberality in sustaining the Sanitary Commission, in aiding the various recruiting and bounty funds. But something additional is demanded. Besides being Americans, they

must not forget that they are Jews." As Jews, they had a special obligation to their brethren. And New York was the leading Jewish community
of the country. "If New York does its duty, Philadelphia, Boston, Baltimore and the other cities . . . will follow its example." Again the *Messenger* volunteered to receive funds for this purpose.[90] Again there was
no response.

The New York editors resorted to severe criticism and sarcasm the
following year in a desperate attempt to badger the Jewish community
into some kind of action. *The Jewish Record* could not contain its indignation when it was informed that only three persons had appeared
for a meeting called for the organization of an association for Jewish
soldiers' relief. Its editor would not even admit that New York Jews were
as charitable as they were said to be. Jewish charitable associations were
very numerous, "but is it not very probable that the cause of so many
persons belonging to these societies may arise rather from the balls and
soirees which they give? . . . [If] it should have been announced that
two or three balls would be annually given by the association, instead of
three, fifty gentlemen would have gathered together for the *benevolent*
purpose."[91]

The *Messenger* wondered if its readers were under the impression that
"somewhere on Broadway a handsome *suite* of apartments are fitted up as
the headquarters of the 'Central Association for the Relief of Jewish
Volunteers,'" that its functions were administered by very able and
trustworthy men, for they were never asked to give an accounting of
the funds at their disposal, and that they were very modest men, because
their names never appeared in print. When would the Jewish community
of New York set itself to the task of meeting the needs of the Jewish
soldiers?

> Will they arouse themselves to the conviction that a war has been going on
> nearly two years for the long desired restoration of peace and harmony to
> our distracted country, and that thousands of Israelites have subjected them-
> selves to the toils, privations and dangers of military life for the glory of as-
> sisting in the good work of maintaining the integrity of the national govern-
> ment, and while every other class of citizens has been prompt in ministering
> to the comforts and religious welfare of the soldier, the American Israelites
> have done just nothing at all in a cause appealing so strongly to their patri-
> otism and sympathy?[92]

VI

Efforts were made to organize Jewish communities for war service in
yet another direction. It was felt in some quarters that Jews should form
their own military companies and regiments in order to demonstrate
Jewish patriotism, just as various other immigrant groups had banded
together for this purpose. A writer who signed himself "Joshua" called

for a meeting to raise funds for a New York Jewish regiment in a letter which he wrote to *The Jewish Messenger* in August 1862.[93] No Jew, the writer said, doubted that his brethren were as loyal to the Union as his neighbors, but

> the Israelites of this city have, as a body, done nothing to evince their faith in the justice of our cause, and their desire to perpetuate our beneficent institutions. It is true, many of them have, individually, borne no small share of the common burden; but does it not behoove them collectively to show the country and the world that they appreciate the blessings they have enjoyed in this country? . . . The Israelites of this city can roll up such an amount of money as will give an enormous impulse to volunteering, and will compel the respect and admiration of the community. . . .

The letter was introduced by editorial comment lending full approval to the proposal, but no one appears to have taken action upon it.

The following month, Colonel William Mayer was busy raising a regiment in the Sixth Senatorial District of New York, to be called the "Perkins Rifles." Col. Mayer hoped that enough Jews would enlist to make it predominantly a Jewish regiment. *The Jewish Record* attempted to stimulate enlistment by its readers:

> It only depends now on the Israelites in this city whether this regiment shall be an organization which they may essentially call "their own" or whether Colonel Mayer shall be compelled to seek support of men and means from others but his co-religionists . . . Arise, then, ye men of wealth and power, stir from your comfortable couches, and if you cannot enlist yourself, call a war meeting of Israelites and create a Jewish bounty fund, to promote enlistments in a regiment which you ought to call "your own."[94]

This editorial was the only support which Mayer received from the Jewish community—individuals enlisted, but there was no Jewish war meeting. New Yorkers apparently did not approve of Jewish enclaves within the army.

At the same time, however, the Jewish communities of Syracuse and Chicago were successfully carrying out such a project. A new regiment was being raised in Syracuse and the members of the Society of Concord Congregation volunteered to recruit and equip one company. Three young men of the community offered to serve as its officers: S. Light was appointed Captain, Samuel Bronner, 1st Lieutenant, and W. Harris, 2nd Lieutenant. The campaign was opened with a war meeting at the synagogue on August 24, 1862, under the chairmanship of Edward Manheimer, and continued for a week, with a recruiting office open during the day, and patriotic meetings at the synagogue at night. One evening the rabbi, the Rev. S. Deutsch, gave the main address. It was a rousing, fiery attack on the "accursed sham confederacy . . . that venomous hydra of rebellion." Deutsch appealed to his congregation to demonstrate their love for the Union by meeting the goal; not only would their efforts assist in defeating the enemy, he said, but they would also be a rebuke to the anti-alienism aroused by the Know-Nothing party. At the end of the week, almost three thousand dollars in cash had been contributed to the fund, and enough men had been recruited to organize the first company of the new regiment. Saturday evening, Company A was sworn in by the regimental colonel after it marched down Mulberry Street to the martial strains of a military band, cheered on by the entire Jewish population of Syracuse.[95]

Several weeks previously, the Jews of Chicago had undertaken a campaign to organize and outfit a Jewish company for the new 82nd Illinois Regiment. A mass meeting was held at the Concordia Club on August 13, and resolutions were drafted pledging those in attendance to support the project:

WHEREAS, The present crisis in the affairs of our nation directly appeals to every citizen enjoying the inestimable blessings of American freedom, to exert himself to his utmost in assisting the government in its effort to maintain the integrity of the Union and the crushing out of the rebellion, which must and shall be done, a number of Israelites of this city, for the first time since their residence here have met together as such, to act upon any public matter whatever, and this time for the purpose of making a united effort in support of a vigorous prosecution of the war. It is hereby

RESOLVED, That as Israelites we disclaim toward each other any and all relations aside from one common religious belief, except as should exist among citizens. In all questions of a political nature the Israelite is untrammelled and free to act for himself, and does exercise his individual judgment and discretion.

RESOLVED, That having contributed individually heretofore, whenever called upon, in support of the war, we are impelled only by the deepest sense of patriotism and a sincere attachment to this land of our choice and love to make an united effort in behalf of our country.

RESOLVED, That we will raise the sum of $10,000, or more, among the Israelites of this city for the purpose of immediately recruiting and organizing a company for active service in the war.

RESOLVED, That an Executive Committee of seven be appointed by the Chairman of the meeting to carry out the object of these resolutions.

RESOLVED, That the Jewish company will join the new Hecker Regiment.

Speeches were made by Major (soon to be Colonel) Edward Solomon and by Henry Greenebaum and Abraham Kohn, two leading Jewish Republicans of Chicago. The sum of $6,200 was subscribed at the meeting and forty-two men volunteered at the recruiting office which was opened the following day. By the end of the week, over $11,000 had been raised in cash and a full complement of ninety-six men had joined the company.[96]

The *Chicago Tribune* paid this tribute after the results of the campaign were announced:

> Our Israelite citizens have gone beyond even their most sanguine expectations. Their princely contribution of itself is a record which must ever redound to their patriotism. The rapidity with which the company was enlisted has not its equal in the history of recruiting . . . Can any town, city or state in the North show an equally good two days' work? The Concordia Guards have our best wishes for their future and hopes that victory may always crown their aims.[97]

No details have been preserved about the activities which resulted in their formation, but two Jewish companies were recruited in the Confederacy: One at West Point, Ga., during the first month of the war,[98] and a second at Macon, in 1862, for the express purpose of sharing in the defense of Savannah.[99]

VII

The raising of Jewish companies in Chicago and Syracuse, Macon and West Point, were effective demonstrations of the capacity of local Jewries for vigorous, united war service. It has been estimated that at least ten thousand Jews served in the Federal and Confederate Armies—4 or 5% of the estimated Jewish population in America.[100] The fact that so few Jewish companies were organized did not stem, then, from any lack of patriotism among Jews, but from a reluctance to form Jewish enclaves in the army. Of course, there were companies like the Light Infantry Blues of Richmond[101] and Company D of the Eighth New York National Guard Regiment[102] in which large numbers of Jews served—but their enlistment in these outfits was on the basis of personal friendship or geographic location, not on the basis of a preference to serve with Jews. In the final analysis, the men who enlisted in the service of the Union and Confederacy exhibited no desire for a segregated minority status.

This also seems to have been the general reaction to the proposals for national Jewish war service organizations. Apathy and indifference were not the only reasons for the failure of American Jewry to respond to the suggestions for the creation of Jewish military hospitals. The majority of American Jews consciously sought to avoid clannish or restrictive actions; the hospital idea undoubtedly struck most of them as unnecessary segregation. Indeed, it would appear that most Jews were quite willing to ignore religious observances, such as the dietary laws which tended to require separate Jewish facilities, rather than create "ghetto" institutions. The entire question was not directly connected with the war but with the adjustment of Jews to the American scene. The manifold charitable and patriotic activities carried on by the synagogues and philanthropic organizations on a local scale, and especially the service of the New York Jews' Hospital, were proof that Jews needed no prodding to do their part in the war effort. But even in this regard, the Rochester community and two of the Jewish periodicals evinced a reluctance to assent to Jewish segregation unless other groups were following a similar procedure.

It was the old question of the nature of Jewishness and of the status of the Jew in a democratic environment. To what extent should Jewish life be organized for purposes other than religious? What line of demarcation separates the Jew's activities as an individual from his activities as a member of the Jewish community? What, if any, are the responsibilities of the Jewish community, *qua* community, to America?

Even in a theoretical vacuum, questions like these are unanswerable. The Civil War Jew was no more able to provide the answers than is the Jew of our own time. But such questions are not completely unrealistic; anti-Jewish prejudice vitalizes and complicates them. Prejudice makes his relations to his people a matter of living concern to every Jew, forces him to create a Jewish rationale for his own life. The Civil War Jew was, unfortunately, confronted with the problem of anti-Jewish prejudice; the gravity of his problem will be weighed in the next chapters.

VI EXODUS 1862

UNTIL 1864, when the Union armies had smashed the Southern fortresses of the Mississippi into submission and the military might of the North was directed eastward towards fateful scenes in Georgia and Virginia, a dual war was fought in the West. Fort Henry, Fort Donelson, Shiloh, and Corinth were military victories over the Confederacy pounded by the pestle of steel and strategy. They were morale-boosting telegraphic dispatches to the Northern newspapers; testing fires for generals and armies in the fury of combat; they were territory captured from the enemy. But there was also a second front: the economic war of greed, exploitation, and treachery, fought by unprincipled individualists who took advantage of the needs of the North and South and battened on the profits.

Northern and trans-Atlantic mills had turned away their workingmen for want of cotton; the Confederacy never possessed, even at the outbreak of war, enough of the stuff of survival: war materiel, medical supplies, manufactured consumer goods, gold and silver specie. And here, at this shifting line of battle through Tennessee and Mississippi, were thousands of bales of King Cotton, for which the South had no use, but which would fetch high premiums in the markets of the factory cities up North. With a frenzy that could only be fathered by greed, speculators, traders, and adventurers descended upon the area like vultures swooping down on carrion. They traded gold and silver, merchandise and arms, quinine and surgical supplies, for cotton and other Southern agricultural products, and found partners in uniform who were eager to share in the profits. Memphis became a notorious center for the trade. (It was charged in Congress that in a two-year period, between $20,000,000 and $30,000,000 worth of supplies had been funnelled to the Confederacy through Memphis[1].) But the traffic was carried on throughout the entire area penetrated by the Union Army.

All trading across the lines should have been banned. General Sherman took the initiative with such a policy, but his order was promptly recalled by the Administration.[2] Many factors tended to prevent the adoption of a forthright, consistent policy: the actual need for cotton and other Southern products in the North and in Europe; the hope of winning the adherence of the Confederate population by permitting a return to normal, unregulated commerce; the interests of big business which, all over the nation, was thriving on the profits of war; the natural desire of military leaders not to be embroiled in social and commercial regulation; the pressure of speculators in and out of uniform. Policies were changed so frequently that their enforcement was vitiated by the brief time they remained in force.[3] Added to all the chaos was the hectic variety of authorities who could issue permits for commercial activities in the close-to-battle areas: the White House, the War Department, the Treasury Department, and the various Commands on the scene. From such a pattern of confusion, nothing but anarchy could result. The anarchy became demoralization when "bribery and corruption," to use the words of the general in command of Memphis, seeped "into every branch of service."[4]

Official reports bulged with charges that almost all the people in the area, civilian and military, including the relatives of the latter, and even the treasury agents sent South to investigate, were implicated in the traffic. Rear Admiral Porter minced no words when he spoke about the Treasury agents: "A greater pack of knaves never went unhung!" But the Western gun-boat crews under Porter's command were equally responsible for cotton speculation. A senator charged them with clearing $100,000,000 during the war. Army officers were also involved; in Tuscumbia, Ala., they captured $2,000,000 worth of cotton and pocketed the proceeds.[5] The President told a friend that "the army itself is diverted from fighting the rebels to speculating in cotton."[6] Jesse Grant was generally understood to be deriving a percentage from the profits of certain cotton-buyers who had obtained their trading permits from his son through his recommendation; a member of Mrs. Grant's family had made a tidy fortune by the time he was asked to leave camp.[7] "Every colonel, captain, or quartermaster is in secret partnership with some operator in cotton; every soldier dreams of adding a bale of cotton to his monthly pay," said Charles A. Dana in a letter to the Secretary of War.[8]

It was in the midst of this nightmare of profiteering that the most sweeping anti-Jewish regulation in all American history was issued. It was wired from General Grant's headquarters in Holly Springs, Miss., on December 17, 1862, and provided for the expulsion "within twenty-four hours" of "the Jews, as a class," without trial or hearing, from the Department of the Tennessee:

General Orders)   Hdqrs. 13th A.C., Dept. of the Tenn.,
No. 11   )   Holly Springs, December 17, 1862.

The Jews, as a class violating every regulation of trade established by the Treasury Department and also department orders, are hereby expelled from the department within twenty-four hours from the receipt of this order.

Post commanders will see that all of this class of people be furnished passes and required to leave, and any one returning after such notification

122

will be arrested and held in confinement until an opportunity occurs of sending them out as prisoners, unless furnished with permit from headquarters.

No passes will be given these people to visit headquarters for the purpose of making personal application for trade permits.

By order of Maj. Gen. U. S. Grant:

Jno. A. Rawlins,
Assistant Adjutant General.[9]

They still tell stories of the expulsion in Paducah, Ky.: of the hurried departure by riverboat up the Ohio to Cincinnati; of a baby almost left behind in the haste and confusion and tossed bodily into the boat; of two dying women permitted to remain behind in neighbors' care.[10] Thirty men and their families were expelled from Paducah, and, according to affidavits by some of "the most respectable Union citizens of the city," the deportees "had at no time been engaged in trade within the active lines of General Grant. . . ." Two had already served brief enlistments in the Union Army.[11]

The Order was also carried out in Holly Springs and Oxford, Miss., where, ironically, Jewish soldiers in Grant's forces were stationed.[12] Three Northern men and the fiancée of one had finally been able to leave the Confederacy, where they were caught at the outbreak of the war. They passed across the lines and, of all days, arrived at Oxford on December 18, the day after General Order Number 11 was issued. Placed under immediate arrest by Colonel Marsh, one of the three was bold enough to ask questions:

JEW: I should like to know the cause of our detention.
COLONEL: I do not feel inclined to give any—in about half an hour you will leave for Cairo and Alton.
JEW: Colonel, can I sell my horse and buggy?
COLONEL: No, sir! You have nothing to sell. You have to leave on the next train under guard.

Their horse and buggy and luggage confiscated, they were taken by train to Holly Springs, then to Bolivar and Jackson, and at last to Cairo, where they were freed and ordered to stay clear of the Department for the duration of the war. For the last time, the reason for all this abuse was requested; finally they received their answer: "Because you are Jews, and are neither a benefit to the Union or Confederacy."[13]

A party of agents for firms in Northern cities, caught in Holly Springs on December 17, were denied rail transportation for their exodus, and had to proceed to Memphis on foot. They still refused to believe that they had really been expelled for being Jews, even though one of their number, a Mr. Silberman from Chicago, had been thrown in prison in Holly Springs for trying to send a telegram to General Grant. In Memphis they were disabused of all doubts: their expulsion had been in accordance with The Order, and their departure had followed the time-table set forth therein.[14]

Since telegrams could not be sent to General Grant, and personal interviews with him were prohibited by The Order, the only recourse was to communicate with the Chief Executive of the nation. So concluded D. Wolff, Cesar Kaskel, and his brother, J.W. Kaskel, of Paducah. They worded a courteous but urgent appeal to the White House, protesting "this inhuman order, the carrying out of which would be the grossest violation of the Constitution and our rights as citizens under it, [and] which will place us . . . as outlaws before the whole world."[15]

Surely the President, "Honest Abe," would recognize their plight, condemn the inhumanity of The Order, and restore them to their homes and livelihoods. But no answer was received, no action was forthcoming, and the Provost Marshal of Paducah proceeded with the expulsion.

Did the President ever receive the telegram? It *did* reach Washington, because eventually it was included in the massive compilation of the official documents of the war. But perhaps it was intercepted at the War Department. . . . Perhaps Lincoln's secretaries set it aside as a misrepresentation of some local action by the military authorities in Paducah. . . . Perhaps it was shown to Lincoln but he could lend it no credence. . . .

Whatever the reason that the Paducah message was ignored, Cesar Kaskel demonstrated a remarkable capacity for imaginative leadership in this unpredictable emergency. He was not content to place his sole hope for redress in a sixteen-line telegram transmitted through military channels. On the boat from Paducah to Cincinnati, the *Charley Bowens*, he spent his time writing letters and telegrams of alarm to Jewish community leaders, and to the publishers of Jewish and daily newspapers; those letters were instrumental in arousing the storm of protest which struck Washington in a few days.[16] But still Kaskel was not content.

Pausing in Cincinnati only momentarily to confer with community leaders and rabbis, and to apprise them of the principal details of the expulsion, Kaskel hastened on to Washington to assure the revocation of The Order. He spent a few moments consulting with Adolphus S. Solomons, Washington member of the Executive Committee of the Board of Delegates of American Israelites,[17] and then requested Congressman Gurley of Ohio, a friend of Rabbi Wise's, to act as his escort to the White House. Gurley secured immediate admission, and together they went up to the famous office on the second floor.

It was obvious that Lincoln knew little or nothing of the facts of the case. Kaskel took the time to explain everything he knew: the persons affected, their clean reputation with the civil and military authorities in Paducah, the military service of several of the deportees. He had even had the foresight to bring some documents along, signed by leading citizens, Republican party members and military authorities, ample proof that if there were any Jews to blame for conditions in the area under Grant's command, they did not live in Paducah.

Then, according to report, a heart-warming, semihumorous, Biblical flavor was introduced by the President:

LINCOLN: And so the children of Israel were driven from the happy land of Canaan?
KASKEL: Yes, and that is why we have come unto Father Abraham's bosom, asking protection.
LINCOLN: And this protection they shall have at once.

And how much longer would Father Abraham, or Moses, or Jeremiah, have to bear upon his shoulders the burdens, and feel in his heart the pains, of all the oppressed and persecuted and exploited? So long as fate permitted, he would listen to such stories, look quizzically at those who sought his help, decide a man's honesty and integrity by the look in his eye, and then, if matters seemed urgent, he would sit at his big table, as he sat now, to write a note.

The note to General-in-Chief of the Army Henry W. Halleck, written, directing him to telegraph instructions for the cancellation of The Order, Lincoln shook hands with Kaskel, told him he was free to return to his home after seeing Halleck, and wished him well.[18]

General Halleck had to hear the whole story repeated, appeared to be as incredulous as the Jews of Paducah, Holly Springs, and Oxford had been, until Kaskel showed him a copy of The Order, countersigned by Captain Wardell, Provost Marshal of Paducah, and even then was not fully convinced. He knew the conditions in Tennessee and Mississippi well, had been Grant's superior there until a few short months before. Was he shocked that Grant had blundered so? Or was there some other motive, more sinister, behind his reluctance to wire Grant? The telegram was worded so tactfully there can be no doubt that Halleck disliked sending it:

> War Department,
> Washington, January 4, 1863.

Major-General Grant,
Holly Springs, Miss.:

A paper *purporting* to be General Orders, No. 11, issued by you December 17, has been presented here. By its terms, it expels all Jews from your department. *If such an order has been issued*, it will be immediately revoked.

> H. W. Halleck,
> General-in-Chief.[19]

Three days later Grant's office transmitted the order of recall, taking pains to state that it was "by Direction of General-in-Chief of the Army, at Washington,"[20] implying that it was sent *only* in accordance with those instructions.

Even when enough time had elapsed for Grant to defend his action, or to apologize, and when he, by failing to do so, took upon himself the complete responsibility for The Order, Halleck still played a mysterious game. He sent a further communication to Grant, not one of censure or warning, but one of explanation with an apologetic tone. Halleck passed the buck for interference onto the President:

> Headquarters of the Army,
> Washington, January 21, 1863.
>
> Major-General Grant, Memphis:
>
> General: It may be proper to give you some explanation of the revocation of your order expelling all Jews from your department. The President has no objection to your expelling traitors and Jew peddlers, which, I suppose, was the object of your order; but as it in terms proscribed an entire religious class, some of whom are fighting in our ranks, the President deemed it necessary to revoke it.
>
> Very respectfully, your obedient servant,
> H. W. Halleck,
> General-in-Chief.[21]

Another indifferent bureaucrat was Attorney General Edward Bates, who forwarded to the President a resolution of protest adopted by the St. Louis B'nai B'rith Lodge, with this illuminating inscription: "I do but comply with [their] expressed wish, in handing you the papers, myself feeling no particular interest in the subject."[22] Was there no one in Washington who objected to an order which "proscribed an entire religious class" except the President? And what if he had not?

Meanwhile, Rabbis Wise and Lilienthal of Cincinnati, Martin Bijur of Louisville, and Moses Strauss of Baltimore had arrived in Washington, with delegations of men from their respective cities, and were making the rounds of Senators, Congressmen, Army officials, and the White House. The very evening the Western delegation arrived—January 7— without even changing their clothes dusty from travel, they sought out Congressmen Pendleton and Gurley of Ohio, and insisted on being taken to the Executive Mansion to thank the President for the revocation of The Order. After accepting their formal thanks, Lincoln went on to express his own reactions to The Order in no uncertain terms. He could not understand what could have impelled the General to issue it. As for himself, he had always believed that "to condemn a class is, to say the least, to wrong the good with the bad. I do not like to hear a class or nationality condemned on account of a few sinners." They liked the President for being so outspoken, and they liked the easy cordiality with which he welcomed them. But after a half-hour of amiable talk they felt they had taken up enough of his time, and so said goodbye.[23]

There was another aim in the minds of the Jewish delegates. They hoped that the Senate and House would be eager to go on record against the kind of bigotry and intolerance which The Order exemplified. But they were sorely disappointed. Political considerations were paramount, and damaged ideals were secondary. The only politicians who took an interest in the case were Democrats—they relished the chance to take a poke at the Republican Administration. The Republicans, on the other hand, vulnerable as was their position in shielding Grant, could not afford to permit the Democrats to attack the only general who seemed to be able to win battles. So the proceedings in both houses of Congress were a sorry display of political fencing.

In the House of Representatives, Democratic Congressman Pendleton of Ohio, who was to be McClellan's running mate in the 1864 election, tried in vain for two days to gain the floor for the introduction of a resolution censuring The Order as "illegal and unjust, and its execution tyrannical and cruel." On January 7, he finally obtained permission to place it before the House, but Republican Congressman Elihu B. Washburne of Illinois, Grant's close friend and consistent champion, made short shrift of its consideration. It "censures one of our best generals without a hearing," he argued, demanding that it be tabled. The fact that the Jews had been *banished* without a hearing did not require his attention. Grant was his friend, Pendleton an enemy of the party, so even though the resolution might be fully justified, it had to be tabled. And tabled it was, by the close vote of 56 to 53, with the division based mainly on political affiliation.[24]

The display of political solidarity was even more pronounced in the upper chamber. There, Democratic Senator Powell of Kentucky had to deal with such Republican stalwarts as Hale, Sumner, Clark, and Henry Wilson. After the first reading of Powell's resolution on January 5, Sumner registered his objection to its being considered immediately and thereby postponed discussion for four days.[25] On January 9, when it was to be read again, Hale thought "it [was] not worth while to read it again;" but Powell insisted, and then proceeded to give a lengthy address in favor of its passage, citing his personal knowledge of some of the Paducah people and referring to the documents which Kaskel had brought to Washington. After the speech, the Republicans took over. None of them defended The Order itself; they all had Jewish constituents. They paid lip-service to the right of the Jew to legal procedure. But Clark thought it was wrong "to condemn the brave General Grant unheard . . . when he and his soldiers are struggling in the field to put the rebellion down." He did not mention the *Jewish* soldiers in Grant's own army and in other combat areas. Neither did Hale, Wilson or Sumner; they were more interested in coming to an agreement on the best parliamentary method for permanently disposing of the resolution of censure—so that the Democrats would have no further opportunity to bring it to the floor. They finally decided to table it.[26]

For all his ringing defense of the Jews, and for all his genuine interest in the welfare of his Paducah constituents (even though Kaskel was vice-president of the Paducah Union League Club), Powell had other interests in mind. When he had warmed up to the subject, he told his fellow members of the Senate what had really attracted him and the Democratic party to the defense of the Jews:

> In my judgment, it is incumbent on this Senate . . . to pass the resolution, and let General Grant and all other military commanders know that they are not to encroach upon the rights and privileges of the peaceable, loyal citizens of this country. Pass the resolution, and the example will be of the greater importance, particularly at this time, when the constitutional rights of the citizens are being stricken down and trodden under foot throughout the entire country by the executive and the military power. We have submitted already too long and tamely to the encroachments of the military upon the civil rights of the citizens . . .

The order against the Jews was of a piece, to the Democrats, with all the other invasions of civil liberties for which they held the Lincoln Administration responsible: the suspension of the writ of habeas corpus, the invoking of martial law in certain areas, and interference with the activities of legally elected city, state and Federal officials. The Jews were being victimized as the whole North had been victimized, in the view of the Democrats.

For Democrats and Republicans alike the resolution censuring Grant for The Order had been transmuted into a symbolic test of party power. It no longer concerned the Jews at all: Powell's speech, the Republican delaying tactics, the vote to table—were concerned with the political issues of January 1863: the administration's conduct of the war, Grant's role as a promising national hero, and the Democrats' frustration at being out of power. The vote to table, 30 to 7, really ignored the violation of Constitutional rights affected by The Order.

With this example of Congressional maneuvering to guide them, the editorial writers of the nation, for the most part, let their bias take them wherever it might. The *Washington Republican* considered Grant infallible. "We believe that in this, as in every other military act, he has consulted his better genius, which has thus far outstripped all the calculations of military science." As to censuring him, the *Republican* figured that Grant was "worth more to the cause than the votes of the whole Jewish nation resident in our midst."[27] No one had threatened to draw Jewish votes away from the party; but a political organ like the *Republican* could only discuss a case of injustice in terms of ballots, elections and offices.

The *Washington Chronicle*, published by John W. Forney, Secretary of the Senate, outdid its contemporary, and featured an editorial which called the Jews "the scavengers . . . of commerce" and gave every shadow

f a doubt to Grant.[28] Jews who lived in the capitol would not permit
his to pass unnoticed and spent many good hours writing letters which
demanded that facts be produced to support the contention of the *Chron-
cle*. They, too, knew that there were Jews, as there were Christians, who
merited punishment, but they insisted that, *as a group*, the Jews were as
honest, dependable and patriotic as any other segment of the Northern
population.[29]

The Order was "one of the deepest sensations of the war," according
to the *New York Times*, usually an administration supporter. The *Times*
referred to the reaction of the more excitable Jewish groups of New York
City to the Western delegations which had thanked the President for his
prompt revocation of The Order. "They say they have no thanks . . .
but grounds for deep and just complaint against the Government, that
General Grant has not been dismissed from the service." Then the *Times*
spoke for itself:

> . . . We are of [the] opinion that there are degrees of rascality developed by
> the war that might put the most accomplished Shylocks to the blush. We
> have native talent that can literally "beat the Jews." Gen. Grant's order has
> the demerit of stigmatising a class, without signalizing the criminals . . . It
> is a humiliating reflection that after the progress of liberal ideas even in the
> most despotic countries has restored the Jews to civil and social rights, as
> members of a common humanity, it remained for the freest Government on
> earth to witness a momentary revival of the spirit of the medieval ages . . .
> We rely on the general principles of republican right and justice for the
> utter reprobation of Grant's order. Men cannot be condemned and punished
> as a class, without gross violence to our free institutions.[30]

All in all, the editorial which appeared in the *Times* was probably the
most fair and least partisan that was printed anywhere in the country.

New York produced the one bizarre aberration in the journalistic world.
The *Sunday Mercury*, which had opposed the war from the first and
was a leading editorial goad in the struggle against the draft, became very
militant in the Jews' behalf and reported that they were "arming themselves to resist further interference with their rights." Unable to discover
any clue to identify the source of this singular report, *The Jewish Messenger* amused its readers by inviting them to witness a dress parade of
the "First Division Jewish Infantry."[31]

In Philadelphia, the *Public Ledger* was reasonably certain that The
Order had been issued "thoughtlessly," but nevertheless demanded that
it be cancelled at once, "for the honor of the country and of humanity
and the nineteenth century," and then proceeded to list for its readers
the Jewish contributions to civilization. Jay Cooke's newspaper, the
Philadelphia Enquirer, acted as though the most satisfactory solution to
the whole problem was to ignore it completely. The Rev. Leeser made
several trips to the editor's office, armed with letters of protest, before he

finally believed what he was told the first time, that the editor would not print anything at all about The Order.[32]

The Republican *Cincinnati Commercial* was rarely reluctant to register an anti-Jewish sentiment or two, and the Grant furore gave it an excellent opportunity. It called the expulsion a "persecution," but proceeded to assure its readers that ". . . Jew traders have been the most adroit smugglers, and have, by their offensive conduct, brought reproach upon the name of their sect."[33] The Democratic *Enquirer*, on the other hand, sidetracked far enough to castigate its Jewish readers for "the vicious character of their politics," i.e., "they are mostly of the party that has Lincoln for its leader," before pontificating that the expulsion was "a wrong and cruelty which military and civil despotism can alone be guilty of."[34] The Cincinnati Jews could do no right: the Republican paper blamed them for their religion, the Democrats for their Republican politics!

Closer to the scene of the operation of The Order, the *Louisville Journal* surmised that if the episode had been "reported to us from Turkey, Russia, Austria, or Morocco [it] would excite the indignation of every liberal man in this free land." The *Journal* asked "how many thousand patriotic soldiers of Jewish descent have laid down their lives upon the altar of this country? And is this miserable, ungrateful order to be the price of their blood?" The *Louisville Democrat*, naturally, felt that The Order was "certainly the most extraordinary, unwarrantable order we have ever heard of."[35]

If most of the newspapers and politicians had slavishly followed the dictates of party interest in their reaction to The Order, the Jews were not so easily trapped into political commitments.[36] The editors, rabbis, and laymen rejected the language of the political campaign and restricted themselves to considerations of history, the meaning of democracy, and the American spirit. Stunned as they were by the implications of The Order, the comment of the Republican press, and the unwillingness of Republican politicians to come to their defense, they did not attempt to herd the Jews of America into the Democratic camp, as the Democrats undoubtedly expected. Even Isaac Mayer Wise, who despised the Republican party and identified it with war-mongering, anti-alienism, and "black" abolitionism, did not raise the standard for a Jewish exodus to the Democratic party. He, like the others, tried to take a supra-political attitude, and appealed to *all* of America to blot out this mark of shame. None of the editors said anything in defense of Grant: he gave them no opportunity, no thread of a chance; but the cause of the Union, the war, and Lincoln continued in the main to receive their support. Wise, the only self-identified Democrat among the editors, was of course an exception.

What, then, was the Jewish reaction? It was one of shock, pain, and anger. The rabbis were burying the bodies of Jewish soldiers who had lost their lives in battle; the charitable organizations were ceaselessly rais-

War Department

Washington City,

January 10th 1863

Sir:—

In reply to your letter of the 5th instant, protesting, against the enforcement, of a General Order, issued by Major General Grant, expelling all Jews from his department,— the Secretary of War directs me to inform you, that the order referred to, has been rescinded by order of the President.

Very respectfully,

I am Obedient Servant

P. H. Watson

Assistant Secretary of War

The Reverend

B. Felsenthal

(Minister of "Sinai Congregation,"

Chicago

Illinois

Facsimile of a War Department official's answer to the Rev. Bernhard Felsenthal's protest against the Grant Order ing funds for the support of war widows and orphans, for the Sanitary Commission, for all kinds of causes; anything that was demanded of any citizen was demanded of the Jews and was forthcoming. And now, in this land of freedom, were they alone to be punished, without a trial, for all the crimes which had been committed in a crime-infested area, and the responsibility for which was clearly to be laid in the lap of the highest authorities in the land? Were they, who had fled, in this generation or an earlier one, from proscription, discrimination, and oppression in lands across the sea, here to be victimized again, here to become the scapegoat again, to bear once again the sins of the nation?

A continual refrain in the stream of editorials and letters was: if there are Jewish law-breakers in the Department of the Tennessee, let them be punished individually for their deeds, but no American law provides for Jewish communal responsibility for the actions of individual members of the community. Let there be a fair trial for every accused individual, Jew and Christian, and, if found guilty, let him pay the penalty prescribed by law.

The editors could not help but reflect on the solicitude of the Republicans for Negro rights, and their apparently illiberal attitude towards the Jews. "Gentlemen," said the pro-Democratic *Jewish Record* in an open letter to Congress, "supposing any general of the United States had issued an order expelling from his command all 'Negroes,' . . . would not 'sympathy for our oppressed brethren, without distinction of color,' have moved you to censure him?"[37] Wise sarcastically remarked that the Jewish deportees were born to the wrong race, if they expected any sympathy from the Republican-dominated Congress;[38] and Leeser believed that The Order had gone unanswered because "the parties threatened with such ill-usage were not Christians, not even Negroes, nothing but Jews!"[39] This was but another indication to them that the humanitarianism which expressed itself in the abolitionist crusade was peculiarly blind to the evil of Jew-hatred.

The Jewish Messenger, cautious and conservative always, was particularly eager to drive home its warning to American Jewry not to permit itself to be caught in a political trap. The Democratic had as little genuine regard for the Jews as the Republican party but would pretend to be their defender to secure their votes. "We warn our co-religionists to beware," said the *Messenger*, "of being *used by designing politicians* for partisan, unpatriotic ends. . . . Shall we, the loyal Israelites of the United States, permit ourselves to be made tools of—we mean what we say—by men who have no love for us, no love for the Union, no respect for constitutional government?" Rather than follow those who posed as their friends, let them prove by their daily lives that "Israelites are among the most valuable, useful and influential members of society."[40]

That warning did not assume its full significance for another five years. Then the election of 1868 made The Order a live political issue once again: the war had been won; Lincoln was dead, and his reconciliation policy buried with him; Grant—the hero of the war—was to be the Republican nominee for the presidency. Jewish memories, always sensitive to threats of oppression, still harbored the pain, anger, and humiliation of January 1863. No matter what party had nominated Grant, no matter what the issues of the campaign, no matter what the name or repute of his opponent—the election would be a critical point in the history of the American Jew. The campaign was bound to reflect the tone of American Jewry's adjustment to American conditions, for it was now confronted with one of the most serious problems a minority ever faces: what influence would or should its own unique experience have on its stand in an election. Could Jews, whatever their previous political beliefs and affiliations, vote for the author of so flagrant an anti-Jewish measure? The election of '68 turned out to be one of the very few American elections in which an issue involving a religious minority assumed major proportions for the entire nation.

The dilemma was not of Jewish making; in every other election Jews had voted as individuals, prompted by their own personal interests, needs, insights, experiences, and loyalties. As we have already discovered, there had been no single Jewish attitude on slavery and abolitionism, war and peace, Democracy and Republicanism. There were only Jews . . . separate entities in a multicolored American society. There were as many different political notions (even anti-alienism)[41] among Jews as there were facets to American political life. The dilemma of '68 was of Grant's making: he had issued The Order; it could not help but be an election issue, not only for Jews, but for all Americans who took part in the electioneering. Newspapers all the way from Corinth, Miss., to Quincy, Ill., published copies of The Order itself, commentaries and letters about it, and even material from the Jewish press. The *Israelite* of Cincinnati was quoted in New York papers, and the *Messenger* of New York was quoted in Chicago papers. Everyone who had an interesting point of information to reveal, or thought he did, took his pen in hand and sent a letter to the press. Democratic papers were publishing appeals to Jews to vote against the traducer of Jewish character; most Republican papers were eagerly publishing pledges by Jewish Republicans to uphold the party; but some, eager to defend the General, accused the Jews of worse crimes than The Order had.[42]

Grant could have dissolved the perplexity of the Jews and dissipated the fog of propaganda. The Jews would have welcomed some forthright statement of apology and explanation. But the General refused to make such a statement, even though, as he told a friend, he had received hundreds of letters begging him to do so. Adam Badeau, Grant's secretary and biographer, General John A. Rawlins, his erstwhile Adjutant, and other intimates wrote letters in his name[43] denying that he was guilty of prejudice against the Jews or any other group, but such letters were manifestly ineffectual. When Grant himself finally did issue a statement,[44] it was not the absolute disavowal that was expected; it could not therefore be the final word on the subject.

Grant's reluctance furnished additional ammunition to Jews who were active in the Democratic party. There was no conflict for them, but they attempted to capitalize on the conflict that might exist in the minds of Jews who were Republicans. In New York, a certain Ph. von Bort published a pamphlet entitled, "General Grant and the Jews," and signed it "in the name of all American Jews." The burden of his open letter was a pledge that "every Jew—no matter of what political party—every Jew, with the votes he can command, will endeavor to defeat, and with God's blessing, *will* defeat you!" An anonymous Jew who signed himself "Max" wrote a letter to the *Boston Post* urging that Jewish self-respect required the defeat of General Grant. In Richmond, M.J. Ezekiel wrote a letter addressed to American Jewry, contending that it was plainly the duty of all Jews "to oppose by every means in their power the efforts that are being made to place a man in power who, by a mere scratch of the pen, can deprive us of all the rights and benefits of a free country." Ezekiel earned for himself a warning to leave Richmond, or face the consequence of his opposition to the Republican party—assassination; the threatening letter was signed by the officers of the Richmond Union League Association.[45]

The Jewish editors opposed the effort to create a Jewish electorate. *The Jewish Messenger* insisted that "there are no 'Jewish votes'" and appealed to Jews to vote as individual Americans, not as members of a Jewish bloc. "If Jews desire to take one side or the other in a campaign that will always be memorable, they can do so as citizens of the Republic. But as Jews they should abstain from bringing religion into politics." These were the sentiments of the editors of *The Hebrew Leader*, who nevertheless announced that they were supporting Seymour. Even Isaac Mayer Wise, inveterate Democrat, did not editorialize as frequently as one would expect, "because," he said, "we feel constrained as far as possible to preserve the character of *The Israelite* as a religious and family journal." Nevertheless, he opposed both Grant's nomination and election because he thought the man was "morally and intellectually unfit through his incapacity to understand the theories and principles of personal liberty which vitalize our Government." None of the editors, including Wise, was willing to make Jewishness the sole issue of the election.[46]

But was it possible? No one knows exactly how many Jews voted for Grant, or how many voted for Seymour; we can, however, evaluate the evidence presented in the periodicals and documents of the period. In only three cases was there an *organized* attempt to use Jewishness as a rallying cry. In Memphis, Tenn., the metropolis closest to the area affected by The Order, an open meeting of the Jewish community was held, attended by the rabbis and other leaders, at which resolutions were adopted castigating Grant as "a man unfit for the high position to which he aspires, and incapable of administering the laws to all classes with impartiality and without prejudice;" pledging those attending to "use every honorable means" to defeat Grant; and urging Jewish communities all over the nation to follow the Memphis example. A similar meeting was held in Nashville.[47] No other community followed suit, but in New York City a group of Jewish Republicans retaliated against Jewish Democrats by forming a "Hebrew Grant and Colfax Club."[48]

Were individual Jews who had identified themselves with the Republican party enticed away from that allegiance by Democratic propaganda? If we may be guided by the public statements of Republican Jewish politicians who announced their position in the marketplace, we are justified in concluding that the great majority of active Jewish Republicans did not change their party affiliation because of The Order.

Adolph Moses, of Quincy, Ill., an ex-Confederate Army officer who had come North, a national officer of the B'nai B'rith Order, and an active politician in the general community, changed his opinions so frequently that the newspapers could not be certain whether he was a Democrat or Republican. Although he was a Republican, early in the campaign he wrote vigorously in condemnation of The Order, pointing it up as a major issue for public consideration. His articles were reproduced in papers all over the country. They were not open appeals for Jewish support of the Democratic candidates; he wanted the Democracy to understand that "the principle would have to be debated and defended in due manly spirit and not with the sole purpose of carrying votes from the Jewish citizens, who, like all others, can draw a correct distinction between the avowal of a manly principle and the hollow lip-service in the interest of party." But he was instrumental, he said later, in convincing certain persons not to vote for Grant.

Moses was not satisfied with his position and eagerly followed developments in the press. When Henry Greenebaum of Chicago, who had known Lincoln and was a devoted Jew, announced his determination to support Grant, Moses felt impelled to reconsider the entire problem. He consulted with Congressman Morris of Illinois, who insisted that he write Grant. This letter, in which he pointed out to Grant the difficult position of Jews who wanted to support him but were deterred by their fear that he was a bearer of prejudice, elicited the only reply which Grant was willing to make to any queries about The Order. It satisfied Moses, and he announced his switch in a long letter tracing the convolutions of his political opinion. He apologized to those to whom he had spoken previously, and said he understood that they might not share his reversal; but for himself, he said, "the burning but just spirit of indignation must give way to the quietly secret feeling of magnanimity which must needs force itself on all intelligent men whose convictions are not debased by the alloy of prejudice, for while it lies in the power of any one to do a wrong act, it requires a higher type of manhood to make a reparation."[49]

Josiah Cohen of Pittsburgh, part-time rabbi, Jewish educator, and able lawyer, who had taken an active role in Republican party politics during the war, wrote a letter to the *Pittsburgh Chronicle* in 1868 in which he expounded his position:

> I have always held political opinions consonant with the Republican plat-
> form, and have therefore always been found in the ranks of the Republican
> party . . . No amount of sophistry can induce me to change my opinions or
> sacrifice my principles by reason of that unfortunate order of General Grant's
> in reference to the Jews. That the order was unjust I cannot deny, but it
> sinks into atomic insignificance when compared with the life of this Govern-
> ment . . . I shall, therefore, vote the Republican ticket . . . however much I
> may object to the leader of the banner of those principles by virtue of the
> prejudice shown to the Jews in his peculiar order.[50]

Mr. (later Judge) Cohen, a highly respectable Pittsburgh citizen, the first Jew to be admitted to the Pittsburgh bar, subordinated his Jewish pride to his political loyalty, and risked his reputation on Grant's good faith.

A certain Noah Green, described by the *New York Herald* as "a lead-ing Israelite of Keokuk, Iowa," knew his Jewish prayerbook by heart. The words and sense he used, in speaking for the Republican party, were words and sense out of the ancient ritual:

> Now on what side do we stand? Shall we array ourselves on the side of equal
> justice, of peace and order, or on the side of war and anarchy? . . . I address
> myself to the intelligent, patriotic Jews, to whom this country and the cause
> of justice and liberty are dearer than the gratification of their indignation,
> however just. I do not ask them to love Grant, but to love their race; to vote
> for Grant, not for his sake, but for the triumph of the idea of justice. For my
> part, if a man had spit into my face publicly, if he had kicked me, if I after-
> wards by voting for him could serve liberty and justice, I would do it. For
> what am I, what is General Grant, what are all of us? We are but like insects
> of the moment, soon passing away . . .[51]

The Order was insignificant, in Green's eyes, when compared with the urgency of the struggle for Negro rights, for the maintenance of the Union, and for the supremacy of Republican principles.

Another Jewish Republican went farther than Cohen and Green in supporting Grant: he defended The Order. This was Simon Wolf, a prominent Jewish and Republican politician in Washington. In 1863 he had no words too harsh for "those time-despised prejudices that have dis-graced the past" and which, he asserted, had been revived by General Grant. But now, in 1868, in a communication to the *Boston Transcript*, he excused Grant's offense to the Jews as unintentional, and even testified on his own account that "I know how many of our people were in-different to the cause, and how many cared only for the spoils." Carried away by his desire to whitewash Grant, Wolf went so far as to misrep-resent the facts of the case. "The order never harmed me—never harmed anyone," he pleaded in its defense, "not even in thought, except those whom *we as Jews despise and hold in contempt*."[52] Rationalization con-trolled his thought processes, even clouded his memory: he ignored the innocent victims of The Order, the folk from Paducah, for instance, whom he must have seen in Washington in 1863. Many Jews must have been disillusioned when they read his comments; and even more dis-illusioned when Grant appointed him Recorder of Deeds for the District of Columbia the very next year.

Still another Jewish political hopeful, who publicly urged Jewish sup-port for Grant on the basis of sympathy for Republican ideas, was David Eckstein of Cincinnati to whom we shall have need to refer again. Eck-stein had been a Republican all through the war, and was embarrassed by The Order; but he would not abandon his party without investiga-tion. So, he wrote in a public letter which was widely reprinted just before the election, he had gone to visit General Grant to confer with him. He was fully convinced after nearly two hours' conversation that he could in all honesty support the General's candidacy. Eckstein did not tell the substance of Grant's explanations, but they were, said he, "suf-ficient to remove and obliterate every vestige of objection against him on the part of every fair-minded and reasonable Israelite, and would impel them to a still more hearty support of the party which put the General in nomination."[53]

Governor John Geary of Pennsylvania credited Eckstein with "bring-ing about an amicable understanding between the Israelites and General Grant," by the publication of this personal guarantee. Two years later, through Geary's insistent representations to Grant, Eckstein was ap-pointed to the consulate at Victoria, British Columbia, in which capacity he served for seven years.[54]

Whatever may have been the motives which impelled Eckstein and Wolf to lend their personal prestige to the Republican party campaign in the face of Grant's prejudiced order, their support plays havoc with the stereotyped superstitions about Jewish solidarity and the "Jewish vote." Even under so great a provocation as the nomination of a presi-dential candidate who was, to all intents and purposes, anti-Jewish, these and other Jews appear to have been more concerned about the national political and economic issues of the day than they were about an insult to the Jewish name. They campaigned and voted as individuals, as poli-ticians, not as members of the Jewish group. Whatever the factors which lead men to vote for a particular candidate in a particular election—eco-nomic class interest, social pressure, habit, personal relationships, honest thought—these same factors operated upon the minds of the Jews.

What had happened was this: the very nature of American life and growth militated against the development of an organically unified American Jewry. America offered its rewards for individual effort and initiative; challenged a man to test his strength in the race for position, wealth, and achievement; caught him up in an overwhelmingly optimistic, expansive, rapid-paced tempo. America was irresistible. Once a man staked his claim in the nation's gamble for glory, all other impulses became secondary. So, from the very first, the freedom to join the race which America offered to the Jew (a comparative freedom, it is true, but one whose imperfections were insignificant to him, moulded as he was by a heritage of unbelievable terror and suffering), that freedom compelled him to abandon the religio-cultural pattern which made him a Jew, and subjected him increasingly to the primary economic, cultural, political, and psychological factors operative in the environment in which he made his home. The antisemite was and is blind to this fact of adjustment; but the rabbi who has attempted to mould a unified Jewish community for the organization of a congregation, knows it; the proponents of Jewish educational and philanthropic activities, on either a local or a national scale, have daily experience with it. The character of American Jewish life for a whole century has been dominated by this one fact: the American Jew has been captured by the mood and modes of American life. The election of 1868 was an effective demonstration of that.

We shall now have to retrace our steps back through the years to 1862 in Tennessee and Mississippi, back to the confusion, corruption and prejudice, out of which The Order issued, to seek out the circumstances of its origin.

1. *Who Was Responsible for The Order?*

During the public discussion in 1862–3 and in 1868, one of the frequent assertions made in Grant's defense was that he himself had not composed The Order, and that he was shielding someone else who was responsible for it. He was too much the gentleman, it was said, to defend himself by casting the blame on its real author.[55]

This explanation was a plausible one. Staff officers more often than not are the authors of orders, reports, and memoranda, to which they sign their commanding officer's name. It was claimed that the name of the officer who did so in this case was known to hundreds of those who served under Grant, and that they considered their chieftain a hero for not revealing that name to the indignant public. This explanation might have received general acceptance had not one of these officers determined to give all of the supposed details to the public in a letter to the *Chicago Evening Journal*, which was widely reprinted throughout the country. He asserted that the responsibility was to be fixed on a Colonel John

DuBois who had written The Order without Grant's knowledge, and affixed his superior's name to it. "I was with Grant's army at the time as a staff officer of one of his Corps Commanders," this informant stated, "and many a laugh we had around the camp fires over what was then called 'Johnny DuBois'' order . . . it was not dictated by General Grant."[56]

These were specific facts, not generalizations. But they were contradicted by DuBois himself, who was at that time stationed at the cavalry fort at Santa Fé. He said he would not sell his good name in order to secure the election for General Grant. He branded the accusation against himself as "untrue in fact, word and inference," and delineated his evidence. He had issued an order dealing with Jews, he admitted, but "this order was revoked by Gen. Grant and I was relieved from command on account of it. I never saw or heard of the notorious 'Jew Order' until it appeared in print. . . . I was never on General Grant's staff, and never signed an order 'by order of Gen. Grant.' "[57]

DuBois did not see the irony of his calling General Order No. 11 "the notorious 'Jew Order' " when his own was equally prejudiced:

> Holly Springs, Miss.,
> December 8, 1862.
>
> General Order.
>
> On account of the scarcity of Provisions all *Cotton Speculators, Jews, and other Vagrants,* having no honest means to support except trading upon the misery of the country, and in general all persons from the North, not connected with the army whatever and having no permission from the commanding General to remain in town, *will leave in twenty-four (24) hours or he will be put to duty in the intrenchments.*
>
> By order of Col. Jno. V. DuBois, U.S. Army Com'd'g.
>> Charles H. Turlu,
>> 1st Lieut., A.A.A. Gen'l.[58]

Now came another anonymous letter, addressed to the *Washington Republican,* purporting to give further evidence in the matter:

> [After the publication of The Order] the Jews as a class united throughout the whole country to resent the insult. They immediately sent deputations to Washington to demand the revocation of the order, and the dismissal of Grant, from the service, and nothing less would satisfy their just indignation. Halleck was a friend of Grant and wished to save him, and enclosed to Col. DuBois, who was then at St. Louis, a copy of his own order, together with a copy of Grant's order, asking him if he was the author, and if he had issued the same with or without the knowledge of Grant. This was a plain invitation to shield Grant, and Col. DuBois, after consulting some friends, concluded to accept the invitation, and in his answer ignored the Grant order, which was the question at issue, and referred only to his own order, which he assumed in full, as he had a right to do. This was used to satisfy the de-

mands of the deputation. Grant revoked his order. DuBois who had been nominated for Brigadier General, had his name withdrawn from the Senate, and was never afterwards permitted to take a conspicuous part in the war ... Generosity thy name is Grant.[59]

Dubois himself copied out this letter, by hand, and deposited it among his personal papers. This might indicate that it was what he wished posterity to believe. It is certainly incorrect in one particular: there is no indication that the Jewish delegations were shown any such letter by Halleck; the reports which Wise and others wrote gave so many of the minor details of their conferences in Washington that it is very unlikely they would have omitted mention of the DuBois letter, if Halleck had shown it to them. But even if he did not use it for that purpose, it is entirely possible that Halleck was attempting to find a shield.

A shield to protect Grant, or someone else?

Five widely divergent sources categorically fixed the ultimate responsibility for The Order upon someone in the War Department. One witness who signed himself "Gentile" wrote, in a letter to the *Cincinnati Commercial*, in January 1863, that:

On the evening of the 17th of December, I was sitting in the General's office at Oxford, Miss., when a telegram was handed in which, he remarked, was instructions from Washington, and read it, as near as I can recollect, as follows: "We are reliably advised that Jews are buying up the gold in the various cities of the Union, for the purpose of investing in cotton in the South. This should be prevented. You will therefore issue an order expelling from your lines *all* Jews who cannot give satisfactory evidence of their honesty of intentions." On this, Gen. Grant issued his order.[60]

This eyewitness deposition is confirmed in an unsigned manuscript found among the papers of David Eckstein, to whom we have already had occasion to refer:

On the 17th of De. 62, I was at Oxford, Mississippi, and saw Gen. Grant receive and open a large number of letters and dispatches that evening received. On opening one of them he remarked: "Here is instructions from Headquarters which I have been expecting," and read as follows: We are reliably informed that the Jews are in the various cities buying up the gold, to take to the South to invest in Cotton. That will place in the hands of the Rebels additional means to carry on the war. That should be prevented. You will therefore take measures to prevent it in your Department. Upon this instruction the Jew Order No 11 was issued. All Jews then within Gen. Grant's lines, who could give a satisfactory account of the honesty of their intentions were relieved from the effect of that order.

Last week I wrote to a gentleman in Washington, that was present at the time assisting the Gen. in looking over his dispatches, to know if my recollection of that circumstance was correct. In reply the gentleman says I am substantially correct. But that the General does not wish any publication made by any special friend. "This statement you can use as you choose, but not give my name as authority."[61]

That Eckstein had been in Oxford at the time, we know from other papers in his family's possession. The words he quotes are approximately the same as those quoted by the unknown contributor to the *Cincinnati Commercial.* This version of the facts would, then, appear to be authentic.

A third witness, however, disagreed and referred to messages of an entirely different nature:

> ... on the evening of December 17, 1862 (the date of the order), the mail brought from Washington a large number of complaints, officially referred to [Grant] by the General-in-Chief of the army, against this class of persons for violations of the [trading] orders. The general felt, on reading them, that some immediate action was demanded of him. He realized to its full extent the critical condition of military affairs, and judged, whether wisely or unwisely, that to meet the exigency action must be immediate, thorough and in a form not to be evaded. The order you refer to was the result. It was written and telegraphed to his subordinates without revision, leaving all persons not justly amenable to its terms to be relieved on their individual application.[62]

This witness probably knew more about The Order than anyone but Grant; he was Colonel (later General) John A. Rawlins, who had countersigned the document as Grant's Assistant Adjutant General. The difference between his testimony and that of the other two witnesses may or may not be significant. If anything, it was his own recollection which was hazy; the Cincinnatian wrote immediately after the event; since Eckstein was a Jew he would be more likely to remember the exact circumstances.

A fourth witness offers very brief, but nevertheless convincing testimony. He was Jesse Root Grant, father of the General, who wrote to his friend, Congressman E.B. Washburne from Covington, Ky., on January 20, 1863. At the end of a lengthy report on conditions down South, as observed by him during a visit with his son from December 13 to January 5, he says, "That Jew order so harped on in congress was issued on express instructions from Washington."[63] The father may or may not have been with his son on December 17, the night The Order was issued; but he was there all during that time and must have heard it talked about a good deal.

The fifth witness made no claim to intimate knowledge of the origins of General Order No. 11; he took it as a matter of general knowledge that instructions had come to Grant from Washington. And eight months later, he claimed, Grant was still attempting to achieve the same objective. Writing from Vicksburg on August 7, 1863, an unidentified correspondent for the *New York World* reported:

... It seems to be the policy of the general of this department to effect what he was instructed by the department at Washington to attempt six months ago, namely, the expulsion of the "Jews." It was one of the few righteous orders originating in Washington, but with the usual vacillation of the same quarter was rescinded, and the odium was cast upon the commander. Had he been a political, instead of a patriotic general, there would have been explanations to "go before the people." If trade was opened now there would be ten thousand of the descendants of Shem here, clogging the wheels of war, and, like vultures at the carcass, no other bird dare venture near. War now and trade hereafter, seems to be the motto of General Grant.

Yesterday, when the boat arrived from above, there were seven Jews with articles purporting to be sutlers' goods. They were examined, and proved to be nearly all contraband. In boxes supposed to contain pickles were flasks of the vinous fluids. In neat lead-foil packages that were marked "solace tobacco" were quinine and morphine. Each boat that arrives brings some sharper who has avoided the provost-guard at Helena, and hopes to make something out of the misfortunes of this people. . . .[64]

Since this reporter agreed with the intention of The Order, he felt no need to defend General Grant because of it; his testimony, though probably based on second-hand knowledge, must nevertheless carry a double weight.

In lieu of more convincing evidence to the contrary we are bound to accept the contention of these five[65] witnesses that Grant issued General Order No. 11 on promptings from Washington, even through no such dispatch or messages as were referred to by the witnesses appear in any known collections of war documents.

No positive identification of the Washington authority who sent the message can be made, but two possibilities exist. One is Halleck. His reluctance to believe Kaskel's testimony about the effects of The Order in Paducah; the apologetic tone in which he explained to Grant the reason for the President's interference; his eagerness to secure an affidavit from DuBois accepting the onus of authorship—all these mysteries are cleared up if it was Halleck himself who suggested that something had to be done about the Jews. If it was he who passed a Wall Street rumor on to Grant —then it was he who had brought the house down on the General's head, and he could not very graciously condemn him for it![66]

The other possible author of the dispatch was an Assistant Secretary of War, to whom Grant wrote a long letter the same day he issued The Order:

> Hdqrs. Thirteenth A. C., Dept.
> of the Tenn.,
> Oxford, Miss., December 17, 1862.

Hon. C. P. Wolcott,
Assistant Secretary of War, Washington, D. C.:

I have long believed that in spite of all the vigilance that can be infused into post commanders, *the specie regulations of the Treasury Department have been violated, and that mostly by Jews and other unprincipled traders. So well satisfied have I been of this that I instructed the commanding officer at Columbus to refuse all permits to Jews to come South, and I have frequently had them expelled from the department,* but they come in with their carpet-sacks in spite of all that can be done to prevent it. *The Jews seem to be a privileged class that can travel everywhere.* They will land at any wool-yard on the river and make their way through the country. If not permitted to buy cotton themselves they will act as agents for some one else, who will be at a military post with a Treasury permit to receive cotton and pay for it in treasury notes which the Jew will buy up at an agreed rate, paying gold.

There is but one way that I know of to reach this case; that is, for Government to buy all the cotton at a fixed rate and send it to Cairo, Saint Louis, or some other point to be sold. Then all traders (they are a curse to the Army) might be expelled.

> U.S. Grant,
> Major General.[67]

Grant may have been answering Wolcott's instructions (though no such instructions were located by the army officers who assembled the documents which were printed in *The Official Records*); he may, on the other hand, have merely been writing down for the record the sentiments which prompted him to issue The Order.

But whoever sent the dispatch from Washington, the letter to Wolcott indicates that Grant needed no instructions, that this was not the first discriminatory order which he had signed, and that he was firmly convinced of the Jews' guilt and was eager to use any means of ridding himself of them. Two other documents are ample evidence of this:

> La Grange, Tenn., November 9, 1862.
>
> Major-General Hurlbut, Jackson, Tenn.:
>
> Refuse all permits to come south of Jackson for the present. *The Israelites especially should be kept out.*
>
> U.S. Grant,
> Major-General.[68]

> La Grange, November 10, 1862.
>
> General Webster, Jackson, Tenn.:
>
> Give orders to all the conductors on the road that *no Jews are to be permitted to travel on the railroad southward from any point.* They may go north and be encouraged in it; but *they are such an intolerable nuisance that the department must be purged of them.*
>
> U.S. Grant,
> Major-General.[69]

For at least a month, then, Grant had been experimenting with techniques for the exclusion of Jews from the area under his command. *General*

Order No. 11 was the logical capstone to a policy of discrimination against Jews which he had deliberately formulated and pursued. It was no accident.

Grant wrote a letter during the campaign of 1868, to Congressman I.N. Morris of Illinois, in which he attempted to make it appear that The Order was written in a moment of spontaneous anger, and that it would never have received his sanction if he had taken the time to consider its implications. The letter read, in part:

> At the time of its publication, I was incensed by a reprimand received from Washington for permitting acts which Jews within my lines were engaged in. There were many other persons within my lines equally bad with the worst of them, but the difference was that the Jews could pass with impunity from one army to the other, and gold, in violation of orders, was being smuggled through the lines, at least so it was reported. *The order was issued and sent without any reflection* and without thinking of the Jews as a sect or race to themselves, but simply as persons who had successfully (I say successfully instead of persistently because there were plenty of others within my lines who envied their success) violated an order, which greatly inured to the help of the rebels.

> . . . I have no prejudice against sect or race, but want each individual to be judged by his own merit. Order No. 11 does not sustain this statement, I admit, but then I do not sustain that order. *It never would have been issued if it had not been telegraphed the moment it was penned, and without reflection.*[70]

The two railroad orders and the Wolcott letter utterly disprove Grant's protestations of innocence. *He had a whole month in which to reflect upon these orders, and they were never withdrawn; one is entitled to conclude that Grant himself was the author of General Order No. 11 and that it never would have been withdrawn if Cesar Kaskel had not organized the pressure campaign against it.*

2. Was Grant Anti-Jewish?

In all fairness to the memory of one of the most skillful generals America has ever placed at the head of its armies in time of war, it is essential that we face this second query. Grant was the author of a blatantly anti-Jewish measure, and, contrary to his own assertions, it was the product of a premeditated and deliberate policy. But was Grant himself anti-Jewish?

During the campaign of '68, when the war of words was being waged over The Order, and the newspapers of the country were printing innumerable articles and letters in an effort to exploit or explain it in terms of their own political interests, various informants strove to locate that experience with a Jew in his earlier days which had made Grant a convinced Judaeophobe. One writer said that the General had been swindled by a Jew named Rosenthal in Galena sometime during 1859; another claimed to know that a Jew refused to buy some farm produce from Grant when he was hard-up for money.[71] It was natural that the public should have searched for a certain experience which would turn Grant against all Jews, but it is entirely possible that Grant had not *decided* to dislike Jews. We know that he had been friendly with at least one Jew in his pre-war years. When he had been stationed at Sackett's Harbor as a Lieutenant in 1849, he came to know and respect Jesse Seligman who was then keeping store in Watertown, N.Y. Seligman said at a public gathering in 1891, "on our acquaintance we immediately became friends, and from that hour until his death I know of no one who was entitled to greater love and respect from not only his immediate friends, but from the people of the entire country." They renewed acquaintance a few years later in California, when Grant was ordered to duty there and found his friend Jesse in business in San Francisco.[72]

Perhaps, then, Grant was not consciously anti-Jewish at all. From the letter which he wrote during the 1868 campaign, it is clear that he believed he was unprejudiced, that he thought he wanted "each individual to be judged by his own merits." How then can we reconcile the man with the action? Only by recognizing the fact that some persons are the victims of unconscious prejudices—that men sometimes assimilate stereotyped images, mythological concepts, bigoted ideas, from their environment, of which they are utterly unaware and which lie dormant in their unconscious minds until called forth by some severe experience. Grant must have been such a man—convinced of his freedom from prejudice and yet completely under its control in a time of stress like the campaigns of Tennessee and Mississippi. So he was willing to believe that all the thievery was due to the presence of Jews—the "bogey-man" of social mythology—and he was willing to banish them from his Department. Then came the unexpected, shocking reaction—forcing him to analyze his own mind, his most secret thoughts. Perhaps, for the first time, he became conscious of the prejudice which he had carried through the years and, also, perhaps he was able by virtue of that consciousness, to root it out from his spirit, although he was too ashamed to admit it.

At any rate, however, he came to bury the prejudice which expressed itself in The Order—Grant never again revealed any antipathy towards Jews. During his presidential terms, he appointed many Jews to minor and major public offices. Among the most significant was his appointment in 1870 of Edward S. Solomon as Governor of the Washington Territory. Solomon had achieved a notable military record during the Civil War, serving as Major in the 24th Illinois Infantry and Colonel of the 82nd. General Carl Schurz commended him for "the highest order of coolness and determination under very trying circumstances at the Battle of Gettysburg;" General J.S. Robinson paid tribute to his "admirable coolness and courage" in the Georgia campaigns. On June 15, 1865, he was brevetted Brigadier-General by Secretary of War Stanton "for distinguished gallantry and meritorious service." Solomon's military record undoubtedly attracted the favor of the General who won the war.[73]

Grant offered a higher appointment to a Jew: the position of Secretary of the Treasury which he tendered to Joseph Seligman, the brother of his old friend and supporter Jesse Seligman. Joseph declined the post, but served the nation in good stead in many financial crises.[74]

Although Simon Wolf's testimony must always be regarded with caution, his pages of pleasant reminiscence about Grant's cordial relations with all manner of Jews cannot be controverted.[75] Wolf undoubtedly was exaggerating when he contended that "President Grant did more on and in behalf of American citizens of Jewish faith, at home and abroad, than all the Presidents of the United States prior thereto or since,"[76] but it is a fact that the State Department took an unusual interest in antisemitic persecutions in Roumania and Russia during the Grant Administration.[77]

In 1870, when pogroms broke out in Roumania with renewed violence, Grant performed a major service for the Jews of the world. He appointed the Grand Master of B'nai B'rith, Benjamin Franklin Peixotto, to serve as Consul at Bucharest, without remuneration, in an effort to bring pressure on the Roumanian government for the cessation of attacks on the Jews. The President added to Peixotto's official credentials a note in his own handwriting:

> Executive Mansion
> Washington, D. C.
> December 8, 1870
>
> The bearer of this letter, Mr. Benjamin Peixotto, who has accepted the important though unremunerative position of United States Consul to Rumania, is commended to the good offices of all representatives of this government abroad.
>
> Mr. Peixotto has undertaken the duties of his present office more as a missionary work for the benefit of the people he represents than for any benefit to accrue to himself—a work in which all citizens will wish him the greatest success. The United States, knowing no distinction of her citizens on account of religion or nativity, naturally believes in a civilization the world over which will secure the same universal view.
>
> U.S. Grant[78]

He had come to recognize the inner meaning of the words he used, and the true contours of the concept of democratic equality.

3. What were the Causes of The Order?

General Grant can in no wise be held responsible, personally and solely, for the anti-Jewish regulations which he dictated and signed. The causes, roots, pressures, and reasons go deep into the nature of the conditions in the Department of the Tennessee.

Grant and Sherman, fast friends and co-strategists, and the officers of their command, were undoubtedly justified in their resentment at the exploitation of the resources of the area, and the conveyance of specie and merchandise to the enemy. It was clearly the responsibility of the Government to regulate all trade on the basis of a well-planned, consistently enforced policy; no need for cotton warranted the accompanying chaos and interference with the strategy of conquest. But if the Government did authorize trading, the Generals should never have been placed in the impossible position of implementing a commercial policy with which they disagreed in principle.

It is essential to recognize the strong opposition which Sherman and Grant voiced against *all* trading and commerce in the area, for it explains much. Sherman swore to "move heaven and earth" to repeal the August 11, 1862, order which instructed him to encourage the trade in cotton even at the risk of permitting gold and silver species to be used as exchange.[79] Grant took an equally blunt position on the entire matter: "I regard a mercenary, pretended Union trader within the lines of our army as more dangerous than the shrewdest spy."[80] He was not referring only to "mercenary, pretended Union traders!" He and Sherman considered all traders rotten to the core; they were all "profiteers," "speculators," and potential "smugglers." It actually became a matter of emotional resistance and hostility to traders, whether or not they abided by Government regulations. The Generals were, of course, entitled to their opinion, and it was their duty to press for the adoption of any policy which they considered conducive to the successful prosecution of the war against the Confederacy; but so long as the administration believed that the industrial and international benefits of a revived trade in the Southland overshadowed all other considerations, Grant and Sherman were duty-bound, in all justice, to carry out the Government's policy. Their reluctance to admit that any of the traders and merchants who came into the area were law-abiding and honest men, performing a service which was essential to the commercial well-being of the area, disqualifies them as objective witnesses for an evaluation of the conditions and factors involved.

Added to this element of conscious opposition to the trading policy was the intangible element of suspicion of Jews. Sherman had been in command of Memphis only nine days before he was dispatching generalized complaints about Jewish traders:

> Hdqrs. Fifth Division, Army of the Tennessee,
> Memphis, July 30, 1862
>
> Col. John A. Rawlins,
> Headquarters Corinth, Miss.:
>
> Sir: ...
>
> I have been very busy in answering the innumerable questions of civilians and hope they are now about through. *I found so many Jews and speculators*

here trading in cotton, and secessionists had become so open in refusing anything but gold, that I have felt myself bound to stop it. This gold has but one use—the purchase of arms and ammunition, which can always be had for gold, at Nassau, New Providence, or Cincinnati; all the guards we may establish cannot stop it. *Of course, I have respected all permits by yourself or the Secretary of the Treasury, but in these new cases (swarms of Jews) I have stopped it.*

All the boards of trade above are shipping salt south, and I cannot permit it to pass into the interior until you declare a district open to trade. If we permit money and salt to go into the interior, it will not take long for Bragg and Van Dorn to supply their armies with all they need to move . . . We cannot carry on war and trade with a people at the same time.
. . .

I am, with great respect, your obedient servant,

W.T. Sherman,
Major-General, Commanding.[81]

Memphis, August 11, 1862.

Hon. S.P. Chase,
Secretary of the Treasury:

Sir:

Your letter just received, at the same time an order from Headquarters of the Army at Washington to encourage the purchase of cotton, even by the payment of gold, silver, and Treasury notes.

I may of course be mistaken, but gold and money are as much contraband of war as arms and ammunition, because they are convertible terms, for you know money will buy any thing for sale at Saint Louis and Cincinnati, and I declare it impossible to keep such articles, be they salt, powder, lead, or anything, from reaching the South. Also, gold will purchase arms and ammunition at Nassau, in the Bahamas, and you know that one vessel out of three can run the blockade. *The flock of Jews had disappeared, but will again overrun us.* I had so arranged that cotton could be had for currency, Tennessee and other banknotes good here but not elsewhere. The whole South is now up, and all they want is arms and provisions. Salt at Grenada is worth $100 a barrel, and if trade is opened Memphis is better to our enemy than before it was taken.

W.T. Sherman,
Major-General.[82]

Headquarters, Fifth Division,
Memphis, Tenn., August 11, 1862.

Adjutant-General of the Army,
Washington, D.C.:

Have just received an order to encourage trade in cotton. Gold, silver, and money are as much contraband of war as powder, lead, and guns because they are convertible terms. Cotton is now procured by Tennessee and Southern bank notes which are unconvertible. If the policy of the Government demands cotton order us to seize and procure it by the usual operations of war, but the spending of gold and money will enable our enemy to arm the horde of people that now swarm the entire South. This cotton order is worse to us than a defeat. *The country will swarm with dishonest Jews who will smuggle powder, pistols, percussion-caps, &c., in spite of all the guards and precautions we can give.* Honest men can buy all the cotton accessible to us with the Tennessee bank notes.

W.T. Sherman,
Major-General, Commanding.

(Copy to General Grant)[83]

Was nine days really time enough for Sherman to ascertain sufficient facts and statistics to prove the generalizations he dictated so glibly? He cited no names or percentages of Jews; he gave no evidence; and what he wrote was in the language of prejudice. Of course there were Jews who entered the area as soon as it had been conquered by the Union armies. It would have been strange if Jewish peddlers and merchants had not taken advantage of the business opportunities which the Government deliberately and consciously extended to the Northern commercial world. The Jews were the business entrepreneurs par excellence; from the peddler with the pack on his back to the proprietor of the incipient department store, they played an indispensable role in the expanding American capitalist economy. One is led to the inevitable conclusion that it was not what they *did*, but what they *were*, that made them so offensive to General Sherman.

Evidence of personal prejudice is difficult to secure, but perhaps General Sherman had long before the War determined the qualities which, for him, the Jews possessed. Witness this excerpt of a letter which he wrote in September 1858:

> . . . Individuals may prosper in a failing community such as San Francisco, but they must be Jews, without pity, soul, heart or bowels of compassion; but in a rising, growing, industrious community like St. Louis, all patient, prudent, honest men can thrive . . .[84]

Such an apparently unprovoked attack, setting up the merciless, unscrupulous Jew in contradistinction to the honest and honorable non-Jew (Sherman was undoubtedly thinking of himself in this connection), appears to brand Sherman as a completely prejudiced person, one who could think nothing good or decent about a Jew.

If Jews were already offensive to Sherman or newspaper reporters, their high visibility made it impossible to overlook them even in the mob. A few Jews, foreign-looking, speaking in European accents, setting up shops or carrying packs and peddling their wares, *would* look like "swarms of Jews" to anyone who objected to their presence. Jews were not the suave purchasing agents who came from Washington with letters of introduction to the commanding officers from important personages, and took rooms in the finest hotels; they were easily within sight, on the streets, at the docks, trudging along the roads, standing in line for permits—visible to anyone who didn't like *any* Jews.

But were they necessarily dishonest because they were Jews? One of the foreign-looking, bearded Jews who spoke with an accent and stood outside his store in Memphis, was named Jacob Peres. He was the part-time cantor as well as president of one of the Memphis synagogues. Undoubtedly he had to apply for cotton-buying permits at the Army headquarters; undoubtedly he was offensive to an officer who disliked foreigners, and especially Jews. But Peres had lived in Memphis before the Union armies captured it, and he was to live there for a long time afterwards. During the final year of the war his fellow-citizens were to demonstrate their profound respect for his learning and administrative ability, despite his accent and origin, by electing him President of the Memphis School Board.[85]

Two brothers, Jules and Jacob Menken, must be added to the "swarms of Jews." They had been in business in Cincinnati before the war, but the slump after the outbreak of hostilities devoured their capital and drove them into bankruptcy. They went to court and made the best settlement they could. Both served in the army but were discharged, one for malaria, the other for a war wound. After Memphis fell to the Union, they moved there and set up shop. During two years of hard work they managed to recoup their losses. In 1864, they journeyed to New York to repay, in full, every debt they owed even though their court settlement had not obligated them to recognize those debts. Their creditors gave them a testimonial dinner in tribute to their high sense of responsibility. Were men of such honor to be spat upon as "dishonest Jews?"[86]

Jews were not all so relatively successful as the Menken brothers. One penniless fellow, named Isaac Meyer, who came to Memphis in 1862, had failed in almost everything he set his hand to do. A German immigrant who arrived in New York in 1854, Meyer had peddled his way across the country to California, engaged in several business ventures, lost his profits and investments by virtue of poor judgment in partners and in fiscal matters, and returned to New York, uncertain as to his next move. A friend told him about the revival of business in Memphis, so he determined to try his luck there. He secured the proper permits, bought a stock of "Dry Goods, Boots, Shoes, Clothing, Hats, Gentlemen's Furnishings and Nursery Goods" on credit and finally arrived in Memphis, after taking oaths of allegiance all along the route. He opened a store, but hard luck seemed to dog his footsteps. First a large part of his stock was stolen, and then:

On the fifteenth day of March, 1863, my store of goods was seized without process of law by the U.S. Military Authorities and I was sent to a Military prison in the center of the City, called Irving Block, among Confederate and Federal prisoners of War. A very filthy and sickly place, not fit for a good dog.[87]

I remained there for sixteen hours and was pushed backward and forward by our own Union Soldiers who refused me a little filthy place to lay down to rest. The Confederates had sympathy with me and offered me their shelter, as clean as they had it.

I was then taken out by one of our own Federal Officers of the Army, Colonel Kanfrom, [Kahn from?] Iowa, a brother Mason who got two Citizens as bondsmen for $10,000 each for my appearance before the Provost Marshal until the case would be tried . . .

On the twenty-fifth of the same month, without any trial, my stock of goods was confiscated and sold at auction.

After reporting twice a day in person before the Provost Marshal for nearly ninety days, a half sheet of paper was read to me by the clerk. This was supposed to be a copy of my sentence from a Military Court. There, a suppose sentence [trial?] had been had without my presence or my knowledge. It said that it was ordered that my stock of goods be confiscated for the use of the U.S. Military forces and that I should be transported beyond the line of the City limits of the Department of Tenn.

This sentence was never enforced, but left me penniless and in a very uncomfortable situation. I was convicted on a false practice of aiding deserters, for selling citizens clothing to one of our own Union Soldiers, a paper collar, a silk neck tie and one colored traveling shirt and a pair of blue jeans pants for the amount of $14.00.

Poor Isaac Meyer had to furnish a bribe of $20 to a clerk to secure a copy of his "sentence," and had to run from office to office for months before he was granted permission to reclaim his personal property—a watch, a ring, a pen-knife, and some cash—which had been taken from him at the time of his arrest and had never been returned. Before long he was drafted into the Army, and served in a unit stationed in Memphis until the end of the war.[88]

Quaint as his telling of the story may be, Meyer and his like were the basis for the generalizations in Sherman's reports, and, ultimately, for the Grant Order. So far as the army was concerned, Meyer was another Jew who was arrested, found guilty, and sentenced. But is there any more reason to accept the version of the officer who presided at the military trial than Meyer's? Sherman did not have to furnish evidence for his allegations; Meyer was so convinced of his innocence that he was willing to have his children and grandchildren learn the facts of his arrest when they read the story of his life!

No Jew of the Civil War era, nor of our own, would attempt to excuse or deny criminal actions committed by Jews. Decent, law-abiding Jews were ashamed that any Americans—Jews or non-Jews—should be guilty of disobeying Government laws and regulations at a time of national crisis. Rabbi Simon Tuska of Memphis was so vehement in his denunciation of some of the Northern Jews who came to Memphis as "greedy birds of prey" that the abolitionist crusader, Rabbi David Einhorn, accused him of being a Confederate sympathizer.[89] Jacob Peres, the other Memphis rabbi, who, as we have seen, was himself in business, had to use Hebrew to express his sorrow and chagrin when he spoke of Jewish law-breakers. "Some time ago," he wrote Isaac Leeser in Philadelphia, "over 20 יהודים [Jews] were in prison for smuggling. It is a great חלול השם [profanation of the name of God.] But אנחנו מה חטאנו [we—how have we sinned?—referring to the Grant Order]?"[90] And when Leeser began his article on The Order, the longest article he ever wrote for *The Occident,* he spoke with shame of "the crowd of needy [Jewish] adventurers, who travel or glide rather through the highways and byways of the land in quest of gain, often we fear unlawful, who in their material labors are perfectly indifferent to the duties of their religion, and not rarely conceal it by a pretended conformity."[91]

On another occasion, Einhorn urged American Jewry to "make war also upon the Amalek in our own midst! Let us meet them that bring shame and disgrace upon us and our religious faith, with the fulness of our moral indignation." He was referring to Jewish smugglers. He admitted that Jews were no guiltier than others, and that "little rogues are brought to punishment whereas big ones are allowed to escape"—but "the crime," he said, "is far greater when committed by a Jew, because he must know that the whole Jewish community is made accountable for his offense, that his act inflicts shame, disgrace and misfortune upon his fellow believers."[92]

These rabbis did not need to be reminded that the people to whose service they devoted their lives and talents were not all saints. They spoke in a spirit of courageous and sincere rebuke to the erring members of the House of Israel. Their honest sense of shame was a challenge to the spirit of intolerance which labeled all Jews wrong-doers, and neglected to specify the religion and national origin of the hosts of others.

Unfortunately the court-martial and prison records of the Tennessee area for the period under discussion are incomplete, but a sufficient number have been preserved in the National Archives at Washington for the purpose of a survey of Jewish offenders. Since no entry concerning a criminal's religion was made by the authorities, names have to be regarded as an index to possible Jewish origin. A margin of error must therefore be underlined in any consideration of these records. It is possible to determine, however, whether generalizations are valid: was there a high incidence of Jewish smugglers and commercial offenders in the Tennessee area?

In the *Report of Citizen Prisoners in the Custody of the Provost Marshal, Memphis Tennessee*,[93] which covers the period from March 1863 to early 1865, a count was made of individuals listed for smuggling offenses. There were 198 such persons. Of these a possible five names may be identified as Jewish. The percentage is 2.5. In the same volume, a special study was made of all those arrested for *any* offense, whose name began with "L"—a letter of the alphabet with which a large number of Jewish names begin. There were 134 arrestees in all, and a possible seven were Jews, all arrested for minor offenses.

In *District of Middle Tennessee, Jail Records*, a study was made for a control period, December 1862 to April 1863, and in *Records of Courts Martial, Memphis District*, for August 1863 to January 1864. The complete number of white men arrested for non-commercial offenses was 104. Of these, two were possibly Jews. The complete number of white men arrested for smuggling and other commercial offenses was 34; one was possibly a Jew. The percentage for the second count is 2.94.

In *Cases Coming Before Wm. Truesdall, Chief of Army Police in Memphis*, from February to May 1863, apparently a volume of special cases requiring such additional records, 44 persons were involved in 37 cases. In two cases three possible Jews were accused of smuggling, and in an additional case, three Jewish brothers were arrested, but no offense was recorded.[94] The percentage of possible Jews, including the latter case, is 13.63.

The average percentage for the three studies is 6.03. If this figure is accurate, and it can certainly not be far wrong for the volumes studied, a possible six of every 100 men arrested (not necessarily convicted) for commercial offenses were Jewish.[95]

In a volume of *Special Orders, District of Memphis*, containing over 350 orders in regard to business and commercial offenses, as well as ordinary civil suits, two Jews were listed as being fined for violating certain liquor ordinances;[96] one Jew was convicted of selling boots without a permit and his two dozen pairs of boots were confiscated;[97] two Jews were charged by a third with extortion in the guise of U.S. Marshals;[98] and one Jew was banished from the city for smuggling while his two Jewish companions, for no stated reason, were permitted to remain.[99] By far the most interesting case in the volume concerns three Jews who were arrested for smuggling on January 12, 1863, and sent to prison at Alton. Their goods were confiscated and ordered sold for the benefit of the Government. On January 27, however, they were released on bond and ordered to appear before the Provost Marshal every day. Their trial was held on February 9, and the court decided that certain drugs and medicine which had been found in their stock did not belong to them, but to a certain John Farley (obviously a non-Jew and otherwise unidentified). Those items were to be confiscated. But the three men were found not guilty and all their own property was ordered restored to them. This was not the end of the case, however, for the findings of the court had to be reviewed by General Hurlbut. He rejected them without detailing his reasons. Although he did not declare the defendants guilty, he ordered certain goods confiscated: buttons, pins, tea, coffee, hats. All other merchandise was to be returned to them. But were the Jews guilty or innocent? Hurlbut evidently believed that they could be found not guilty and still deserve to have their property confiscated! Why? Perhaps their guilt was in being Jewish![100]

One other illuminating example of the influence of prejudice upon General Hurlbut's decisions was detailed by Rabbi Wise. On November 30, 1863, General Order No. 162 was issued by his Headquarters of the 16th Army Corps at Memphis, prohibiting fifteen clothing houses, which "are reported to have stocks of military clothing on hand, and not having the necessary authority to trade in the same from these headquarters," from selling those stocks and ordering them to send their goods north of the lines of the Department. All fifteen stores were owned by Jews.[101] One of them wrote and urged Dr. Wise to protest:

> . . . the goods were bought and shipped on legal permits, and five percent duty was paid thereon, which is a clear loss . . . Most wonderful, however, in this matter, is that two non-Jewish houses, of Memphis, Tickner & Co., and Waggner and Cheek, were not included in this order. On the contrary, it is maintained, on good authority, that Tickner and Co. not only knew in advance that such an order was to be issued, but were given permits to bring such military goods to Memphis and monopolize the trade.[102]

It is doubtlessly impossible to locate any conclusive evidence in either direction, but the order *was* issued, and the description of it which was furnished to Dr. Wise is verified by Hurlbut's General Order No. 162, published in the *Official Records*. The fifteen merchants *were* all Jewish. Unless one finds it logical that fifteen Jewish merchants could be guilty of illegal practices, while two non-Jewish competitors were not, the only conclusion is the one expressed by Wise's informant: prejudice was the controlling factor.

Since prejudice exists in the realm of the emotions, it is hardly possible to identify and isolate its indirect influence. We have no way of discovering the number of cases in which prejudice against the Jews and economic gain combined to produce confiscations, prison terms, or expulsions.[103] This was one of the interpretations given to The Order, however, by contemporary writers who suspected that the expulsion of the Jews had been foisted upon Grant and Sherman by influential cotton buyers and their officer-partners, to pave the way for higher profits for themselves. The *Cincinnati Enquirer* was prepared to assert editorially that Grant was imposed upon by malicious misrepresentations of interested parties . . . with whose arrangements for speculating in cotton certain Israelites, engaged in the same business, interfered. It is well-known, that in more than one instance, military officers took to themselves a monopoly of the cotton trade . . . and made fortunes for themselves and relatives . . . It may be that the Israelites at Memphis and other points, have been purchasing cotton without any regard for the nice little percentage which it is expected cotton traders should pay for the protection of Federal bayonets and the use of Government transportation.[104]

Isaac M. Wise thought he had proof of this in the fact that the price of cotton was lowered from 40¢ to 25¢ a pound the day after The Order was issued. The meaning was clear to Wise:

> The Jews bought cotton of planters at 40 cents a pound; the military authorities with their business partners, agents, clerks, portiers, &c., intend to buy that staple at twenty-five cents a pound . . . They could sell it in Eastern cities just as high as the next man—and the Jews must leave, because they interfere with a branch of the military business.[105]

No verification of these suspicions and accusations is possible. *But only Jews, and not all traders were banished; cotton traders as a group were never expelled.* The question, therefore, which was asked by so many Jews and Christians alike, "Who stood to profit most from the departure of Jews?" was not an unfair or irrelevant question. And the answer, "The other traders and speculators, civilian and military," was in itself the only possible explanation of The Order.
. Why stigmatize the Jews? Because for Grant and all the others who paved the way for The Order, the Jews were a scapegoat already prepared and identified, handed down from one age to the next, hounded and hunted from one country to another; the Jews were a myth, a people branded as the purveyor of all manner of wickedness. Few would question the guilt of Jews for any crime or evil; few could doubt that they were capable of anything of which the clichés accused them. The Jews were the natural scapegoat, even in the United States, because they had already been the scapegoat for almost two millenia.

VII AMERICAN JUDAEOPHOBIA
1861-1865

HAD THE GRANT AFFAIR been the one unique instance of anti-Jewish prejudice in action during the Civil War period, it would have to be recorded as an inexplicable aberration, an isolated freak of irrationality; but an extensive reading in the daily press and occasional literature of the period demonstrates that The Order was only one example of a series of anti-Jewish libels which were propagated during the War in both the Union and the Confederacy. Anti-Jewish prejudice was actually a characteristic expression of the age, part and parcel of the economic and social upheaval effectuated by the war.

No satisfactory study of the history of anti-Jewish prejudice in America has yet been written. While it is quite true that the almost total absence of legal disabilities and of overt acts of violence indicated an enlightened attitude toward the Jew by the United States as a nation, it is equally true that there was always a subtle undercurrent of prejudice which flowed through the American civilization. There was prejudice in New Amsterdam in 1654 when Peter Stuyvesant battled with his superiors in Holland for the right to expel the first Jewish immigrants to his colony;[1] in Maryland in 1658 when Jacob Lumbrozo was tried for blasphemy;[2] in 1737 when the members of the New York Assembly prohibited Jews from voting;[3] in Maryland and North Carolina, where Jews were forbidden to hold office, long after the ratification of the Constitution.[4]

In periods of social and political crisis, such as the Federalist-Republican strife at the turn of the nineteenth century, this prejudice became a political weapon. Jews and non-Jews who belonged to the Jeffersonian movement were smeared *as Jews* by their opponents. In Philadelphia a Federalist said that "A Jewish Tavern Keeper, with a very Jewish name [Israel Israel—a non-Jew] is chosen one of the Senators of this commonwealth for the city of Philadelphia solely on account of his violent attachment to the French interests."[5] In New York City a Federalist thought he would permanently damn the Democratic-Republican Society by saying that "all seem, like their Vice-President, of the tribe of Shylock."[6] In Pittsburgh, a Federalist broadside played upon the name of John Israel (a non-Jew) in an effort to disarm the effectiveness of his anti-Federalist paper, the *Tree of Liberty:*[7]

Have you heard	of the New Press?
Echo	of the Jew Press.
What, is it published,	and by a Jew?
Echo	and by a Hugh.
Of the Aurora	Another edition?
Echo	a mother of sedition.
Jacobinism imaginary is	or is real
Echo	Israel.

American Jewry was not large enough to warrant the violent passions which were aroused against the Catholic immigrants in the 1820s and 1830s, and later in the 1850s by the Know-Nothing party, but Jewish individuals who were conspicuous in the journalistic, political, or economic world, bore the brunt of prejudice. Mordecai M. Noah, dramatist, politician, journalist, and newspaper editor, was one of those who frequently had his religion thrown into his face. United States Consul to Tunis in 1815, he was recalled by Secretary of State Monroe, apparently on orders from President Madison, in a brief, curt note which began:

> At the time of your appointment, as Consul at Tunis, it was not known that the Religion which you profess would form any obstacle to the exercise of your Consular functions. Recent information, however, on which entire reliance may be placed, proves that it would produce a very unfavorable effect . . .[8]

In 1842, Horace Greeley used Noah's religion as a point in an anti-slavery argument:

> We choose our own company in all times, and that of our own race, but cherish little of that spirit which for eighteen centuries has held the kindred of M. M. Noah accursed of God and man, outlawed and outcast, and unfit to be the associates of Christians and Musselmen, or even self-respecting Pagans. Where there are thousands who would not eat with a Negro, there are (or lately were) tens of thousands who would not eat with a Jew. We leave to such renegades as the Judge of Israel the stirring up of prejudices and the prating of "usages of society," which over half the world make him an abhorrence, as they not long since would have done here . . .[9]

One of the strangest cases in legal history occurred in Philadelphia in 1849–51, when Warder Cresson, U.S. Consul to Jerusalem and an eccentric student of obscure religious sectarian views, went on trial for insanity because he had decided to become a Jew. His wife and children were convinced that anyone who converted to the Old Testament faith must be demented, especially if he was the scion of a proud Quaker family. It required two long trials to free him from the charge, restore his property to him, and permit him to return to Palestine so that he could live out his days in piety and good works.[10]

Uriah P. Levy fought against prejudice all through his years in the regular navy, and had to testify at a special court of inquiry ordered by Congress before he was cleared of charges which he said were trumped up because he was a Jew.[11] Almost every political opponent of Judah P. Benjamin referred to his name and faith. A typical case was that of Nicholas Davis of Alabama who, in the heat of a political campaign, denounced the Louisiana Senator as that "infamous Jew . . . Judas P. Benjamin. . . ."[12] Practically every Jew who rose above the ordinary level had to realize that he would pay for his conspicuous position by suffering attacks on his background and the faith of his folk.

It is the writer's impression, however (and until a thorough research has been made of the entire field, impressions will have to serve), that although specific individuals were abused as Jews by those who opposed, hated, or envied them, it was not a common habit to attack all Jews for whatever anyone found wrong with life in the United States. That remained for the Civil War period.

I. UNION VERSION

An indication of the anti-Jewish tendency of the age was the common practice of Northern newspapers to identify as a "Jew," "Israelite," or, worst yet, a "German Jew," any Jew who was apprehended in or suspected of carrying on disloyal activities. Jews who enlisted in the Army, or whose names were reported in the casualty columns were never identified as such; but a wrong-doer was promptly catalogued for the public mind, whether it was in Dubuque, Iowa, Rochester, N.Y., or Burlington, Vt.[13] A dispatch from St. Albans, Vt., for instance, referred to "Mrs. Meyer, the wife of a German Jew residing in N.Y., who had been acting as a messenger between the rebels who congregate in Montreal and the South"[14] At the other end of the Union, in Cairo, Ill., an AP writer wired a story to the *New York Herald* about "a Jew named Morrison . . . who had been arrested at Memphis as a rebel spy."[15]

This journalistic technique was at one and the same time the product of prejudice and an agency for its dissemination. It fixed ever more strongly in the mind of the reader the myth of the dishonest, law-breaking Jew. But it could never have been used unless there had been an acquaintance with the myth in the first place. As one reporter put it, "How could you expect a Jew quartermaster to be honest?"[16] Omit the word "quartermaster" and the question would be representative of the habit of mind with which some citizens approached the Jewish question.

In the political sphere, the fact that Judah P. Benjamin, high statesman of the Confederacy, was a Jew, provided a convenient slur with which all Jews could be defamed. Crude and insulting references to his religious origins were commonplace at the very beginning of the war and during election campaigns. A catalogue of public figures who attacked him *as a Jew* would include, among others, Senator Andrew Johnson, of Tennessee;[17] General Benjamin F. Butler;[18] Senator Henry Wilson of Massachusetts;[19] Governor John Brough[20] and Senator Ben Wade of Ohio.[21]

At the very outbreak of secession, the *Boston Transcript* directed its criticism of Southern intransigeance at Jewish figures:

> The Children of Israel—It is stated that Mr. Mordecai, a wealthy Jew of Charleston, S. C., has presented to his belligerent state and city $10,000, to aid the purpose of secession, with the offer besides of a large number of negroes to work in the cause. Mr. Benjamin of Louisiana, a member of the same faith, is *the* disunion leader in the U. S. Senate, and Mr. Yulee of Florida, whose name has been changed from the more appropriate one of Levy, has always been one of the hottest leaders of the ultra fire-eaters. Can it be possible, that this peculiar race—the old Catholics used to call them "accursed"—having no country of their own, desire that other nations shall be in the same unhappy condition as they are themselves? . . . This "stiffnecked generation," by its principal men, takes a lead in attempting to destroy a Constitution which has been to them an Ark of refuge and safety.[22]

It could only be prejudice and bigotry which would prompt an editor to single out prominent Southern Jews for special treatment.

The same conclusion must be reached in a consideration of those Republican journals and papers which accused all Northern Jews of being enemies of the Union. Articles by the "Lounger" in *Harper's Weekly* said that all Jews were secessionists, copperheads, and rebels.[23] During the 1864 election, the *Newburg* (N.Y.) *Journal* matched the "Lounger" in this wise:

> Show me the descendants of that accursed race who crucified the Savior and who are always opposed to the best interests of the Government in every land in which they roam; who never enter our armies but for the purpose of depleting the pockets of the soldiers, and who hang around the camps to take every advantage of their necessities; and I will show you the men who, ninety-nine out of a hundred, will vote for the Modern Democracy this fall, and would support Vallandigham or the infamous butcher Quantrell in preference to General Butler or Abraham Lincoln.[24]

The *Harrisburg* (Pa.) *Telegraph* published a paragraph about a certain Lazarus Barnhart, a Jewish tavern-keeper of the city, who participated in a Democratic party parade. Then came this appeal to prejudice: "Will Rabbi Barnhart please inform his Christian fellow copperheads who murdered the Savior and who shed the blood of the early Christians? Our Irish friend, Pat Ryan, occupied a seat in this carriage and looked as if he was out of place (which he was) sitting side by side with a Jew copperhead."[25] In Indiana, the *Evansville Journal* swore that "it is a fact that our fellow citizens of the Hebrew persuasion are, with a few honorable exceptions, all afflicted with the Copperhead mania."[26] In California, the *American Flag* of San Francisco announced that "a large majority of the wealthier Jews of California, and particularly of San Francisco, are copperheads . . . adherents of the last, lingering, horrid despotism of the Dark Ages, which were dismal with the wail of their forefathers."[27] The Jews, apparently, whether there were many or few who preferred the Democratic party's policies, were not to be permitted the choice accorded to other citizens.

August Belmont was a particular target for the Republican press and party spokesmen, even though (or perhaps *because*) he had married into one of America's most distinguished non-Jewish families, was rearing his children as Christians, and maintained no affiliation with Jewish activities or religious life.[28] His participation in national affairs as the Chairman of the Democratic National Committee, not to say his great wealth and contacts with the bankers of Europe, made him extremely vulnerable to those Republicans who disliked Jews. It was he, they said, who paid all the bills for the Democratic party, and he expected to collect handsomely after the Union had been surrendered to the South.[29] In Philadelphia, a Union League speaker made it a point to refer to "the Jew banker of New York;"[30] an orator at the Cooper Institute in New York made some insulting comments about Belmont and his "knot" of German Jewish bankers;[31] the *Weekly Mirror* of Manchester, N.H., said that the "Jew brokers" who gathered around Belmont were doing all they could to help the Confederacy.[32] The *Chicago Tribune*, approaching the election of November '64, wanted to know "how much is McClellan to get from the Rothschilds . . . if he succeeds in betraying his country and handing it over to [the Confederates'] tender mercies? . . . Will we have a dishonorable peace in order to enrich Belmont, the Rothschilds, and the whole tribe of Jews . . . ?"[33] The small *Vincennes* (Ind.) *Weekly Gazette*, as well as the powerful *New York Herald*, spoke as though all the Jewish bankers in the world, with Belmont in the lead, were joined together for the support of the Confederacy.[34]

It was true that the European banking firm of Erlanger had negotiated for a six million dollar loan to the Confederacy, and had sent three of its agents to Richmond,[35] but that the Jews should be attacked on Erlanger's account by the *Harper's Weekly*, the *Cincinnati Gazette*, and other papers,[36] was too much like rubbing salt into a wound. Erlanger had long ago been converted to Christianity! And were the Jews still to be blamed for his actions? *The Jewish Record* asked, "Apropos—does *it pay* to send out missionaries, and convert Jews, if 'Christianity' teaches such things as Mr. Erlanger appears to have learned?"[37] Isaac M. Wise wanted his neighbors to know that "Baron Erlanger is not one of those common Jews and usurers . . . he was baptized many years ago!"[38]

The accusation that the Rothschilds were pro-slavery was printed so often that the American Consul at Frankfort decided to set the American press straight. His letter must have been a shock to the *Harper's Weekly* and other journals:[39]

> In your paper of February 28, you do a great injustice to the eminent firm of Rothschilds here, when you hint that they are like a certain Rabbi [Raphall] who held opinions that some men were born to be slaves. I know not what the other firms—and there are many of the Rothschilds, all related—in Europe, think of slavery, but here the firm of M. A. Von Rothschild & Son are opposed to slavery and in favor of Union. *A converted Jew*, Erlanger, has taken the rebel loan of £3,000,000, and lives in this city; and Baron Rothschild informed me that all Germany condemned this act of lending money to establish a slaveholding government, and that so great was public opinion against it, that Erlanger & Co. dare not offer it on the Frankfort Bourse. I further know that the Jews rejoice to think that none of their sect would be guilty of lending money for the purpose above named; but it was left, they say, for apostate Jews to do it.
> I hope you will correct the statement you made about this firm.
> Yours truly,
> W. W. Murphy.

The *New York Tribune*,[40] *Herald*,[41] and *Commercial*,[42] the *Patterson Press*,[43] and the *Detroit Commercial Advertiser*[44] were only a few of the papers which alleged that Jews were responsible for the speculation in gold: "all Jews are gold speculators;" "the Jews are engaged in destroying the national credit, in running up the price of gold;" "those hook-nosed wretches speculate on disasters;" "the great majority of those engaged in gold speculation are of the Jewish race." The *New York Dispatch* said that if you walked to the corner of Williams Street and Exchange Place, all you would see were the "descendants of Shylock," and all you would hear would be "Up to shixty-five, up to sheventy-one! Mine God, it vill go up to von hundred!"[45] There was as little truth in this accusation as in any other blanket generalization; the New York Jewish editors dared their secular colleagues to walk to the gold curb and count Jews, so certain were they that a very small proportion of Jews could be found there.[46]

There were Jewish bankers, of course. One Jewish banking firm in New York was Seligman Brothers. Joseph and Jesse Seligman, both Republicans, had made a fortune in clothing manufacture early in the War —at one time the Government owed the firm over one million dollars for merchandise already delivered. Joseph was so eager to be of assistance to the Union cause that he went to Frankfort to sell securities, and succeeded in disposing of $200,000,000 in Union bonds—a feat which W.E. Dodd said was "scarcely less important than the Battle of Gettysburg," because it turned the tide on the financial-diplomatic front.[47] An indication of Seligman's personal opinions is to be found in a letter which he wrote his family in 1863 about the Democratic party and the draft riots:

Although I know the character of the party and people opposed to our present Government and the country I have yet confidence enough in the wisdom and patriotism of the masses to hope of an early putting down of all "Copperheads!" . . . I am really anxious to see your remarks respecting the late riots in N. Y. That Seymour had telegraphed to Washington to stop the Draft is of a piece with the known Copperheadism of the once "Democratic" party. In place of putting down rebellion at home and at the South, they advise stopping drafting and thereby give Jeff Davis their moral support, and another straw of hope . . .[48]

This was one of the "Jew bankers" who were said to be wrecking the country!

Even Belmont, the completely devoted Democrat, was eager to use his talents and contacts for the benefit of the Union. In 1861 he corresponded with Secretary of the Treasury Chase, advising him on the wisest course to follow in attempting to secure the support of European capital. In July, on his way to Europe, he wrote:

If by that time [when Belmont would be in Europe] Congress has passed the measures you propose, or that in anticipation of what Congress intends to do, you have made up your mind as regards the disposition of your foreign loan I shall be very happy to devote my best energies toward the furtherance of your views if you deem proper to confide them to me. I mean to act in these promises not as the Banker & Correspondent of foreign Banking firms but as an American citizen, anxious to do his share in the crisis which has overcome our dear Country. If you should deem it advisable & conducive to the public interest to empower me with the negotiations of the loan & place me in full possession of your views & limits I shall do my utmost to watch & promote the interests of my Government . . .[49]

This banker-politician so irresponsibly attacked as a Confederate sympathizer and traitor had already recruited and equipped the first German-American regiment in New York.[50]

It was not only the Jewish bankers of New York who were disloyal to the Government, and devising ways of plotting the economic ruin of the country, so the rumors ran—but at every geographic point of contact between the Union and the Confederacy, Jews were supposed to be doing the actual work of supplying the South with goods and the necessities of war. The Grant affair was the capstone of this accusation in the Memphis area, but the accusation was current in other areas as well. In Cincinnati and Louisville, the early centers of trade with the Confederacy, and the geographical, political, and emotional borderline between the two sections, the libel made its appearance even earlier than in Tennessee. A reporter in Covington, Ky., concluded an article on the Jews with the statement that "the people whose ancestors smuggled for eighteen centuries smuggle yet."[51] In Louisville, an anonymous writer told the readers of the *Louisville Journal* that Jewish smugglers were pouring into the city. "It is remarkable what a flight of these birds of passage the contraband business has brought to this city."[52] Dr. Felsenheld, who answered the charge, demanded that the anonymous writer identify the Jews by name; he insisted that to his knowledge "not a single Jew has settled here since the smuggling commenced."[53]

Grant had only banished the Jews from his area; an Associated Press writer in New Orleans would have had them all executed if he had his way. He told the story of three Jews who were caught on Lake Pontchartrain carrying "a large quantity of medicine for the rebels, and also letters from forty or fifty leading citizens of New Orleans to persons high in authority in the Confederate Government." And then this sorry exhibition of prejudice: "The Jews in New Orleans and all the South ought to be exterminated. They run the blockade, and are always to be found at the bottom of every new villainy."[54] Anti-Jewish prejudice was apparently rife in New Orleans. A few weeks later, a Cincinnati Jew returning north from Louisiana told Isaac M. Wise that "local editors and correspondents of northern papers, residing temporarily in [New Orleans], frequently ventilate their stupid prejudice against our race in revolting newspaper hoaxes and downright lies."[55]

When a Confederate privateer put in at Curaçao in 1861, the *Philadelphia Public Ledger* reported that the Dutch had permitted the ship to touch port with great reluctance, but felt that the dangerous condition of the ship's keel spelled disaster unless it could be repaired. This harmless incident was perverted into an attack on the Jews by the *New York Post*. The Jews of Curaçao had defrauded all the non-Jews of their wealth, and were completely in control of trade in the West Indies, said the *Post;* they are only "too glad to furnish the Confederate pirates with all they need. . . . There is small doubt that these people are favorably inclined toward our insurgents, being, like them, slaveholders and unscrupulous and eager for trade of whatever kind."[56] An anti-Jewish flavor could be injected into any obscure report if the editor was so inclined.

Anti-Jewish accusations during the war ran the gamut from the ridiculous to the tragic:

All the commissary officers in General Sigel's division were dishonest Jews, making fortunes by fraud.[57]

Jews were buying up commissions and living in luxury in Washington.[58]

If a non-Jew was engaged in disloyal activities, it was only because "he was made a tool of by his friends of the Hebrew faith."[59]

The Jews favored the draft; therefore they suffered more severely than others from the New York draft riots in July, 1863.[60]

The Jews were prepared to "crucify Abraham Lincoln" as they had "crucified the Savior."[61]

Columbia, South Carolina, had been set afire by Jews.[62]

Some of the most prominent persons in the Union were imbued with prejudice against the Jews. One of these was Major General Benjamin F. Butler of Massachusetts, conniving careerist and political opportunist of major proportions, who was given the title of "Beast" by the Confederacy for his severity during the early military occupation of New Orleans. One of his better-known victims in New Orleans was Mrs. Philip Phillips, wife of the Alabama Congressman, a fire-eating secessionist in skirts. Butler ordered her to be imprisoned on Ship Island for months because:

> . . . having been once imprisoned for her traitorous proclivities and acts at Washington, and released by the clemency of the Government, and having been found training her children to spit on officers of the United States, for which act of one of those children both her husband and herself apologized and were again forgiven, [she] is now found on the balcony of her house during the passage of the funeral procession of Lieut. DeKay, laughing and mocking at his remains, and upon being inquired of by the Commanding General if this fact were so, contemptuously replies, "I was in good spirits that day."[63]

The war which Butler waged upon this Jewess and other Southern women made him the Confederacy's "Public Enemy Number One," with a price upon his head.

The Jews found reason to take issue with him in early 1864, when, as the commanding officer at Fortress Monroe, Va., he released a report announcing the capture of "150 rebels, 90 mules, 60 contrabands [Negroes] and 5 Jews."[64] The obviously intentional stratification which evaluated Jews lower than rebels and mules and slaves had a remarkable touch of maliciousness about it. Lincoln laughed at the report, because he thought it was a joke.[65] But it was not funny to Jews. One of the Jewish editors, Myer S. Isaacs, curbed his anger and wrote Butler a moderate, patient letter of protest, calling the unfairness to his attention. Isaacs and Butler then engaged in a protracted correspondence. The General revealed the extent to which he had imbibed prejudicial conceptions of the Jews. They were a tightly-knit and highly-organized nation who set themselves apart and defended themselves against others even when one of their group was wrong. They were all "traders, merchants, and bankers." He said that the only Jews he ever knew had "been principally engaged in the occupations [i.e. smuggling] which caused the capture which has occasioned this correspondence."[66] They were supporting the Confederacy with whole heart—"two of them certainly are in the Confederate Cabinet."

Isaacs wondered who the Cabinet officers were . . . the progenitor of "the tribe of Benjamin, the Jewish Secretary of State," as Butler referred to him in another connection;[67] and then a highly inaccurate report: "I refer to Mr. Memminger as the other member of the Confederate Cabinet. I have been informed that Mr. Mallory is also of the Jewish faith or nationality."[68] It was apparent that Butler was one of those who, without further investigation, adopt any rumors which support their prejudices.

Butler ultimately apologized for the dispatch which had provoked the correspondence, and thanked Isaacs for the bird's-eye-view of contemporary Jewish life which he wrote for his information and which has become a classic of its kind.[69] He also apologized to Simon Wolf, who had shown the dispatch to Lincoln and then went to see Butler in person. The General had written Isaacs, in his first letter, that "since my attention has been drawn to it by your comments, and others of the press, I really do not see any reason for changing the phrase." But he apparently gave Wolf another story: "He, like so many other generals who have made mistakes, claimed that he knew nothing of the message, that it had been sent by a subordinate, and that he would have the error corrected at once."[70]

But it was too late to change the references to Jews in the Butler-sanctioned *History of the Administration of the Department of the Gulf in the Year 1862* which James Parton wrote in his behalf. There Butler was quoted as saying that "the most active agents and most effective supporters [of the Confederacy], have been the same quasi-foreign houses, mostly Jews, and other correspondents, principally in Havana and Nassau, who all deserve at the hands of the Government what is due to the Jew Benjamin, Slidell, Mallory, and Floyd." He also had harsh words for J.P. Benjamin's brother-in-law, whom he called "a Jew famed for a bargain."[71] In his diary and reminiscences, published in 1892, Butler made further references to Jews. Curbstone transactions in Confederate money had been legalized in New Orleans because Butler hoped to get reliable information from the variations in price. Those who traded in the paper money, he said, "were principally Jews, and as Benjamin, the Confederate Secretary of State, was a Jew, and his brother-in-law was a broker, I supposed that there were some of the Jew brokers who would get true intelligence from Richmond."[72] In a letter to Secretary of War Stanton, Butler wrote,

. . . is the profitableness of the investment to be permitted to be alleged as a sufficient apology for aiding the rebellion by money and arms? If so, all their army contractors, principally Jews, should be held blameless, for they have made immense fortunes by the war. Indeed, I suppose another Jew—one Judas—thought his investment in the thirty pieces of silver was a profitable one, until the penalty of treachery reached him.[73]

This was in connection with a tax on brokerage firms which he instituted on July 4, 1862. It was always a good argument for a policy to predict that it would prevent Jews from making too much money!

Butler may even have activated his prejudice to the extent of discriminating against those Jews who fell into his hands at Fortress Monroe. *The Jewish Record* of New York thought so, and reported that Butler had said "he could suck the blood of every Jew, and he will detain every Jew as long as he can." The editor of the *Record* said he was afraid to publish details of Butler's mistreatment of Jewish prisoners because it would only give him a chance to "increase his severities" against them.[74] After he was transferred from the post, the *Record* said it hoped that certain Jews who had been confined in prison for over a year, at his orders, would finally have a trial or at least a hearing so that they would discover the reason for their arrest.[75] President Lincoln was convinced that at least one of them, Abraham Samuels, had not been given a fair hearing at Fortress Monroe, and instructed Butler to give him an opportunity to prove that he was not a Confederate agent. Samuels defended himself so ably that Lincoln ordered his unconditional release.[76]

It would be idle to speculate on the reasons for Butler's prejudice against the Jews. Perhaps part of the explanation, however, is to be found in the fact that he himself had an unsavory reputation: he was the one General who was never able to free himself of the suspicion of using his power to amass a fortune for himself, his family, and his intimate friends, while he controlled New Orleans with an iron fist.[77]

It remains only to be recorded that, being a typical politician, when the Jews of Boston asked him to give an address at a huge Hebrew Fair for charity in 1877, General Butler was pleased to accept the invitation, and in his address paid glowing tribute to the noble character of the Jewish people![78]

Fitting company for Benjamin F. Butler in terms of character, temperament, and the number of enemies he made during his lifetime, was another Union leader possessed of a nickname: "Parson" William Ganaway Brownlow of eastern Tennessee. A Methodist circuit-rider in his early years, later a staunchly partisan newspaper editor and publisher, Brownlow was a vociferous propagandist for causes all his life.[79] In 1856, he set the seal to a vigorous Know-Nothing crusade against Catholics and aliens in editorials and speeches with the publication of a book titled at length, in the style of the day, *Americanism Contrasted with Foreignism, Romanism, and Bogus Democracy, in the Light of Reason, History, and Scriptures; in which Certain Demagogues in Tennessee and elsewhere, are Shown up in their true Colors.* It was a revelation of a man goaded to hatred. Less a religious zealot than a fanatic who latched his neurosis on to a religious vehicle, more a demagogue than an orator, more a propagandist than a journalist, Brownlow was a dangerous enemy for anyone to make, whether it was the editors of the opposition, the Baptists and Presbyterians, or Andrew Johnson.

A man like Brownlow whose career was erected on hatreds could not avoid being a Jew-hater. His *Knoxville Whig* demonstrated it when Congress, in February 1860, for the first time invited a rabbi to open a House session with prayer. That a Jew, a member of "the people that killed Christ," should pray for the national welfare was too much for the "Parson" to bear. "It was not until an old *Jewish Rabbi, Father* Raphael, by invitation of the *Democracy,* opened the proceedings of the House with prayer, that they were enabled to organize, by the election of Pennington. [When] they called into their aid one of the *murderers of Christ*, their hearts and minds were prepared for anything . . . Let *Jews* and *Catholics* pray for Democrats, if you want the prayers to have effect," he wrote.[80] The readers of the *Whig* were quite accustomed to the "Parson's" opinions about the Jews,[81] and might almost have predicted that he would take Judah P. Benjamin's high status in the Confederate Government most personally.

When Tennessee seceded from the Union, Brownlow was one of the organizers of anti-Confederate forces in the Tennessee highlands. The resistance movement of which he was a leader was like a thorn in the flesh of the Confederacy, and Benjamin, as Secretary of War, was determined to see it quelled. Confederate troops moved in and Brownlow was one of those captured. Instead of having Brownlow imprisoned or executed as a traitor, Benjamin preferred not to add his name to the Union martyrology, and gave orders to have him sent North.[82] It was an act of clemency as well as statesmanship, but Brownlow counted his arrest and exile a score to settle with Benjamin.[83]

Once he had reached Union territory, he became a national hero and made a triumphal tour of the North. Everywhere he spoke he took a poke at "the little Jew" who had persecuted and oppressed him. The North virtually lionized him and he capitalized on his popularity by writing a book about his experiences. It was known as *Parson Brownlow's Book*, its real title being *Sketches of the Rise, Progress, and Decline of Secession; with a Narrative of Personal Adventures among the Rebels*. In that book he continued his campaign against Benjamin, repeating the tale about his expulsion from Yale for stealing, and denouncing him as the leading enemy of the Union.[84] In another book which he published some time later, he said that he had expected "no more mercy from [Benjamin] than was shown by his illustrious predecessors towards Jesus Christ,"[85] and in one of his speeches he said that Benjamin had "threatened to hang [me] with or without evidence. My only wonder was that he did not threaten to crucify me."[86]

One who was willing to say of Southern clergymen that "a more unmitigated, God-forsaken set of scoundrels do not live than the preachers of the Gospel down South,"[87] could not be expected to use restraint in discussing the Jews. When Grant issued his General Order Number Eleven, Brownlow was one of the few public figures who actually applauded. After a long, tongue-in-cheek pretense at being free of prejudice against any group of individuals, in a letter to the *Cincinnati Daily Times*,[88] Brownlow set his justification of Grant on record: "It is useless to disguise the fact that nineteen out of every twenty cases brought to light, of all this smuggling, turns out to be the work of certain *circumcized Hebrews*." Not as content as General Grant with making generalizations, the "Parson" proceeded to enumerate names and cases—but these "facts" were promptly investigated by a Cincinnati Jew who wrote to the *Times* six days later that the two Jews Brownlow mentioned were not doing business in Knoxville, but in Louisville and New York, and "that of the several boxes, marked 'Sanitary Stores', that have been lately seized by our authorities and confiscated, not one is, nor ever has been claimed as the property of certain *circumcized Hebrews*."[89] Brownlow had caught a tartar!

It would be pointless to attempt to accumulate a list of all those persons who expressed unfavorable opinions of the Jews, but it is essential that we understand how widespread and common those expressions were among individuals who were high in authority and influence.

Senator Henry Wilson of Massachusetts, an abolitionist Republican, had achieved office by way of the Know-Nothing agitation against aliens and Catholics. He later disclaimed any positive allegiance to the prejudiced principles of the party, but the fact remains that, when he withdrew, it was on account of the slavery issue, not on account of anti-alienism.[90] This background of political affiliation may explain the ease with which Wilson attacked Judah P. Benjamin, as a Jew, in the Senate, after the Louisiana Senator's famous farewell speech:

> His bearing, the tone of his voice, his words, all gave evidence that the spark of patriotism, if it ever existed, was extinct in his bosom; that his heart was in this foul and wicked plot to dismember the Union, to overthrow the government of his adopted country, which gives equality of rights even to *that race that stoned prophets and crucified the Redeemer of the world.*[91]

Wilson spoke of Jews in derogatory terms again a year later, when he said in a Senatorial debate on fiscal measures that "you will have every curbstone Jew broker . . . and the class of men who fatten upon public calamity . . . using all their influence to depreciate the credit of the government." The entire question of the nation's financial structure was, to him, "a contest between those curbstone brokers, the Jew brokers, the money-changers, and the men who speculate in stocks, and the productive, toiling men of the country."[92] Here again the appeal to prejudice was utilized as a weapon in debate, a diverting tactic to win the opposition.

On the evening of February 28, 1861, Charles Francis Adams, of the distinguished Boston family, was chatting with Senator Andrew Johnson, later to become the seventeenth President of the United States. Johnson discoursed on many subjects, and finally came around to two of his Senatorial colleagues:

> He [writes Adams] was amusingly severe over the secession of Florida. "There's that Yulee," he said, "miserable little cuss! I remember him in the House—the contemptible little Jew—standing there and begging us—yes! begging us to let Florida in as a State. Well! we let her in, and took care of her, and fought her Indians; and now that despicable little beggar stands up in the Senate and talks about *her* rights." Towards Jews, he evidently felt a strong aversion; for, after finishing with Yulee he began on Benjamin, exclaiming: "There's another Jew—that miserable Benjamin! He looks on a country and a government as he would on a suit of old clothes. He sold out the old one; and he would sell out the new if he could in so doing make two or three millions!"[93]

Thirteen years later ex-President Johnson was an honored guest at the dedication of the new synagogue in Nashville, Tenn. He rode in a carriage with Rabbi Kalisch of the Nashville congregation, and Rabbi Isaac M. Wise, and was accompanied by them to the pulpit. After the two dedicatory addresses, the chairman introduced him to the assemblage. He said he would not take much of their time, according to the report in the *Nashville Republican Banner*, because they had already heard two very stimulating speeches. "No one felt a deeper interest in the success and prosperity of them and their temple than he did. He hoped that it would ever remain a monument to the industry, prosperity, and welfare of the Jewish citizens of Nashville. He thanked them for their attention and retired amidst applause."[94] The thought never entered Johnson's mind that these people whom he was complimenting and congratulating were the people who had produced Yulee and Benjamin.

One of the most distrusted men in Washington was Colonel LaFayette C. Baker, chief of the Detective Bureau of the War Department, the secret service. Those who knew him pictured him as a cruel and ruthless man. He was notorious for his disregard of civil liberties and was flatly accused of gaining personal profit from the persecution of the innocent and the protection of the guilty.[95]

Jews were surely not alone or unique in suffering hurt at the hands of this man, but his anti-Jewish feelings were apparent in the narratives of Jewish cases in the boastful book he wrote about his war experiences. He tells, for instance, of the capture of three men, one a Jew, who had been running military goods from Baltimore to the Confederacy. He seems to applaud when one of them turns to the Jew and blames him for their capture. "You're a ——— Jew, and it's you who have brought all this trouble on me."[96] And then later, Baker's relish at the Jew's discomfiture is obvious: "The Israelite was so played upon that he is not yet aware of the enemies who ruined him."[97] Prejudice and a touch of sadism. . .

Baker was the man who had Simon Wolf arrested because he was a member of the B'nai B'rith, which Baker was convinced was "a disloyal organization, which has its ramifications in the South . . . [and] is helping the traitors." Wolf was acting as attorney for a number of Southern Jews arrested in Washington on the charge of spying for the Confederacy, and his membership in the Jewish fraternal order was the clinching argument against his loyalty, to Baker's way of thinking. It took Secretary Stanton's personal intercession to free Wolf from arrest.[98]

The expression of prejudice against the Jews in so many quarters did not go entirely unchallenged. Some non-Jews had a clear vision of the meaning of democratic equality. Not every statement was answered; there were dozens of inflammatory libels for every editorial in the press which defended the Jews—but more than a few editors and officers in high places set themselves against the anti-Jewish formulas of the day.

When the AP writer in New Orleans urged that the Jews of the South be "exterminated," both the *Commercial* and *Daily Times* of Cincinnati called attention to the flagrant prejudice of the writer, insisted that most Jews were loyal and law-abiding, and called for a halt to Jew-baiting. The *Cincinnati Enquirer* went one step further and ventured to suggest that the report must have been "planted" by jealous Yankee traders who had been out-smarted by Jews in New Orleans and took out their resentment in this way.[99]

Butler may have been prejudiced against the Jews; his successor, General N.P. Banks, was not. Rabbi Bernard Illowy of New Orleans established friendly relationships with the General, and was successful in securing a hearing for Jews who did not feel able to speak for themselves. The rabbi's son, Henry, recalls that

> . . . I was kept busy day by day writing applications and recommendations for poor peddlers for relief from the various forms of taxes, state, city and national that were exacted at the time. So numerous were these applications that a collector of one of these taxes wrote to my father to be good enough and not send him any more applications or supplications, but to just indorse his name on the notice and the party would not be troubled any more.

Rabbi Illowy once tried for weeks to see the General in an effort to secure a pardon for a Jew whom Butler had sentenced to six years in prison. When he finally did see the General and told him how long it had taken to do so, "the General turned to his orderly, and directed him to instruct the men at once, that no matter at what time the Rabbi came, he was to be admitted immediately and without ceremony." The Jew had been sentenced for receiving stolen property, but still insisted he had not known the nature of the item he bought; he was freed by Banks because of Illowy's intercession. This General did not assume that every Jew was a thief.[100]

Nor did the *Baltimore Clipper* see eye to eye with anti-Jewish propaganda. When "Parson" Brownlow visited that city on his long speaking tour, the editor of the *Clipper* gave him a verbal whipping:

> Parson Brownlow is not generally very choice in his language . . . but it is in extreme bad taste, and obnoxious to the censure [*sic*] of every right-minded man, thus to identify a great religious and national people with such a consummate rogue and hangman as this Benjamin . . .[101]

It was, obviously, not out of respect for the Confederate Secretary of War that the editor criticized Brownlow!

The "Parson's" prejudice was rejected again some years later by the *Memphis Bulletin* which said that a letter which Brownlow had written against the Jews was "a coarse and vulgar vituperation, narrow-minded, illiberal, unjust and uncalled for, containing misstatements of fact, undignified abuse, and insidious attacks upon the liberty of conscience, and showing a worldly, ungodly ambition in conspiring against the best interest of the State, entered into to advance his own schemes of political ambition and power. . . ."[102] Brownlow was *persona non grata* with the *Bulletin* anyway, but his anti-Jewish prejudice gave the paper another opportunity to subject him to public censure.

When the *American Flag* of San Francisco set out on its campaign to convince the public of the disloyalty of Jews to the Union, various California newspapers threw down the gauntlet to the *Flag*. The *Placerville News* said: "We suggest to the *Flag* that such a course may do in the dominions of King Jeff, but is hardly the thing in a civilized community. The day for unreasoning bigotry has gone by."[103] The *Maysville Appeal* said that the talk about "disloyal Jews, disloyal Catholics, and disloyal Irishmen," "only impl[ies] prejudice and hatred to Jews, Catholics, and Irishmen. . . To cry 'disloyal farmers' or 'traitor boot-blacks' and 'traitor tailors,' would be as intelligible . . . as to use the terms 'disloyal Irishmen' or 'traitor Jews.' "[104] The *San Francisco Morning Call* conveyed good logic in its editorial on "Religion and Patriotism":

> . . . What is there in the faith of the Hebrew to make him a loyalist or a rebel? . . . And how does it happen that some of the most ardent Unionists, both at the South and North, may be found in citizens of Hebrew faith, while Benjamin and others of the same religious creed are aiders of Rebellion? It is locality, and local institutions and teachings, the influence of surroundings, habits and tone of the community, which chiefly govern . . . In this country there can be no classification of patriotism or treason, upon the basis of sectarian creeds. To attempt doing so would be as unjust as unphilosophical and neither likely to aid religion nor the causes of the Union.[105]

The *Alta California* suggested that the anti-Jewish campaign of the *American Flag* was a scheme to sap away the strength of the Union party:

> The only effectual method of reducing the strength of the Union Party in California is by making religious intolerance part of its creed. It is not pretended that there is anything in the Bible, in the writings of the rabbis, or in the proceeding of the synagogues, which renders loyalty to the Government impossible . . . But, throughout the whole proceeding, common sense is repudiated . . . The object is to weaken the Union Party.[106]

The reaction of these California editors was an exception to the general run of newspaper opinion. In no other section of the Union was bigotry so generally condemned.

But isolated papers did object. In Washington, the *Daily Times* ran an editorial on "Assailing Nationalities," identifying anti-Jewish prejudice as a legacy of the old Know-Nothing party, and defending the Jews against the accusations of the rabid bigots.[107] In Springfield, Ill., the *Daily Illinois State Journal* insisted that "the Jews of this country have shown their full share of patriotism since the war began," and cited military statistics in proof of this contention.[108] In Franklin, Ind., the *Herald* criticized the mayor for calling only on Christians to observe the October 1861 Fast Day. "The Israelites here," said the *Herald's* editor, "as well as elsewhere, are industrious and peaceable citizens, their loyalty to this government has never been questioned, and why our Mayor should give them the cold shoulder is more than we can say . . ."[109] On several occasions, editorials of protest in Jewish periodicals were reprinted in the daily press. The *Boston Post* quoted at length from Isaac M. Wise's editorial answer to the *Boston Transcript's* discourse on Yulee, Benjamin, and Mordecai;[110] and the *Times* and *Herald* of New York as well as other papers, reprinted the Butler-Isaacs correspondence.[111] Said the *Times:*

> We admit, as Christians, that too many of us are in the thoughtless habit of alluding, quite as opprobriously as General Butler, to "Jews," as though we were speaking of a nationality, not of a religious denomination, and Mr. Isaacs has therefore given us all a salutary lesson which it would be well for us, as just persons, to remember."[112]

There *were* some editors who were open-minded enough to examine the tenor of the times and find it contrary to the ideals of the nation.

It is entirely possible that the vast majority of Americans, journalists and others, did not share the prejudices against the Jews—but those who registered their protest were in the minority. The Jews, of course, were disappointed that so few rose to their defense. They wanted no praise, no soft-soaping, no honorific tributes; they knew that there were Jews who brought ill repute to the people's name; but they expected the American people to judge them as individuals, and not as a class apart. If the majority of public officials and journalists would not come to their active defense, they would have to defend themselves. This was not an age for ostrich attitudes towards prejudice. The Jews of the 1860s were not so fearful or insecure that they were afraid to defend themselves. Silence in the face of so many libelous attacks could only be interpreted as assent. They, therefore, answered their slanderers vigorously, but with dignity and logic.

The Jewish newspapers led the fight and acted as clearing-houses of information. Jews all over the country sent clippings and documents to the editors; and the editors promptly printed the data and analyzed it. It was important to know who and what and where. In many cases, the editors sent copies of these issues to the guilty ones, or letters of protest. The Butler-Isaacs correspondence is an example of this type of counter-attack, where a Jewish editor was not content to write editorials but challenged a bigot to stand before the public with whatever evidence he had at his command.

A similar tactic was employed by Simon Wolf when he conferred with Butler in person, and by the editor of the *Messenger* when he went to see the staff of the *New York World* to discuss a specific case of libel and left with the assurance that the vilification would not continue.[113] When the *Cincinnati Enquirer* reported, on October 20, 1861, that a "combination of Jewish clothing houses in this city" had been organized "to take advantage of the pressing necessity of our Western soldiers for blankets, etc.," the Jews of Cincinnati insisted that a reporter interview the businessmen involved, examine their records, and give an unbiased version of the facts. The *Enquirer* printed a retraction, admitting that its information had been unreliable. It said that one firm "had made contracts at an early period in the war, when prices were down, and were now uncomplainingly living up to them, since prices had materially raised. [The owner's] figures were sufficient assurance of his truthfulness."[114]

Sometimes there were protest meetings, as in New York, Cincinnati, and St. Louis, during the heat of the Grant affair, or in Washington, when the Washington Hebrew Congregation sent a resolution to Senator Wilson condemning his ungenerous statement in the Senate about Jewish brokers.[115]

But Jews could not spend all their time running to newspaper offices, or attending meetings of protest. Moreover, most of the accusations were so general that little or no evidence could be adduced to prove the Jewish contention that they were false. Josiah Cohen of Pittsburgh thought that concrete evidence of patriotism on the part of the Jews might dispel the fog of propaganda. Said Professor Cohen at a meeting of Pittsburgh Jews for the benefit of the Sanitary Commission:

Let us prove, by our liberality here this evening, that the Jewish heart beats as strongly in favor of the restoration of the Union as any of America's other sons. Let us prove that, in spite of the rumored lethargy on the part of the Israelites, we are invoking every means in our power to advance the cause of our country; and when the veil of prejudice, which hides our true character, shall be torn from the eyes of those who would malign us, then they will find that Israelites, forgetting their creed in their patriotism, unmindful of slander in their loyal efforts, are as anxious and earnest in their efforts in behalf of the Union as those of any other creed . . .[116]

These sentiments were expressed frequently at Jewish organizational meetings and synagogue services; many Jews believed that, if they participated in patriotic activities, the non-Jews would have to recognize their claims to equality.

One idea which was consistently advanced for combatting anti-Jewish propaganda was the collection of statistical data about the service of Jews in the Army. As early as 1862, an Indianapolis Jew wrote a letter to *The Israelite* in favor of such a counter-propaganda move:

It is only a few days ago, that a gentleman mentioned incidentally to me that he thought that there were very few Jews in the Army, for, said he, "he never heard of none!" I replied that in my opinion, there had not a single regiment left the state of Indiana, but some Israelites can be found in any of them, and to my positive knowledge, there were some six Jewish soldiers in the 11th Indiana Regiment for the three months service. We ought to be able to speak with certainty upon these points, it would be to our credit, and would silence the calumnies . . .

So he offered the suggestion that Jews in various cities send to *The Israelite* as much information as they had about the war service of Jews.[117] All of the Jewish periodicals, particularly *The Jewish Record* of New York, published lists of Jewish soldiers and casualties. But the effort was so desultory and unorganized that it could not be accurate or conclusive. In 1865 the Executive Committee of the Board of Delegates of American Israelites recommended that "a committee of three be appointed to draft a suitable circular to be sent to the President of each congregation throughout the United States requesting him to ascertain the names and history of those who have left their home for the field and their fate."[118] But nothing came of this suggestion, nor of Isaac M. Wise's far-fetched scheme in 1868 for Jewish communities to "have every dead soldier exhumed and buried in our cemeteries, and let the monuments to the deceased Soldiers of our persuasion put to shame all those who slandered the Jews in a dangerous and excitable time." It was not actually until J.M. Rogers wrote a letter to the *North American Review* in 1891, asserting that he had never met a Jew in uniform during the Civil War, or heard of one afterwards, and challenging Jews "to give the names of the regiments they condescended to accept service in,"[119] that Simon Wolf belatedly attempted to gather whatever statistics were still available and published his results in a book which listed the names of 7038 Jews who had served in the Union and Confederate forces, together with as many particulars as he could unearth.[120]

But all this Jewish defense was beside the point. No matter how much Jews protested, actually, they did not touch the root of the matter. It was all very well for them to plead, as did Isaac Mayer Wise:

> Our sons enlisted in the Army, our daughters sew and knit for the wounded soldiers and their poor families, our capitalists spend freely, our hospitals are thrown open to the sick soldiers of all creeds, our merchants represented at every benevolent association contribute largely to the wealth and prosperity of the cities, give bread and employment to thousands; we keep from politics, gambling houses, public-offices, penitentiaries, and newspaper publications— what else must we do to heal these petty scribblers from their mad prejudice?[121]

And Isaac Leeser:

> During the continuance of the unfortunate war which desolates the South of the Union and brings mourning and distress to almost every household at the North, a spirit of intolerance has gradually been developed which seeks to wreak its spite on our defenseless heads . . . Newspapers have aided some military satraps to spread a spirit of personal dislike against us . . . No doubt some worthless creatures who were born Jews have done unworthy things during the war; they may have smuggled on both sides, been spies for everyone who would pay them, and thus disgraced by their shameful conduct the noble name of Israel. But we venture to assert that in all the dealings which the Government has had with Jews, they have acted on the whole as honorably as the same class of other persuasions. In the ranks, many of our brethren have enlisted, and many have met their death . . . Even since we commenced writing this article a lonely widow with her little orphan boy in her arms, has applied to us for aid, her soldier husband having died in Virginia after serving nearly the full term of his enlistment. Everywhere in the hospitals the maimed and sick of our faith are found . . . Is it therefore fair that political journals should hold us up as a class to public odium? . . .[122]

But they knew deep within their hearts that it would do little or no good. All they could do was to pray for a speedy end of hostilities and a return to a more peaceful life for the nation as a whole. They knew that there had been almost no public vilification of the Jews before the war; they could only hope there would be none after it. Only a removal of the causes of economic, social, and personal tension, it appeared, could deliver the Jews from such irrational prejudices as were directed against them during the tumultuous war years.

II. CONFEDERATE VERSION

There was a certain historical symbolism in the fact that the leading Union general issued his Order No. 11 in Southern territory: the same psychological, social, economic, and political factors which brought latent prejudices against Jews into the open in the North were creating a similar pattern of scapegoatism in the Confederacy. Economic tensions, personal fears and frustrations, and mass passions required an outlet and a victim in the South just as in the North.

Additional social factors peculiar to life in the South tended to strengthen and heighten the reaction to Jews: a general dislike of all aliens and foreigners which, during the War, created the legend that the Union Army was a band of German and Irish hirelings and mercenaries, while the Confederate Army was said to be exclusively native;[123] a wide-spread suspicion of the merchant and storekeeper, typical of a society dominated by the plantation owner and farmer; a deeper commitment than existed in the North to fundamentalist "Bible" Christianity; the intensified emotional depression as the War dragged on from year to year and Confederate chances for victory became more slight with each passing month. Granted an original suspicion and dislike of the Jew before the War, the four-year-long travail of the Confederacy was certain to emphasize it.

Two examples have been preserved of discrimination against Jews in the military forces. Captain R.E. Park tells us that his Colonel was so prejudiced against Jews that he attempted to block the promotion of Captain Adolph Proskauer of Mobile, Ala. Proskauer insisted on taking an examination in military strategy and discipline so that he might be able to demonstrate his qualifications. The Colonel agreed, but, according to Captain Park, instructed the Committee of Examiners to make the test as difficult as they could. Let Captain Park continue his story:

> During the day of the examination there was an unusual interest felt by the officers of the camp, and especially by the Colonel. Late in the afternoon, after an all-day examination had been concluded, one of the officers rode rapidly up to Col. Pickens' headquarters and in reply to an anxious inquiry, was told that the Committee had done all they could to defeat Capt. Proskauer, but that after an examination [in] squad drill, in company drill, in regimental drill, in brigade drill, in drill by echelon, and in the army movements as suggested in Jomini's tactics, Captain Proskauer did not fail to answer promptly and accurately every question. The General [chairman of the Examining Board] added, "he knows more about tactics than any of the Examining Committee, and we were forced to recommend his promotion.[124]

When a Jewish Colonel was assigned to a Texas regiment, newly arrived in Virginia, the enlisted men did not attempt to hide their feelings. Two said in voices loud enough for all to hear: "What? What is it? Is it a man, a fish or a bird?" "Of course it is a man, don't you see his legs." The Colonel swallowed his pride. But when he found, the next day, that his horse's tail had been cut off, he threw up his hands at an impossible task and left forthwith. His departure was a signal for a regimental celebration.[125]

If a Jewish officer would have difficulty, what could a Jewish cabinet member expect? Judah P. Benjamin was a popular target all through the war, in the Confederacy as in the North. Those who disliked all Jews took especial pleasure in being able to blame him for all the problems of the Confederacy, its defeats in the military sphere while he was Secretary of War, and its failures in diplomacy while he was Secretary of State.[126] A citizen of North Carolina swore that "all the distresses of the people were owing to a Nero-like despotism, originating in the brain of Benjamin, the Jew."[127] A writer to the *Richmond Enquirer* believed it blasphemous for a Jew to hold so high an office as that of Secretary of State, and thought that the prayers of the Confederacy would have more effect if Benjamin were dismissed from the cabinet.[128] A Confederate Brigadier General and member of the Provisional Congress, Thomas R.R. Cobb of Georgia, said of him: "A grander rascal than this Jew Benjamin does not exist in the Confederacy, and I am not particular in concealing my opinion of him."[129] A Tennessean denounced him as the "Judas Iscariot Benjamin" of the Confederacy.[130] A man from Virginia was heard to assail President Jefferson Davis in violent language, "and the sole offense alleged against him was that he had appointed one Jew a member of his cabinet."[131] These were only a few of the recorded denunciations of Benjamin in which his Jewish origin played a large role. Popular and Congressional disfavor seemed to pursue Benjamin more than any other Confederate official, and it was undoubtedly his Jewishness which made him so vulnerable. But it is to be counted to the everlasting credit of President Davis that he steadfastly refused to sacrifice Benjamin's administrative talent as a sop to prejudice, and that he retained his Jewish friend and confidant as a trusted lieutenant all through his service as the Confederate chief of government. It was inevitable, but nonetheless sad and disheartening, that under the stress of war the public should utterly forget Benjamin's record as a loyal servant of the South in state and national affairs.

Prejudice against Jews was revealed most frequently in connection with the economic life of the Confederacy, and here again Benjamin's Jewish origin was a feature of the attacks. Anti-Jewish mythology had always described the Jew as grasping, thievish, and unscrupulous in business practices; now, in a period of severe economic crisis, the old canard appeared with renewed vigor. A sizable number of references in contemporary diaries and memoirs, as well as in the columns of Confederate newspapers, attests to the widespread belief that Jews were the chief source of the Confederacy's economic troubles.[132] "Extortion" was the word commonly applied by citizens of the Southern states to the high prices charged by merchants and shopkeepers, and it was alleged that Jews were the chief "extortionists."

In the Confederate House of Representatives, during a heated debate on January 14, 1863, concerning the question of drafting foreigners into military service, Congressman Henry S. Foote of Tennessee made a major pronouncement on this subject. The Jews had flooded the country, he said, and controlled at least nine-tenths of the business of the land. They were engaging in all kinds of illegal trade with the enemy without any official hindrance. Why was this permitted to continue? Because, he said mysteriously, the Jews had been invited to come to the Confederacy "by official permission" and were under official protection. Here he was obviously alluding to Judah P. Benjamin, whose appointment to high office always irritated him. He was not yet prepared, he said, to make any specific charges, but would continue gathering evidence, and he hoped eventually to be in a position to expose the powerful influence which was transferring all of Southern commerce to the hands of "foreign Jews." He concluded by quoting a friend of his who had said that "if the present state of things were to continue, the end of the war would probably find nearly all the property of the Confederacy in the hands of Jewish Shylocks."[133]

Foote never made good his threat to expose Benjamin, nor did he ever produce any statistics to bear out his contentions, but three months later he was still calling the attention of his fellow Congressmen and of the public to the deplorable condition of affairs. "Foreign Jews," he stated, "were scattered all over the country, under official protection, engaged in trade to the exclusion of our own citizens, undermining our currency." He predicted that "by the close of the war they would have the control of all the cotton and tobacco."[134]

Foote was not the only Confederate Congressman to speak of the Jews in such terms. On various occasions, Chilton of Alabama,[135] Miles of South Carolina,[136] and Hilton of Florida, voiced similar sentiments. Hilton said that the Jews swarmed all over the country, like locusts, eating up its resources and monopolizing its trade. The only way to control them was to draft them into the army. There was really no shortage of goods; demand had not created the high prices. It was "competition among buyers for the purpose of extortion," which was responsible for the rising cost of living! Hilton gave an example of Jewish persistence: a blockade-runner had landed on the Florida coast and its cargo was confiscated by the authorities, but somehow the Jews had heard about it and "at least one hundred" of them "flocked there, led even to this remote point by the scent of gain, and they had to be driven back actually at the point of the bayonet."[137]

John Beauchamps Jones, a clerk in the Confederate War Department, was another who attributed the inflation to Jewish extortioners and speculators. In his diary, which has become familiar to students of social and economic conditions in war-time Richmond, Jones indulged in almost daily tirades against the Jewish merchants. During a critical military campaign in 1862, for instance, he noted that the people of the capital showed little interest in the course of events. The Jews were, as always, busy speculating on the street corners, he said; every once in a while there would be a loud burst of laughter, "when a Jew is asked what will be the price of his shoes, etc., tomorrow." Jones believed that the Jews did not care "which side gains the day, so they gain the profits."[138] Eight days later, he summarized his feelings about them:

> The illicit trade with the United States has depleted the country of gold and placed us at the feet of the Jew extortioners. It still goes on. Mr. Seddon has granted passports to two agents of a Mr. Baumgartien—and how many others I know not. These Jews have the adroitness to carry their points. They have injured the cause more than the armies of Lincoln. Well, if we gain our independence, instead of being the vassals of the Yankees, we shall find all our wealth in the hands of the Jews. [139]

Foote's allegations against Jewish merchants in the arena of national politics had their counterpart in various local areas. In Thomasville, Ga., for instance, on August 30, 1862, a public meeting was called for the discussion of the "unpatriotic conduct" of Jewish merchants. Resolutions were passed in which "German Jews [were] denounced in unmeasured terms . . . prohibited from visiting the village, and banishing all those now resident in that place."[140] Unfortunately, there were no Jewish periodicals in the South; if there had been, they might have preserved further details of this episode. A Georgia Jew wrote, however, that denunciations of Jewish merchants were frequent in the area, and that the habit had spread from town to town throughout the state.[141] In Talbotton, the seat of Talbot County, a grand jury completed its session with a presentment referring to "the evil and unpatriotic conduct of the representatives of Jewish houses."[142] And in another Georgia town, according to a letter preserved in the Duke University Library, the wives of soldiers away with the army became so desperate that they raided Jewish stores and took whatever they wished at pistol point, accusing the Jewish merchants of speculating on the shortages and making fortunes while the men were fighting for the life of the nation.[143] These examples indicate a trend which was characteristic of many sections of the Confederacy—the Jews being held responsible for the inflation of prices and the shortages of goods—a pattern which bears a remarkable likeness to the background of the Grant Order.

That there was widespread acceptance of the alleged guilt of the Jews cannot be gainsaid. Diarists and letter-writers throughout the South attested to this. One correspondent wrote, "I should despise myself if in this time of our country's need I should do anything to put up the price of a single article of necessity. I leave that to the Jews and extortioners of whom there are unfortunately too many among us."[144] Another charged that cotton was "a favorite article with Jews, and the country swarms with them—and other speculators."[145] Frequent were the accusations that Jews were largely engaged in passing counterfeit money, running the blockade, aiding the inflation by charging outrageous prices, driving well-established "Anglo-Saxon" firms out of business by unfair competitive methods, and, in general, "batten[ing] and fatten[ing] upon speculation to the misery of the population."[146]

Natives of the South very quickly transmitted these opinions to visitors from other countries, particularly England. One writer, who called himself "An English Combatant," wrote:

> . . . The Israelites, as usual, far surpassed the Gentiles in shrewdness at the auspicious moment, and laid in stocks (procured on credit) which, in almost every instance, were retailed at rates from five hundred to one thousand per cent above ordinary prices; cash being always exacted. Many of these gentry proved unscrupulous knaves during the war; for having husbanded their goods for one or two years, and converted them into coin, if they did not decamp from the Confederacy altogether, they found a thousand and one excuses for not bearing arms . . . This is true of Hollanders generally, and of Dutch Jews almost universally . . .[147]

"An English Merchant," speaking of Charleston as a center for blockade-run goods, marveled that there seemed to be "more Jews in Charleston than . . . in Jerusalem," so thoroughly had he been indoctrinated with prejudice.[148]

That these and other descriptions of the Jews of the South were the result of prejudice, and not of a realistic consideration of the actual facts, was recognized by many who tried to be fair minded. The editor of the *Richmond Sentinel*, for instance, acknowledged the fact that "intolerant and illiberal views and prejudices" against the Jews "prevail to some extent . . . in no wise affecting their [the Jews'] individual and personal merits and character."[149] A Missionary Chaplain to the Army wrote to the *Savannah Daily Morning News* that he was saddened by the "many unfair, and, to my mind, very unjust, as well as injudicious *flings* at this part, no unimportant part, of our fellow citizens."[150] A Jew who wrote a lengthy letter of defense to a Richmond paper began his plea with these words:

> I have marked with sorrow and dismay the growing propensity in the Confederacy to denounce the Jew on all occasions and in all places. The press, the pulpit, and grave legislators, who have the destiny of a nation committed to their charge, all unite in this unholy and unjust denunciation.

Then he continued:

> That a man like Foote should habitually denounce the Jew is to be expected; he denounces everybody and every thing; his mouth is a "well spring" of

slander; and I should doubt the beauty of virtue, itself, should he chance to praise it. But that the whole press of your city (your paper excepted) should add fuel to these fires of persecutions, and should seek to direct public opinion in such foul channels, surpasses my comprehension . . .[151]

A year after the war had ended in defeat for the Confederacy, the editor of the *Augusta* (Ga.) *Sentinel,* in commenting on North Carolina's refusal to abandon the religious test for public office, defended the Jews against "the charges which we have frequently heard made by our street-corner gossipers and windy patriots, that the Israelites of the South failed to perform their duty during the recent war."[152]

So frequent and bitter were the verbal attacks on the Jews that the Rev. Maximilian J. Michelbacher, rabbi of Beth Ahabah Congregation of Richmond, delivered a public answer to them in a sermon which he preached at a Confederate Fast Day service in Fredericksburg in 1863 and which was printed in the daily papers and even found its way up North.[153] He said that accusations against Jewish merchants were so common that he could no longer keep silent. If the Jews were guilty, he said, they would find no defender in him, because he prided himself on the fact that "I always speak of your faults without fear, favor, or affection." He had investigated the conduct of Jewish merchants and was convinced that "the Israelites are not speculators nor extortioners." How could they be? The Jewish merchant specialized in rapid turnover sales, he said; the speculator made his fortune by hoarding. Besides, Jews did not deal at all in the basic commodities in which speculation was most common: "Flour, meal, wheat, corn, bacon, beef, coal and wood." For that matter, if the Jews actually were the extortioners, how could they stay in business? Wouldn't the trade go to non-Jews who were, by implication, free of all taint of profiteering? How, then, could one explain the uproar against the Jews? Michelbacher said he was prepared to assert that the condemnation of the Jews was deliberately *instigated*—"cunningly devised after the most approved mode of villainy"—to shield the real extortioner and speculator, "who deals in the miseries, life and blood of our fellow citizens," from the pent-up indignation of the Confederate populace. The "monstrous and evil thing that draws its nourishment from the heart's blood of men, women and children" was blamed on the Jews so that those who were actually guilty could escape punishment!

Was Michelbacher defending the Jews because they were his people and he had to speak out in their behalf? Or was his contention that prejudice and profit were the roots of the accusation, valid and demonstrable?

Before we can attempt to assay the evidence, a clear picture of the Southern economy must be kept in mind. Although industrialization had proceeded farther than is commonly supposed, it is nevertheless true that the South was basically an agricultural society. Its entire life and conception of life were founded on a maintenance of the slave system and the plantation standard. The section had never produced anything approaching the equivalent of its consumption of manufactured goods; imports from Europe and the North were always required to supplement local production. This need for the importation of the products of modern industry gave rise to certain significant items in the South's brief against the North: resentment against the tariff system which protected Northern industry but penalized the South; and the widespread belief that the South was being exploited only for the benefit of the Northern industrialist empire.[154]

An obvious impasse was reached with the outbreak of the war. Supplies from the North were cut off. The blockade of Southern ports by the Union Navy prevented the importation of European products. Whatever trend there had been, before the war, towards increased industrialization was necessarily channeled into the production of war materiel. The result was, of course, an instantaneous shortage of all kinds of goods, and a rapid inflation of prices. Buying agents from the larger cities scoured the interior in search of stocks which might still be unsold in the rural stores; blockade runners earned fantastic prices for cargoes taken on in the Caribbean area; illegal trade along the borders increased by leaps and bounds as smugglers risked life and liberty to get valuable merchandise across the lines.

The process of attrition had been an inevitable one. The only corrective would have been a completely authoritarian control of economic affairs by the Confederate government. Such a regime would have pegged prices, but there would still have been no safeguard against the development of a black market. Price controls could not have produced more goods.[155]

Everyone who produced or sold commodities was involved in the inflationary spiral: farmers, manufacturers, merchants, tradesmen, Jews and Gentiles, natives and foreigners, traitors and patriots. This was the way the *Macon Daily Telegraph* put it: "It is doubtful if any man in these times can pursue a speculative or money-making business consistently with his duty to his country."[156] Unless they changed their means of earning a livelihood, or entered military service, they had to participate in the economic system. Were they to blame, however, for the scarcity and the inflation? Should the responsibility not be ascribed to the fire-eaters who had assured their compatriots that the South could maintain itself militarily and industrially in peace *and in war*, that the slave system was not only an advantage to the Southern economy but that it was worth fighting for, that the South could live as an independent nation and had to fight for the right to do so? Far more guilty than the farmers and merchants were the men who led the South into secession and war without calculating fully the realistic problems of a war crisis, and the legislative and executive leaders of the Confederacy who failed to grapple with the serious economic struggle for survival on the home front.

It is not difficult to prove that, in at least a few cases, the accusations against Jews were motivated by a climate of prejudice rather than an objective consideration of the facts. We are fortunate, for instance, in possessing the memoirs of a Talbotton Jew.[157] He was Isidor Straus who was later to become one of the outstanding merchant princes of the nation. In 1862 he was seventeen years old, living with his father and family: *they were the only Jewish family in Talbotton and theirs was the only Jewish store in the county!* Isidor recalled in after days how hurt and bewildered his father had been when he was informed of the grand jury's condemnation of Jewish merchants. Lazarus Straus had believed that he had earned the respect of the fellow-townsmen, that they were fond of him and his family. But how wrong he had been. So he immediately determined to move away from a town "which had cast such a reflection on him as the only Jew living in their midst." The reaction to the announcement of his imminent departure was bizarre: his fellow citizens waited upon him in large numbers, seeking to persuade him to remain; every member of the grand jury which had issued the pronouncement called upon him; every minister in town asked him to change his mind. They assured him that there had been no intention to reflect upon *his* business ethics or *his* faith—although they now saw that it was possible for their action to be so interpreted! Nevertheless, the Straus family moved on to Columbus, Ga. One is moved to pity and compassion for these folk who were so possessed by prejudice that they could not anticipate Lazarus Straus' reaction to their denunciation of his people.

Congressman Foote, on the other hand, does not deserve pity. It was generally known that he disliked Jews and took advantage of every opportunity to vent his hatred upon them, no matter how flimsy the evidence. On January 7, 1864, for instance, the *Daily Richmond Examiner* printed a rumor that an unnamed Congressman had obtained passports out of the Confederacy for three Jews.[158] According to the report, he had been paid three thousand dollars for his helpfulness. That very morning, Foote jumped to the floor and demanded the appointment of a committee to investigate the charges and to bring the culprits to the bar of justice. He wished it understood in advance that he had no desire to become a member of the committee because, said a newspaper report, "many members thought him already too fond of ferreting out abuses and frauds." The resolution was adopted and the committee appointed forthwith.[159] Its members reported back to the House on January 25. They had found "nothing to sustain the charge." When they had asked the editor of the *Examiner* for evidence, he told them a long, involved story. The article had originally been written by one of his reporters, but when he asked the reporter for the evidence and became convinced by his silence that there was no truth to the story, he had forbidden its publication. Some slip-up had occurred, however, and the article found its way into print. He was still unable to furnish any proof, and said that he "knew nothing of the truth of it."[160]

The House had not been interested, of course, in investigating a story about three Jews; the purpose of the committee was to ascertain the truth of a report about a Representative's dishonesty. Foote never suggested that a committee be appointed to investigate any of his other charges against Jews, nor did the House ever trouble itself to do so. This was the only investigation which was ever ordered to track a rumor about Jews to its source—and it proved to be without foundation.

It is interesting to note in passing the contrasting tone of the Confederate loyalties of Congressman Foote and the Jew he disliked so deeply, Secretary Benjamin. The latter fled the Confederacy at the very last, after Lee's surrender and the transfer of the capital from Richmond, with the vow never to be taken alive by the Union forces. He made good his pledge and established a new life in England. Foote's political career reached its zenith on February 27, 1865, when he was expelled from the Confederate House of Representatives for deserting the Stars and Bars and crossing the lines to the Union.[161]

The appointment of the investigating committee, at Foote's behest, was grist for J.B. Jones' mill. It earned a typical flourish against the Jews in his diary.[162] But he did not feel it necessary to mention the committee's report which proved the *Examiner* article to be a fabrication. Jones could not, by any stretch of the imagination, be regarded as a detached observer when it came to Jews. He appears to have been driven by a psychopathic Judaeophobia. The word "Jew" appears in his diary more than forty times—each time part of an unfriendly reference to an individual Jew or to all Jews. Some psychological compulsion forced him to label Jews as though they were members of a curious species; if there was any uncertainty about a person's religion, he would hazard a guess to be on the safe side: (*Jew?*)[163] or (*Jew name*)[164] or *perhaps a Jew*[165] or (*another Jew, I suppose*).[166] So he assured himself that if it came to a test he could not be accused of missing a single one. Any testimony by Jones about J.P. Benjamin, or Quartermaster General Myers, or any or all Jews, ought to be accorded the credence which his hostility deserves.[167]

The reaction of the Jews to the public outcry against them was similar to that in the North: bewilderment, hurt pride, anger, rebellion. In Savannah, they held a public meeting, passed resolutions against the people of Thomasville who had banished Jews from their town, and urged their non-Jewish neighbors to repudiate the citizens of that place as "enemies of human liberty and freedom of conscience."[168]

In Richmond, the two congregations, Beth Ahabah and Beth Shalome, held consultations for the discussion of possible courses of action "to vindicate our character as Jews and good citizens, which has been repeatedly and grossly assailed in public prints, etc." The Board of Beth Ahabah suggested that the Jews raise a special fund to be distributed among the poor of the city, apparently in the belief that this would earn the gratitude of Richmond citizens. A meeting of Beth Shalome congregation was called to consider the project, and unanimously rejected it in the conviction that the poor were the responsibility of all denominations, not only of the Jews. The Beth Shalome members probably suspected that unilateral generosity would be regarded as an evidence of guilt, rather than of charity. In regard to the existing prejudice, they resolved:

> That while this meeting denounces the unfounded aspersions made against the Israelites of this city, and feels satisfied that the acts of our co-religionists can well bear the test of comparison with those of any other denomination in this community for patriotism, charity, or freedom from selfishness; yet think the best and most dignified course to be adopted, will be to treat them with silent contempt, confident that the enlightened and unprejudiced do not join in this crusade against our people.[169]

Letters were written to the editors of newspapers,[170] and one Jew even challenged an editor to a duel. Colonel Adolphus H. Adler of the Confederate Army, a Hungarian who had served as an officer in Garibaldi's army, was so incensed at the editor of the *Richmond Examiner* for printing libelous statements about the Jews that he wanted to settle the matter with his sword. The editor is said to have made an apology in lieu of an appearance with seconds.[171] The answers of the Jews were the same as they have always been: Jews were individuals; many were fighting in the Confederate Army; some had given their lives in the conflict; Jews were as patriotic as their neighbors; blanket condemnations are unjust. These arguments would always be brought forward by a people hounded by slander.

In the Confederacy as in the Union, there were fair-minded non-Jews who were convinced that the generalized accusations were unjust, and that they were motivated by prejudice and dislike. The editor of the *Richmond Sentinel* felt that Jews, like all others, should be judged as individuals, and that the Confederacy ought to defend this principle of fair play especially at this time of crisis in the national epic. Loyal citizens should, he felt, be wary of spurning any support—no class of the population should be insulted and, perhaps, alienated, by prejudiced statements. "We consider it a duty to hail every good citizen as a brother. We ask him not where he was born or what his faith." The editor went on to question the loyalty of those who were activated by prejudice; they were espousing principles foreign to America, and though they were born in America, their identification with the nation might be judged by the Irishman's remark: "a man's being born in a stable doesn't make him a horse."[172]

The missionary chaplain who wrote a letter of protest to the *Savannah Daily Morning News* had long wanted to reply to the complaints about Jews, he said, but his service with the military forces had consumed all his time. Now the formation by the Jews of Macon of a company for the defense of Savannah, had reactivated his interest in the question. He did not intend to be an apologist for the Jews. They needed none. But he wished it understood that he had concluded, from his own personal experience and contact with Jews, that they were "pretty largely represented" in the military, and that they made "good, enduring, hard-fighting soldiers." He had seen them in camp, in battle, on long marches, sharing all the privations and hardships of their fellows. In civilian life, he knew them to be "true patriots . . . giving as much towards supporting the Government, clothing the troops, administering comforts for the sick and wounded, &c., as any other class of citizens."[173]

An editorial in the *Augusta Sentinel*, in 1866, said that its editor had been in a position to observe Jewish conduct during the war, and that he was certain that the charges of Jewish disloyalty were "most gratuitous and unfounded slander upon that people." He gave examples of Jewish officers and soldiers who played outstanding roles in the front lines, and cited the names of young Augusta Jews who had served in the army.[174]

One of the fairest answers to the anti-Jewish libels came from the pen of the editor of the *Richmond Dispatch*. He would have no part in the campaign of propaganda against Jews. He agreed with the Rev. Michelbacher's assertion that, though Jews may have speculated in certain merchandise, they had not profiteered in flour, grain, or any other food products, in which category the most ruthless speculation was done. He suggested that the so-called Christians who were the leading speculators, "starving people to death by their horrible extortions in the staff of life," and who were "grieving their righteous souls over the audacity of Jews in speculating in jewels and other luxuries," should read their New Testaments somewhat more frequently. Jews were as good and as bad as non-Jews, and for every Jew who left the country with a fortune, there were many non-Jews guilty of the same thing. So far as he could tell, Jews had contributed money and support and blood to the Confederate cause in their correct proportion, and Christians had better look to the guilty in their own midst before criticising Jews. These were the opinions of a non-Jewish editor.[175]

Yet another eminently just comment on the outcry against the Jews came from the editor of the *Charleston Courier*:

We have said, and shall say, and urge our opinions against extortioners and bloodsuckers and prowling beastly bipeds of prey under whatever guise they come, but we protest earnestly and emphatically against any wholesale denunciation of Germans or Jews, or of German Jews. We have no more and no less opposition to an extortioner who happens to be a German and a Jew, than one who is an Englishman, or a Frenchman, or a Welchman, or a Yankee, and a so-called Christian. If there is such an animal as a Christian extortioner, we hate and abhor it, and would gladly exterminate it. Let the offenders and all who trouble our political Israel, and devour people, be rebuked, denounced, execrated, imprisoned, or expelled, if it can be done, but let us hear of no more abuse of a class as a class.[176]

In these impassioned phrases, the Charlestonian came to the crux of the problem, seeing clearly that it was a question of fanatical prejudice versus fair-mindedness.

Although the evidence relating to anti-Jewish propaganda in the Confederacy is less voluminous than that which has been gathered for the North, its total cumulative effect is equally damning. Continued research in the periodical and journalistic literature of the Confederacy will undoubtedly uncover hosts of items which will offer further substantiation of the pattern of prejudice.

The North and the South, despite provincial and sectional loyalties and hostilities were, after all, part and parcel of the same country. The people who dwelt in Alabama were not so vastly different from those residing in Illinois or New Hampshire that they should be diametrically opposed in culture and thought patterns. This is especially true in regard to their conceptions of the Jewish people. It would actually be unaccountable if anti-Jewish prejudice had not appeared with equal virulence in both halves of the sundered nation.

The war was the key, the secret combination, which unleashed heretofore dormant prejudices. If there had been no leading public figures who were anti-Jewish, if all the Jews had been law-abiding patriots, the emotional, economic, and social frustrations of the war years would still, in all likelihood, have been directed against them. Society had to have scapegoats, in the South and in the North, for all its pent-up passion, frustration, anger, disappointment, fear, insecurity, anxiety, shame, jealousy. Lincoln was the outstanding scapegoat in the Union, while Davis occupied a similar position in the South; both suffered bitterly from the senseless slander which was directed against them. There were other scapegoats during the war, as well: Yankees who were caught in the South at the outbreak of the hostilities, German settlers in Texas, sincerely loyal Democrats in the North; but, apparently, the Jews were a more popular scapegoat in all areas than any of these.

There were no realistic causes, no justified reasons, no logical bases, for the war-time rise of prejudice—as there never have been—except the unconscious roots of hostility, transference, and anxiety which the psychiatrist uncovers, and the deliberate hate-promotion of men who hope to profit when a competitive group loses caste in the public eye. Many of the economic libels against Jews were undoubtedly set forth by men who stood to gain from the removal of Jewish business men. But for all, consciously or unconsciously, an escape-valve was necessary. General Sherman was telling more of the truth than he realized in a letter which he wrote to Grant about the smugglers, in 1862: "The great profit now made is converting everybody into rascals, and *it makes me ashamed of*

187

my own countrymen every time I have to examine a cotton or horse case. . ."[177] Sherman's shame was wiped away by imputing the major responsibility for smuggling to the Jews.

Consciously or unconsciously, citizens both North and South absolved themselves of guilt and cleansed themselves of fear, and projected their anxiety, by blaming their scapegoats for all the evils of American life and the dangers and hurts of war. A British visitor to the Confederacy was saying this, perhaps without realizing it, when she wrote:

> . . . [T]hese extortioners were generally known to be "Northern men with Southern sympathies" (for Southern dollars), or German Jews . . . No perquisites, no money-making contracts and frauds were heard of in the South, but such as were traced to Jews or Yankees . . .[178]

Could she not have carried this thought to its logical conclusion by saying: the average Southerner would have lost faith in himself, his fellows, and his cause, were he to admit to himself that the economic and social evils unleashed by the war were, in the final analysis, his own responsibility; foisting the blame upon "traitorous" Jews and Yankees saved him from the emotional agony of such realism.

If no Jews whatever had lived in the Union and Confederacy, some other group—perhaps the Catholics, as in the recent days of Nativism—would have served as a major escape-valve. The Jews were an insignificant feature of the story. The fact that any scapegoat was necessary was an important commentary on the nature of the American ethos in time of stress.

VIII LINCOLN AND THE JEWS

Brethren, the lamented Abraham Lincoln believed himself to be bone from our bone and flesh from our flesh. He supposed himself to be a descendant of Hebrew parentage. He said so in my presence.[1]

These words were spoken by Rabbi Isaac M. Wise during the eulogy which he delivered five days after the assassination of the President. There is no shred of evidence to substantiate Wise's assertion, and Lincoln is not known to have said anything resembling this to any of his other Jewish acquaintances. He could not, however, have been any friendlier to individual Jews, or more sympathetic to Jewish causes, if he had stemmed from Jewish ancestry.

The roll of Jews who knew Lincoln grows with the years, as researchers delve deeper into the documents and records of the age. The Robert Todd Lincoln Collection of Lincoln Papers in the Manuscript Division of the Library of Congress, opened for public inspection in 1947, has provided another source for the elucidation of Lincoln's contacts with various Jews. In particular, these papers indicate how intimately Abraham Jonas and Isachar Zacharie were associated with Lincoln the Illinois lawyer and Lincoln the war-time President.

I

On April 29, 1861, Lincoln appointed his old friend and political coworker, Abraham Jonas, to the postmastership of Quincy, Ill. In a sense this was a partial payment of a political debt, for Jonas had been Lincoln's consistent champion in central Illinois over a long period of years; but it was also a token of respect for a man whom Lincoln regarded as "one of my most valued friends."[2]

Lincoln and Jonas had probably struck up a friendship shortly after the latter's arrival in Quincy in 1838. Both had already served their apprenticeship in politics: Lincoln for two terms in the Illinois State Legislature and Jonas for four in the Kentucky House. It was natural that the two young politicians should gravitate towards each other, even though their personal backgrounds were so different.

Jonas had come to Cincinnati from England in 1819, with a sizable group of Jews from Plymouth and Portsmouth, after his brother Joseph, the first Jew to settle in the town, sent back the news that life on the

189

western frontier showed much promise.[3] After a few years in the growing Queen City, Abraham decided to move on. Perhaps it was the sudden death of his young wife, a daughter of the Revolutionary War patriot rabbi, Gershom Mendes Seixas, in 1825; perhaps it was the pioneering spirit which made him seek out less crowded land; perhaps it was for business reasons that he moved. At any rate, in 1828, he opened a store in Williamstown, Kentucky, and began to flex his political muscles. Four years of service in the fledgling state legislature taught him the practical lore of political life. Within a few years he had risen to the position of Grand Master of Kentucky Masons, a state-wide tribute to his capacity for leadership. He would undoubtedly have gone far had he remained in Kentucky.

But again the pioneering instinct would not let him rest. Illinois beckoned to him as it did to so many other Kentuckians. After his arrival in Quincy in 1838, he divided his time between store-keeping and the study of law, except for a brief period in 1840–41 when he moved to Columbus, Ill., to take the leadership in a movement which favored the transference of the county seat of Adams County from Quincy to Columbus. During this unsuccessful venture he edited the *Columbus Advocate*, organ of the pro-Columbus forces.[4] In 1842, he made his first bid for political office, running for the state legislature on the Whig ticket. Twenty-one candidates were seeking five places in the Adams County representation; Jonas ran third in the race, receiving 1297 votes, a good showing for a man who had lived in the district only four years.[5] The following year he was admitted to the bar and gave the management of his business over to two brothers who had meanwhile joined him in Quincy. That year also saw the establishment of a partnership with Henry Asbury that was to be terminated only by Jonas' death.

Jonas sought elective office only once more. In 1844 he ran for a seat in the Illinois Senate, but was defeated by the Democratic candidate. The results were extremely close: 106 more votes would have gained the election for him.[6] From 1849 to 1852 he served as postmaster of Quincy under appointment from Presidents Taylor and Fillmore, in recognition of his continuing services to the Whig Party in Illinois.

What kind of man was this British Jew who was accepted so wholeheartedly by the people and by his fellow-workers in the field of politics in a day when there were so few Jews in the area that you could count them on the fingers of both hands?[7] Gustav Körner, a German immigrant who was later to serve as justice of the Illinois Supreme Court and as lieutenant-governor, said in his diary that one of the secrets of Jonas' success was his talent as a public speaker. In Körner's judgment, Jonas was "the best debater and best politician" of all the Whig members of the legislature. "His quickness of perception, his readiness of speech, his plausibility made him a very formidable opponent" in political debate and election rallies. Körner described Jonas as having a "slender figure, brilliant dark eyes, an aquiline nose, black hair and a very good voice."⁸

By 1854, when Lincoln visited Quincy for the first time, Jonas was his closest friend in town. Indeed, Lincoln had agreed to make the trip from Springfield to address a Whig Party meeting only because Jonas had written him an importunate letter urging his personal support for the district's Whig candidate for Congress. Stephen Douglas was to speak in Quincy in behalf of the Democratic nominee, and Jonas was convinced that a speech by Lincoln in reply to Douglas "would be more effective, than any other." "Be assured," Jonas had written, "that nothing will afford greater pleasure to your personal friends and the Whigs generally than you consent to visit us—and the Douglasites would as soon see old nick here as yourself." When Lincoln arrived by stagecoach from Springfield, Jonas was on hand to meet and escort him to the hall where the rally was to be held. Afterwards, in company with others, the two friends went to an oyster house for refreshments and political talk. Then Jonas walked Lincoln back to the Quincy House, where he was staying for the night.

There must have been many more interchanges of correspondence between Jonas and Lincoln than have been preserved by the historical societies and libraries, and many more meetings between the two than have been recorded. By December of the same year, 1854, Jonas was doing political spade-work for Lincoln, sounding out powerful Whigs for their reaction to the Springfield lawyer's candidacy for the national Senate in the next election. For himself, Jonas wrote,

> I have no pretensions for that or any other office at this time—and Browning and Williams not being in the way, I should prefer you to any other—and should be pleased to render you any service in my power.

The old Whig Party finally died in the sectional strife over the slavery issue, and Jonas and Lincoln decided to enlist in the ranks of the new Republican Party. Both served as presidential electors on the Fremont ticket in 1856, that first bid of the new party for national power. During the campaign, as was his wont, Jonas traveled the district delivering lengthy, impassioned political speeches. He was, apparently, one of the most successful political orators in central Illinois.⁹

In July 1858, Jonas summoned Lincoln post-haste to give another one of his "*sledge hammer speeches*," at a district convention in Augusta, Hancock County, this time in behalf of James Stark, the Republican candidate for Congress. Douglas was again on the scene, and Jonas was certain that an address by Lincoln would "effect wonders." He promised "the tallest kind of a crowd" if his Springfield friend could see his way clear to making the trip. Lincoln trusted Jonas' political judgment and, as in 1854, did not hesitate to take Jonas' word for it that his services were needed by the party. Even though he was in the midst of his exhausting series of debates with Douglas, the political turning-point of his life, he wrote back to Jonas that "my mind is at once made up to be with you." Two months later Jonas proudly signed his name as Chairman of the Republican Committee of Arrangements to an advertisement which invited "The Friends of Hon. Abraham Lincoln" to "hear the true principles of the Republican party expounded, and the unsound doctrines of the Douglas Democracy exposed" at the Quincy debate between the two great contenders for popular favor.[10]

In December 1858, Horace Greeley came to Quincy to deliver a public lecture. Afterwards, the leading Republicans of the town—Wood, Williams, Browning, Bushnell, Asbury and Jonas—closeted themselves with the New York editor and talked about the presidential election of 1860. Henry Asbury mentioned Lincoln as a possible nominee of the party. Asbury later wrote that "my suggestion fell flat, it was not even discussed, none of them seemed for Lincoln. I felt a little mortified,— finally, some one said Lincoln might do for Vice President—at this point Mr. Jonas probably to relieve my embarrasment [*sic*] or probably because he concurred—said: Gentlemen there may be more in Asbury's suggestion than any of us now think. Here the whole subject was dropped and the caucus dispersed."[11] Whatever Jonas then thought of Lincoln's chances for the nomination, by early 1860 he was unquestionably in the Lincoln camp. On February 3, he wrote to his Springfield friend for a copy of the published version of the Lincoln-Douglas debates, assuring him that "with proper exertions and judicious selections at Chicago in June, we shall be able to carry the day and in November proclaim *victory* to all the world."

Shortly after Lincoln was nominated at the Chicago convention, Jonas wrote him a confidential letter conveying the news that Douglas' cohort, Isaac N. Morris, was collecting false affidavits to prove that Lincoln had been a member of the old Know-Nothing Party, which affidavits would be published in an effort to draw the foreign vote away from him in the coming election. Lincoln had denied the charge previously, but Jonas felt that the whole matter was too dangerous to ignore. Ironically enough, the accusation centered around Lincoln's visit to Quincy back in 1854 when he had hardly been out of Jonas' sight long enough to attend the Know-Nothing meeting which had supposedly been conducted that night. In his answer to Jonas, Lincoln recalled the details of his visit to Quincy and, without saying it in so many words, suggested that Jonas was the logical man to make public denial of the accusation. Lincoln was too clever a politician to repudiate the old Know-Nothing voters at such a crucial time, but the foreign vote had to be safeguarded under all circumstances. There is no record of Jonas' statements on the subject, but it is entirely possible that he went to the Democrats and threatened to expose their attempt to misrepresent Lincoln's political affiliations unless they called a halt to the scheme. Whatever Jonas' course of action, the affidavits were not published.

During the campaign, Jonas again took to the political platform, traveling the area which he knew so well in behalf of Lincoln's candidacy. Orville Hickman Browning, a close political friend of both Jonas and Lincoln and Senator from Illinois for a brief period during the war, accompanied Jonas to three important meetings and shared the stump with him. Browning recorded in his diary that Jonas' speech before ten thousand persons at Stones Prairie on August 25, 1860, "occupied an hour."[12] He agreed with Körner that Jonas was one of the ablest orators in the area.

In December, after Lincoln's election had been interpreted by the slave states as the signal for secession, Jonas wrote Lincoln another "confidential" letter. He apologized for taking up the President-Elect's time "when you have so much to think of and so many things to perplex you." But the matter was urgent. Jonas had many relatives and friends in the South; he had just received a letter from New Orleans warning him of a plot by prominent Southerners to assassinate Lincoln before the inauguration. Jonas regarded the writer of the letter as a cautious, sober, and reliable person who would transmit such information only if he were convinced that it was authentic. He pleaded with his friend to take all precautions for "your personal safety and the preservation of our National Integrity." Jonas, needless to say, was not among those who laughed and sneered a few months later when news leaked out that Lincoln had arrived at Washington under secret guard to avert a threatened attack upon his train in Baltimore. Jonas believed that the life of the Chief Executive was really endangered by the fanatics of the South.

Jonas was not one to ask favors for himself. But his friend Browning knew that he would like to be appointed to the Quincy Postmastership again. He wrote, on December 9, 1860, to the President-Elect, that "when the time arrives for appointing to offices throughout the country, I would be glad to have our mutual friend Abram [sic] Jonas remembered in connection with the Post Office at Quincy. He wishes the place, and, I think, ought to have it."[13] Only a short time after the inauguration, Lincoln obliged his Quincy colleague with the desired appointment; perhaps he would have done so whether or not Browning had written.

In 1862, Lincoln turned to Jonas for a favor. A Missourian charged with disloyalty had been held in prison in Quincy despite a flock of petitions for his release. Lincoln decided to leave the decision to his friends Abraham Jonas and Henry Asbury, and so wrote in his order:

> Will the Secretary of War please direct that Mr. Thoroughman may be disposed of at the discretion of Abram Jonas and Henry Asbury of Quincy, Illinois, both of whom I know to be loyal and sensible men?[14]

In May 1864, Jonas' family turned to Lincoln, through Orville Browning, for a final favor. Like Lincoln's, Jonas' was a "house divided." Four of his sons were fighting on the Confederate side. One, Charles, had been captured and confined in a prisoner-of-war camp. Jonas had made no attempt to secure his son's release, but now he was on his death-bed and the physicians had given up all hope for his recovery. So Mrs. Jonas wired to Browning and asked him to intercede with Lincoln for Charles' release to pay a last visit to his father.[15] Lincoln must have been shocked to hear the news of his friend's fatal illness; directions were immediately issued for Charles' furlough:

> Allow Charles H. Jonas now a prisoner of War at Johnson's Island, a parol[e] of three weeks to visit his dying father, Abraham Jonas, at Quincy, Illinois. June 2, 1864.
>
> A. Lincoln[16]

It was none too soon. Charles reached Quincy on the day of his father's death, but, as he wrote later with a thankful heart, "in time to be recognized and welcomed by him."[17]

One final act of friendship and the Lincoln-Jonas story was closed. Two days after Jonas' death, Browning went to see the President and obtained his promise to appoint Mrs. Jonas to serve out her husband's unexpired term in the Quincy Post Office.[18] Again we do not know whether Browning's prompting was necessary or not. But Lincoln did make the appointment and so paid another tribute of friendship to his comrade whose life had paralleled his own in many ways, who had shared many interests and principles with him, and who had been so loyal to him during all the disappointing years which had preceded his election to the highest office in the land.

II

One of the most enigmatic intimates of President Lincoln during the war years was Isachar Zacharie, an obscure British-born physician and chiropodist who, according to the *New York World*, "enjoyed Mr. Lincoln's confidence perhaps more than any other private individual . . . [and was] perhaps the most favored family visitor at the White House."[19]

It all began in September 1862, when Zacharie, who had already removed corns and bunions from some of the most distinguished feet in the country, including those of Henry Clay and William Cullen Bryant, journeyed to Washington for an interview with Secretary of War Stanton. Whether it was to treat Stanton's feet or for another purpose, is not known; but the Jewish chiropodist first looked to Stanton's pedal comfort, and then proceeded to discuss the foot health of the army. He proposed to organize a corps of chiropodists for army service, "a corps of corn doctors, or foot soldiers," as the punning *New York Herald* would have it. The Secretary of War apparently thought more of Zacharie's professional treatments than he did of his military proposals, for he passed him on to the President not to discuss the chiropodists' corps, but to relieve Lincoln's feet.[20]

After the treatment, Zacharie requested a recommendation from his distinguished patient. The President promptly wrote the following testimonial:

> Dr. Zacharie has operated on my feet with great success, and considerable addition to my comfort.
>
> A. Lincoln[21]
>
> Sep. 22, 1862.

According to the newspapers, Zacharie then proceeded to remove corns from the feet of Generals McClellan, Banks and Burnside, and of various cabinet members and other high officials. Punsters and satirists had the time of their lives when word got around about Zacharie's professional success in Washington:

> ... In the certificates furnished to the chiropodist by the President, Secretary Seward and other members of the Cabinet, and by Generals McClellan, Banks and Burnside, we have a cornucopia of information about the secrets of this war. The President has been greatly blamed for not resisting the demands of the radicals; but how could the President put his foot down firmly when he was troubled with corns? There have been rumors of personal animosities and ill-timed bickerings among the members of the Cabinet; but undoubtedly these have been caused by the honorable Secretaries inadvertently treading upon each other's bunions under the council board. Some of our generals have been reproached for their slow movements; but is celerity of motion to be expected of persons whose toe nails are growing into the flesh? No human being could be expected to toe the mark of our expectations under such circumstances ... General Pope, who by a singular paradox placed his headquarters in the saddle, made a few rapid evolutions, during which he nearly succeeded in using up himself, the enemy and our army; but Jackson's barefooted rebels, who do not know the need or the value of a chiropodist, got the better of him at last ... It would seem, therefore, that all our past troubles have originated not so much with the head as with the feet of the nation. Dr. Zacharie has shown us precisely where the shoe pinches ... [22]

This was just the kind of nonsense that the President liked to read to his friends. Perhaps the editorial jokers were partly responsible for the development of a cordial relationship between the Chief Executive and his corn doctor.

We do not know what Zacharie told Lincoln while he was removing his corns, or how many times he returned to the White House, but four months later Zacharie was in New Orleans on a special mission entrusted to him by the President. He hardly practiced his profession at all, except for General Banks' personal convenience; the rest of his time was devoted to readjusting the exchange rates of Louisiana and Union currency, to interviewing local people in an effort to gauge public opinion, and to penning reports for the presidential eye on the state of affairs under the military government of General Banks. In his reports Zacharie retailed stories of Butler's regime, related military gossip, and praised Banks' moderate policy towards the residents of New Orleans. His duties apparently combined those of a special presidential envoy, special assistant to the Military Governor, and intermediary between the military government and the civilian population.[23] In the latter capacity he took special pains to secure a generous hearing for Northern Jews who had been caught in New Orleans by the outbreak of war, and for New Orleans Jews who had to depart for the Confederacy upon their refusal to take the oath of allegiance to the Union. Indeed, this connection with his co-religionists in the Louisiana port was a key to another role which the chiropodist was destined to play, as we shall see very shortly.

In March 1863, Zacharie returned to the North to convey special reports and secret memoranda to Lincoln. Within ten days he was on his way back to New Orleans with Lincoln's replies. On the eve of his departure Zacharie wrote the President a note in which he referred to his agitation over "the great responsibility resting on me." We have no way of ascertaining the nature of "the great responsibility." Perhaps Lincoln had charged him with the duty of fostering the activities of the Union associations in New Orleans, for after his arrival in Louisiana the chiropodist began to report on the success of these groups. But perhaps he had already broached a much more important subject to the President, a subject which had undoubtedly been the focal point of much of his activity in New Orleans: *a negotiated peace with the Confederacy!*

General Banks conceived himself to be a peace-maker. He had already sent one emissary, Martin Gordon by name, to Richmond to sound out official and popular opinion on the question of a peaceful settlement to the war.[24] So encouraging was Gordon's report that Banks determined to make an official effort to bring the men at Washington and at Richmond together around a conference table. It is not clear whether Zacharie or Banks took the initiative in formulating their joint plan for peace; in his letters to Banks, Zacharie frequently refers to himself as the author of the scheme.[25] At any rate, on July 2, 1863, Banks instructed his Quartermaster to issue five-thousand dollars in Confederate currency to Zacharie,[26] wrote a letter of introduction to Secretary of State Seward for Zacharie to deliver in person,[27] and sent the chiropodist off to the North.

The letter which the General wrote to the Secretary of State indicated the importance of Zacharie's Jewish contacts in New Orleans:

> The return of Dr. Zacharie to New York offers me an opportunity to say that he has enjoyed many opportunities of obtaining information which are not open to Officers of the Government, and that I am satisfied he is a zealous supporter of the Government. His connection with the Jewish Com-

munity of New Orleans which is very large and very powerful both by its numerical strength, and the activity which distinguishes its leading members has given him great advantages in this respect. He has been considerate and attentive to many of the families that have been recently required to leave the Department as Registered Enemies and enabled the Officers of the Government to perform some acts of grace trifling in themselves, but of service to all parties. These attentions have won from persons who have great influence with leading men of the Rebel Government expressions of gratitude and secured for him such endors[e]ments as will enable him to do that which other men cannot do, and which perhaps could not be given to a man of more commanding social or political position . . .[28]

Armed with such a letter, Zacharie could not fail to obtain an interview with Seward, who thought enough of his plan to send him on to Lincoln. The President was delighted to renew acquaintanceships, listened carefully to the details of his scheme, and then referred him back to Seward for arrangements for his trip into the Confederacy. Several days later, however, the Secretary of State very coldly informed him that the Cabinet had rejected the proposal. So far as Zacharie knew, the scheme had been killed.[29]

But Lincoln was not one to leave any stone unturned. Apparently on his own responsibility, and without consultation with his Cabinet officers, he called Zacharie back to Washington about a month later, discussed his ideas with him for two days, and then authorized him to cross over into the Confederacy for a meeting with Confederate officials.[30] Arrived in Richmond, he was met by Benjamin, the Secretary of State, Mallory, the Secretary of the Navy, Seddon, the Secretary of War, and General Winder, Provost-Marshal of Richmond, and began consultations which lasted for several days.[31] What the actual proposals were which Zacharie presented to the Confederate high command during his stay in Richmond is not known, but he returned to Washington happy in the thought that "the interview was of the most friendly nature."[32] To Banks he wrote, confidentially, that "Benjamin & Mallory spoke of you in the *kindest manner,* and Benjamin said that he was under many obligations to you for your kindness towards his *sister.*"[33]

Sometime later the *New York Herald* caught wind of the episode and reported a fantastic version of the Zacharie peace-plan:

. . . Davis, the rebel Cabinet and the rebel armies are to go to Mexico. Our government is to furnish them with transportation to that favored land and with rations on the way. Jeff Davis calculates to land in Mexico with one hundred and fifty thousand veteran fire-eaters, each of whom can devour a Frenchman at a meal, without salt and without the slightest injury to his digestion. With this force he will drive away Napoleon's hordes and proclaim himself President of the new Mexican republic. Simultaneously the seceded Southern States will return to the Union with whatever negroes are left in them. This will end the war satisfactorily to all concerned . . .[34]

Apparently *anything* Zacharie did brought the press' sense of humor into play. It is unlikely that such a plan as the *Herald* reported should have received Lincoln's serious consideration, or the Confederate statesmen's either.

At any rate, as Zacharie wrote to Banks, "on my first arrival Mr. Lincoln detained me 2 hours, locking his doors and preventing any person from having access to him. He seemed to be delighted with my revelations."[35] If the President was pleased, his Cabinet was not. Seward was angry that Lincoln had gone ahead with the scheme over his disapproval; Chase was opposed to any negotiations with the Rebels.[36] Despite this, Lincoln talked with Zacharie again; he seemed reluctant to forego any chance for a peaceful settlement:

> ... the President is true and is perfectly delighted with my success. But how to act he does not know. *He reminds me of the man that won the Elephant at a Raffle.* He does not know what to do with it ...[37]

Lincoln sent Zacharie to see Seward several times, but the Secretary of State had an objection for every alternative suggestion Zacharie made, although so far as he was concerned, he said, Zacharie was free to carry on the negotiations:

> ... He said go to New York and keep quiet—if you wish to go down to see *Benjamin* again to do so, that I could do whatever I liked, that the President was satisfied with whatever I [had] done, and when the time came & all was ready he could clintch [*sic*] the matter ...[38]

He received many kind words from both Lincoln and Seward, but neither was willing to activate the follow-up Zacharie recommended, namely, that General Banks be recalled to Washington for the express purpose of continuing the consultations with Richmond. There was a plaintive note in Zacharie's frustrated plea to Banks: *"Now what is the use of my going to see Benjamin, if we are not ready to do any thing."*[39]

The chiropodist was convinced that his plans were thwarted by two groups of officials: the radicals who would not relent from their determination to destroy the South, and jealous bureaucrats who would not permit Banks' emissary to proceed because they feared that the popularity which would result from success would guarantee the Presidency to Banks in 1864. And, indeed, Zacharie's letters to his chieftain were chock full of assurances that the people were anxiously awaiting the opportunity to elect him in '64. Whatever the reason for the rejection of the Zacharie-Banks peace plans, the Jewish chiropodist was now a member of that remarkable group of fanatics, thieves, visionaries and idealists who believed that they could have ended the war if the Government had only supported their activities.

Back to New York and the comparatively unexciting job of cutting toe-nails and removing corns! But Zacharie's services to the Jews in New Orleans was not overlooked. According to a laudatory article in *The Jewish Messenger*,[40] in May 1864, a group of New York Jews, headed by A.R.B. Moses, Samuel A. Lewis, Jacob S. Cohen, and Lewis J. Phillips, tendered him a testimonial evening and presented him with an expensive silver tea service and salver in appreciation of his "noble and fraternal efforts" in behalf of the Jews of New Orleans and other Confederate Jews whom he had helped.

Samuel A. Lewis had good reason to be among the group who were expressing their gratitude to Zacharie. He was the uncle of Ada Jackson, fiancée of Goodman L. Mordecai of Charleston, S.C., who had been imprisoned in Washington as a Confederate commercial agent on his way to Nassau. The chiropodist had made a personal trip to Washington to see the President about the case and convinced Lincoln to order the young man's release. Mordecai insisted on going to the White House to thank the President. During the interview, Zacharie mentioned the fact that Mordecai's father had contributed $10,000 to South Carolina immediately after its secession from the Union and was one of the most active participants in all of Charleston's war activities. With a typical touch of his quixotic humor, Lincoln grasped the young Confederate veteran's hand and said: "I am happy to know that I am able to serve an enemy!"[41]

After appropriate speeches by the members of the committee, who had originally hoped to give a testimonial dinner for their honored guest (which idea he rejected), and the reading of congratulatory messages from General Dix, Rabbi Raphall, and others who could not be present, Zacharie himself arose to speak. He touched on various subjects, his love of the Union, the high place which Jews had achieved in the modern world, his own humble origin and struggle to better himself, and his gratitude for being honored by his fellow Jews for doing his duty to his adopted country. Zacharie then invited his friends into the dining room "where a sumptuous collation was prepared . . . [and] appropriate toasts were given and responded to, among them, the health of Dr. Zacharie and family, his aged father, now absent, the Committee, the Jewish press, the ladies, the President of the United States, Maj. Gen. Banks, Sir Moses Montefiore, and many other sentiments. . ." One wishes that details were available about other cases in which Zacharie used his personal influence to intercede for persons in trouble. There must have been a sizable number to warrant the expression of gratitude by a whole committee of New Yorkers.

During the next few months Zacharie spent his time electioneering for Lincoln and the Republican party. The practice of his profession never seems to have satisfied him. He conferred with local party officials, took their demands and queries to the President, and obtained statements from him designed to quiet the more restless spirits among his fellowing. He even undertook several political trips through Pennsylvania and New York, but it is not clear whether it was to consult with local politicians, to speak at rallies, or merely to propagandize for Lincoln as a private citizen. Here, as on previous occasions, it is difficult to define the chiropodist's relationship to the President. We cannot tell from their correspondence whether Zacharie undertook these missions on his own initiative, or whether the President assigned them to him.

In a report to the White House on November 3, Zacharie indicated that he had been concentrating on the Jewish voters of New York City:

> As regards the *Isrelites* [*sic*]—with but few exceptions, they will vote for you. I understand them well, and have taken the precaution, to see that they do as they have promised. I have secured good and trustworthy men to attend on them on Election Day. My men have been all the week seeing that their masses are properly Registered. . . .

Zacharie evidently did not agree with the Jewish press in its campaign against a "Jewish vote." As in other elections, the *Messenger* was insisting that "nobody is authorized to speak for our co-religionists on political questions; there is no such thing as a 'Jewish vote.' "[42] The *Record* agreed, with the reservation that Jews should be advised to vote against candidates who appeared to approve of the agitation for a Constitutional amendment recognizing Christianity as the official religion of the country.[43] Myer S. Isaacs, co-editor of the *Messenger*, wrote an indignant letter to Lincoln, the month before the election, when daily papers printed a report that certain New York Jews had gone to Washington to pledge the Jewish vote to Lincoln. John Hay answered reassuringly that

> No pledge of the Jewish vote was made by these gentlemen and no inducements or promises were extended to them by the President. They claimed no such authority and received no such response as you seem to suppose—The President deems this statement due to you . . .[44]

The *Messenger* would not have been so eager to record the honors given to Zacharie if it had been aware of his efforts to shepherd the Jewish vote into the Republican fold.

The final recorded contact between the chiropodist and the President occurred after the fall of Savannah. Zacharie's family had lived there all during the war and Lincoln had promised his friend that he would arrange permission for him to go there as soon as the Union armies captured it. On January 25, 1865, therefore, he instructed the Secretary of War to see that Zacharie was granted a pass to enable him to proceed to Savannah.

The last letter which the chiropodist wrote to the White House was a message that he was leaving for the South and would happily undertake any mission which Lincoln would want to entrust to him! For the first time, the President found no business at hand worthy of the chiropodist's inventiveness; he set out for Savannah without a presidential mission. Lincoln was assassinated before Zacharie returned from the South.

What manner of man was this chiropodist-presidential envoy who sent baskets of bananas, oranges, and pineapples to the White House, conveyed his "kind regards" to Mrs. Lincoln, and, after two years of correspondence, began to address the President as "My Dear Friend"? What was the nature of the friendship which led the *New York World* to say that "the President has often left his business-apartment to spend an evening in the parlor with this favored bunionist"?[45]

The *New York Herald* described him as a man of charm and grace:

> Dr. Zacharie is distinguished by a splendid Roman nose, fashionable whiskers, an eloquent tongue, a dazzling diamond breastpin, great skill in his profession, an ingratiating address, a perfect knowledge of his business and a plentiful supply of social moral courage . . .[46]

The *World*, on the other hand, thought him a conniving "toe-nail trimmer," and accused him of speculating in cotton in New Orleans, and of taking bribes for the favors he obtained from the President.[47] Rumors of his speculation *were* widespread. He himself told the President of their currency and warned him not to believe them. Banks, in his letter of introduction to Seward, repudiated the suspicion by assuring the Secretary of State that "I can only say that Doctor Zacharie has had no favors whatever from the Government and has asked for none at my hands."[48] Suspicion of dishonesty in captured Southern territory was not unusual; a General's personal character reference was very unusual.

Undoubtedly the chiropodist had high expectations of reward. He was actually on two political band-wagons at almost the same time, supporting both Lincoln and Banks. In his letters, Zacharie continually assured Banks of his loyal support, and promised over and over again that he would permit no one to steal "the honour" of achieving peace: it belonged to his Commanding General and himself. When, later, he worked actively for the re-election of Lincoln, practically every letter contained a hint that his services to the Chief Executive merited some tangible recognition. In what directions did his ambitions tend? Perhaps he was revealing a hidden hope when he spoke in this wise to the Jews who honored him in May 1864:

> . . . Let us look at England, France, Russia, Holland, aye, almost every nation in the world, and where do we find the Israelite? We find them taken into

the confidence of Kings and Emperors. And in this republican and enlightened country, where we know not how soon it may fall to the lot of any man to be elevated to a high position by this government, why may it not fall to the lot of an Israelite as well as any other? ...

Did he conceive of himself as another Jewish premier, like Judah P. Benjamin, wielding the power of statecraft for an affectionate President? It is not altogether unlikely.

But whatever Zacharie's secret ambitions, the two men who trusted him and took him into their confidence, Banks and Lincoln, were not credulous, naive men. Lincoln, in particular, had a profound insight into human character. What he saw beneath the chiropodist's charm and glibness struck him as sound enough to warrant opening the White House doors to him whenever he came to Washington, sending him to New Orleans to work out policy with Banks, listening seriously to his analysis of political developments, while all the time he was an unknown, unimportant foreigner, with no mass following or well-placed backers. Whatever Zacharie's motivation for ingratiating himself into the presidential favor—even if it was only social-climbing—Lincoln liked him well enough and believed in his integrity enough to discuss high matters of state policy with him and to while away hours of despondency in his company.

Zacharie dropped back into obscurity after Lincoln's death, returning eventually to his native England, where he passed away in 1897.[49] Whatever his role—sycophant, court-jester, politician, spy or sincere friend— his relationship with Lincoln was one of the strange corners in the personal and public life of the Civil War President.

III

In March 1863, Lincoln conferred with a strange and visionary man, Henry Wentworth Monk, the Canadian-born Judaeophile and early Zionist, who had come to Washington to urge upon the President a plan for the abandonment of the war. Lincoln was not seriously disposed to listen to his proposals, so Monk went on to discuss one of his pet projects: the restoration of European Jewry to Palestine. The President agreed that the vision which Monk had of a Jewish state in Palestine was worthy of consideration, but protested that the United States was in no position to take a leading role in international affairs until it had set its own house in order and reunited the two warring sections. This is what he said of the Jews:

> ... I myself have a regard for the Jews. My chiropodist is a Jew, and he has so many times "put me upon my feet" that I would have no objection to giving his countrymen "a leg up." ...[50]

This passing reference to Zacharie was the only known opinion Lincoln ever registered in regard to the Jews, beyond the general comments to Wise and his friends in connection with the Grant Order and to Fischel concerning the chaplaincy clause. In those two cases he had expressed an interest in seeing justice done to the Jews, and was willing to take upon himself the responsibility for the necessary action. He understood the quality of democratic equality well enough to know that no group could be deprived of its rights without endangering the whole structure of democracy. Indeed, his personal dealings with Jews in his Illinois years, with Abraham Jonas the lawyer, Julius Hammerslough the merchant,[51] and Henry Rice the clothier,[52] undoubtedly helped him to realize that Jews were no different from other human beings, despite the widespread prejudices against them.

The wide variety of Jews whom he met during the election year and in the White House deepened his understanding of Jews as individuals. Henry Greenebaum, another Illinois politician who had long been an abolitionist;[53] Sigismund Kaufmann[54] and Abram J. Dittenhoefer,[55] both Republican presidential electors; Moritz Pinner, the St. Louis abolitionist;[56] Simon Wolf, the lawyer,[57] and Adolphus S. Solomons, the printer and photographer,[58] both of Washington; Edward Rosewater, the War Department telegrapher;[59] Gustavus A. Myers, the Richmond lawyer[60]—these were only a few of the many Jews whom Lincoln met, some of whom saw him frequently on official or personal business. A man with Lincoln's broad understanding of human beings could not have been prejudiced against Jews at the first; meeting so many Jews only served to broaden his experience with them.

Lincoln met four rabbis, according to the record. Three we have already mentioned: Wise, Fischel, and Szold. The fourth was Morris J. Raphall of New York, the divine whose pro-slavery sermon had aroused such controversy in early 1861. One wonders if Lincoln, who once told an Army chaplain that he "sometimes thought that Moses didn't quite understand" the Almighty's instructions on slavery,[61] might not have discussed the matter with Raphall if he had known of Raphall's sermon on the subject. As it was, Raphall and Adolphus Solomons, who introduced him to the President, were given only a brief interview. The rabbi had come to ask for a promotion for his son. It happened to be one of the National Fast Days which Lincoln proclaimed for public prayer in behalf of the armed forces. After Raphall told his story, Lincoln said, as Solomons recalled it, "As God's minister is it not your first duty to be at home today to pray with your people for the success of our arms as is being done in every loyal church throughout the North, East and West?" Lincoln could not know that Raphall was one of the rabbis who never failed to conduct services on such public occasions. "My assistant is doing that duty," the rabbi replied. "Ah, that is different," said the President, as he turned to his table to write out a message to Stanton on one of his small cards:

> The Secretary of War will promote Second Lieutenant Raphall to a first Lieutenancy.
> A. Lincoln.

"Now doctor," he said, "you can go home and do your own praying."[62]

One of the most interesting Jewish experiences in Lincoln's life was the presentation to him of a Hebrew souvenir by Abraham Kohn, President of the KAM Congregation and City Clerk of Chicago. Kohn had been introduced to Lincoln, shortly after the nominating convention, as a Republican stalwart who would help to marshall votes for the Lincoln ticket. They talked, it is said, not only of politics, but also of the Bible. In February 1861, one month before the Inauguration, Kohn, a pious and learned Jew, was pondering the fate of the nation and its leader. What message of encouragement could he send to the President-Elect? He turned to the Bible and found in the first chapter of the Book of Joshua words whose meaning the President would take to heart:

> Moses My servant is dead; now therefore arise, go over this Jordan, thou, and all this people, unto the land which I do give to them, even to the children of Israel. Every place that the sole of your foot shall tread upon, to you have I given it, as I spoke unto Moses. From the wilderness, and this Lebanon, even unto the great river, the river Euphrates, all the land of the Hittites, and unto the Great Sea toward the going down of the sun, shall be your border. There shall not any man be able to stand before thee all the days of thy life; as I was with Moses, so I will be with thee; I will not fail thee nor forsake thee. Be strong and of good courage; for thou shalt cause this people to inherit the land which I swore unto their fathers to give them. Only be strong and very courageous, to observe to do according to all the law, which Moses My servant commanded thee; turn not from it to the right hand or to the left, that thou mayest have good success whithersoever thou goest. This book of the law shall not depart out of thy mouth, but thou shalt meditate therein day and night, that thou mayest observe to do according to all that is written therein; for then thou shalt make thy ways prosperous, and then thou shalt have good success. Have not I commanded thee? Be strong and of good courage; be not affrighted, neither be thou dismayed; for the Lord thy God is with thee whithersoever thou goest.

He painted a replica of the American flag, and upon it, in Hebrew, the verses from the Book of Joshua.

Lincoln was probably unfamiliar with Kohn's address in Chicago, for he appears to have sent a note of appreciation to Kohn through the agency of J. Scammon Young, who misplaced it for almost six months before forwarding it to Kohn:

Chicago, August 28, 1861.

Abraham Kohn, Esq.

My dear Sir: The enclosed acknowledgement of the receipt of your beautiful painting of the American flag by the President got lost among my letters or it would have been sent to you before. Regretting the delay, I am,

Truly your friend,

J. Scammon Young.

Unfortunately Lincoln's letter was lost again, this time irretrievably. It must have been an interesting one. Lover of the Bible that he was, he must have been deeply moved by Kohn's quotation of the inspiring words of Scripture.[63]

In late 1862, a New York paper printed a report that some local Jewish women had presented a flag to Mrs. Lincoln. A.S. Cohen, editor of *The Jewish Record*, attempted to discover the details, but no one seemed to know the source of the report, so he took his pen in hand and wrote to the President. John Hay answered the query:[64]

Executive Mansion,

Washington, November 28, 1862.

My Dear Sir:

The paragraph to which you refer was altogether erroneous.

The "flag" referred to was a small painting of the American banner, inscribed in Hebrew characters with a passage from the 1st Chapter of Joshua, from the 4th to the 9th verse. It was presented to the President in February, 1861, before his departure from Illinois, by Abraham Kohn, City Clerk of Chicago, who had himself painted it. It has been in the Executive Mansion ever since the President's inauguration.

Your obt. Servant,

John Hay,

Assist. Priv. Sec.

A. S. Cohen & Co.,

&c., &c.

Lincoln's attitude towards the Jews must be measured in part, at least, by his opinions of the Know-Nothing movement. The overwhelming majority of Jews were, after all, immigrants, and although the Nativists never mentioned Jews as a specific target, they were undoubtedly included in the general classification of unwanted aliens. The 1860 letter to Jonas, already mentioned, was a carefully written political document, not a personal opinion. In 1855, at the peak of the Know-Nothing crusade against Catholics and aliens, Lincoln had expressed himself more fully in a letter to Joshua Speed:

I am not a Know-Nothing. That is certain. How could I be? How can any one who abhors the oppression of negroes, be in favor of degrading classes of ·

205

white people? Our progress in degeneracy appears to me to be pretty rapid. As a nation, we began by declaring that *"all men are created equal."* We now practically read it "all men are created equal, *except* negroes." When Know-Nothings get control, it will read: "all men are created equal except negroes, *and foreigners and Catholics."* When it comes to this I should prefer emigrating to some country where they make no pretense of loving liberty—to Russia, for instance, where despotism can be taken pure, and without the base alloy of hypocrisy . . .[65]

In answer to a query from a German editor as to his estimation of the Massachusetts provision for the restriction of the citizenship privileges of aliens, Lincoln wrote:

I say, then, that as I understand the Massachusetts provision, I am against its adoption in Illinois, or in any other place, where I have a right to oppose it. Understanding the spirit of our institutions to aim at the *elevation* of men, I am opposed to whatever tends to *degrade* them. I have some little notoriety for commiserating the oppressed condition of the negro; and I should be strangely inconsistent if I should favor any project for curtailing the existing rights of *white men,* even though born in different lands and speaking different languages from myself . . .[66]

The Lincoln who urged his countrymen to banish all thoughts of vengeance against the foes who had embroiled them in a four-year-long holocaust, whose words "with malice towards none, with charity for all" ring with a noble biblical tone—that Lincoln had friendship in his heart for all men—foreign-born and native, Negro and white, Jew and Catholic and Protestant. His dealings with Jews were another dynamic demonstration of his truly democratic spirit.

IV

It was the eve of the fifth day of the Passover festival and Union Victory evening: April 14, 1865. Jews were gathered in their synagogues to celebrate the two-fold holiday and to thank God for the deliverance of their forefathers from Egyptian slavery and the return of peace to the United States. In his sermon that evening, Rabbi Max Lilienthal of Cincinnati spoke of the weary struggle through the years and of the aims of the Union in the war. It was, he said, a victory for freedom and democracy all over the world. He pleaded that all thoughts of vengeance and hatred against the Confederacy be expunged from the hearts of true Unionists, and that friendship and kindness be offered to the Southern rebels. He spoke also of the President:

Four years ago the President-elect, the scorned rail-splitter, on his way to Washington, had to disguise himself as a Scotchman, in order to elude the assassin's dagger that awaited him in Maryland . . . And four weeks ago the same man, re-elected to the same office, in spite of having signed the declaration of emancipation, now respected and revered, now considered as a man of manifest destiny and heroic immortality— renders the oath into the hands of another Chief Justice, the advocate of universal freedom . . .[67]

At about 10:15 that evening the President was shot in Ford's Theater in Washington. A short time after dawn the next morning he died without regaining consciousness.

Jews were on their way to synagogue or already worshipping when tidings of the assassination reached them. Black draperies were quickly hung on the altars; Yom Kippur hymns and chants were substituted for Passover melodies; Jews who had not planned on attending services hastened to join their brethren in the sanctuaries where they could find comfort in the hour of grief. The rabbis put their sermon notes aside, and spoke extemporaneously, haltingly, reaching out for the words to express their deep sorrow. But no matter how words were multiplied, they could not say more than Dr. Lilienthal that morning, in the spirit of David's lament over Abner, "Indeed a great man has fallen in Israel."[68]

Rabbi Samuel Adler of Temple Emanu-El, New York, the newspaper said, began to deliver a sermon, but he was so overcome that he could not continue.[69] Alfred T. Jones, *Parnas* of Beth El-Emeth Congregation of Philadelphia, asked Isaac Leeser to say something to comfort the worshippers; he did, but it was so disconnected that he had to apologize: "the dreadful news and its suddenness have in a great measure overcome my usual composure, and my thoughts refuse to arrange themselves in their wonted order."[70] The tidings took longer to reach San Francisco. The Rev. Elkan Cohn was just rising to deliver his sermon when a member of the congregation handed him a note conveying the news. He burst into tears, said the *Daily Alta California*, and then in sobbing voice told the congregation of the national tragedy.[71]

During the next days, synagogue boards, B'nai B'rith lodges, and other Jewish communal organizations met to affix in words their declaration of unity with the nation in its time of sorrow. The Hebrew Young Men's Literary Association of St. Louis resolved to wear the badge of mourning for thirty days in memory of "our great, worthy Chief Executive, a man of generous impulses and of noble nature."[72] Montefiore Lodge No. 54 of B'nai B'rith in New York City draped its charter and lodge symbols in black cloth, and lauded "the irreproachable character of Abraham Lincoln, as a man, his purity of purpose as a statesman, his exalted patriotism and his magnanimity in the hour of triumph."[73] The resolutions of the Hebrew Benevolent Society and Orphan Asylum spoke of the "kind-heartedness [and] humility" which had characterized the President's personal dealings with men, urged that they become an example to all Americans.[74] Beth Israel Congregation, of Jackson, Mich., like many others throughout the country, resolved to drape the altar in mourning cloth and to recite memorial prayers in the President's memory for six weeks. Its resolutions asked Him "who ruleth all the People of the Earth, in His Providence, to work out His Purpose in this appalling Calamity, that has gone so near to the heart of the American people, and to decree and hasten that end which our lamented President has so nearly consummated, religious Liberty, and the Restoration and perpetuation of the American Union."[75]

The columns of the Jewish periodicals, encased in heavy black border lines, added their voice to the keen of sorrow. *The Israelite* compared the assassinations of Caesar and Lincoln: "Caesar was slain to restore the Roman Republic; Lincoln and Seward fell victims of revenge to crushed slavery. Liberty or slavery, patriotism or revenge—here is the difference between Brutus and the assassins of Lincoln and Seward." Forgotten was Wise's partisan sniping at Lincoln the man: "Attired in a garb of simplicity and good humor, his modest worth lay concealed under a rough and uncouth exterior. He was an upright, honest, unassuming man, possessing the extraordinary skill of hiding his individuality behind the mighty deeds planned in his great intellect. . . He was forgiving in his nature, gentle as a child. . ."[76] *The Jewish Record* compared the passing of Lincoln before he could see the fruits of his war-year labors with Moses' death on Mount Pisgah in sight of the Promised Land. And yet the *Record* could not lay aside its opposition to his policies: "This is no hour for carping criticism. Posterity will pass judgment upon his virtues and his foibles. He was a man of energy, of perseverance; his sternest enemies never denied that his actions were based upon firm conviction. Of his schemes and the modes of execution others, at a later date, will speak with historical impartiality. Meantime, be it enough for us to state that the news of his assassination had shed a gloom over the country that time alone can dispel. The most inveterate haters of the principles with which he ever identified himself, bow their heads with sorrow at the decree of Providence. . ."[77]

The texts which the rabbis chose for their memorial sermons on April 19, the day of the funeral services in the White House, and on June 1, the Day of National Mourning appointed by President Johnson, were loving biblical tributes to the Lincoln who drew strength and comfort from Holy Writ.[78]

David Einhorn of Philadelphia[79] and Isaac M. Wise of Cincinnati[80] thought of the martyred President as another patriarchal Abraham departing from familiar surroundings at the divine behest, holding fast to the promise that his people would be a blessed nation:

Now the Lord said unto Abram: "Get thee out of thy country, and from thy kindred, and from thy father's house, unto the land that I will show thee. And I will make of thee a great nation, and I will bless thee, and make thy name great; and be thou a blessing. And I will bless them that bless thee, and him that curseth thee will I curse; and in thee shall all the families of the earth be blessed." So Abram went, as the Lord had spoken unto him . . .

Samuel M. Isaacs of New York[81] took his text from a biblical verse which many had regarded as almost a Presidential motto during the war:

Fear not, Abram, I am thy shield, thy reward shall be exceedingly great.

King David's lament for Abner was the passage to which Henry Vidaver of St. Louis[82] and Bernard Illowy of New Orleans[83] turned for their expression of sorrow:

And the king lamented for Abner, and said: "Should Abner die as a churl dieth? Thy hands were not bound, nor thy feet put in fetters; as a man falleth before the children of iniquity, so didst thou fall." And all the people wept again over him. And all the people came to cause David to eat bread while it was yet day; but David swore, saying: "God do so to me, and more also, if I taste bread, or aught else, till the sun be down . . . Know ye not that there is a prince and a great man fallen this day in Israel? . . ."

David's rebuke to the Amalekite who slew Jonathan was the question which Max Schlesinger of Albany[84] asked in the name of all Americans:

"How wast thou not afraid to put forth thy hand to destroy the Lord's anointed?"

Bernhard Felsenthal of Chicago[85] commenced his sermon with Isaiah's stirring proclamation of hope:

"Then shall thy light break forth as the morning,
And thy healing shall spring forth speedily . . ."

The sermons were as varied in text and in thought as their authors in character and interest. But there was a uniformness, a sameness about them, nonetheless. They dealt with the inscrutability of God's ways; the inevitability of death; the hope of immortality. Lincoln's death was compared over and over with Moses': the work of one era done, the transference of leadership to another generation. The rabbis sought to find a lesson for America in the murder of a beloved chief executive: everyone who had committed a sin or swerved from the ethical life shared Booth's responsibility for the assassination; Lincoln's death was a visitation from God, punishment of America for all the evil of the war. There was thanksgiving and gratitude for Lincoln's deeds and character; his noble work was a legacy to the nation—the abolition of slavery and the reconstruction of the Union; but his habits of heart were also an inheritance to be passed on to future generations.

Many of the memorial sermons referred to Lincoln's relationship with the Jews. Isaac Leeser said that the action taken by the President in reference to Jewish chaplains and the Grant affair "speak loudly for the natural kindness of the late President, which all can cheerfully acknowledge, whatever their political opinions may be, and let us hope that all in authority in America may be animated by the same spirit of justice and liberality."[86] Col. Philip J. Joachimsen of New York, who was invited to deliver the memorial address at the Temimi Derech Synagogue in New Orleans, said that "we, as Jews, had a distinct ground to love, respect and esteem him. I know that he, in his high position, appreciated those of our creed who had come forward to sustain him. His mind was not subject to the vulgar clamor against Jews, and when . . . an order was made to banish Jews as a class from a particular Department . . . our deceased President at once reversed an unauthorized command so harsh and . . . condemnable."[87] Alfred T. Jones, President of Beth El-Emeth Congregation of Philadelphia and an outspoken Democrat during the war, said that

> While many occupying high positions have either ignored our existence or turned a deaf ear to our claims for protection or redress, his just, kind and generous nature was never appealed to by us in vain. On every occasion (and he has been several times appealed to) he promptly recognized our claims as a religious body to national protection, and acceded unhesitatingly to all our just demands. So strong and noble a contrast to others did he exhibit in this respect, that we should be guilty of gross ingratitude not to acknowledge it.[88]

The Jews were not ungrateful for the President's fairmindedness towards them.

Isaac M. Wise tried to grasp the meaning of Lincoln as a human being, and spoke of "the passions, feelings, struggles, victories, motives and thoughts of . . . the man who stood at the head of affairs during this gigantic struggle, his cares and troubles, his sleepless nights and days of anxiety, his thoughts and his schemes, his triumphs and mortifications, his hopes and fears, and ten thousand more sentiments, feelings and thoughts. . ." But it was impossible, he said, to describe the inner Lincoln in words or pigment or stone. One would have to be satisfied to emulate the spirit and principles of the man.

> Let us carry into effect and perpetuate the great desires which heaved the breast of Abraham Lincoln; let us be one people, one, free, just and enlightened; let us be the chosen people to perpetuate and promulgate liberty and righteousness, the union and freedom of the human family; let us break asunder, wherever we can, the chains of the bondsman, the fetters of the slave, the iron rod of despotism, the oppressive yoke of tyranny; let us banish

strife, discord, hatred, injustice, oppression from the domain of man . . . and we set him the most durable monument in the hearts of the human family . . .[89]

Sabato Morais was chagrined at the efforts of some Protestant divines to prove that Lincoln was a religious man.

Why, my friends, [he said] if the essence of religion is what the great Hillel taught us, then I unhesitatingly say that the breast of our lamented President was ever kindled with that divine spark. "To forbear doing unto others what would displease us," was his golden rule. It is the maxim he illustrated in the immortal document of emancipation that bears his honorable signature. It is that which he exemplified by his numerous acts of clemency towards the unworthy, by remitting criminal offenses, by restoring the child of guilt to a widowed mother, or a desolate household. It is that which is breathed in every line of his last official message. He who penned these soul-elevating words needs not an open declaration of faith to evince his piety. "With malice towards none, with charity for all, with firmness in the right, as God gives us to see the right, let us finish the work in which we are engaged, to bind up the nation's wounds, to care for him who shall have borne the battle, and for his widow and orphans; to do all which may achieve and cherish a just and lasting peace among ourselves and with all nations."[90]

Max Lilienthal saw in Lincoln "the first laborer-President." He had risen from the lowliest of origins to the highest office in the land. His election had unfolded, for the first time, "the full meaning of American liberty and equality."

Do not give up the work, says his example, because you are born in an obscure station; do not get disheartened, because you have to wrestle with the disadvantages of a want of education—life is the best school, energy and perseverance the best teacher, honesty of purpose the best means for obtaining success; follow his example, and we shall finally, and in fact, establish the equality of mankind. He has achieved this triumph, and a whole world stands there, first amazed and then admiring the man, who, by his own indomitable energy, proved the greatness and glory of our institutions.

Lilienthal found in the personal story of Lincoln an object-lesson for his congregation of immigrants. They, too, might share in the realization of democracy patterned on the life of "the people's President."[91]

Rabbi Samuel Adler of Temple Emanu-El, New York, thought that Lincoln resembled Moses in the rare quality of meekness.

Man cannot create meekness; it is natural; it comes with and remains with him. He was the great spirit which sheltered and protected this whole nation . . . Like Moses, he was ever thoughtful of the duty allotted to him, to bring his people back to enjoy the whole land. For land and people were the desires and determinations of these men. Both lived lowly in spirit, both were respected, loved, and adored, and both died with the same qualities. How terrible that Abraham Lincoln, having performed a portion of his duty, should be taken away by the hand of destiny before he completed it. This sad event was the will of God, and we must bear it calmly, as if a prophet had died. . . .

As if a prophet had died! Not one who peered into the future, but one who by the depth of his spiritual insight and the universality of his compassion, brought a divine message to his fellow-men.[92]

In the estimation of Rabbi Bernard Illowy of New Orleans, Lincoln's memorable qualities were his honesty and goodness.

No, thy hands were never bound by the wiles of others, by the ties of flattery or by the galling manacles of fear; thou didst hear nothing but the wishes of thy people, thou didst fear none but God who alone was thy guide and trust . . . Thy hands were always active, always stretched forth to help, when and where thy help was needed. Thy feet were not put in chains, never restrained by selfishness, never checked by ambition, but with self-denial, with noble ardor, with paternal love and a brave and courageous heart didst thou walk before thy people, to save their honor, to guard their rights and to restore peace and harmony to their gates; and thou hast succeeded . . . Thou hast wound thyself lovingly around the hearts of millions with gentle ties, which even the destructive tooth of time can never loosen. Ages will roll upon ages, but thy memory will still live in the hearts of thy countrymen until the latest generations. . . .[93]

For John Wilkes Booth, the rabbis found no word too harsh. Samuel M. Isaacs asked his congregation if they would have believed a week ago that "here on earth, in this century, monsters could be found to deprive so valuable, so good, so religious a being of his life? Yet it is a fact, that in our boasted age of civilization and intellect, there are yet hearts so depraved, intellects so stunted as to harm the nation's benefactor."[94] Max Lilienthal thought that the War Department was at fault for not having kept its eye on Booth. "To allow a man like Booth—a man who, on the stage of New Orleans, trampled upon our flag, spat at it and disgraced it—to allow such a man to go about free and unmolested in our capital, was a fatal error, a disastrous mistake, and the whole country has to suffer and to mourn for it."[95] Illowy thought Booth was an "infernal fiend;"[96] Wise called him a "mad villain;"[97] Vidaver said he was an "imbruted assassin;"[98] to Morais he was an "execrable wretch [who] has robbed liberty of its staunchest defender, and nature of its noblest creation."[99]

In their mourning over the loss of the martyred leader, and their anger at the psychopathic deed of his assassin, all of the rabbis were humane enough to urge restraint on extreme ideas of vengeance.

Justice, [said Lilienthal] but no vengeance! Do you wish to honor his memory? Try to finish that part of his work he left undone ... The South lies conquered and subjugated at our feet. She has sown the wind, and has reaped the whirlwind. But now she is no longer our foe; she is part and parcel of our family. We must assist her in healing her deep and sore wounds. With charity to all, we must help her to recover her former flourishing condition. We must feed and clothe her; we must take care of her widows and orphans; by the hand of free labor we must redeem her devastated territory. We must learn not only to forgive, but also to forget, so that the South, seeing her sin repaid by love and charity, may come back in sincere repentance, and resolve to wipe out, by future deeds of loyal patriotism, the shame and disgrace of past rebellion. The Union—then a Union, not of the law and the sword, but of sentiment and brotherly feeling—will inscribe, with tears of joy and gratitude, on Lincoln's monument the appropriate words: "The United Nation to the savior of the country."[100]

So, too, Elkan Cohn of San Francisco expressed the hope that Booth's crime might not arouse the North to exact vengeance from the entire Southland:

And we pray that He, in His infinite love, may graciously avert the dreadful consequences of this calamity, calm the passions of the people, so justly aroused at this atrocious crime, soothe the grief and sorrow so deeply cutting in the very heart of our nation, and speak to the Angel of Destruction: "Enough! The noblest victim may be the last. Henceforth, the great work for which they bled stands under my divine protection ... I will now seal their work with the great blessing of peace!" O God! Thou who hast given victory to Thy people, may it please Thee to bless thy people with peace.[101]

Echoing the sentiments of his rabbinical colleagues, Sabato Morais called upon the people of America to immortalize Abraham Lincoln in the only real way a human being could be immortalized by his fellow-men.

It is not by polished marble that the memory of our sainted chieftain can be extolled. The heart that sorrows for his untimely decease; the heart that glows with gratitude at the recollection of his labor and services, is the acknowledgement that becomes one so good. We must bear his name with a blessing upon our lips. Teach our children to pronounce it with the reverence inspired by that of the immortal father of this Republic. Picture it in their presence, as an incentive to virtue, his unostentatious goodness. Show how he adhered to truth amid appalling trials; how he met death for the sake of principles. The precious blood will then, indeed, bear fruits of sublimity. ... Oh, blessed be the grief we feel, if it will adjust all differences, bury away all animosities, make an end of party strife, and raise a high and exalted throne to enduring peace in the country of Lincoln and Washington.[102]

In many cities throughout the nation, Jewish organizations took part in community-wide memorial exercises. The two Memphis congregations participated in a union memorial service in the city park; 167 members of Euphrates Lodge of B'nai B'rith marched in the procession preceding the service, and Rabbi Tuska spoke briefly as the Jewish representative.[103] Congregation B'nai B'rith of Los Angeles was one of the organizations which sponsored a memorial procession in that city. Since the congregation had no synagogue, its members met at the home of Rabbi Abraham Edelman after the public exercises for a Jewish memorial service.[104] Congregations in Chicago[105] and Boston[106] also participated in civic processions and memorial services.

As "the lonesome train" made its way from city to city, and millions of citizens bade a last farewell to the fallen leader, special committees were appointed to escort the train from one area to another. Josiah Cohen of Pittsburgh,[107] Abraham Kohn of Chicago[108] and Julius Hammerslough of Springfield,[109] were members of these civic committees in their respective communities.

The greatest demonstration of all was held in New York City. About three thousand Jews marched in the civic procession, representing Jewish Masonic lodges, the B'nai B'rith and other Jewish fraternal orders, the Ceres Union and other Jewish social and literary organizations. Meanwhile other Jewish groups met at the Shearith Israel Synagogue for special exercises, after which they proceeded to the public memorial meeting in which the Rev. S.M. Isaacs represented the Jews. He read some passages from Scripture and an original prayer. *The Jewish Record's* report of these activities is reprinted as Appendix D.[110]

To all this outpouring of grief by Jewish congregations and rabbis, only one voice of objection was raised, not on political but on traditional grounds. A New Jersey gentleman, writing to *The Occident*, rebelled against the recitation of memorial prayers for Lincoln:

> I have heard that in one of our congregations, an Escava [memorial prayer] was repeated by the Hazan. If not sinful, is this not most absurd and ridiculous? If we are to maintain our form, and perpetuate the peculiar ideas of our faith, should we not be careful to guard against innovations under any pretense whatever? It was entirely right and proper that the Jewish congregations should express their sorrow at the death of the Chief Magistrate of the country, and their detestation of perpetrators of the horrible deed which deprived him of life; but is it necessary for this purpose to run counter to the opinions and religious views of their co-religionists? Is there a Jew in this whole land, educated in the history and traditions of his people, who would consider a Christian deserving of any of the *religious* services appertaining to Jewish worship or who in a moment of calm reflection can find any comparison between the late President and their great law-giver, "whom the Lord knew face to face"? . . .[111]

By their resolutions and services, the Jews of America showed themselves to be far more liberal than this narrow sectarian from New Jersey. The

Rev. Leeser gave his answer to this letter in his memorial sermon in Washington on April 22:

> It is, indeed, somewhat unusual to pray for one not of our faith, but by no means in opposition to its spirit, and therefore not inadmissible. We pray for the dead, because we believe that the souls of the departed as well as of the living are in the keeping of God . . . The prayers, therefore, offered up this day for the deceased President are in accordance with the spirit of the faith which we have inherited as children of Israel, who recognize in all men those created like them in the image of God, and all entitled to His mercy, grace, and pardon, though they have not yet learned to worship and adore Him as we do who have been especially selected as the bearers of His law. . . .[112]

Prominent citizens of the town from which Lincoln had gone forth to lead the nation in war met together on May 2, 1865, to form the Lincoln Monument Association, for the purpose of erecting a monument which would honor Illinois' most distinguished son.[113] Julius Hammerslough, a Springfield merchant who had been on intimate terms with the late President and was the first president of Temple B'rith Sholom, was asked to represent the Association in an appeal to the rabbis and synagogues of the nation. His letter asked Jews to contribute to the fund out of a desire to prove themselves patriotic citizens as well as out of reverence for Lincoln's memory. "Let it be remembered," he said, "that we have, as a race, despite the advanced and enlightened age, to meet the prejudices still existing in the minds of many. Let us quell this feeling, and vindicate ourselves by contributing to this holy national work, in a manner that shall prove that the Hebrews are, as they have ever been, the staunch friends of freedom and liberty, and the foes of all oppression and wrong."[114]

The response which Hammerslough received was a gratifying indication of the eagerness of Jews to unite with their fellow citizens in memorializing the late President. Special committees collected funds for the monument in Philadelphia and Cincinnati.[115] The duplicate receipts for contributions to the Monument Association are so organized that it is not possible to ascertain the total sums collected by these committees, but Hammerslough himself received a total of $260.25 from his appeal, and the congregations in Alton, Ill., LaPorte, Ind., Louisville, Ky., Quincy, Ill., and St. Joseph, Mo., sent additional sums totaling $225 directly to the Association. Congregations Keneseth Israel of Philadelphia, and K.A.M. and B'nai Sholem of Chicago, forwarded another $150. This does not, of course, include contributions from individual Jews.[116]

New York and Philadelphia had plans for their own monuments in Lincoln's memory. Sabato Morais was delegated to send Mikveh Israel's contributions of $300 to the Mayor of Philadelphia.[117] The Rev. J.J. Lyons of Shearith Israel Congregation of New York made a personal appeal to his congregation at services, asking each member "to assist in the furtherance of so noble and commendable an undertaking, which will in [the] future bear testimony of your love of a good man, and your appreciation of the services of a faithful officer—peace be unto his memory."[118] *The Jewish Messenger* printed the names of ninety-nine New York Jews who had forwarded their contributions to its office for transmission to the proper authorities.[119]

So American Jewry paid a last tribute to the President who had appointed the first Jewish chaplains and ordered the revocation of the most sweeping anti-Jewish regulation in American history.

IX EPILOGUE

INTO THE FOUR YEARS of the Civil War were compressed the experiences and lessons and pain of generations. Events of our own day continue to be motivated by political, economic and psychological forces which were created by the catastrophe of 1861–1865. Such contemporary problems as the social backwardness of many areas of the Southland, the recognition of the civil rights of the Negro in many sections of the country, the tremendous discrepancy between the economic productivity of the North and that of the South, the effect of Southern sectionalism upon national political issues—these and many other problems demonstrate over and over again the vital relevance of the Civil War to our own age.

The experiences of the American Jewish community during the Civil War also had far-reaching effects. Out of the crucible of those emotion-laden years came trends which were to shape the life of American Jewry for several generations.

The first of these was the highly accelerated pace of Americanization which resulted from Jewish participation in the war on both the individual and communal levels. In less critical periods of the national life, the immigrant tends to assimilate the atmosphere of his new home slowly, cautiously, unhurriedly. He savors the mores and manners and ideas of his environment gradually, as a stranger, with a mixture of fear and reluctance, retaining as a safeguard the bulk of his older heritage. In some periods and areas, several generations have had to pass through the assimilatory process before the change-over from immigrant to American has been completed. During the fratricidal blood-bath of the Civil War, however, the most desperate, fearsome period in American history, almost every inhabitant—citizen, immigrant, visitor—was drawn into the fray, emotionally even more than physically. Psychologically it was almost impossible for the alien to remain aloof from the strife which was disrupting the nation. In the South and in the North, the average immigrant became a partisan—generally sharing the ideas and attitudes of his neighbors, opposing them in a few, rare instances, but making an emotional commitment whatever his stand. The national defeats and triumphs were part of his daily life; the high excitements of victory and the depressions of tragedy drove deeply into his nature. Enduring the hardships of battle, burying sons and husbands and friends, participating in the multifarious welfare activities of the home front, taking sides in political arguments—these and a thousand other aspects of life in a nation at war with itself Americanized the large immigrant population at a much more rapid rate than that of more peaceful times.

Jews, like other immigrants, felt that they had earned their stake in the country. They belonged to it. This feeling of being a part of America played a major role in the inner life of American Jewry in the post-war generation. Reform Judaism, for example, which many regarded as a conscious adaptation of the Jewish tradition to the American climate, entered its greatest period of expansion and growth with the end of the war. When the floods of Jewish refugees from the pogroms of Eastern Europe began to beat against the shores of America in the late Seventies, the German immigrants of the previous generations had practically completed the process of acculturation. Reform Judaism had, in fact, become estranged in many ways from the major currents of Jewish thinking and practice. The amazing antipathy between the Eastern European, Orthodox Jewish immigrants and the Americanized Reform Jews, which has been a significant feature of American Jewish communal life almost to our own day, was at one and the same time a result and a demonstration of this rapid pace of assimilation. Another indication of this same factor was the attempt of the Reform communities to accelerate the natural, slow process of adjustment in the lives of the East-European immigrants. But classes and organizations and clubs and centers could not hasten assimilation in the same manner as the emergency of a war. Many of the new immigrants remained aloof, looking askance at what they considered to be the sacrifice of the essentials of Jewish tradition by the Americanized Reform Jews.

But those self-same immigrants who were shocked at the Protestant-like behavior of the Reform Jews were subjected to yet another stunning blow: the emotional furore of the first World War speeded up the assimilatory process in the lives of their own children, who began to take on the coloration of the environment with the same haste as the German immigrants after the Civil War.

One important feature of the process of acculturation is a realistic appraisal of the conditions of the new life. During the Civil War, American Jewry had learned much about the problems which it would have to solve. It had been confronted with two critical challenges: the denial of equal rights in connection with the chaplaincy legislation, and the increasing onslaughts of anti-Jewish prejudice. In the two specific cases of the Jewish chaplaincy and Grant's General Order Number 11, the Jewish communities made public demand for rectification and achieved their objective. In the one case, Congress recognized the principle of equality, and in the other, President Lincoln cancelled the offensive regulation as soon as it came to his attention. American Jewry knew that it need have no hesitation about using the right of petition; its faith in the American safeguards of the rights of religious minorities was upheld. The government was not indifferent to victims of bigotry.

But could one legislate against the misrepresentation of Jews by newspaper editors and other prejudiced individuals? American Jewry knew that it would not be free from attack; but it also knew that those attacks were not typical of America. This was a major lesson of the Civil War period; one which would have to be learned again and again. It was not a question of black or white; one could not say that all Americans respected the Jews, nor that they all disliked the Jews. In certain quarters prejudice would arise; in others there was fairmindedness. Each occurrence of discrimination had to be dealt with as a specific case. In 1867, for instance, five insurance companies announced that they would no longer issue policies to Jews. Many prominent non-Jews denounced the action as intolerant and un-American. Public protest meetings conducted by non-Jews as well as Jews were held in many cities. Other firms made hasty announcement of their opposition to the policy of the five. By and large, the newspapers and the public took a determined stand against the offending companies. America as a whole had, perhaps, learned something from the excesses of the Civil War.

Another result of the Civil War experiences of the American Jewish community was its heightened consciousness of the need for national organizations and institutions. The impulse towards nation-wide unification of effort had been halted, temporarily, by the outbreak of hostilities in 1861. But the events of the war years had strengthened the determination of Wise, Leeser and Isaacs to reach the objectives for which they had been striving through several decades. The crises of the war had demonstrated to them and to many other Jews throughout the land how feeble American Jewry actually was without representative organizations. Now, with the end of the conflict, the leaders returned with renewed vigor and conviction to the task of creating a climate which would be favorable to cooperative endeavors. Their success was noteworthy. Leeser and the eastern Traditionalists opened the doors of Maimonides College, the first American Jewish academy of higher learning, in 1867. Within a few years it had graduated the first two American-trained Jewish spiritual leaders. Wise, working desperately to unite the congregations throughout the mid-West and South, finally realized his dream when the Union of American Hebrew Congregations held its organizational meeting in 1873. Two years later the Union established the Hebrew Union College in Cincinnati.

American Jewry had been, in 1860, inchoate and immature, uncertain of its needs and unsure of its strength, almost completely unprepared to solve the most elementary of its problems. Time alone would serve to give it the understanding and wisdom, the courage and self-discipline it required. But the process of time was assisted by the devastating experience of the Civil War. In 1865 American Jewry was more than five years older; it had learned the lessons and gained the insights of several generations.

APPENDIX A

List of Printed Sermons, Speeches and Prayers Dealing with the Civil War

Bondi, Jonas: Prayer. Philadelphia; *Occ.*, XXII, No. 9, p. 403, Dec. 1864.

Cohn, Elkan: Prayer. San Francisco; *HEB* I, No. 46, p. 1, Oct. 28, 1864.

DeCordova, R. J.: Sermon. New York; *Occ.*, XVIII, No 42, pp. 253-4, 260-1, Jan. 10, 1861. *Isr.*, VII, No. 29, pp. 228-9, Jan. 18, 1861.

DeCordova, R. J.: Sermon. New York; *Mess.*, IX, No. 20, pp. 154-5, May 24, 1861.

DeLeeuw, M. R.: Prayer. New York; *Mess.*, XVI, No. 21, p. 164, Dec. 2, 1864.

Deutsch, Solomon: Speech. Syracuse; *Isr.*, IX, No. 11, p. 83, Sept. 19, 1862. No. 15, pp. 116-7, Oct. 17, 1862. No. 17, p. 130, Oct. 31, 1862.

Einhorn, David: Sermon. Philadelphia; *Sinai*, VII, No. 7, pp. 183-192, Aug. 1862.

Einhorn, David: Sermon. Philadelphia; Published separately, Phila. 1864.

Felsenthal, Bernhard: Sermon. Chicago; *HL*, VII, No. 11, p. 1, Dec. 22, 1865.

Fischel, Arnold: Sermon. New York; *Mess.*, IX, No. 2, p. 11, Jan. 11, 1861.

Fischel, Arnold: Sermon. New York; *Mess.*, X, No. 7, p. 51, Oct. 4, 1861.

Gunzberg, A.: Prayer. Rochester; *Mess.*, XV, No. 20, p. 157, May 27, 1864.

Gutheim, J. K.: Prayer. Montgomery; Newspaper Clipping. I. Solomon Collection. Duke University Library.

Hochheimer, Henry: Sermon. Baltimore; *Isr.*, VII, No. 30, p. 236, Jan. 25, 1861. *Occ.*, XVIII, No. 44, p. 268, Jan. 24, 1861.

Huebsch, Adolf: Sermon. New York; *Mess.*, XX, No. 22, p. 3, Dec. 7, 1866.

Illowy, Bernard: Sermon. Baltimore; *Occ.*, XVIII, No. 44, pp. 267-8, Jan. 24, 1861.

Isaacs, S. M.: Sermon. New York; *Mess.*, VIII, No 22, p. 173, Dec. 7, 1860.

Isaacs, S. M.: Sermon. New York; *Mess.*, IX, No. 2, pp. 12-13, Jan. 11, 1861.

Isaacs, S. M.: Prayer. New York; *Mess.*, IX, No. 20, p. 157, May 24, 1861.

Isaacs, S. M.: Sermon. New York; *Mess.*, X, No. 7, p. 51, Oct. 4, 1861.

Isaacs, S. M.: Sermon. New York; *JR*, I, No. 12, pp. 2-3, Nov. 28, 1862.

Isaacs, S. M.: Sermon. New York; *Mess.*, XIII, No. 18, pp. 152-3, May 3, 1863.

Isaacs, S. M.: Sermon. New York; *Mess.*, XIV, No. 21, p. 187, Dec. 4, 1863.

Isaacs, S. M.: Sermon. New York; *Mess.*, XVI, No. 6, p. 44, Aug. 12, 1864.

Isaacs, S. M.: Sermon. New York; *Mess.*, XVI, No. 21, pp. 164-5, Dec. 2, 1864.

Isaacs, S. M.: Sermon. New York; *Mess.*, XX, No. 22, pp. 2-3, Dec. 7, 1866.

Jacobs, George: Prayer. Richmond; *Occ.*, XVIII, No. 42, p. 253, Jan. 10, 1861. *Richmond Daily Dispatch*, Dec. 31, 1860. *Mess.*, IX, No. 3, pp. 20-1, Jan. 18, 1861.

Jacobs, George: Prayer. Richmond; *Richmond Daily Dispatch*, Feb. 19, 1861. *Mess.*, IX, No. 9, p. 69, March 1, 1861.

Jacobs, H. S.: Sermon. Augusta, Ga.; *Occ.*, XXIII, No. 10, pp. 462-8, Jan. 1866.

Lasker, R.: Sermon. New York; *Mess.*, X, No. 12, p. 91, Dec. 13, 1861.

Leeser, Isaac: Sermon. Philadelphia; *Occ.*, XVIII, No. 38, pp. 227-9, Dec. 13, 1860.

Leeser, Isaac: Prayer. Philadelphia; *Occ.*, XVIII, No. 39, pp. 237-8, Dec. 20, 1860.

Lilienthal, Max: Sermon. Cincinnati; Philipson, *Max Lilienthal*, pp. 398-414. *Isr.*, XI, No. 44, pp. 349-50, April 28, 1865.

Lilienthal, Max: Sermon. Cincinnati; *Isr.*, XIII, No. 40, p. 4, April 12, 1867.

Lyons, J. J.: Sermon. New York; *HL*, VII, No. 11, p. 2, Dec. 15, 1865.

Michelbacher, M. J.: Prayer. Richmond; *Occ.*, XVIII, No. 43, p. 260, Jan. 17, 1861.

Michelbacher, M. J.: Prayer. Richmond; Printed in Text, pp. 88-90.

Michelbacher, M. J.: Sermon. Richmond; *JR*, II, No. 13, p. 1, June 5, 1863.

Morais, Sabato: Sermon. Philadelphia; *Mess.*, X, No. 7, pp. 52-3, Oct. 4, 1861.

Morais, Sabato: Sermon. Philadelphia; *Mess.*, X, No. 12, p. 91, Dec. 13, 1861.

Morais, Sabato: Sermon. Philadelphia; *Mess.*, XI, No. 16, pp. 129-30, May 2, 1862.

Morais, Sabato: Sermon. Philadelphia; *JR*, II, No. 9, p. 1, May 8, 1863.

Morais, Sabato: Sermon. Philadelphia; *Mess.*, XIV, No. 2, pp. 12-13, July 10, 1863.

Morais, Sabato: Sermon. Philadelphia; *Mess.*, XV, No. 2, pp. 9-10, Jan. 15, 1864.

Morais, Sabato: Sermon. Philadelphia; *Mess.*, XIII, No. 19, p. 165, May 15, 1865.

Moses, M.: Sermon. Peoria; Reprinted from *Peoria Morning Mail* in *Isr.*, X, No. 13, p. 88, Sept. 25, 1863. *JR*, III, No. 2, p. 1, Sept. 25, 1863.

Myers, M. H.: Prayer. New York; *Mess.*, XVII, No. 6, p. 44, Feb. 10, 1865.

Noot, Isaac: Prayer. Philadelphia; *Occ.*, XIX, No. 4, p. 142, June, 1861.

Pape, G.: Prayer. Philadelphia; *Occ.*, XIX, No. 12, p. 561, March, 1862.

Raphall, M. J.: Sermon. New York; *Mess.*, VIII, No. 22, p. 173, Dec. 7, 1860. *Occ.*, XVIII, No. 38, pp. 229-30, Dec. 13, 1860.

Raphall, M. J.: Sermon. New York; *Mess.*, IX, No. 2, p. 11, Jan. 11, 1861. Printed separately, 1861, New York.

Raphall, M. J.: Sermon. New York; *Mess.*, IX, No. 20, pp. 156-7, May 24, 1861.

Raphall, M. J.: Sermon. New York; *Mess.*, X, No. 7, p. 51, Oct. 4, 1861.

Raphall, M. J.: Sermon. New York; *JR*, I, No. 12, p. 2, Nov. 28, 1862.

Raphall, M. J.: Sermon. New York; *JR*, II, No. 9, p. 1, May 8, 1863. *Mess.*, XIII, No. 18, p. 154, May 3, 1863.

Raphall, M. J.: Sermon. New York; *HL*, VII, No. 11, p. 2, Dec. 15, 1865.

Raphall, M. J.: Sermon. New York; *Mess.*, XX, No. 22, pp. 2-3, Dec. 7, 1866.

Szold, Benjamin: Sermon. Baltimore; *Isr.*, VII, No. 28, p. 220, Jan. 11, 1861.

Wise, I. M.: Prayer. Cleveland; Quoted from *Cleveland Plain Dealer*; *Occ.*, XVIII, No. 40, p. 243, Dec. 27, 1860.

Wise, I. M.: Sermon. Cincinnati; *Isr.*, XI, No. 43, pp. 340-1, April 21, 1865.

APPENDIX B

Jonas-Lincoln Correspondence

Quincy Ills Sep 16. 1854

A Lincoln Esq
Springfield Ills

My Dr Sir—We are in the midst of what will probably be the warmest contest for Congress that we have ever had in this district—if the election was near at hand—Williams, I think would be elected beyond a doubt. This district is to be the great battle field, the defeat of Richardson at this time, would be the downfall of Douglas, standing and occupying the same position on the Nebraska humbug—every foul and unfair means will be brought to operate against Williams. Douglas is to be here and will [speak?] in this and other counties of the district. Williams has just left for Oqua[w]ka—it being court in Henderson on Monday next—and has requested me to say to you, that he, as well as *all the Whigs* here, would be much gratified if you could make it convenient and pay us a visit, while the little giant is here. It is believed by all who know you, that a reply from you, would be more effective, than from any other. I trust you may be able to pay us the visit and thereby create a debt of gratitude on the part of the Whigs here, which they may at some time, have it in their power, to repay with pleasure and with interest. We do not exactly know when Douglas will be here—but you can consent to come, we will let you know in time. I will thank you to answer this as soon as convenient—and be assured that nothing will afford greater pleasure to your personal friends and the Whigs generally than you consent to visit us—and the Douglasites would as soon see old nick here as yourself. The present indications here are good. This county will do better, or I am much mistaken, than it has done for many years. Pike will give a decided majority for us. Brown will do as well as on former occasions although Singleton is doing all in his power against us. We hear favorably from all parts of the district—and I think with your assistance, we can check mate them

Trusting to hear from you soon

I remain Yrs truely

A Jonas*

* Robert Todd Lincoln Collection of Lincoln Papers, Manuscript Division, Library of Congress.

Quincy Dec 2. 1854

A Lincoln Esqu

My dear Sir

Yrs of the 27th ultimo is at hand. I have seen Mr. Sullivan. I can get nothing out of him except that he will act altogether with the Whig party in regard to Senator and will make no pledges.

He would of course support Williams or Browning—and no doubt would prefer either of these gentlemen to any others—and I am inclined to think though he did not say so, that you would be his next choice—and I think, that Browning & Williams out of the question, you may rely on him—although I am not authorized to say so.

I have no pretentions for that or any other office at this time—and Browning & Williams not being in the way, I should prefer you to any other—and should be pleased to render you any service in my power.

Yrs truely

A Jonas*

=====

Urbana, Oct. 21. 1856

A. Jonas, Esq

My dear Sir:

I am here at court, and find myself so 'hobbled' with a particular case, that I can not leave, & consequently, can not be with you on the 23rd. I regret this exceedingly, but there is no help for it. Please make the best apology, for me, in your power.

Your friend as ever

A. Lincoln.†

=====

Quincy July 30. 1858

A Lincoln Esqu

Springfield Ills

My dear Sir

You will see by the enclosed slip that we hold a district convention at Augusta in Hancock Co, on the 25th of August. This town is quite near the line of Adams & Schuyler and on the Quincy and Chicago Rail Road—36 miles from this city. You are of course aware that a Senator has to be elected from the counties of Hancock, Henderson & Schuyler. This is one of the most im-

* Robert Todd Lincoln Collection of Lincoln Papers, Manuscript Division, Library of Congress.

† Paul M. Angle (ed.), *New Letters and Papers of Lincoln*, p. 164.

portant districts and the result in the Senate in my opinion, depends on it. The fight will be a desperate one; James Stark of Augusta will be the Rep Candidate and with the proper exertions can be elected. Can you make it convenient to be [in?] Augusta on the day of the convention, we can get to hear you the tallest kind of a crowd, and one of *your sledge hammer speeches*, will effect wonders—it is I think a very important point, and you ought not to miss being there. Answer me, on this subject immediately, so that we may make it known in time. Things are working well here. Jac Davis is an Independent democratic candidate in opposition to Morris he and his friends—will canvass the District. The anti Douglas and anti Morris feeling is greatly on the increase—many of the Leaders are openly out for the Administration. Brooks of the Herald will be removed from the P.O. in a few days, and WH Carlin, who is anti-Douglas and anti Morris, will be appointed, it is said—the most bitter feeling prevails between the different factions—pray God it may result in good.

God speed you in your fight

Yrs sincerely

A Jonas*

don't fail answering

———————

Springfield, Aug: 2. 1858—

A. Jonas, Esq

My dear Sir

Yours of the 30th July is just received. My mind is at once made up to be with you at Augusta on the 25th of August, unless I shall conclude it will prevent my being at Freeport on the 27th when and where, by appointment, I am to meet Judge Douglas. I suppose there will be no difficulty in getting from Augusta to Freeport in due time.

Yours very truly

A. Lincoln.†

———————

Quincy Ills Augt 5/58

Hon A. Lincoln

Springfield Ills.

My dear Sir

There will be no difficulty in the world in your getting to Freeport on the 27th after being at Augusta on the 25th. I have therefore had it announced that you will be there—and you may expect the tallest kind of a crowd.

* Robert Todd Lincoln Collection of Lincoln Papers, Manuscript Division, Library of Congress.

† Lincoln Collection, Illinois State Historical Library.

Things look well here, and the split is widening daily between the two branches of the unterrified. The Buccaneers supporting Jac Davis and the Douglasites, I N Morris—the latter will poll by far the largest vote, but the *Stinkfingers* are daily gaining strength—the great difficulty with us is in getting a Candidate for Congress. Browning could I think be elected, but he will not consent to run under any circumstance, what we shall do on the 25th I can hardly say?—but like Macawber—hoping that something will turn up—

I remain   Yrs truely

A Jonas*

Quincy Feb 3/60

Hon A Lincoln

My dear Sir

I want to get a copy of the book publishing in Ohio containing the speeches of your self and Doug in the Campaign of last year, can you procure me a copy, or advise me, how and where I can get one.

Let me congratulate you on the election of Speaker—and indications are that with proper exertions and judicious selections at Chicago in June, we shall be able to carry the day and in November proclaim *victory to all the World*.

Yrs &c   A Jonas†

Springfield. Feb. 4 1860

Hon: A. Jonas

My dear Sir:

Yours of the 3rd inquiring how you can get a copy of the debates now being published in Ohio, is received. As you are one of my most valued friends, and have complimented me by the expression of a wish for a book, I propose doing myself the honor of presenting you with one, as soon as I can. By the arrangement our Ohio friends have made with the publishers, I am to have one hundred copies gratis. When I shall receive them I will send you one by Express. I understand they will not be out before March, and I probably shall be absent about that time. So that you must not be disappointed if you do not receive yours before about the middle of that month

Yours very truly

A. Lincoln‡

* Robert Todd Lincoln Collection of Lincoln Papers, Manuscript Division, Library of Congress.

† Robert Todd Lincoln Collection of Lincoln Papers, Manuscript Division, Library of Congress.

‡ Lincoln Collection, Illinois State Historical Library (which also possesses a copy of the book, inscribed, "To Hon. Abraham Jonas/ with respects of/ A. Lincoln").

JONAS-LINCOLN CORRESPONDENCE

"Confidential"

Quincy Ills. July 20/60

Hon A Lincoln—

My dear Sir

I have just been creditably informed, that *Isaac N. Morris* is engaged in obtaining affadavits and certificates of certain Irishmen that they saw you in Quincy come out of a Know Nothing Lodge—the intention is to send the affadavits to Washington for publication. I do not know if there is any truth in the matter, neither do I care, but thought it best to let you know about it—the object is to work on the Germans—and Morris can get men to swear to any thing—my informant saw one of the affadavits or certificates.

Yrs truely

A Jonas*

if it all false, let me know

═══════════════════

Confidential

Springfield Ill July 21st 1860.

Hon. A. Jonas
My Dear Sir—

Yours of the 20th is received. I suppose as good, or even better men than I may have been in American or Know-Nothing lodges; but in point of fact, I never was in one, at Quincy or elsewhere. I was never in Quincy but one day and two nights while Know-Nothing lodges were in existence, and you were with me that day and both those nights. I had never been there before in my life; and never afterwards, till the joint debate with Douglas in 1858. It was in 1854 when I spoke in some hall there, and after the speaking, you with others took me to an oyster saloon, passed an hour there, and you walked with me to, and parted with me at the Quincy House, quite late at night. I left by stage for Naples before day-light in the morning, having come in by the same route, after dark the evening previous to the speaking, when I found you waiting at the Quincy House to meet me. A few days after I was there, Richardson, as I understood, started this same story about my having been in a Know-Nothing lodge. When I heard of the charge, as I did soon after, I taxed my recollection for some incident which could have suggested it; and I remembered that on parting with you the last night, I went to the office of the Hotel, to take my stage passage for the morning, was told that no stage office for that line was kept there, and that I must see the driver before retiring, to insure his calling for me in the morning; and a servant was sent with me to find the driver, who after taking me a square or two, stopped me, and stopped perhaps a dozen steps farther, and in my hearing called to some one, who answered him, apparently from the upper part of a building, and promised to call with the stage

* Robert Todd Lincoln Collection of Lincoln Papers, Manuscript Division, Library of Congress.

226

for me at the Quincy House. I returned and went to bed, and before day the stage called and took me. This is all.

That I never was in a Knownothing lodge in Quincy, I should expect could be easily proved, by respectable men who were always in the lodges and never saw me there. An affidavit of one or two such would put the matter at rest.

And now, a word of caution. Our adversaries think they can gain a point if they could force me to openly deny the charge, by which some degree of offence would be given to the Americans. For this reason it must not publicly appear that I am paying any attention to the charge

Yours Truly
A. Lincoln*

"Private"

Quincy Dec 30/60

Hon A Lincoln

My dear Sir

The purport of this communication, must be my apology for troubling you—and my great anxiety in regard to your personal safety and the preservation of our National integrity will I think justify me on this occasion, when you have so much to think of and so many things to perplex you.

You perhaps are aware, that I have a very large family connection in the South, and that in New Orleans I have six children and a host of other near relatives. I receive many letters from them, their language has to be very guarded, as fears are entertained that the sanctity of the mails, is not much regarded. On yesterday I received a letter from N.O. from one who is prudent, sound and careful of what he writes and among other things, he says "things are daily becoming worse here, God help us, what will be the result, it is dreadful to imagine. One thing I am satisfied of, that there is a perfect organization, fearful in numbers and contrauled by men of character and influence, whose object is to prevent the inauguration of Lincoln, large numbers of desperate characters, many of them from this city, will be in Washington on the 4th of March and it is their determination, to prevent the inauguration, and if by no other means, by using violence on the person of Lincoln. Men, engaged in this measure are known to be of the most violent character, capable of doing any act, necessary to carry out their vile measures." The writer of this, I know, would not say, what he does, did he not believe the statement above given to you. I cannot give you, his name, for were it known, that he communicated such matters to persons in the North, his life would be in danger—and I trust you will not communicate, having received any such information from me. I had seen rumors in the Newspapers to the like effect, but did not regard them much—this however alarms me, and I think is worthy

* Robert Todd Lincoln Collection of Lincoln Papers, Manuscript Division, Library of Congress.

of some notice. What ought to be done—you are more capable of judging, than any other person—but permit me to suggest—ought not the Governors of the free States, and your friends generally to adopt at once some precautionary measures—no protection can be expected from the damned old traitor at the head of the Government or his subordinates—something should be done in time and done effectually.

With great esteem and devotion

I am truely yrs—

A Jonas*

* Robert Todd Lincoln Collection of Lincoln Papers, Manuscript Division, Library of Congress.

APPENDIX C

*Zacharie-Lincoln Correspondence**

St Charles Hotel
New Orleans Jany 14th 1863

To his Excellency
A Lincoln President
of the United States

Dear Sir

In my last communication I promised to give you further details related to Genl Butler & now embrace the opportunity

What I now relate I get from one of the party in person. Several Gentlemen were called before Genl Butler to further some certain purpose of his, to which they would not however agree, when as a threat he told that by a wave of his hand from the top of the St Charles Hotel he could make New Orleans a second St Domingo, and if it suited his purpose he would yet make the Streets of the City run with blood

I now relate a pecuniary transaction. Messer Hyde & Goodrich the principal Jewelers here, remited to a relation in the City check on one of the Banks for five thousand dollars, payable to a relation here by the name of Norton, the proceeds of the check to be paid over to the clerks in their establishment for salary due. The letter containing the afore mentioned check fell into the hands of Genl Butler, who sent for Mr Norton, who he made endorse the check under threat of sending him to Fort Jackson. The check was paid, but is there any record of how the money was applied? I know another transaction for twenty one hundred dollars of the same kind.

Mr. I P Davis President of the Bank of New Orleans, one of the most esteemed gentlemen of this city, who Genl Butler threatened with hanging, & who he confined in a criminals cell for over two weeks, has entirely lost his mind. This is looked upon here by all classes of people as an unjustifiable act of severity

Some parties robbed the Jesuit church of two sets silver candellabras & other silver articles. The day after Genl Banks took command they were returned

---

* All of these letters are taken from manuscript originals in the Robert Todd Lincoln Collection of Lincoln Papers, Manuscript Division, Library of Congress, with two exceptions noted.

The practice of my profession & as I have before mentioned my habits of life, has thrown me among all classes of people. At the same time it has been my good fortune to have secured the friendship of many of our most distinguished statesmen, commencing in my boyhood with the great Henry Clay. But I have never known a person better fitted both by nature & education for his position than Genl Banks is for the one he now honors. You can not imagine the vast amount of business he gets through with each day, never loosing his self possession, listening patiently to all. I some times wonder that his health stands it as well as it does. For my own part I have endeavored to assist him all in my power. My great desire is that our efforts may prove of benefit to your administration, any action you may suggest be assured will have my most cordial & heart felt cooperation. My desire is to serve you in such a manner that my services may rebound to your honor.

So far I feel flattered at the success I have met with not only among my own people but among the most wealthy & influential of citizens. Do not think it egotism on my part what I write. One of the most prominent gentleman remarked yesterday—Doctor had the President sent six missionarys amongst us like you it would have more effect upon us than hundreds of cannon

As regards Genl Banks, the only persons who I have heard mention a word here against him, are those connected with Genl Hamiltons staff, why this should be I cant say, such however is the fact

Very Respectfully

Your Obt Servt

I Zacharie M D

St Charles Hotel
New Orleans Feby 19th 1863

To his Excellency
   A Lincoln
President of the United States

    Dear Sir

I must apologize for not writing more punctually. Perhaps I'm some what like the Irish Biddy who remarked to the lady of the house, "Shurr Mistress darlent a poor gal that works hard likes to know if she gives satisfaction to youz"

Now I can only repeat what I have previously written, & I am gratified in being able to do so. The people every day are becoming more favorably disposed to the Government, not only in this City but through the different Parishes. This I know from personal observation

The reported return of Genl Butler has created intense excitement among all classes, & from information which I have, am fearful should he reach here he never will return

The same favorable feeling manifested towards Genl Banks which I mentioned in former letters continues—only today a gentleman remarked to me. The people just yet cannot openly express their good feeling towards him, but they nevertheless appreciate his honesty, his uprightness, & his true patriotism, & trust before long when the proper occasion offers to express themselves publicly

The policy which he has adopted in regard to Negroes laboring upon plantations, meets with much favor by both black & white. Through its beneficent influence I hope to see an increase in the production of those commodities which are of the utmost importance to the happiness & comfort of the human family

A friend of mine just from Baton Rouge informs me that our army there is in excellent condition, of its movements you are no doubt fully informed. Port Hudson is very strongly fortified

For two weeks past it has taken considerable of my time attending to the currency. Certain parties here have used every effort to depreciate United States Treasury notes in comparison with Louisiana Bank bills, & have endeavored to influence planters not to dispose of their produce without it was for City Bank notes. This had to be stopped. Some seemed unwilling to sell without receiving specie in payment. This delusion had to be removed. You must know the commerce of this city is rapidly increasing. Large quantities of Sugar & Molasses reach here daily. Seldom a day passes without two or three hundred bales of Cotton arriving. With such diversified interest, it took time & labor to bring the currency to an equalized point. I have done so, & that too without having closed a Banking house, or seriously interfering with the rights of any merchant or tradesman

In doing this, I doubtless have made some enemies, men who came here to speculate, & cared not how they made money even at the expense of the Government. I mention this, as I have understood that parties here have written to Washington, stating that I too have been speculating—which I most earnestly deny. Never since I have been here, have I bought sold or bartered, or been interested in any speculation to the value of one cent. My profession thank God has always given me a competency. Since I have been here I have not practiced it—Genl Banks deeming my time could be better occupied. On the other hand, should I be so disposed there is nothing here now to make money out of, unless it were to go to plantations & take Horses, Mules, Cotton or Sugar, or to the houses of these unfortunate people & rob them of their furniture & plate, which I regret to say has been done. But Heaven forbid that I or any friend of mine, should be guilty of such an act, even if they had permission from the Commanding General. Therefore should it at any time be brought to your notice that I have been speculating here, I trust you will out of justice towards me deny the charge

I came here to use my best efforts, humble though they be, in aiding to unite our country, should I in any way be instrumental in consumating so great a result, my ambition will be gratified. For I shall know full well my name will not be forgotten either by the United States Government or the people of Louisiana

With my best wishes for your health & happiness

Most respectfully

Your Obt Servt

I Zacharie, M D

Office of U. S. Military Telegraph,
War Department.

The following Telegram received at Washington *1.15 P. M.*
17th March 1863,
From *New York*　M.
Dated, *March 17th* 1863.

President of the U.S.
　Washington D. C.
　Arrived here last night. Am quite unwell. Will have the honor of seeing you in day or two.

I. Zacharie
M. D.

Washington City
Friday morning
March 27 1863

To the President

Dear Sir

Policy prevents my seeing you, which I greatly regret. I would wish to have said adieu in person

My mind is much agitated on account of the great responsibility resting on me. I trust everything will be consumated to realize your best wishes. If it does not the fault shall not be mine

I hope you will aid my efforts by giving such orders as will tend to carry out the suggestions contained in my memorandum

Thanking you for the prompt & kind manner you have acted towards me

Believe me most
Faithfully, Your
Obt Servant
I. Zacharie, Md.

St Charles Hotel
New Orleans April 25th 1863

To his
Excellency   A Lincoln
President of the United States
Washington D C
Dear Sir

After an absence of five weeks I find but little change in the condition of affairs in this city. The Levee & some parts of the business streets are less lively. This is to be accounted for in the decreased receipts of produce. The crop of Sugar within our lines has been brought to market & disposed of   The crop of Cotton in Southern Louisiana has never been of much importance. The high prices ruling in January Feby & March brought every bale to market. Thus the Planter having disposed of his produce we cannot look for a revival of business until the country now regained by Genl Banks throws of[f] its shackles & is agained [*sic*] opened to the commercial world.

As regards the feelings of the people—which I have given much attention to—I find the kind disposition evinced towards Genl Banks continues. There are a few that will complain, but the feeling towards yourself & the general Government is improving. The Union associations of the city have five thousand names enrolled, & there are *many* good Union men here who have not yet enrolled

The recent rapid & effective movements of the Army under the leadership of the General commanding in person, has given courage, new life as it were, to all true lovers of the Union, while to its enemies, it has astonished & disheartened. The country regained is the finest portion of the State, & the people there yield submissively to the Government. The despondency of the secessionists is very marked. They complain of the cream of their country being given up without a struggle, & the little preparation made for its defence. They say their only hope now is Magruder who they look for from Texas with a body of thirteen thousand men. He can't [have?] raised half the number. That they may receive reinforcements from Texas is true, but they have a long ways to march over bad roads & poor means of transportation, & before they reach the Red River country it is to be hoped our troops will have permanent possession

My reception here by the citizens, particularly the creole, has been very kind, & I trust my influence among them will be of benefit to the Government

I have communicated with Genl Banks & wait his pleasure

Trusting your in the enjoyment of good health

Most Respectfully
Your Obt Servt

I Zacharie M D

Private & Confidential

Willards Hotel
Washington D C
July 20 1863

To the President

Sir!

On my interview with the Hon Secretary of State, he informed me he could not grant my—or rather General Banks'—request at present, which was to give me a pass to proceed to Ackin's Landing Va. This determination disarranges all my plans, as it was my intention to proceede from Richmond to Mobile & from there to New Orleans & rejoin General Banks so as to keep him fully advised of all proceedings both Military & Political

I am fearfull that in my short interview both with yourself & Mr. Seward my intentions have been misunderstood, & was anxious to see you today on the subject, regret not having been able to do so, as I have matters of importance to communicate only for your ears

What I wish to do is for the benefit of yourself & my country. I have no other aspirations. I leave for home this evening. Should you wish at any time to listen to me, or if I can serve you I am at your command

Very Respectfully
Your Obt Servt

I Zacharie M. D.
760 Broadway
New York

Office U. S. Military Telegraph.
War Department.
The following Telegram received at Washington, *6.35* P M.
Sept 29 1863
From *Fort Monroe*   M.
Dated *September 29*   1863.

His Excellency
A Lincoln P. U. S.
Just returned. Will be with you tomorrow afternoon.
Zacharie

SDH

760 Broadway

New York Oct 22, 1863.

His Excellency A. Lincoln
    President of the United States

        Dear Sir

On my way home in the cars last evening I was amazed on reading the Herald Newspaper to find the article concerning my recent visit to you

I embrace this first opportunity to write to you in reference thereto, for fear you might imagine that I had betrayed the confidence you so kindly reposed in me.

I pledge you that I have not lisped a word respecting this matter, except to Mr Seward, Genl Bowen of New Orleans and yourself.

I am of the opinion that my movements since my return from New Orleans have been watched by some person in your immediate vicinity, and the matter stated in the Herald drawn from the writers immagination as to the purport of my visits to you.

I beg you will not for a moment harbor any idea but that I have kept faithfully within my own breast all that has passed between us.

From casual remarks made by persons here it is looked upon as a sensation article and as little importance is attached to it as the belief in its correctness.

Do you think it advisable for me to write the *fact* that you did not give me any pass to Richmond, or shall I let the paragraph die a natural death?

Please assure Mr Seward that I had neither directly nor indirectly any knowledge of the article in the Herald until I read it.

I have not seen Mr Bennett or any one connected with the Herald for the last six months.

        Yours very Respectfully

          I. Zacharie, M.D.

Phila. Feb. 13th 1864

Hon A. Lincoln

    Dear Sir.

Some time ago, I purchased a *Barral* of *Homminy* in this city, to be forwarded it to you, and to my astonishment I found on my return here, that it had not gone.

Now Dear Sir, I send it, hoping you will find it good, and eat it with much enjoyment.

With kind regards to Mrs Lincoln.

Yours Respectfully
I. Zacharie. MD

P.S. prehaps I will take a run over to see you, in a few days,

I.Z.*

---

760 Broadway

New York

May 13th 1864

To His Excellency
  A.Lincoln.

Dear Friend.

I sent you some days ago a Box of five *Pine apples*, which I hope you received. With kind regards to Mrs. Lincoln,

I remain

Yours Truly

I. Zacharie MD

---

760 Broadway
New York. Sept 21st 1864

Dear Friend.

Yours of the 19th came duly to hand, it has had the desired effect, with the friends of the Partie.

I leave tomorrow for the interior of Pennsylvania, may go as far as Ohio. One thing is to be done, and that is for you to impress on the minds of your friends for them not to be to[o] sure.

Yours Truly

I. Zacharie, MD

To His Excellency
  A Lincoln,
    Washington
    D. C.

* Nicolay Papers, the Library of Congress, from photostat in Collection of the Abraham Lincoln Association.

760. Broadway,
New York. Nov. 3d 1864

My Dear Friend.

I just returned to this city after a trip of 9 days through Pennsylvania and New York States, and I am happy to inform you, that I am satisfied that I have done much good. *I now think all is Right*—and if we can reduce the Democratic majority in this city, I shall be satisfied. As regards the *Isrelites* [*sic*]—with but few exceptions, they will vote for you. I understand them well, and have taken the precaution, to see that they do as they have promised. I have secured good and trustworthy men to attend on them on Election Day. My men have been all the week seeing that their masses are properly Registered. So that will be right on the 8th ins.

As Regards Pennsylvania, if you knew *all*—you and your friends would give me much credit, for I flatter myself I have done one of the sharpest things that has been done in the campaign. Will explain it to you when I see you.

I wish to God all was over for I am used up, but, 3 years ago, I promised I would elect you, and if you are not it shall not be my fault.

Raymond will inform you that I am doing all I can for him but his chances are very doubtful—I should feel very bad if your chances was like his. I have much to say to you but have been up almost every night—that I am used up. I hope to see you after the fun is over, when I hope you will say
"Well done, My good and faithful servant."

With kind regards to Mrs. Lincoln.

Yours truly,

I. Zacharie, MD

P. S. did you receive the oranges.

Office U. S. Military Telegraph.
War Department.
The following Telegram received at Washington, *12* M.

Dec 26 1864.
Dec 26 1864.

From *New York*
His Excellency A Lincoln
Allow me to congratulate you on the fall of Savannah
My family are crazy with joy

I Zacharie

15   111 Pd

Executive Mansion

Washington Jan 25. 1865

Hon Secretary of War

My dear Sir

About Jews. I wish you would give Dr. Zacharie a pass to go to Savannah, remain a week and return, bringing with him, if he wishes, his father and sisters or any of them. This will spare me trouble and oblige me—I promised him long ago that he should be allowed this whenever Savannah should fall into our hands.

Blumenberg, at Baltimore. I think he should have a hearing. He has suffered for us & served us well—had the rope around his neck for being our friend—raised troops—fought, and been wounded. He should not be dismissed in a way that disgraces and ruins him without a hearing.

Yours truly

A. Lincoln*

———————————

760. Broadway
New York.

My Dear Friend

I leave on Saturday for steamship *Arago* for Savannah where I hope to find my Dear old Father and friends—if you have any matters that you would have properly attended to, I will consider it a favour for [you] to let me attend to it for you.

Please inform me if you received the *Bananas.*

God bless you is the sincere prayer of

Yours Truly

I. Zacharie, MD

* Paul Angle (ed.), *New Letters and Papers of Lincoln,* p. 368.

APPENDIX D

The Jewish Record's Description of Jewish Participation in the New York Lincoln Memorial Exercises

THE FUNERAL PAGEANT

THE LAST SAD TRIBUTE OF RESPECT—JEWISH CITIZENS IN THE RANKS—THE MEETING IN UNION SQUARE, &C., &C., &C.

WITH ORIENTAL BRIGHTNESS and warmth did the sun shine down, on Tuesday last, upon crowded house-top and groaning balcony, haughty monument and unpretending dwelling, glorious banners, the emblems of victory, and trailing draperies, sombre evidences of woe. Never before had the historian to chronicle so unaffected a display of universal sorrow, so grand a pageant testifying respect for a departed chief. Not in the old world could a monarch, with his unnumbered legions, command the payment of any such tribute of admiration even to the memory of a fallen hero. Nor could the new world have beheld such an outpowering of its masses, had the object of popular recognition been a great conqueror or a great king. It was reserved for the people of this land thus to honor the recollection of one who had sprung from their midst. It was reserved for this country, through the masses, its true and sole representative, to drop a tear in the yawning grave soon to be closed upon the mortal remains of the late President of the Republic. Everywhere the seemingly silent grief of the people had found utterance in a display of draperies of woe. Everywhere huge banners with bindings of dark crape, forming a strange contrast with the crimson and azure of the stripes and fields, tiny bannerets, with appropriate inscriptions, epitaph-like mottoes, wreaths of *immortelles*, pendent festoons, golden eagles enshrouded, as it were, by a cloud of gloom, pillars as sombre as those of the catafalco itself, badges of mourning, saddened faces and sorrowing hearts. Artistic skill, the poetry of woe, the tenderness of women were alike brought into requisition to further demonstrate to the eye how solemn was the occasion.

The funeral was a grand pageant. Cavalry that had charged on many a battlefield, artillery-men that had planted their batteries and stared death full in the face, infantry that had shared the forced marches incident to the strategical combinations of war, benevolent and protective associations having for object the assisting of the weak, the guarding of the helpless, the healing of mental and physical ills, all professions, all trades and social organizations were hand in hand testifying by their presence in the ranks to the respect they bore the deceased Chief Magistrate. It was a grand, an impressive scene; one which the youngest will remember to the last hour of life, with the recollection of the darkly-brilliant scene undimmed by the lapse of years.

The funeral pageant started from City Hall a few minutes before two o'clock, the military cortege forming the vanguard, followed by the representatives of the City, County and State governments and of the United States Department. Then came the clergy, the press, the bar and several political organizations. The Fourth Division, in charge of General J. H. Hobart Ward, numbered in its ranks hundreds of Jewish citizens. Foremost of these came the

FREEMASONS,

in whose ranks were noticeable three organizations numbering none but Jewish members: the Adelphi Lodge, headed by P. M. W. Asheim; Mount Neboh Lodge, in charge of W. Bro. J. Sulzberger, and King Solomon Lodge, under the guidance of Bro. Koch. In direct sequence advanced the

INDEPENDENT ORDER OF RED MEN,

in whose van there were borne three massive links of a chain, enshrouded with black crape, their banner being also draped in black. The order comprised some eighteen lodges, numbering in all about fifteen hundred members. In direct sequence marched the members of the

INDEPENDENT ORDER OF B'NAI B'RITH

represented by fifteen lodges and in charge of P. W. Frank, Esq., Grand Marshal, J. Ballin and N. Schainwald, Aids. Each lodge was preceded by its respective officers and all advanced in the following order: New York Lodge, No. 1; Zion, No. 2; Saran, No. 3; Hebron, No. 5; Lebanon, No. 9; Beer-Sheba, No. 11; Jordan, No. 15; Palestine, No. 18; Canaan, No. 29; Rhehoball, No. 38; Arnon, No. 39; Isaiah, No. 41; Mordecai, No. 57; Hillel, No. 28; Tabor, No. 31. The order numbered in all from twelve to fourteen hundred members.

THE ORDER OF B'NAI ABRAHAM,

was represented by Abraham Lodge No. 1, mustering about fifty members.

THE ORDER OF B'NAI MOSCHE

mustered some four hundred members who bore in front two magnificent banners, bearing the mottoes of the Order, with the brilliancy of the gilding and the brightness of the hue dimmed by the sombre shroud that embraced the folds.

THE I. O. FREE SONS OF ISRAEL

numbered ten lodges under the command of the M. W. Grand Master Bro. Pettenger. In the ranks were the Constitution Grand Lodge; Noah Lodge,

No. 1; Reuben, No. 3; Levy, No. 5; Arich, No. 6; Issachar, No. 7; Zebulon, No. 8; Dan, No. 9; Napthali, No. 10, and Gad, No. 11, turning out in all some nine hundred members.

THE CHEBRA ANSHE EMUNO

numbered about one hundred representatives, headed by Mr. M. Stark, who brought up the rear in the Jewish department of the Fourth Division. In the Seventh Division, the

CERES UNION

one hundred and twenty-five strong, presented a good appearance, wearing a badge of white satin ribbon, with a heavy black border, bearing the inscription:

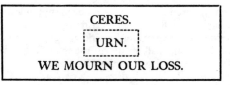

CERES.

URN.

WE MOURN OUR LOSS.

THE NATIONAL GLEE CLUB,

a combination of the Henry Clay Debating Society, the Webster Literary Association, made a creditable display, and brought up the rear of the procession, inasmuch as their co-religionists were participants in its grandeur. The dense mass marched onward and upward, the sad music ever and anon swelling in volume and dying away upon the spring breeze and, at length, the lower portions of the city resumed its wonted aspect, no vestiges left of the mighty throng that so recently had invaded every foot of tenable ground.

AT UNION SQUARE.

At four o'clock precisely were assembled at the Nineteenth street Synagogue, delegates from a number of congregations and associations who, in charge of Benj. I. Hart, Esq., marshal, and M.S. Isaacs, Esq., aid, marched to Union Square. In the ranks of this large deputation were representatives of the congregation B'nai Jeshurun, Shaary Tefila, Anshi Chesed, Rodef Sholem, B'nai Israel, Ahavas Chesed, Beth Israel Bikur Cholim, Poel Tsedek, Bikur Cholim u Kadisha, Aderath El, Mishkan Israel; of the Hebrew Benevolent Y.M.H.B. Fuel, Hebrew Free School, Hebrew Mutual Benefit, Mutual Benefit and Burial, Jerusalem and Purim associations; and deputies from the Orphan Asylum and Board of American Delegates. In all, the representatives numbered about two hundred; they proceeded through Fifth avenue to Fifteenth street, thence to the Maison Doree. The meeting was just being called to order.

On the speakers' platform we noticed the Rev. Drs. Raphall, Bondi; the Rev. Mr. Kramer; Henry Josephi, Esq., President of the Board of American Delegates, B. I. Hart, Esq. and several other co-religionists. After a prayer by the Rev. Dr. Tyng, an oration by the Hon. George Bancroft, the reading of the late President Lincoln's last inaugural address, the further reading of a psalm by the Rev. Mr. Boole, and the offering up of a fervent prayer by the Rev. Dr. Rogers, the Rev. S.M. Isaacs stepped forward and prefaced his prayer to the throne of grace, by the following passage from the scriptures:

"Remember, O Lord, thy tender mercies and thy loving kindness; for they are eternal. Grant us to be among those who die by thy hand, O Lord! those who die by old age, whose lot is eternal life; yea, who enjoy even here Thy hidden treasures. His soul shall dwell at ease, and his seed shall inherit the land. Therefore will we not fear, though the earth be overturned and though the mountains be hurled in the midst of the seas.

"He redeemeth thy life from destruction; He crowneth thee with [loving] kindness and tender mercies. Wherefore doth living [man] complain, he who can master sins? Small and great are there; and the servant is free from his master. For He remembered that they were but flesh; a wind that passeth away and cometh not again. All flesh shall perish together, and man shall return unto dust—who rejoice even to exultation and are glad when they find a grave.

"And such a frail mortal, shall be more just than God? Shall man be more pure than his maker? In God I will praise His word; in the Lord, I will praise His word. Man is like to vanity; his days are as a shadow of thing that passeth away. Be kind, O Lord, unto those that are good, and unto them that are upright in their hearts. Let the pious exult in glory; let them sing aloud upon their couches. Then shall Thy light break forth as in the morning, and Thy health shall spring forth speedily, and Thy righteousness shall precede Thee; the glory of the Lord shall be thy reward. The Lord shall preserve thee from all evil. He shall preserve thy soul.

"Behold, the keeper of Israel doth neither slumber nor sleep. The Eternal killeth and maketh alive; He bringeth down to the grave and bringeth up. Wilt Thou not turn and revive us, that we may rejoice in Thee? Let us, therefore, trust in the Lord; for with the Lord there is mercy, and with Him is plenteous redemption.

"One generation passeth away and another generation cometh; but the earth abideth forever. For the word of the Lord is upright, and all his works are done in faithfulness. The dust shall return to the earth as it was, and the spirit shall return unto God who gave it. His seed shall be mighty upon earth: the generation of the upright shall be blessed. The Lord gave, and the Lord hath taken away. Blessed be the name of the Lord.

"And as for him, righteousness shall precede him and form steps for his way.

"Ye are blessed of the Eternal, who made heaven and earth."

The reverend gentleman then delivered the following impressive prayer:

"Thou, whose attributes are omnipotence, Thy eye unseen, sees, Thy direction unknown, guides; Thy mercy unbounded, upholds; our God, our Father. From hearts penetrated by grief, we pray; oppressed by the weight of our feelings, bruised in spirit, we most earnestly implore Thee, visit us not in Thine anger, nor chastise us according to our works. Enter not into judgment with us, look not to our iniquities. As frail, erring creatures, in faltering accents we confess our guilt. Who can be justified before Thy immaculate purity? In humble and reverential awe, we approach Thee, invoking Thee to inspire us with a proper spirit and temper of heart and mind under the powers of Thy providence. God of Abraham, of Isaac, and of Jacob, millions of beings Thy will has created this day fall prostrate at Thy throne, offering the overflowing of their hearts and their resignation to Thy will, as the homage of their adoration. The inhabitants of this land are overburdened with grief. The good being who, like Aaron of old, "stood between the living and the dead," so that the war which decimated the land might cease. Alas! he is no more. Thy servant, Abraham Lincoln, has, without a warning, been summoned before Thy august presence. He has served the people of his afflicted land faithfully, zealously, honestly, and, we would fain hope, in accordance with Thy supreme will. O that "his righteousness may precede him and form steps for his way" to the heavenly abode of bliss; that Thy angels of mercy may be commissioned to convey his soul to the spot reserved for martyred saints; that the suddenness with which one of the worst beings deprived him of life may atone for any errors which he may have committed. Almighty God! every heart is pierced with anguish—every countenance furrowed with grief, at our separation from one we revered and loved. We beseech Thee, in this period of our sorrow and despondency, to sooth our pains and calm our griefs; and, as in days of old, before the sun of Eli went down, Thou didst cause that of Samuel to beam upon Israel, so it may be thy divine will, as the sun of our deeply lamented Abraham Lincoln had scarcely set, and darkness covered the people, that the sun of Andrew Johnson, which has burst upon the gloom, may shed its brilliant rays as sparkling it is borne amid purity and innocence. Our Father, who art in Heaven, show us this kindness, so that our tears may cease to depict our sorrow and give peace to the joyful hope that, through Thy goodness, peace and concord may supersede war and dissension, and our beloved Union, restored to its former tranquility, may be enabled to carry out Thy wish for the benefit and the happiness of humanity. We pray Thee do this; if not for our sakes, for the sake of our little ones unsullied by sin, who lisp Thy holy name, with hands uplifted, with the importunity of spotless hearts, they re-echo our supplication. Let the past be the end of our sorrow, the future the harbinger of peace and salvation to all who seek Thee in truth. Amen."

At the conclusion of this prayer, two poems by William Cullen Bryant were read by Dr. Osgood, "Old Hundred" was sung by the entire assemblage and the benediction was announced by Rev. Dr. Hitchcock. Then the crowd slowly dispersed in every direction, ebbing down tributary streets, descending and ascending the great thoroughfare, and in an hour thence, as evening closed in, the statue of the Father of his country gazed calmly down on a deserted and seemingly limitless waste.

ABBREVIATIONS
USED IN NOTES

Asm The Asmonean

DAB Dictionary of American Biography

HL The Hebrew Leader

HUCA Hebrew Union College Annual

Isr The Israelite

JCCS Journal of the Confederate States of America, 1861–1865

JE The Jewish Encyclopedia

JISHS Journal of the Illinois State Historical Society

JR The Jewish Record

JSH The Journal of Southern History

Mess The Jewish Messenger

MVHR The Mississippi Valley Historical Review

Occ The Occident

PAJHS Publications of the American Jewish Historical Society

SHSP Southern Historical Society Papers

UJE The Universal Jewish Encyclopedia

WROR War of the Rebellion ... Official Records of the Union and Confederate Armies

CHAPTER NOTES

Notes to Chapter 1

1. The statistical estimates of the Jewish population and congregations in this and the following paragraphs were taken from the very careful compilations made by Rabbi Allan Tarshish for his unpublished doctoral dissertation, *The Rise of American Judaism.* Rabbi Tarshish brought together various estimates (for specific cities and states) from widely separated periodical sources and combined them into the best available charts of American Jewish population statistics for the nineteenth century. A good survey of governmental census statistics is to be found in H. S. Linfield, "Statistics of Jews and Jewish Organizations in the United States," pp. 65–72. Other authorities, including Dr. Jacob Lestschinsky, one of the outstanding students of Jewish statistical data, are agreed on the rough estimates given in the text.

2. See Dr. Hyman Grinstein's listing of New York congregations in his *Rise of the Jewish Community of New York 1654–1860,* pp. 472–4; *Mess,* V, No. 15, p. 4, Apr. 15, 1859, states that there were 160 permanent congregations in the country, and about 50 more for the Holy Days in the fall. The official census reports, as digested by U. Z. Engelman in "Jewish Statistics in the U.S. Census of Religious Bodies (1850–1936)," pp. 129–30, list 37 synagogues in 11 different states in 1850, 77 synagogues in 19 states and the District of Columbia in 1860. These listings are at sharp variance with contemporary data and the research of scholars like Grinstein and Tarshish.

3. Jacob R. Marcus, "Light on Early Connecticut Jewry."

4. J. J. Benjamin, *Drei Jahre in Amerika,* pp. 40ff., 341ff.

5. See B. D. Bogen, *Jewish Philanthropy,* and M. J. Karpf, *Jewish Community Organization in the United States,* for material on the development of Jewish philanthropy in America.

6. Grinstein, *op. cit.,* pp. 109–14.

7. B. Rabinowitz, "The Young Men's Hebrew Associations (1854–1913)," pp. 223–32.

8. See, for instance, Israel Goldstein, *A Century of Judaism in New York,* pp. 115–8; J. G. Heller, *As Yesterday When It Is Past,* pp. 42–54; H. Morais, *The Jews of Philadelphia,* pp. 154–5; J. Trachtenberg, *Consider the Years,* pp. 149–51; Grinstein, *op. cit.,* pp. 225–59.

9. *DAB,* XI, 137–8.

10. *DAB,* IX, 513–4.

11. *DAB,* XX, 426–7; M. B. May, *Isaac Mayer Wise;* D. Philipson and L. Grossman, *Isaac Mayer Wise; Life and Selected Writings;* I. M. Wise, *Reminiscences.*

12. *DAB,* VI, p. 65; *David Einhorn Memorial Volume.*

13. See R. C. Hertz, *The Rabbi Yesterday and Today*, for an interesting survey of the changing rabbinate.

14. Solomon Jackson's monthly paper, *The Jew* (1823–25), the first Jewish periodical in America, was issued to combat the activities of the Christian conversionist group, the American Society for Ameliorating the Conditions of the Jews. Robert Lyon's *Asmonean* (1849–58) and Isidor Busch's *Israel's Herold* (1849) were the other exceptions. Although edited by a layman, whose premature death brought his publishing venture to a sudden end, the *Asmonean's* contributors were, in the main, the rabbinical leaders of the time. The fact that rabbis sprang to the fore even in a paper edited by a layman is another indication of the reluctance and/or inability of laymen to take an active role in Jewish leadership.

15. A copy of the circular appeal has been preserved in the archives of Mikveh Israel Congregation, Philadelphia. Photostat in American Jewish Archives.

16. See Grinstein, *op. cit.*, pp. 423–39, for details of these activities.

17. *JE*, IX, 35–6.

18. Grinstein, *op. cit.*, pp. 433–9.

19. See Temple Emanu-El circular of opposition, AJHS Library.

20. B. A. Elzas, *The Jews of South Carolina*, pp. 147–65, 208–19; L. C. Moise, *Biography of Isaac Harby*; C. A. Rubenstein, *History of Har Sinai Congregation of the City of Baltimore*; M. Stern, *The Rise and Progress of Reform Judaism . . . A History . . . Of Temple Emanu-El of New York. . . .*

21. D. Philipson, *The Reform Movement in Judaism*, pp. 339–53.

22. See, for example, Wise's comments on the atheists in *Reminiscences*, pp. 272, 302, 327.

23. *Archives Israelites*, XXI (1870), p. 412.

24. *Isr*, VII, No. 5, p. 34, Aug. 3, 1860.

25. See *JE*, III, 194–201, for various types of European Jewish community organizations.

26. The circular referred to above in Note 19 leans heavily upon possible non-Jewish reactions to the organization of the Board.

27. One might make a good case for the contention that attempts to convert American Jews were actually helpful to the Jews. Many Jewish activities were instituted, directly or indirectly, in response to groups like the American Society for Ameliorating the Conditions of the Jews. Leeser began answering the Society's propaganda in the very first issue of *The Occident* (I, No. 1, pp. 43–7, Apr., 1843). See Grinstein, *op. cit.*, pp. 381–6, for some interesting data on the attitude of New York Jews to conversionist movements.

28. See Albert M. Friedenberg, "Calendar of American Jewish Cases," for a number of interesting examples of court cases in which Jews pleaded their rights as Jews, and L. Hühner, "The Struggle for Religious Liberty in North Carolina, With Special Reference to the Jews," pp. 46–52, for the story of Jacob Henry's struggle to occupy his seat in the State Legislature.

29. Grinstein, *op. cit.*, pp. 414–65; S. W. and J. M. Baron, "Palestinian Messengers in America, 1849–79."

Notes to Chapter II

1. *Annual Report of the American and Foreign Anti-Slavery Society*, pp. 114–5.

2. E. Donnan, *Documents Illustrative of the History of the Slave Trade to America*, III, 21 ff., cited by A. V. Goodman, *American Overture*, p. 50.

3. For the statement that the largest house for the sale of slaves in Richmond was owned by Jews, see Hermann Schuricht, *History of the German Element in Virginia*, II, pp. 92–3.

4. See M. Vaxer, "Haym M. Solomon Frees His Slave," pp. 447–8, for the text of one indenture. Schappes, *A Documentary History of the Jews in the United States*, pp. 118 *passim*, lists a sizable number of Jews who freed their slaves under the auspices of this Society.

5. Isaac Goldberg, *Major Noah*, pp. 251–2, 265–8.

6. M. J. Kohler, "The Jews and the American Anti-Slavery Movement," pp. 152–3, gives the details of Pinner's abolitionist activities, as well as much interesting data about other Jews who participated in the abolitionist movement.

7. See R. D. Meade, *Judah P. Benjamin, Confederate Statesman*, pp. 100–3.

8. Yulee letter to *East Floridian* reprinted in *St. Augustine Examiner*, Nov. 17, 1860.

9. J. A. Wax, "Isidor Bush, American Patriot and Abolitionist."

10. Kohler, *op. cit.*, p. 152.

11. A facsimile of a broadside of a sale of slaves by Moses, dated Nov. 14, 1859, was printed in Charles F. Heartman, *Americana Catalogue* (1947), p. 145. The word "Negro" has been capitalized here and in subsequent citations, in keeping with current practice.

12. Letters, Kakeles to Smith, Nov. 13, 1850, and Jan. 26, 1851, Numbers 447 and 481 of the Gerrit Smith Papers.

13. Leon Hühner, *Judah Touro*, p. 69.

14. Gustav Pollak, *Michael Heilprin and His Sons*, pp. 169–70.

15. Morris J. Raphall, *The Bible View of Slavery*, reprinted in E. M. F. Mielziner, *Moses Mielziner 1823–1903*, pp. 212–24. Mrs. Mielziner performed a genuine service by reprinting this controversial sermon together with three other items bearing upon the subject, to be referred to below, in her volume on her father-in-law.

16. Raphall, *op. cit.*, pp. 27–8; Mielziner, *op. cit.*, p. 219.

17. *Ibid.*

18. Raphall, *op. cit.*, pp. 37–8; Mielziner, *op. cit.*, p. 223.

19. Raphall, *op. cit.*, p. 30; Mielziner, *op. cit.*, p. 220. See Schappes, *op. cit.*, p. 683, for the intriguing discovery that Raphall was made an honorary member of the American Society for Promoting National Unity, a group of pro-slavery Northerners and Southerners, including in their number the Reverends George Jacobs, James Gutheim and J. Blumenthal.

20. For text and comment, see *New York Tribune*, Jan. 5, 14, 18, 22, 1861; *New York Daily News*, Jan. 5; *New York Herald*, Jan. 5, 1861.

21. *Richmond Daily Dispatch*, Jan. 7, 1861.

22. L. G. Tyler (ed.), *Encyclopedia of Virginia Biography*, II, p. 52.

23. *Richmond Daily Dispatch*, Jan. 29, 1861.

24. *Memphis Daily Appeal*, Jan. 23, 1861.

25. Quoted *ibid.*, May 12, 1861.

26. *New York Tribune*, Jan. 15, 1861, reprinted in Mielziner, *op. cit.*, pp. 224–34. For various answers to Raphall by non-Jews, see Schappes, *op. cit.*, pp. 685–7. Most effective of all, perhaps, were the lines of a poem written by R. S. H. for *The Independent* and entitled "Rabbi Raphall":

> He that unto thy fathers freedom gave—
> Hath he not taught thee pity for the slave?

Reprinted in Schappes, *ibid.*

27. Pollak, *op. cit.*, pp. 3–9.

28. Mielziner, *op. cit.*, pp. 224–5.

29. *Ibid.*, pp. 21–23; treatise reprinted pp. 64–103.

30. G. Gottheil, *Moses Versus Slavery: Being Two Discourses on the Slave Question.*

31. *Ibid.*, p. 4.

32. *Sinai*, I, No. 9, pp. 258–9, Oct. 1856; No. 11, pp. 353–9, Dec., 1856; II, No. 6, pp. 599–601, July, 1857; see also VII, No. 7, pp. 183–92, Aug. 1862.

33. *Sinai*, VI, No. 1, pp. 2–20, Feb., 1861; No. 2, pp. 45–50, 60–1, Mar., 1861; No. 3, pp. 99–100, Apr., 1861. The first article is reprinted in Mielziner, *op. cit.*, pp. 234–50.

34. Mielziner, *op. cit.*, p. 241.

35. *Ibid.*, p. 250.

36. David Einhorn, *War With Amalek*, pp. 4–5.

37. *Ibid.*, p. 4.

38. *Sinai*, I, No. 9, pp. 258–9, Oct. 1856; VII, No. 7, pp. 207–9, Aug. 1861.

39. *Sinai*, VII, No. 5, pp. 135–42, June, 1861; *Isr*, VII, No. 48, p. 382, May 31, 1861.

40. *Sinai*, VII, No. 5, p. 140, June, 1861.

41. Letter, Einhorn to R. Oppenheimer, Aug. 13, 1861, Marcus Collection.

42. *Sinai*, VII, No. 10, p. 319, Dec., 1862; letter, Einhorn to Felsenthal, Sept. 3, 1862, in AJHS Library.

43. Letter, Felsenthal to M. J. Kohler, Oct. 25, 1901, American Jewish Archives.

44. Emma Felsenthal, *Bernhard Felsenthal, Teacher in Israel*, p. 23.

45. *Ibid.*, pp. 33–4.

46. Reprinted from the *Chicago Republican* in *HL*, VII, No. 11, p. 1, Dec. 22, 1865.

47. *Sinai*, VI, No. 7, p. 208, Aug. 1861.

48. Felsenthal, "The Jews and Slavery," letter to *Illinois Staatszeitung*, June 6,

1862, reprinted in *Sinai*, VII, No. 6, pp. 158–63, July, 1862; also *HL*, VI, No. 25, p. 1, Sept. 8, 1865. The German-language abolitionist press made frequent anti-Jewish comments about Jews who supported the Confederacy. Felsenthal sought to defend his people, recognizing that the attacks were not realistic discussions of the issue, but were motivated by hostility to the Jews brought from Germany. Isaac M. Wise understood this thoroughly, and delivered himself of some blistering rebuttals to Felsenthal's defense as well as the German attacks, in *Isr.*, IX, No. 4, pp. 3–4, July 25, 1862. The specialist in immigrant adjustment to life in the United States will be interested in comparing the political affiliation and activities of German non-Jews and Jews during this period. The Germans were much more a compact, unified body, than were the Jews. See Ella Lonn's excellent study, *Foreigners in the Confederacy*, for material on German refusal to support the Confederacy, and on the strong prejudice against Germans which existed in the South.

49. *Mess.*, IX, No. 17, p. 133, May 3, 1861. Julius Eckman's San Francisco *Weekly Gleaner* disagreed with the *Messenger's* "ungenerous" attitude towards Einhorn and told its readers that Einhorn was "a martyr." *Mess.*, X, No. 1, p. 5, July 12, 1861.

50. *Mess.*, IX, No. 3, p. 21, Jan. 18, 1861; No. 4, p. 28, Jan. 25; No. 5, p. 37, Feb. 1. The editors were not entirely consistent. On the same day that Raphall had delivered his sermon, *Mess.* published an article by one of its regular contributors, "Judaeus," completely siding with the South:

> . . . No matter how patriotic and unpartisan Mr. Lincoln may be, the mass of the Southern people, relying on the statements of their political leaders, believe him to be an uncompromising abolitionist . . . Northern men must leave their Southern brethren to regulate their own internal concerns . . . It was designed [in the Constitution] that wherever slavery existed, it should be protected and not disturbed . . . [Abolitionism] is the primary cause of the present dissatisfaction at the South. The interference of abolitionists was entirely uncalled for . . . That the country will pass safely through the present ordeal, I am confident . . . (*Mess.*, IX, No. 1, p. 2, Jan. 4, 1861).

51. *Mess.*, XIV, No. 13, pp. 108–9, Oct. 9, 1863.

52. *Mess.*, XVII, No. 5, p. 36, Feb. 3, 1865; XIX, No. 4, p. 1, Jan. 26, 1866; No. 5, p. 1, Feb. 2. The editors of the paper had changed their tune by the end of the war, and printed, every week, a digest of national news in which the editorial policy was consistently conservative and anti-vindictive. One cannot help feeling that S. M. and Myer Isaacs were afraid to take an editorial stand in the pre-war months, rather than convinced that they should not.

53. *Occ.*, XVII, No. 43, p. 259, Jan. 17, 1861; No. 44, p. 268, Jan. 24; No. 45, p. 274, Jan. 31. It was somewhat typical of Leeser's cast of mind that, in one breath, he should say he will not take a public stand, and in the next reveal his substantial agreement with Raphall by differing with him on minor points.

54. *Occ.*, XVIII, No. 33, p. 197, Nov. 8, 1860. For Frederick Law Olmsted's comments on this problem, see Chapter 7, Note 132, of the present work.

55. See the writer's essay on "Isaac Mayer Wise On the Civil War," for a fuller discussion of the subject.

56. *Isr.*, VII, No. 22, p. 173, Nov. 30, 1860; No. 24, p. 188, Dec. 14; No. 26, p.

205, Dec. 28; No. 31, p. 244, Feb. 1, 1861; No. 37, p. 292, Mar. 15; No. 48, p. 381, May 31; VIII, No. 16, p. 124, Oct. 18; No. 30, p. 236, Jan. 24, 1862. Lincoln agreed, at least in part, with Wise's judgment of the role of the clergymen. He said, to a visitor in 1863, "Sir . . . the parsons and the women made this war." D. Barbee, "President Lincoln and Doctor Gurley," p. 11.

The degree to which misinformation about the Jews found its way into print was indicated by an editorial in the *Memphis Argus*, in March, 1861, accusing Wise of being an abolitionist! "This paper," said the *Argus*, "ostensibly devoted to the religious needs of the editor's Israelitish brethren is, in truth, little more than a Jewified repeater of the doctrines of Beecher & Co. The editor . . . has . . . deduced two prominent facts: First, that the nigger is superior to the white race, even 'the chosen race' of God, which He once held in bondage, and secondly, that the abolition of slavery is as much enjoined by Moses as by Theodore Parker." Wise was as likely to be anti-slavery as the *Argus* itself. How it came to print such nonsense must remain a mystery. *Isr.,* VII, No. 40, p. 318, Apr. 5, 1861.

57. *Isr.,* VII, No. 26, p. 205, Dec. 28, 1860.

58. *Isr.,* VII, No. 29, p. 230, Jan. 18, 1861; XIV, No. 52, p. 4, July 3, 1868. M. J. Kohler in his essay on "Jews and the American Anti-Slavery Movement," p. 150, and Philip S. Foner in *The Jews in American History, 1654–1865,* p. 60, both state erroneously that Wise endorsed Raphall's sermon. As late as 1897, Wise himself, still alive, felt impelled to print a formal denial that he "shared the opinion of Dr. Raphall . . . that slavery was a divine institution, sanctioned by the Old Testament Scriptures, or that there is on record one paragraph to show that the said Isaac M. Wise ever was a pro-slavery man or favored the institution of slavery at any time." *Isr.,* LXVIII, No. 52, p. 4, June 24, 1897, in answer to charges by the *London Jewish Chronicle.*

59. *Isr.,* XI, No. 20, p. 156, Nov. 11, 1864, to No. 26, p. 204, Dec. 23. The series is entitled "On the Provisional Portion of the Mosaic Code, with Special Reference to Polygamy and Slavery." Around the same time, Lewis N. Dembitz, one of Wise's Louisville friends and supporters, published an article "On Slavery and Polygamy Tolerated by the Bible," in one of the Louisville newspapers. Its conclusions were similar to Wise's. *Isr.,* XI, No. 19, pp. 148–9, Nov. 4, 1864.

60. *Isr.,* XI, No. 26, p. 204, Dec. 23, 1864.

61. *Isr.,* XI, No. 25, p. 196, Dec. 16, 1864.

62. See Korn, *op. cit.,* pp. 639–40.

63. *Isr.,* X, No. 5, p. 36, July 31, 1863.

64. *Indianapolis Hebrew Congregation Trustees Minute Book,* May 3, 1863, called to the writer's attention by Rabbi Morris M. Feuerlicht of Indianapolis.

65. *Occ.,* XVIII, No. 44, pp. 267–8, Jan. 24, 1861.

66. *Isr.,* VII, No. 38, p. 301, Mar. 22, 1861; VIII, No. 35, p. 278, Feb. 28, 1862. The Rev. A. Gunzberg of Rochester was another rabbi who was convinced that the Jews were a peculiar blind spot in the liberal thinking of the abolitionists and so he wrote in a letter to G. F. Train, referring to "high standing politicians who are very zealous for the half-civilized Negro, [but] so illiberal against our nation." *Isr.,* XI, No. 46, p. 364, May 12, 1865; No. 48, p. 381, May 26; No. 49, p. 388, June 2, 1865.

67. *JR*, I, No. 18, p. 2, Jan. 9, 1863.

68. *JR*, I, No. 20, p. 2, Jan. 23, 1863.

69. *Ibid.*

70. *JR*, I, No. 21, p. 2, Jan. 30, 1863; No. 22, p. 2, Feb. 6.

71. *JR*, VI, No. 2, p. 2, Mar. 24, 1865. Benjamin Szold was one rabbi who disagreed with the *Record*. After Maryland freed her slaves, H. L. Bond and others organized "The Baltimore Association for the Educational and Moral Improvement of the Colored People." A letter was sent to the ministers asking for their support, because the sponsors felt it was a project which should appeal to "every Christian man's charity." It did not; many ministers did not answer; others wrote bitter attacks against the society. Rabbi Szold mailed fifty dollars to the Association, noting that it appealed to his "*Jewish* charity." His note made so forceful an impression on the officers that they elected him to their Board. H. L. Bond, "Dr. Szold and Timbuctoo."

72. Lilienthal's Victory Sermon, printed in *Isr.*, XI, No. 44, pp. 349–50, Apr. 28, 1865, a profoundly revealing expression of Lilienthal's personal opinions.

73. Sophie Lilienthal, *The Lilienthal Family Record*, pp. 56–7.

74. Receipts for payment of slave rental fees in George Jacobs Scrapbook; information supplied by Miss Rebecca Jacobs.

75. Sermon printed in *JR*, II, No. 13, p. 1, June 5, 1863. The *Record's* editor found it difficult to understand how Michelbacher could be so loyal to the Confederacy. Isaac M. Wise had little to say about the sermon except that it was "a partisan rigamarole dictated by some partisan stump speaker," but criticised the *Record* for saying Michelbacher was a rabbi:

... "The Rev. Rabbi Michelbacher" never was and is not now a rabbi, never made any studies to this end, never received any such title of any authorized person or persons, and to the best of our knowledge never claimed any such title ... Mr. Michelbacher could as easy write a work on astronomy as he writes a sermon. He can do neither. He can sing and chant ... (*Isr.*, IX, No. 50, p. 394, June 19, 1863).

76. There had been one pardonable error in the 1853 report of the Anti-Slavery Society. Its officers could hardly have been expected to read every issue of the Jewish periodicals. Robert Lyon's *Asmonean* had already committed itself to a pro-slavery position in 1850–1, by defending the wisdom of the Fugitive Slave Law, (*Asm.*, III, No. 1, p. 6, Jan. 10, 1851; IV, No. 12, p. 92, Oct. 12, 1851) and by registering itself against the abolitionist crusade. Lyon felt that England was responsible for fostering the anti-slavery movement in order to weaken the young republic. He was fearful of the results of the agitation for emancipation, warning his readers that events in Jamaica and Haiti foreshadowed what would occur in the United States, if the Negroes were to be given their freedom. Lyon adopted that line of reasoning which regarded the slaves as property, and therefore inviolate:

Let our citizens, one and all, resolve this day, to put down Abolitionism, in whatever shape or form it may present itself, to discountenance it, by whomsoever its principles may be advocated, and to crush out at once and forever this attempt to plunder our Southern citizens of their property ... Once more, Down with Abolitionism! Let us stand by the Union, and nothing but the Union. (*Asm.*, IV, No. 11, p. 88, July 4, 1851.)

Although Lyon had said nothing about Judaism, the very fact that he had printed such sentiments in a professedly Jewish newspaper subjected him to abolitionist rebuttal. The *Christian Freeman*, edited by the Rev. Sylvanus Cobb of Boston, thought it ill became Jews to favor slavery:

Well done, Mr. Israelite . . . Had not our government better make slaves of you and all your people we can catch? For this we might plead some sanction from the word of God, which declares that you shall be trodden underfoot of all nations! Jehovah never said this of Africans. (*Asm.*, IV, No. 13, p. 104, July 18, 1851.)

Not in the least disconcerted, Lyon turned tables and accused Cobb of being a poor Christian, thus to threaten the Jews with slavery. The Bible, said he, did not teach abolition, but respect for property!

77. The only congregational action on record was the adoption by the Beth Elohim Congregation of Charleston, S. C., of a provision in its 1820 constitution that all duly converted proselytes be accepted as members of the Congregation "provided he, she, or they are not people of color." B. Elzas, *The Jews of South Carolina*, p. 153.

78. W. W. Sweet, *The Story of Religions in America*, pp. 412–47. See also C. B. Staiger, "Abolitionism and the Presbyterian Schism of 1837–1838."

79. *Report of the Proceedings of the Thirteenth Annual Meeting of District Grand Lodge No. 2, Independent Order of B'nai B'rith, Held in Cincinnati Ohio, on July 9, 1865, and Following Days*, pp. 6, 20.

Notes to Chapter III

1. *Isr.*, X, No. 13, p. 88, Sept. 25, 1863.

2. *Mess.*, X, No. 8, p. 63, Oct. 17, 1861.

3. *Isr.*, IX, No. 11, p. 83, Sept. 19, 1862.

4. *Isr.*, X, No. 47, p. 371, May 20, 1864.

5. J. Trachtenberg, *Consider the Days*, p. 166.

6. A. E. Frankland, "Fragments of History," p. 94.

7. *Occ.*, XVIII, No. 43, p. 260, Jan. 17, 1861.

8. *Mess.*, X, No. 6, pp. 44–5, Sept. 18, 1861.

9. Letter, A. Hart to Morais, Sept. 21, 1862, Morais Collection.

10. *Shearith Israel Trustees Minutes*, VI, p. 441, May 5, 1861.

11. *Mess.*, IX, No. 17, p. 133, May 3, 1861; No. 20, pp. 156–7, May 24.

12. *Cleveland Leader*, May 18, 1861; S. Wolf, *The Presidents I Have Known, From 1860 To 1918*, pp. 33–5.

13. *Easton Argus*, May 23, 1861, quoted by Trachtenberg, *op. cit.*, p. 166.

14. A. E. Frankland, *op. cit.*; *Mess.*, XXI, No. 18, p. 5, May 10, 1867.

15. *Easton Argus, op. cit.*

16. *Mess.*, IX, No. 17, p. 133, May 3, 1861.

17. *Mess.*, X, No. 7, pp. 52–3, Oct. 4, 1861. It has been stated that Morais was anti-slavery (see Kohler, *op. cit.*, p. 151) but there is no indication of this in his sermons. The phrase "the adversaries of human brotherhood," quoted in the text undoubtedly refers to the secession of the South from the "brotherhood" of the Union, not to the evils of slavery.

18. *JR*, II, No. 9, p. 1, May 8, 1863.

19. *Mess.*, XI, No. 16, pp. 129–30, May 2, 1862.

20. *Ibid.*

21. Nos. 15646–7, Robert Todd Lincoln Collection.

22. Letter, May 13, 1862, Morais Collection.

23. *Mess.*, XV, No. 2, pp. 9–10, Jan. 15, 1864; letter, John Hay to Hart, Jan. 9, 1864, Morais Collection.

24. *Mess.*, XIII, No. 19, p. 165, May 15, 1865.

25. *Mess.*, XV, No. 2, pp. 9–10, Jan. 15, 1864.

26. *Mess.*, XIV, No. 2, pp. 12–3, July 10, 1863. According to a letter to the writer, March 9, 1950, from J. William Hardt, Pres. of the Union League of Philadelphia, League minutes do not record Morais' election to honorary membership, but do list him on the special Clerical Roll, which appears to have been the equivalent of honorary membership.

27. All of the sermons in *Mess.* were reprinted from Philadelphia newspapers. The copy of the Fast Day sermon which was sent to Lincoln (note 21) was a clipping from an unidentified Philadelphia daily.

28. Letter, Morais to Lieberman, Dec. 15, 1864, Morais Collection.

29. *Ibid.*

30. *Mikveh Israel Adjunta Minutes*, Feb. 5, 1865.

31. *Ibid.*, Apr. 7, 1865.

32. *Mikveh Israel Congregation Minutes*, Apr. 9, 1865.

33. *Mess.*, XVIII, No. 19, p. 165, May 15, 1865; H. S. Morais, *The Jews of Philadelphia*, pp. 62–3.

34. *Isr.*, VII, No. 27, Jan. 4, to No. 32, Feb. 8, 1861.

35. *Isr.*, VII, No. 42, p. 334, Apr. 19, 1861.

36. *Isr.*, IX, No. 4, p. 46, July 25, 1862.

37. *Isr.*, IX, No. 19, p. 147, Nov. 14, 1862.

38. *Isr.*, VII, No. 33, p. 262, Feb. 15, 1861.

39. *Isr.*, VII, No. 37, p. 294, Mar. 15, 1861.

40. *Isr.*, VII, No. 50, p. 396, June 14, 1861. In XIII, No. 1, p. 5, July 6, 1866, Wise said:

> The war broke out and broke my staff of existence in two. Half of my subscribers resided in the Southern States, and of those who resided in the North nearly half stopped payment for my support . . . I lost every thing I had, and I lay prostrated, crushed to the ground . . .

The Occident had been published weekly in 1860–61, but had to return to monthly issues because of a similar problem. Leeser probably had more subscribers in the South than in the North. *Occ.,* XX, No. 1, p. 1, Apr., 1862. The *Messenger* was published only every other week for the second half of 1861 because of its sudden loss of subscribers, but managed to survive the rest of the war as a weekly, with a raise in price several times. *Mess.,* IX, No. 25, p. 196, June 28, 1861; XI, No. 1, p. 1, Jan. 5, 1862; XVII, No. 1, p. 4, Jan. 6, 1865.

41. *Isr.,* VII, No. 48, p. 381, May 31, 1861; XIII, No. 1, p. 5, July 6, 1866.

42. See Jacob R. Marcus, *The Americanization of Isaac Mayer Wise,* pp. 10–8, for a detailed treatment of Wise's political ideas. Wise probably voted for Douglas in 1860, although he supported no candidate in his paper. See his eulogy of Douglas in *Isr.,* VII, No. 49, p. 386, July 7, 1861. Wise, in his *Reminiscences* (p. 327) states that he was present at the Ohio organizational meeting of the Republican party, but withdrew because of its identification with the leading (non-Jewish) German atheists of Cincinnati.

43. *Cincinnati Daily Enquirer,* Sept. 6, 1863.

44. *Cincinnati Daily Gazette,* Sept. 7, 1863.

45. *Isr.,* X, No. 12, pp. 92–3, Sept. 18, 1863, reprinted in *JR,* III, No. 2, p. 1, Sept. 25, 1863, which says that they were also printed in the *New York Times* of Sept. 10.

46. *Ibid.*

47. *Cincinnati Daily Gazette,* Sept. 11, 1863.

48. *Ibid.*

49. *Cincinnati Daily Enquirer,* Sept. 11, 1863.

50. *Isr.,* XI, No. 8, p. 60, Aug. 19, 1864.

51. *JR,* III, No. 3, p. 2, Oct. 9, 1863.

52. The Conference of Rabbis which met in Pittsburgh in November, 1885, produced one of the earliest social justice pronouncements by any religious group. European Reform Judaism had been liberal theologically, but took no group interest in liberal political movements. It is interesting to compare the Race Relations statements by the Commission on Justice and Peace of the Central Conference of American Rabbis, as well as those of the Rabbinical Assembly of America, issued annually on Race Relations Day, with the rabbinical statements on slavery analyzed in the previous chapter.

53. *Occ.,* XVIII, No. 33, p. 197, Nov. 8, 1860; No. 47, p. 286, Feb. 14, 1861.

54. *Occ.,* XVIII, No. 43, p. 257, Jan. 17, 1861.

55. *Occ.,* XVIII, No. 39, pp. 237–8, Dec. 20, 1860.

56. *Ibid.*

57. *Ibid.*

58. *Occ.,* XIX, No. 3, pp. 92–3, May, 1861.

59. *Occ.,* XX, No. 5, p. 238, Aug., 1862.

60. *Occ.,* XXIII, No. 8, pp. 276–7, Nov., 1865.

61. *Occ.,* XXV, No. 9, p. 461, Dec., 1867.

62. *Isr.,* XIV, No. 33, p. 2, Feb. 21, 1868.

63. Morais, *op. cit.*, p. 256; C. Adler, *Lectures, Selected Papers, Addresses*, pp. 48, 51.

64. *Occ.*, XIX, No. 3, pp. 92–3, May, 1861.

65. Rough draft of letter, Leeser to Henry, June 3, 1861, Leeser Collection.

66. *Ibid.*

67. Letter, Henry to Leeser, June 5, 1861, Leeser Collection.

68. Manuscript Thanksgiving Sermon, delivered Nov. 29, 1860, Gutheim Papers.

69. A large collection of Gutheim's manuscript sermons was given to the American Jewish Archives on permanent loan by Temple Sinai of New Orleans, through the courtesy of Rabbi Julian B. Feibelman and Mr. Leonard Levy.

70. Manuscript Thanksgiving Sermon, delivered Nov. 29, 1860, Gutheim Papers.

71. Letter, Leeser Collection.

72. Gutheim was not exaggerating. Another New Orleans Jew wrote to friends in England that "almost the entire Jewish population daily leave, and two-thirds of the Portuguese Congregation with their Rabbi have already departed." Reprinted from the *London Jewish Chronicle* in *JR*, II, No. 22, p. 2, Aug. 21, 1863. *The Israelite* said that over seven-eighths of the congregation had left, X, No. 1, p. 2, July 3, 1863.

73. *Occ.*, XXI, No. 5, pp. 234–5, Aug., 1863.

74. *Mobile Advertiser and Register*, May 29, 1863.

75. *Kahl Montgomery Minutes*, pp. 59, 61, 63, 66, 92.

76. *Ibid.*, p. 97.

77. Clipping from unidentified Montgomery paper, May 16, 1862, I. Solomon Scrapbook.

78. *Kahl Montgomery Minutes*, p. 106.

79. *HL*, VI, No. 22, p. 2, Aug. 18, 1865.

80. *Occ.*, XXII, No. 6, p. 238, Aug. 1865.

81. Max Heller, *Jubilee Souvenir of Temple Sinai, 1872–1922*, p. 52.

82. T. E. Dabney, *One Hundred Great Years*, p. 236.

83. *SHSP*, X (1882), pp. 248–50.

84. *New Orleans Daily Picayune*, May 7, 1904.

85. How ironic that on April 29, 1863, the Confederate House of Representatives should have passed a resolution encouraging New Orleans residents to defy Butler and thereby testify "to the patriotic spirit and *Christian* faith of our people." *JCCS*, VI, p. 461.

86. *Mess.*, IX, No. 3, p. 19, Jan. 18, 1861.

87. *Mess.*, IX, No. 19, p. 148, May 17, 1861.

88. *Mess.*, IX, No. 16, p. 124, Apr. 26, 1861; see also No. 21, p. 164, May 31, for a quotation from the *New York Independent*, congratulating the *Messenger* on its editorial position, saying in part: "This tone of manly, independent patriotism might well be imitated by certain professedly Christian editors, who,

though born and educated [in] the United States, study just now to maintain a neutral ground . . ."

89. *Mess.*, X, No. 1, p. 4, July 12, 1861.

90. *Mess.*, IX, No. 22, p. 172, June 7, 1861.

91. Letter, Jacobs to Leeser, Nov. 21, 1865, Leeser Collection.

92. Speech on life of Penina Moise by her niece, at South Carolina State Federation of Sisterhoods convention, in Marcus Collection.

93. See H. Hennig, *The Tree of Life*, pp. 4–6, for data on the Columbia congregation during the war. According to a manuscript deposition, Jan. 16, 1866, N. Y. Public Library, the Beth Elohim Congregation of Charleston deposited its Torah scrolls and other ceremonial objects with the Columbia congregation; these were, of course, destroyed in the fire.

94. *Mess.*, XVIII, No. 11, p. 85, Sept. 15, 1865. In this letter, Jacobs offered the hand of friendship to Isaacs in deference to the latter's age and long years of service to Jewry. He did not intend to perpetuate war-time enmities. According to Hennig, *op. cit.*, the Jews of Augusta also sent a contribution to assist their brethren in Columbia.

95. *Occ.*, XXIII, No. 3, p. 142, June, 1865.

96. Elzas, *op. cit.*, pp. 219–21, 260.

97. *Occ.*, XXIII, No. 11, pp. 462–81, Feb., 1866.

Notes to Chapter IV

1. See *The United States Army Chaplaincy*, for a detailed study of the historical development of the Army Chaplaincy.

2. See statistics and lists of Jews in the Union and Confederate armies and navies in Simon Wolf, *The American Jew as Patriot, Soldier and Citizen*.

3. *JCCS*, II, pp. 160, 196. Ella Lonn (*Foreigners in the Confederacy*, p. 265) erroneously refers to the Rev. Jacob Frankel, who is discussed below, pp. 77 ff., as a Confederate chaplain. Miss Lonn obviously misread a vague phrase in the authority which she cites, Mrs. Townes R. Leigh, "The Jews in the Confederacy," p. 178, where it is not clearly stated that Frankel was a Union chaplain. *UJE.*, IX, pp. 519–20 (cited in Schappes, *op. cit.*, p. 439) referring to the Rev. Julius Lewin of Shreveport as having served in the Confederate Army, appears to be without warrant. Neither the Adjutant General of the War Dept. nor the Archivist of the Adjutant General of the state of Louisiana has any record of his service. No rabbi is known to have served as a chaplain in the Confederate Army.

4. *WROR*, III, I, p. 154.

5. *Congressional Globe*, 37th Congress, 1st Session, p. 100.

6. *Isr.*, VIII, No. 3, p. 23, July 19, 1861.

7. *Philadelphia Sunday Dispatch*, Oct. 20, 1861. There were undoubtedly many other cases in which the appointment of chaplains of minority faiths was at-

tacked publicly. Carl Sandburg, in *Abraham Lincoln: The War Years*, II, p. 230, records the visit to Washington of a delegation of Philadelphia clergymen to urge Lincoln not to appoint a certain Universalist minister as chaplain, because "he believes that even rebels themselves will be finally saved."

8. His resignation was accepted on Sept. 26. Special Orders No. 79, Headquarters, Army of the Potomac, in *Records of the War Dept., Office of the Adjutant General, Vol. 403, Orders and Special Orders.*

9. Wolf, *op. cit.*, pp. 484–5. The law was passed only a few days before Allen enlisted (July 18, 1861, according to *Records of the Veterans Administration*, WO 1204831). The officers could hardly have known of the prohibitory clause. *New York Tribune*, Oct. 31, 1861.

10. Certificate in possession of Mrs. Clarence M. Allen, New York.

11. *Mess.*, XIX, No. 23, p. 4, June 15, 1866.

12. *Mess.*, X, No. 7, p. 52, Oct. 4, 1861; Henry S. Morais, *The Jews of Philadelphia*, p. 245.

13. P. 5 of an eleven page diary kept by Allen during the weeks his regiment was encamped near Washington, in the possession of Mrs. Clarence Allen of New York, printed, with an introduction, by Dr. David deSola Pool, in *PAJHS*, No. 39 (1949), pp. 177–182.

14. In a letter to the *Philadelphia Sunday Dispatch*, Oct. 20, 1861.

15. *Philadelphia Sunday Dispatch*, Oct. 27, 1861.

16. *Philadelphia Enquirer*, Oct. 12, 1861, p. 8.

17. *WROR*, III, I, p. 728.

18. Henry N. Blake, *Three Years in the Army of the Potomac*, p. 43.

19. *Presbyterian Banner*, cited in *Isr.*, IX, No. 2, p. 14, July 11, 1862.

20. *Isr.*, VIII, No. 6, p. 45, Aug. 9, 1861; No. 9, p. 70, Aug. 30, 1861. For further data on atheist chaplains see Ella Lonn, "The Forty-Eighters in the Civil War," in Zucker, *The Forty-Eighters.*

21. W. O. Stoddard, "White House Sketches," in *New York Citizen*, Oct. 6, 1866, quoted in Barbee, *op. cit.*, p. 7.

22. Practically nothing is known of Fischel's life beyond the fact that he was a native of Holland and that he returned there in 1862. *JE*, V, p. 400.

23. *Mess.*, X, No. 12, p. 93, Dec. 13, 1861; *Isr.*, VIII, No. 25, p. 196, Dec. 20, 1861, and various items in the Board of Delegates of American Israelites correspondence files (notably Letter No. 37, from Myer S. Isaacs, Secretary of the Board, to the Rev. Fischel, Nov. 27, 1861) establish the authenticity of his appointment by the officers of the regiment. Some of Fischel's activities are chronicled in the mis-named article by Myer S. Isaacs, "A Jewish Army Chaplain." The Rev. Fischel's contract as lecturer at the Shearith Israel Synagogue in New York was about to expire on Oct. 31, 1861, and was not expected to be renewed. He was, therefore, seeking a new position. *Shearith Israel Trustees' Minutes*, VI, p. 477, *passim*.

24. *Mess.*, X, No. 12, p. 93, Dec. 13, 1861.

25. *Isr.*, VIII, No. 20, p. 157, Nov. 15, 1861; No. 23, p. 177, Dec. 6, 1861; No. 25, p. 196, Dec. 20, 1861; No. 44, p. 348, May 2, 1862.

26. *Occ.*, XIX, No. 9, pp. 417–20, Dec., 1861; XX, No. 5, pp. 236–7, Aug., 1862.

27. *Mess.*, X, No. 9, p. 68, Nov. 1, 1861; No. 12, pp. 92–3, Dec. 13, 1861; XI, No. 17, p. 136, May 9, 1862.

28. *Isr.*, VIII, No. 22, p. 172, Nov. 29, 1861; No. 39, p. 308, Mar. 28, 1862; *Mess.*, X, No. 13, p. 101, Dec. 27, 1861; *Occ.*, XX, No. 5, pp. 236–7, Aug., 1862.

29. *Isr.*, VIII, No. 39, p. 308, Mar. 28, 1862.

30. *Congressional Globe*, 37th Congress, 2nd Session, Part 1, p. 156; Fischel letter, Dec. 27, 1861 (see note 22).

31. Quoted in *Isr.*, VIII, No. 19, p. 146, Nov. 8, 1861; No. 22, p. 172, Nov. 29, 1861.

32. Quoted in *Isr.*, VIII, No. 27, p. 212, Jan. 3, 1862; *Sinai*, VII, No. 1, pp. 23–5, Feb., 1862.

33. Quoted in *Sinai*, VI, No. 10, p. 321, Nov., 1861.

34. *Isr.*, VIII, No. 26, p. 206, Dec. 27, 1861; No. 27, p. 215, Jan. 3, 1862. The only unfavorable reaction which the Jewish editors recorded came, not from an American journalist, but a British journalist, Sir William Howard Russell, American correspondent for the *London Times*, who felt that the Jewish agitation for a change in the chaplaincy law was a "hoax," and wrote to England that there were few enough Jews in the whole army, at best only a "slight sprinkling" in the Cameron's Dragoons, and that there was no justification for the Jewish request for the right to chaplains. Russell did not quite understand the deeper implications of the Jewish campaign. *Mess.*, XI, No. 5, p. 41, Feb. 7, 1862.

35. *Isr.*, VIII, No. 20, p. 157, Nov. 15, 1861, *passim*.

36. *Isr.*, VIII, No. 23, p. 177, Dec. 6, 1861.

37. *Congressional Globe*, *op. cit.*, pp. 25, 67, 219, 444.

38. *Baltimore Clipper* quoted in *Isr.*, VIII, No. 26, p. 206, Dec. 27, 1861; No. 27, p. 215, Jan. 3, 1862.

39. *Isr.*, VIII, No. 28, p. 223, Jan. 10, 1862.

40. *Isr.*, VIII, No. 29, p. 230, Jan. 17, 1862.

41. *Isr.*, VIII, No. 30, p. 239, Jan. 24, 1862. Other towns from which petitions were sent were: Louisville, Ky., Trafalgar, Ind., Laporte, Franklin, and Iowa City, Iowa.

42. For New York, see *Mess.*, X, No. 10, p. 72, Nov. 15, 1861 and *Temple Emanu-El Board of Directors Minutes (1851–1862)*, entry for Dec. 1, 1861. For Philadelphia, see *Sinai*, VI, No. 11, pp. 255–7, Dec., 1861; No. 12, p. 381, Jan., 1862. For Cincinnati, see *Isr.*, VIII, No. 22, p. 172, Nov. 29, 1861.

43. *Mess.*, X, No. 12, p. 93, Dec. 13, 1861.

44. Letter No. 37, Board of Delegates to Fischel. The Board apparently believed that it would later appoint a similar chaplain to be attached to the military forces in the Mississippi River area, and so wrote to A. J. Latz of St. Louis, asking his reaction. Copy of Letter, No. 43, Board of Delegates to Latz. No further mention of the project was made, but it is likely that it was dropped due to lack of funds.

45. Most of the material for the remainder of this section is taken from the Fischel reports to the Board of Delegates, unless otherwise noted. The reports

are dated Dec. 11, 13, 15, 20, 27, 1861; Jan. 2, 7, 8, Mar. 10, Apr. 3, 1862. Some of them are printed, in part, in Myer S. Isaacs, "A Jewish Army Chaplain," pp. 127–137, and L. M. Friedman, *Jewish Pioneers and Patriots*, pp. 46–48. Fischel's own interest in American Jewish history (he was collecting material in 1860–2 for "a comprehensive history of the Israelites in America," *Mess.*, X, No. 9, p. 68, Nov. 1, 1861; XI, No. 11, p. 88, Mar. 21, 1862) was undoubtedly responsible for the care with which he wrote these reports, and the wealth of detail which he included in them. He knew he was participating in an historic campaign.

46. Letter, Fischel to Hart, Dec. 15, 1861.

47. *Ibid.*, Dec. 11, 1861.

48. *Ibid.*, Dec. 13, 1861.

49. *Ibid.*, Dec. 15, 1861.

50. *Congressional Globe, op. cit.*, pp. 156–7.

51. A copy of the original bill, in printed form, was sent by Fischel to the Board in New York, and preserved with its other records.

52. Letter, Fischel to Hart, Apr. 3, 1862.

53. *Congressional Globe, op. cit.*, p. 299.

54. *WROR*, III, III, pp. 175–6.

55. This text of the protest is taken from *Sinai*, VII, No. 1, pp. 2–3, Feb., 1862. Leeser answered it in the *Philadelphia Enquirer*, Jan. 13, 1862 (reprinted in *Occ.*, XIX, No. 11, pp. 503–11). He was at a loss to explain the motives of "the six." What harm or hurt were they protesting against? His answer to the protest asserted that: 1) the Board of Delegates never pretended to represent all Jews; 2) the Board did represent *some* congregations, more than "the six," at least; 3) Dr. Fischel was actually accomplishing something in connection with the chaplaincy restrictions—"the six" had done nothing but talk!

Felsenthal continued the campaign against the Board in the *Illinois Staatszeitung* (Chicago), July 12, 1862 (reprinted in *Sinai*, VII, No. 7, pp. 200–1, Aug., 1862), denying that Fischel's activities had anything to do with Congress' final revision of the chaplaincy clause. He gave the credit to Senator Wilson. Of course the Senator had introduced the bill which included the revised regulation, but it is questionable whether anything would have been done in Washington if Fischel himself had not been there to lobby in behalf of the Jewish position. Protests and letters and petitions could easily be pushed aside in the rush of events, but Fischel could not be so neglected.

Those who supported the Board were not entirely objective in their bickering with the Reformers. When a writer to *Mess.*, (XII, No. 1, pp. 4–5, July 4, 1862) attacked the "Protest Rabbis," he descended to the lowest level of *ad hominem* arguments, suggesting that American congregations should refuse to call German and Polish rabbis (the six protestors were all immigrants from Central Europe) and should, in the future, call their rabbis from a civilized country like Great Britain (Raphall and Isaacs, supporters of the Board, had come to America by way of England, though neither was born there). He further suggested that the only explanation of the protest was that "the six" were jealous of the Board's success. Fischel himself was greatly exercized when he wrote in a letter to Hart, Mar. 10, 1862, that he had heard a rumor that the Reform rabbis were attempting to secure a chaplaincy appointment for one of their own group!

56. Letter, Fischel to Hart, Jan. 8, 1862. The bulk of the material in this section also, except as noted, is derived from the Fischel reports to the Board of Delegates.

57. Also noted in *Mess.*, XI, No. 2, p. 17, Jan. 17, 1862. In his report of April 3, 1862 (published in full in *Occ.*, XX, No. 5, pp. 219–222, Aug., 1862), Fischel commented: "Most of the Jewish soldiers, seeing that no provision had been made for them, had joined the Society of Odd Fellows and other associations, that undertake to return the bodies of the dead to their relatives, and one instance came under my notice in which a messenger was sent from California to recover the body of a soldier, who was a member of some association in that State."

58. Fischel letter to Hart, Mar. 10, 1862.

59. Fischel letter to Hart, Dec. 20, 1861.

60. Quoted in *Mess.*, X, No. 13, p. 100, Dec. 27, 1861. Printed copies in Board of Delegates files and Leeser Collection.

61. See letter to Joseph Abraham, Cincinnati, Dec. 17, 1861, No. 44 in the Board of Delegates' correspondence files.

62. *Mess.*, XI, No. 1, p. 4, Jan. 10, 1862; No. 18, p. 144, May 16, 1862. Anshi Chesed Congregation of New York, in what was probably a typical action, tabled the Board's appeal for funds. *Anshi Chesed Board of Trustees Minutes (1856–1866)*, p. 437.

63. *Mess.*, XI, No. 6, p. 49, Feb. 14, 1862. Two weeks previously, the *Messenger* printed the news that a collection was about to be taken up in Pittsburgh for the support of the "Jewish chaplaincy mission." It is hoped that the childrens' contribution of $5 was not the result of a widespread collection throughout the Jewish community of Pittsburgh! *Mess.*, XI, No. 4, p. 33, Jan. 31, 1862.

64. See *Mess.*, citations above; *Occ.*, XIX, No. 10, pp. 476–80, Jan., 1862, where Leeser wrote, ". . . it cannot be expected that he [Fischel] should forego lucrative engagements to devote himself to the ministry at large, while our own people do nothing and contribute nothing . . ."

65. *Mess.*, XI, No. 20, p. 161, May 30, 1862. The identity of the author is not known, but it is very possible that it was the Rev. Fischel himself, who liked to write and was known as a literary person. The scrupulous avoidance of any mention of Fischel's name or his activities, as well as the reference to a British boy killed in a recent battle, might point to Fischel as the author of this eloquent plea.

The bitterness of this essay was matched by that of an editorial which appeared in *JR*, I, No. 23, p. 2, Feb. 13, 1863, entitled "Shortcoming of our Clergy," which commented, after a discussion of the activities of the U. S. Christian Commission, on the failure of the rabbis to take an interest in the spiritual needs of Jewish soldiers, particularly those who were patients in hospitals:

> . . . Have our clergy manifested such efficiency in behalf of the scattered Hebrews in the Republic? Let the thousands of Israelites in the army, who are as destitute of the consolations of their faith as if they resided among the Esquimaux, reply,—and bring a blush, if possible, over the features of a ministry who are partially answerable to the Almighty for their souls.

Our clergy, with an etiquette which the holy prophets would spurn as an irrecoverable leprosy, will not go beyond the pave of the synagogue to perform their labors. They may yet insist on imitating the Episcopal Church by demanding a rectory which shall communicate with their temples.

We respectfully suggest to our clergy that they should follow the example of the Christian Commission, and make an effort to provide our co-religionists in the army with the instruction and ministrations of their faith. If they do not, their culpable inactivity will be noticed more forcibly by our people than by a simple editorial.

It may be stated, however, that application has been made for Jewish army chaplains and refused. Has the application ever been tried on the part of a United Jewish Clergy Army Commission? No minister needs official permission to visit any hospitals, where as much good can be accomplished as on the "tented field."

Allowing for the anti-clerical opinions of the only lay Jewish editor, all of whose competitors were rabbis, we must still admit that there was some truth to Cohen's allegations. Not all of the rabbis were as eager as Fischel to endure discomfort and inconvenience in order to minister to the soldiers.

66. *Mess.*, XI, No. 18, p. 144, May 16, 1862.

67. *Occ.*, XX, No. 7, pp. 325–8, Oct., 1862. The actual letter, No. 7870-1 of the Robert Todd Lincoln Collection, indicates that Lincoln's secretary wrote the Surgeon General for his opinion of "the legality and propriety of the request," concluding: "If possible the President would like this to be done." The Surgeon General approved.

Markens, in "Lincoln and the Jews," p. 116, states that the Rev. Sabato Morais of Philadelphia "had previously declined an appointment as Chaplain." Unfortunately Markens did not annotate his article. The writer has found no evidence for this assertion in the contemporary periodicals; but a letter from John Hay, Lincoln's secretary, to A. Hart, president of Morais' congregation, Jan. 9, 1864, (in Morais Collection), stating "your petition for his appointment is on file," probably indicates that Morais *sought* a chaplaincy appointment unsuccessfully. This is far different, however, from his *declining* a proffered appointment!

68. *Ibid.* The appointment was signed by the President on Sept. 10, and forwarded by the Surgeon General on Sept. 15. *Records of the War Dept., Office of the Adjutant General.* The commission, which is now in the possession of his grandson, was sent to Frankel two years later when his appointment was renewed.

69. Morais, *op. cit.*, pp. 73–4; Edward Davis, *The History of Rodeph Shalom Congregation, Philadelphia, 1802–1926*, pp. 61, 98–100.

70. *Records of the War Dept., Office of the Adjutant General.*

71. See the Rev. Leeser's pass, addressed to "Surgeons in Charge of USA General Hospitals, Department of the Susquehanna," requesting that he be permitted to visit sick Jewish soldiers, signed Mar. 30, 1864, Leeser Collection. See facsimile on p. 79.

72. *Occ.*, XXII, No. 5, pp. 234–5, Aug., 1865. Other details from miscellaneous clippings in the possession of Mr. Joseph Frankel of New York, grandson of Jacob.

73. *General Orders of the War Department, 1861–1863*, I, p. 177. Allen wore a uniform, as did certain other chaplains, because he had enlisted as an officer of the line before his election as chaplain.

74. For the military orders concerning the appointment and assignment of hospital chaplains, see *WROR*, III, II, pp. 67, 222, 276; IV, III, p. 496.

75. See Sandburg, *op. cit.*, II, p. 44, for pertinent quotations from Lincoln's correspondence on this subject.

76. *WROR*, III, I, pp. 712, 721.

77. *Occ.*, XX, No. 7, pp. 325–8, Oct., 1862.

78. No. 18878–9 of the Robert Todd Lincoln Collection. The reply is contained in No. 19222–3.

79. Isaacs, *op. cit.*, pp. 130–1. *JR* reported several times that Fischel intended to return to America, but these expectations were never fulfilled. See, for example, V, No. 22, p. 2, Feb. 24, 1865.

80. Markens, *op. cit.*, quotes the letter from Usher to Dessar. No source is given. Could Kalisch have been the Reform rabbi whose chaplaincy application had worried Fischel a year earlier?

81. *Isr.*, IX, No. 45, p. 357, May 15, 1863; *Records of the War Department, Office of the Adjutant General, Vol. XI, Officers of Signal Corps and Hospital Chaplains.*

82. Letters from Rabbi Stanley Brav, Vicksburg, Oct. 23, 1947, and Mr. Harold Gotthelf (grandson of the rabbi), Vicksburg, Nov. 18, 1947; *Keneseth Israel 90th Anniversary Booklet.*

83. Cited in *Isr.*, IX, No. 45, p. 357, May 15, 1863.

84. *Isr.*, XI, No. 30, p. 237, Jan. 30, 1865.

85. *Isr.*, XI, No. 34, p. 269, Feb. 17, 1865.

86. *Isr.*, XI, No. 39, p. 309, Mar. 24, 1865.

87. *Records of the War Dept., Office of the Adjutant General*, and the Records of the Adjutant General of the Division of Military and Naval Affairs of the State of New York, Albany.

88. *Isr.*, IX, No. 43, p. 338, Apr. 31, 1863; *Occ.*, XXI, No. 2, May, 1863, p. 96.

89. This is the date on his passport. He told the army authorities at the time of his enlistment in 1863 that he was then 38! He undoubtedly wanted to avoid any question of his being too old to enlist.

90. *Anshi Chesed Board of Trustees Minutes, 1856–1866*, p. 414.

91. *Mess.*, VIII, No. 18, p. 141, Nov. 1, 1861. One of Sarner's plays (the only one registered in the Library of Congress' Union Catalogue) was published in New York in 1871. It is entitled *Prinzessin von Cariola, oder; Liebe und Zeistesstörung. Drama in 5 akten.*

92. Copy of the certificate in the *Records of the War Dept., Office of the Adjutant General.*

93. *A Record of the Commissioned Officers, Non-Commissioned Officers and Privates of the Regiments which were organized in the State of New York . . . To Assist in Suppressing the Rebellion*, II, pp. 407-27.

94. Both documents are found in the *Records of the War Dept., Office of the Adjutant General*. Manuscript evidence can be disconcertingly erroneous: the board of chaplains also certified that Sarner was "a regularly ordained minister of the Lutheran Church"!! Were we not certain that he was a rabbi previous to and subsequent to his service in the army, and did we not know that he was in contact with contemporary Jewish periodicals (which would surely have received reports of his apostasy if such had been the case), there might be a possibility that the chaplains knew better than we. Perhaps they too assumed that a regiment composed of a majority of German Gentiles would elect a Protestant chaplain. It is barely possible that Sarner spoke such poor English that he could not make them understand he was a rabbi. Whatever the reason for such an error, it is enough to make a researcher shudder for the accuracy of other "certified" evidence.

95. *Archives Israelites*, XXV, p. 135, Feb. 1, 1864.

96. *Headquarters of the Army, Adjutant General's Office, Special Orders No. 330, Paragraph 36, Oct. 3, 1864*. Dr. Sarner apparently left camp before this order had been transmitted to him, under the impression that it would be forwarded. This made him technically absent without leave, and in March 1869, the Adjutant General's Office finally compared its records of his service, revoked the order for his honorable discharge on account of disability, and listed him as discharged for being absent without leave. *Records of the War Department, Office of the Adjutant General, Special Orders No. 63, Mar. 18, 1869.*

97. *Occ.*, XXII, No. 9, p. 420, Dec., 1864.

98. *JR*, V, No. 15, p. 2, Jan. 6, 1865.

99. *Isr.*, XI, No. 31, p. 244, Jan. 6, 1865.

100. *Isr.*, XI, No. 34, p. 269, Feb. 17, 1865.

101. For six months he was partner with S. H. Kleinfeld in directing a New York boarding school. *HL*, XVI, No. 3, p. 5, May 6, 1870; XVII, No. 4, p. 6, Nov. 11, 1870. He preached in Brevoort Hall, New York, on the High Holy Days of 1872. *Mess.*, XXXII, No. 15, p. 2, Oct. 11, 1872.

102. *Mess.*, XI, No. 5, p. 41, Feb. 7, 1862.

103. *Isr.*, XI, No. 5, p. 37, July 29, 1864.

104. The text is taken from a printed copy in the Confederate Museum, Richmond, inscribed "To Max Myers from his friend & well wisher M. J. Michelbacher." Many Christian organizations issued volumes of prayers and devotions during the war. It was not until the first World War that special volumes of Jewish prayers were published for use by soldiers.

105. Letter, Edwin Kursheedt to Sarah [?], Dec. 28, 1864, American Jewish Archives.

106. *Mess.*, XIX, No. 13, p. 2, Mar. 30, 1866.

107. Letter, Isaac J. Levy to Leonora Levy, April 24, 1864, American Jewish Archives. "Passover," "*Matzot*," and "*Seder*" are printed in Hebrew letters in

the original manuscript. Unleavened bread for Passover was scarce in the latter years of the Confederacy—as was all manner of food! See the *Major Hart Diary*, April 8, 1865, (p. 18) where Hart, trying to get to Mobile from Richmond in those last desperate days, stops off in Charlotte, N. C., to celebrate the Passover with friends—having brought *Matzot* along from Richmond to supply his friends as well as himself with that rare commodity!

108. *Mess.*, XIII, No. 23, p. 195, June 12, 1866.

109. *Isr.*, IX, No. 15, p. 118, Oct. 17, 1862.

110. Told by Myer Levy's niece, Miss Miriam E. Levy of Philadelphia, in a letter to the writer, Mar. 22, 1949.

111. *Aunt Sister's Book*, pp. 7, 13. Isaac Lowenberg later moved to Natchez and became one of the town's leading figures, president of a local bank and mayor of the town in 1882–6. *UJE*, VII, p. 218. For a similar story, with Richmond as its locale, and "a pleasant, quiet, home *Shabbas*" the ambition, see Philadelphia *Jewish Exponent*, I, No. 11, p. 7, June 24, 1887.

112. Two letters from Lee are reprinted from Jones, *Personal Reminiscences, Anecdotes, and Letters of Gen. Robert E. Lee*, pp. 443–4, in Ezekiel and Lichtenstein, *The History of the Jews of Richmond from 1769 to 1917*, pp. 161–3; a third, the one we have quoted, is in the possession of LeRoy R. Cohen, Jr., of Richmond. Also reprinted by Ezekiel is a statement by a certain M. Goldsmith about the Rev. Michelbacher's attempts, in 1864, to secure such furloughs on the basis of personal interviews with various political and military figures. The Jones volume is quoted as authority for a further story about religious furloughs: A company commander disapproved a Jewish soldier's application for leave to attend synagogue services with the comment, "If such applications were granted, the whole army would turn Jews or shaking Quakers." Lee is said to have endorsed it, "Approved, and respectfully returned to Captain ————— with the advice that he should always respect the religious views and feelings of others" (Ezekiel, *op. cit.*, pp. 164–5). An answer to a letter by Michelbacher concerning Holy Day furloughs from General Beauregard's Assistant Adjutant General, Thomas Jordan, is printed in *JR*, I, No. 23, p. 2, Feb. 13, 1863. There is, unfortunately, no evidence as to the number of times that Michelbacher made such applications; those which are recorded, however, were spaced over the entire period of the war: Rosh Hashonah, 1861; Passover, 1863; Rosh Hashonah, 1864.

At least once, it would appear, the military situation was sufficiently static for General Lee to accede to the Rev. Michelbacher's request. L. Leon, a private in Company C of the First North Carolina Bethel Regiment, wrote in his diary, under date of Sept. 29, 1863:

> All quiet today. Brother Morris returned from Richmond yesterday, where he had been for ten days on a furlough. Before our Jewish New Year there was an order read out from General Lee granting a furlough to each Israelite to go to Richmond for the holidays if he so desired. I did not care to go. (L. Leon, *Diary of a Tar Heel Confederate Soldier*, p. 49).

Leon was not so careless of his Jewish heritage as might seem. His diary is replete with references to other Jewish soldiers and officers whom he met, to the dates of Jewish holidays, and other such items (see pp. 12, 47, 48). He records with pride how curious some people were to see him, after they heard of his capture of a deserter: "Is there a Jew in your detachment that caught a deserter yesterday?" (p. 46).

113. *Isr.*, X, No. 29, p. 229, Jan. 15, 1864.

114. *Mess.*, XI, No. 7, pp. 4–5, Feb. 12, 1862.

115. *Isr.*, XI, No. 5, p. 37, July 29, 1864.

116. *Isr.*, VIII, No. 18, p. 141, Nov. 1, 1861. This letter was written by Herman Kuhn of Phoenixville, Pa., *Herman Kuhn*, pp. 42–3. See also *Mess.*, XI, No. 16, p. 125, Oct. 24, 1862: A Christian chaplain wrote a New York Jew about his son, "He is seriously ill, and I fear will not survive. All that medical skill can do, will be done for him. As to his *spiritual* welfare, I will see to that." The *Messenger's* editorial comment: "This from a Christian to a Jew! Will not this—by no means isolated—case arouse our co-religionists to the necessity of providing for the spiritual interests of Jewish soldiers?" It was, naturally, a cause for concern among sensitive Jews, that some Christians might take advantage of impressionable young men suffering from wounds and disease in the military hospitals.

117. *Mess.*, XI, No. 5, p. 41, Feb. 7, 1862.

118. *Occ.*, XXIII, No. 7, pp. 293–4, Oct., 1865. There was a widespread impression in the post-war days that Jews had been taunted about their religion, especially in the hospitals. See *Mess.*, XIX, No. 3, p. 2, Jan. 19, 1866, for B. F. Peixotto's short story "The Ben Berith—A Reminiscence of the Late War," in which a Jewish soldier hospitalized for war wounds is urged to convert to Christianity to aid his recovery.

119. *Memoirs of Henry Beck, 1864–5*, pp. 1–7.

120. Letter, Emanuel to his mother, Apr. 9, 1864.

121. *Mess.*, XIII, No. 20, pp. 170–1, May 22, 1863.

122. *Autobiography of August Bondi 1833–1907*, pp. 71–2, 82, 87–8, 101, 123.

123. One wonders if this category would include the only rabbi known to have served as a line officer—Captain John Salominsky of the cavalry, who came to the United States in 1860 after participation in a Polish uprising, and joined the Union Army in 1861, intending to return to the rabbinate at the end of the war. His marriage to a Swedenborgian lady apparently made this impossible, so he remained in the military service, and was stationed at Fort Humboldt, Dakota, when last heard from. *Isr.*, XVI, No. 6, p. 6, Aug. 13, 1869.

Notes to Chapter V

1. Brief resumes of the activities of the Sanitary Commission are to be found in A. C. Cole, *The Irrepressible Conflict*, pp. 331–3, and J. G. Randall, *The Civil War and Reconstruction*, pp. 634–5. It is surprising that no adequate study of the Sanitary Commission has been made.

2. Sandburg, *op. cit.*, II, p. 609.

3. *JR*, I, No. 6. p. 2, Oct. 15, 1862. Fifteen other firms gave a total of $1,305.

4. *Isr.*, IX, No. 50, p. 398, June 19, 1863.

5. No. 38395, Robert Todd Lincoln Collection; *Denver Daily News*, July 27, 1897; *Baltimore Sun*, Apr. 27, 1865; Grossmayer Papers. Grossmayer's will, written during the Civil War, provided that his estate should be turned over to Lincoln for war relief purposes. It was, of course, changed after the war ended.

6. Elzas, *op. cit.*, pp. 220–2.

7. Moses Papers.

8. *Occ.*, XXIII, No. 12, p. 568, Mar., 1866; XXIV, No. 3, p. 144, June 1866.

9. Mrs. T. R. Leigh, "The Jews in the Confederacy," p. 179.

10. Mary Boykind Chesnut, *A Diary From Dixie*, p. 176.

11. Manuscript Division, Library of Congress; another fine expression of women's war work is to be found in Mrs. Commodore Levy's speech when she presented a flag to a New York artillery company; *JR*, I, No. 13, p. 2, Dec. 5, 1862.

12. *Isr.*, VIII, No. 16, p. 126, Oct. 18, 1861; *PAJHS*, No. 17 (1920), p. 124; *Mobile Tribune*, quoted in *Occ.*, XXIV, No. 3, p. 143, June, 1866; *Mess.*, IX, No. 21, p. 165, May 31, 1861; Selig Adler, "Zebulon B. Vance and the 'Scattered Nation'," p. 362.

13. Letter, Morais to Smith, May 11, 1863, Morais Collection.

14. *Philadelphia Enquirer*, quoted in *JR*, II, No. 9, p. 1, May 8, 1863; *Mess.*, XIII, No. 20, p. 171, May 22, 1863.

15. Quoted in *Sinai*, VII, No. 6, p. 172, July, 1862.

16. *JR*, VI, No. 10, p. 1, May 26, 1865.

17. Letter in Cohen Papers.

18. *JR*, III, No. 16, p. 1, Jan. 8, 1864.

19. *Isr.*, X, No. 26, p. 204, Dec. 25, 1863.

20. *Ibid.*

21. *Ibid.*

22. Clipping from an unidentified San Francisco newspaper, Marcus Collection.

23. *Mess.*, XV, No. 24, p. 190, June 24, 1864; letter, Alfred H. Adler to his cousin, Mar. 30, 1864, Marcus Collection.

24. *Mess.*, XV, No. 12, p. 98, Mar. 25, 1864.

25. *Anshi Chesed Board Minutes (1856–1866)*, pp. 410, 413, 415; *Mess.*, IX, No. 20, p. 157, May 24, 1861.

26. *Temple Emanu-El Board Minutes (1848–1868)*, May 11, 1862; *Sinai*, VII, No. 4, p. 116, May, 1862. On Purim, 1861, Emanu-El raised $130.75 "in aid of the sufferers in Kansas," entry Mar. 3, 1861.

27. *JR*, III, No. 23, p. 3, Feb. 26, 1864.

28. Kohler, *op. cit.*, p. 151.

29. Typical contributions: Philadelphia Society for Visitation of the Sick and Mutual Assistance, $25 to the Volunteer Refreshment Establishment, Dec. 1861, and $100 to the Sanitary Commission, Sept. 1862 (*Society Minutes*); Anshi Chesed Congregation, New York, $50 to Soldiers' Relief Society, June 1862 (*Board Minutes*, pp. 450–1); Buffalo congregation, $175 to the Sanitary Commission, Dec. 1863 (*JR*, III, No. 14, p. 5, Dec. 25, 1863); Jewish Charity Ball of

Philadelphia, $25 to Volunteer Refreshment Establishment, Jan. 1862 (unidentified clipping in American Jewish Archives); Beth Elohim Congregation, $250 to Brooklyn Sanitary Fair (*Mess.*, XV, No. 9, p. 67, Mar. 4, 1864).

30. *Isr.*, X, No. 23, p. 182, Dec. 4, 1863; No. 24, p. 187, Dec. 11; No. 26, p. 203, Dec. 25; No. 27, p. 21, Jan. 1, 1864; No. 31, p. 246, Jan. 29.

31. *Mess.*, XV, No. 17, p. 134, May 6, 1864.

32. *Mess.*, XV, No. 24, p. 190, June 24, 1864.

33. *Mess.*, XV, No. 22, p. 174, June 9, 1864.

34. *Mess.* XV, No. 8, p. 58, Feb. 26, 1864.

35. *Mess.*, XV, No. 17, p. 133, May 6, 1864; *JR*, III, No. 23, p. 2, Feb. 26, 1864.

36. *JR*, III, No. 25, p. 2, Mar. 11, 1864; *Mess.*, XV, No. 13, p. 102, Apr. 1, 1864.

37. *Mess.*, XV, No. 12, p. 98, Mar. 25, 1864.

38. See, for instance, *Isr.*, VIII, No. 34, p. 270, Feb. 21, 1862, where Wise reprints in full a Sanitary Commission speech by Judge Hoadly.

39. *JR*, III, No. 16, p. 1, Jan. 8, 1864. Two years earlier the Jews of Rochester had organized several benefits for war relief: *JR*, I, No. 4, p. 6, Oct. 3, 1862; *Isr.*, IX, No. 17, p. 131, Oct. 31, 1862.

40. *JR*, III, No. 26, p. 2, Mar. 18, 1864.

41. *Mess.*, XV, No. 9, pp. 66-7, Mar. 4, 1864. See also Myer S. Isaacs' letter, Nov. 19, 1863, to Rev. H. W. Bellows, Pres. of the New York Sanitary Commission, suggesting a policy of non-segregation, Schappes, *op. cit.*, pp. 493-4.

42. *Isr.*, X, No. 24, p. 187, Dec. 11, 1863.

43. *The Story of the First Fifty Years of the Mount Sinai Hospital, 1852-1902*, pp. 1-28.

44. *Isr.*, VII, No. 44, p. 350, May 3, 1861.

45. *Mess.*, XI, No. 9, p. 151, May 23, 1862; No. 23, p. 184, June 20, 1862.

46. *Mess.*, XII, No. 6, p. 46, Aug. 8, 1862; *JR*, I, No. 5, p. 2, Oct. 8, 1862; *Occ.*, XX, No. 8, p. 383, Nov. 1862; No. 10, p. 375, Jan., 1863; No. 11, p. 526, Feb., 1863; *Mess.*, XV, No. 23, p. 182, June 17, 1864; XVI, No. 6, p. 44, Aug. 12, 1864; *Occ.*, XXII, No. 7, p. 331, Oct., 1864; *Mess.*, XVII, No. 2, p. 13, Jan. 13, 1865.

47. *New York Tribune*, quoted in *JR*, I, No. 13, pp. 2-3, Dec. 5, 1862.

48. *Temple Emanu-El Board Minutes (1854-1862)*, May, 1862; *Mess.*, XI, No. 19, p. 151, May 23, 1862.

49. *Mess.*, XI, No. 24, p. 194, June 27, 1862; XII, No. 2, p. 14, July 11; No. 3, p. 22, July 18; No. 4, p. 30, July 25; No. 6, p. 46, Aug. 8; No. 8, p. 54, Aug. 15; *Anshi Chesed Board Minutes (1856-1866)*, pp. 450-1.

50. *Mess.*, XII, No. 3, pp. 20-1, July 18, 1862.

51. *Mess.*, XII, No. 24, p. 187, Dec. 19, 1862.

52. *New York Tribune*, *op. cit.*

53. *New York Times*, quoted in *JR*, I, No. 3, p. 2, Sept. 24, 1862.

54. *Mess.*, XII, No. 3, pp. 20-1, July 18, 1862.

55. *Mess.*, XVIII, No. 22, p. 169, Dec. 8, 1865.

56. *Isr.*, VIII, No. 15, p. 118, Oct. 11, 1861; No. 28, p. 222, Jan. 10, 1862; IX, No. 33, p. 258, Feb. 20, 1863.

57. *Occ.*, XIX, No. 9, pp. 415–6, Dec. 1861.

58. *Occ.*, XV, No. 9, pp. 412–3, Dec. 1862.

59. *Isr.*, IX, No. 16, p. 123, Oct. 24, 1862; No. 17, p. 134, Oct. 31.

60. *Occ.*, XIX, No. 9, pp. 422–3, Dec. 1861.

61. *Mess.*, IX, No. 25, p. 196, June 28, 1861. The Jews of Washington found difficulty in raising funds to purchase a building to be used as a synagogue. On Feb. 17, 1863, they wrote other congregations, asking for help. This appeal was endorsed by Richard Wallach, Mayor of Washington, a member of the congregation. (Copy of appeal in Mikveh Israel Archives, Philadelphia.) Very few answers were received. *Occ.*, XXI, No. 7, pp. 273–285, Sept. 1863.

62. *Mess.*, XIII, No. 25, p. 211, June 26, 1863.

63. *Mess.*, XVII, No. 8, p. 59, Feb. 24, 1865.

64. Anne Marcovitch, "A History of Temple Beth El," pp. 3, 10.

65. *Savannah Daily Morning News*, Apr. 25, 1862.

66. Barnett R. Brickner, *The Jews of Cincinnati*, p. 165.

67. *Occ.*, XXIII, No. 5, pp. 234–5, Aug. 1865.

68. *Isr.*, XI, No. 20, p. 157, Nov. 11, 1864; XVI, No. 1, p. 6, July 9, 1869.

69. *Baltimore Sunday Herald*, May 24, 1896; *JR*, II, No. 23, p. 2, Aug. 28, 1863. In *The Autograph Collectors' Journal*, I, No. 2 (Jan. 1949), pp. 14–15, Alden S. Condict and Rhea Barzilay print the text of a letter Lincoln wrote to General Meade about the five condemned men: ". . . I understand these are very flagrant cases, and that you deem their punishment as being indispensable to the service. If I am not mistaken in this, please let me know at once that their appeal is denied."

70. *Mess.*, XIV, No. 9, p. 69, Sept. 4, 1863; *JR*, II, No. 24, p. 2, Sept. 4, 1863. Another eye-witness records additional details, although he is probably in error in referring to *two* Jewish men:

> The band of the regiment played the "dead march" while the procession was moving to the scene; and each prisoner, with his hands manacled behind him, walked in the rear of his coffin, which was carried by four soldiers, and placed in front of the grave. Two were Jews, and two were Roman Catholics; and the rabbi and priest who accompanied them had a dispute about precedence, and urged their respective claims upon theological tenets; but the commander of the provost-guard viewed the subject in a military light, and decided the novel question by allowing the rabbi to walk first, because his faith was the oldest and outranked the other. The last solemn rites were celebrated; each culprit sat upon his coffin; their eyes were bandaged; within a second the bullets from fifty muskets pierced them, and soon five mounds of earth covered their bodies. . . . H. N. Blake, *Three Years in the Army of the Potomac*, pp. 238–40.

71. See *Isr.*, XV, No. 22, p. 4, Dec. 4, 1868 for the Cincinnati monument; and *Isr.*, XIV, No. 21, p. 6, Nov. 29, 1867 for one in Chattanooga, Tenn.

72. Clipping from unidentified Richmond paper, George Jacobs Scrapbook.

73. Copy of circular in George Jacobs Scrapbook.

74. Rebekah Kohut, *My Portion*, p. 26.

75. *Occ.*, XXIV, No. 5, p. 239, Aug. 1866.

76. *Isr.*, X, No. 16, p. 122, Oct. 16, 1863; XI, No. 11, p. 124, Oct. 14, 1864.

77. *Isr.*, VIII, No. 35, p. 278, Feb. 28, 1862.

78. See, for instance, General Butler to M. S. Isaacs, Apr. 9, 1864, Aug. 3, 1864, Board of Delegates correspondence files. Nathan Grossmayer secured a pardon for Moses Waldauer, a Jewish deserter who had gone AWOL to visit a dying mother; papers in American Jewish Archives. Other cases will be referred to in later chapters.

79. *Mess.*, XVII, No. 9, p. 171, Mar. 3, 1865; No. 12, p. 98, Mar. 24, 1865; James A. Wax, *History of United Hebrew Congregation, St. Louis*, p. 33; *Shearith Israel Trustees Minutes*, VI, p. 520; Letter, Rev. Henry Kuttner to Leeser, Mar. 13, 1865, Leeser Collection; *Savannah Daily Herald*, Mar. 29, 1865, for the arrival of the *Matzot* in Savannah.

80. *Shearith Israel Trustees Minutes*, VI, p. 523.

81. *JR*, VI, No. 7, p. 2, June 5, 1865; *Occ.*, XXIV, No. 4, pp. 184–5, 189, July 1866.

82. *Ibid.* See also *Mess.*, XVII, No. 5, p. 36, Aug. 4, 1865.

83. *Occ.*, XXVI, No. 1, p. 44, Apr. 1868.

84. *Mess.*, IX, No. 21, p. 165, May 31, 1861.

85. *Ibid.*

86. *Mess.*, IX, No. 22, p. 172, June 7, 1861.

87. *Mess.*, IX, No. 23, pp. 181–2, June 14, 1861.

88. *JR*, I, No. 1, p. 4, Sept. 12, 1862.

89. *Mess.*, XII, No. 15, p. 114, Oct. 18, 1862; *JR*, I, No. 4, p. 4, Oct. 3, 1862.

90. *Ibid.*

91. *JR*, I, No. 22, p. 2, Feb. 6, 1863.

92. *Mess.*, XIII, No. 8, pp. 60–1, Feb. 11, 1863. See *Mess.*, XV, No. 24, p. 190, June 24, 1864, where a wounded Jew in a hospital at Portsmouth, Va., asks for help.

93. *Mess.*, XII, No. 9, p. 67, Aug. 29, 1862.

94. *JR*, I, No. 3, pp. 3–4, Sept. 24, 1862. See also the *Record's* editorial urging Synagogues and Jewish lodges to collect funds to provide substitutes for the Jewish poor, *JR*, VI, No. 3, p. 2, Mar. 31, 1865.

95. *Isr.*, IX, No. 11, p. 83, Sept. 19, 1862; No. 15, pp. 116–7, Oct. 17. The members of the Cincinnati "Allemania Society" organized the Second Company of the Second Ward Home Guard. All of its officers and members were Jewish. A large proportion of the Third Company were also Jewish. These outfits, of course, did not see action. Many of the men involved subsequently enlisted in the Army itself. *Mess.*, IX, No. 17, p. 133, May 3, 1861.

96. *Chicago Tribune* quoted in *Isr.*, IX, No. 8, p. 59, Aug. 22, 1862, and *Sinai*, VII, No. 8, pp. 228–9, Sept. 1862; see also *Annals of Ramah Lodge No. 33*, pp. 12–3.

97. *Chicago Tribune*, Aug. 16, 1862.

98. *Memphis Daily Avalanche*, May 20, 1861.

99. *Savannah Daily Morning News*, Feb. 23, 1863.

100. S. Wolf, *The American Jew As Patriot, Soldier and Citizen.*

101. *Mess.*, XIX, No. 19, p. 4, May 16, 1866.

102. *JR*, V, No. 15, p. 2, Jan. 6, 1865, story of the presentation of a sword to Captain Isaac Cohen by the company.

Notes to Chapter VI

1. Senator Chandler, quoted in E. Merton Coulter, "Commercial Intercourse with the Confederacy in the Mississippi Valley, 1861–1865," p. 386.

2. Joseph H. Parks, "A Confederate Trade Center Under Federal Occupation: Memphis, 1862 to 1865," p. 295.

3. See, for instance, *WROR*, I, XVII, Pt. II, pp. 123, 130, 155, 158, 163, 357, 368, 400, 522–3, 569, 575–6. A merchant would have had to employ a secretary to keep files of the regulations which were issued by headquarters!

4. General Hurlbut, in *WROR*, I, XVII, Pt. I, p. 230.

5. Coulter, *op. cit.*, pp. 391–2.

6. Sandburg, *op. cit.*, III, p. 15. The President was writing to his friend, Congressman William Kellogg of Illinois, explaining the reason for his refusal to issue cotton-buying permits which Kellogg had requested for certain of his friends.

7. William B. Hesseltine, *Ulysses S. Grant: Politician*, pp. 30–1; Sandburg, *op. cit.*, II, p. 538.

8. *WROR*, I, LII, Pt. I, p. 331. Dana also mentioned the "vast population of Jews and Yankees" in the Memphis area. His motives in writing this letter to Stanton are not difficult to ascertain. He was dramatizing his reliability as a government-supporter in this hair-raising report in order to return to the good graces of Stanton, who had withdrawn his appointment as Assistant Secretary of War after Dana made a premature announcement of his good fortune.

Dana's own role as a cotton speculator is not very clear. He formed a partnership with Congressman Roscoe Conkling of New York and an obscure cotton expert, procured letters of introduction to Hurlbut, Grant, and Curtis, and proceeded on to Memphis, where he took up residence at "the Gayoso House, at that time the swell hotel of the town and the headquarters of several officers." Dana does not indicate whether he wrote his report to Stanton before or after he tried to capitalize on his political connections. It is entirely possible that he had supposed he would have a clear field in cotton-buying, and that his letter was a way of making the best of a bad bargain. In a post-script, Dana noted that Grant had been shown the letter and agreed "with all my statements and suggestions [about the Government's taking over the cotton business itself], except that imputing corruption to every officer, which of course I did not intend to be taken literally." Charles A. Dana, *Recollections of the Civil War With the Leaders at Washington and in the Field in the Sixties*, pp. 16–21.

9. *WROR*, I, XVII, Pt. II, p. 424.

10. Told by Mrs. William Fineshriber of Philadelphia.

11. Speech by Senator Powell, Jan. 9, 1863, *Congressional Globe*, 37th Congress, 3rd Session, Pt. I, pp. 245–6; *New York Times*, Jan. 3, 1863.

12. There were, of course, many Jews in the mid-western regiments which took part in the Tennessee-Mississippi campaigns. Colonel Marcus M. Spiegel of the 120th Ohio Infantry Regiment was probably the highest ranking Jewish officer in the Department. He was wounded at Vicksburg only a few weeks after The Order was issued, rejoined his regiment over a doctor's protest, and died in action at Snaggy Point, La., in 1864. It is said that he was about to be promoted to Brigadier-General at the time of his death. *Occ.*, XX, No. 1, pp. 41–2, Apr. 1863; Simon Wolf, *The American Jew as Patriot, Soldier and Citizen*, p. 340.

Another young Jew in the Department, Lieut. Jacob C. Cohen of the 27th Ohio Infantry, had a literary bent which he indulged at a moment's notice. From August 1, 1862 to July 16, 1863, he wrote a number of articles for the *Messenger* describing the Tennessee and Mississippi campaigns from the viewpoint of a soldier who was bored to tears between battles, eager to meet people, happy when battles were ended. He described life at Corinth, Holly Springs, and Oxford, spoke of the speculators and of "the vast cotton operations which have disgraced our management of the conquered territory, and enriched a class of speculators generally of doubtful loyalty." *Mess.*, XIII, No. 16, p. 135, Apr. 24, 1863.

According to Cohen (*Mess.*, XIII, No. 23, p. 195, June 12, 1863), there were only about one thousand Jews, men, women and children in Memphis. They supported "two synagogues, three charitable societies, two clubs, besides a literary society, etc." These organizations had existed before the war. Apparently Cohen was not conscious of the flood of Jews supposed to have been swept into Memphis with its capture.

Cohen made no mention of The Order at the time of its promulgation. Later on, he contributed an amusing group of puns to entertain the *Messenger's* readers:

... it is not strange that your correspondent should attempt to find something new to relieve the *ennui* which was making him a "used-up man." Consequently I honored the august U. S. Grant, commanding this department, with an application for a leave of absence. In a few weeks it came back with an ominous endorsement in Arnold's carmine, "not granted." I was not to be discomfited so easily, taking it for *Grant*ed that *Grant* would not *Grant* me a leave. I consequently took a circuitous path, avoided red-tape, obtained a leave (how, it is nobody's business), and in twelve hours thereafter one of U. S. Grant's "as a class" friends was speeding homeward.

Mess., XIII, No. 16, p. 135, Apr. 24, 1863.

After his discharge from the Army because of physical disability, Cohen remained in Memphis and became Assistant Adjutant General and Chief of Staff of Memphis' "Enrolled Militia." *Mess.*, XV, No. 6, pp. 42–3, Feb. 12, 1864.

13. From an interview with one of these men in *JR*, I, No. 19, p. 2, Jan. 16, 1863.

14. Communicated to Wise from Memphis by the men involved. *Isr.*, IX, No. 26, p. 202, Jan. 2, 1863.

In 1868, during the election revival of the episode, it was asserted that no Jews had actually been harmed. A Mr. A. Z. Rosenthal, then a notary public in Louisville, made a deposition swearing that he had been one of the deportees. *Louisville Jewish Sentinel*, June 12, 1868.

15. *WROR, op. cit.*, p. 506.

16. See, for instance, *Memphis Daily Bulletin*, Jan. 6, 1863, which published The Order and Kaskel's letter immediately following the Emancipation Proclamation.

The "storm" took many forms: delegations of Jewish notables from various cities; copies of the Jewish periodicals devoted almost exclusively to a consideration of The Order, and which were sent by their editors to the President, the War Department, and various Congressmen; letters and resolutions to the President from Jewish organizations and individuals.

The Board of Delegates of American Israelites was active, but played no essential role in having The Order rescinded. Kaskel had achieved his purpose before the Board even heard of The Order; Wise and the Western delegations were already in Washington. When the executive committee of the Board met, then, on Jan. 8, it was observing a ritual rather than considering an urgent problem. The resolutions which were sent to Lincoln (Nos. 21089–90, 21159 of the Robert Todd Lincoln Collection; *JR*, I, No. 19, p. 4, Jan. 16, 1863), protesting The Order and thanking him for his prompt action in rescinding it, reinforced Lincoln's supposition that the Jews were united in objecting to it; but the persons most intimately affected by The Order actually were responsible for the action which was taken by the President.

Wise naturally took up the cudgels against the Board in conection with the Grant affair. Events in Washington had proved to him, he said, that the Board was unnecessary; and their resolution of thanks, in the name of the Jews, was a misrepresentation of their position in Jewish life. And beyond that, Halleck deserved no thanks! *Isr.*, IX, No. 31, p. 244, Feb. 6, 1863.

The Jewish Messenger, on the other hand, closely allied with the Board, used the Grant case as an argument for strong support of the Board. If Washington was to be deluged by rabbis, synagogues, and laymen "with reams of foolscap, detailing the individual sentiments of a thousand or more independent, petty communities on this or that question, can we wonder that the officers of Government pay no attention to this mass of papers and signatures?" A strong, united American Jewry was needed to protect the Jewish name—"Gen. Grant would *never* have issued an order expelling 'all Jews' from his Department, if he were conscious that the Jews were an influential, a powerful community . . . had individuals remained at home and left it to a central organization properly sustained to represent the general body, the offending General might have been sternly reprimanded, perhaps dismissed." *Mess.*, XIII, No. 3, p. 20, Jan. 16, 1863.

17. Solomons was a close friend of Henry Hart, President of the Board of Delegates, and, naturally, Hart wired him for exact information on the status of The Order. See the exchange of telegrams and letters in the Board of Delegates files.

18. The details of Kaskel's activities and experiences in Washington are taken from *Isr.*, IX, No. 28, p. 218, Jan. 16, 1863, and from Markens, *op. cit.*, pp. 117–9.

19. *WROR, op. cit.*, p. 530. Emphasis added.

20. *Ibid.*, p. 544.

21. *WROR*, I, XXIV, Pt. I, p. 9.

22. No. 21003 of the Robert Todd Lincoln Collection. Emphasis added. Bates might well be listed in the next chapter as one of those high officials who were victims of Judaeophobia. The B'nai B'rith resolution had been sent to him by Isidor Bush, an active Republican in St. Louis, who apparently thought Bates liked him: Bush signed his covering letter "with the highest esteem and true affection." In his note forwarding the resolution and letter to Lincoln, Bates also commented, "The writer of the within letter, *tho' a Jew*, is a man of personal respectability in St. Louis, & a member of the State convention." (Emphasis added.) Bates was an active Presbyterian; perhaps a religious prejudice moved him to dislike Jews. An entry in his diary for Mar. 17, 1862, refers to a recently published document proving that David (Levy) Yulee, Senator from Florida, had been involved in a "conspiracy of senators and others, to dissolve the union." Bates comments:

> That treacherous Jew, Yulee, has, for months back, been trying to "ly [*sic.*] low and keep dark [.]" But this letter, if it be genuine, spoils his disguise.

(Editorial marks by Howard K. Beale, editor, *The Diary of Edward Bates, 1859–1866*, p. 243.)

23. *Isr.*, *op. cit.* Strauss, nowhere mentioned in the published reports, told Prof. Selig Adler of the University of Buffalo, that he, together with other Baltimoreans, had taken the short trip to Washington. It is entirely possible that representatives from other cities did the same.

24. *Isr.*, IX, No. 28, p. 218, Jan. 16, 1863. The previous day Washburne had proven himself even more staunchly Grant's defender, if in less conspicuous a manner. He had written to the President, urging him not to revoke The Order:

House of Reps.
Jany. 6, 1863.

Mr. Lincoln:

  I see a report that you have revoked Grant's order touching the Jews.—I hope not. I consider it the wisest order yet made by a military command, and from my own personal observation, I believe it was necessary. As the friend of that distinguished soldier, Genl. Grant, I want to be heard before the final order of revocation goes out, if it be contemplated to issue such an order. There are two sides to this question.

Truly yrs.

E. B. Washburne.

(Robert Todd Lincoln Collection, Nos. 21026–7)
Washburne himself was not utterly free from suspicion as a speculator and investor in war commodities. See *Letters from Lloyd Lewis*, pp. 22, 27.

25. *Congressional Globe*, 37th Congress, 3rd Session, Pt. I, p. 184.

26. *Ibid.*, pp. 245–6.

27. Cited in *JR*, I, No. 19, p. 2, Jan. 16, 1863.

28. Cited in *Occ.*, XX, No. 11, pp. 491–3, Feb. 1863.

29. *Washington Star*, Jan. 7, 1863; *Washington Chronicle*, Jan. 8, 1863.

30. *New York Times*, Jan. 18, 1863.

31. *Mess.*, XIII, No. 3, p. 20, Jan. 16, 1863.

32. *Occ.*, *loc. cit.*, pp. 497, 501–2.

33. *Cincinnati Commercial*, Jan. 6, 1863; *cf. Isr.*, XV, No. 5, p. 4, Aug. 7, 1868, for a citation of the *Commercial's* defense of The Order at the time of the 1868 election.

34. *Cincinnati Enquirer*, Jan. 5, 6, 1863.

35. Both quoted in *Isr.*, IX, No. 27, p. 210, Jan. 9, 1863.

36. The opinions condensed into the next paragraphs are to be found in *Occ.*, *Isr.*, *Mess.*, and *JR*, for the various issues of Jan. and Feb. 1863.

37. *JR*, I, No. 20, p. 2, Jan. 23, 1863.

38. *Isr.*, IX, No. 34, p. 268, Feb. 27, 1863.

39. *Occ.*, *op. cit.*, p. 493.

40. *Mess.*, XIII, No. 3, p. 20, Jan. 16, 1863.

41. Because the Know-Nothing Party never took any position in reference to Jews, but concentrated on Catholics and foreigners, Jews were perfectly free, if they too were prejudiced, to support that party. Congressman Lewis C. Levin of Philadelphia, a national Know-Nothing spokesman, delivered several inflammatory speeches in Congress against Catholics and in praise of the Native American party. (*Congressional Globe*, 29th Congress, 1st Session, pp. 46–50, 63; 30th Congress, 1st Session, pp. 418–421.)

Congressman Philip Phillips of Mobile, on the other hand, was a staunch opponent of the Know-Nothing Party. A long article which he wrote against "Religious Proscription of Catholics," published in the *Mobile Register*, was a challenging analysis of the nature of prejudice; it was widely reprinted in the Jewish press. *Occ.*, XIII, No. 6, pp. 274–81, Sept., 1855; *Asm.*, XII, No. 15, July 27, 1855. Leeser praised the article but warned Jews against taking part in politics *as Jews;* the person who sent the article in to the *Asmonean*, on the other hand, urged a united Jewish opposition to the Know-Nothing Party.

It was ironic that Congressman Levin's wife and son should have been converted to Catholicism after his death. *American Catholic Historical Researches*, VII (1911), p. 189, cited in Ray A. Billington, *The Protestant Crusade, 1800–1860*, p. 217, the authoritative study of anti-Catholic prejudice during those years.

42. *Corinth* (Miss.) *Caucasian*, July 9, 1868, referred to in *PAJHS*, No. 34, p. 275; *Quincy* (Ill.) *Herald* quoted in *New York Times*, Oct. 13, 1868; *Chicago Tribune*, Sept. 2, 1868 (Lewis Mss.); *Illinois Staatszeitung*, quoted in *HL*, XII, No. 15, p. 2, July 17, 1868; *Kansas City* (Mo.) *Evening Bulletin*, quoted in *Isr.*, XIV, No. 39, p. 4, Apr. 3, 1868; *London Jewish Chronicle*, Sept. 6, 1872. An unidentified Richmond, Va., paper published an article entitled "A Contrast—Washington and Grant to the Hebrews," which included the following documents: The Order, the well-known letter of the Jewish congregations of Phila., New York, Charleston and Richmond to George Washington, and Washington's answer, which begins with the sentence, "The liberality of sentiment toward each other which marks every political and religious denomination of men in this country, stands unparalleled in the history of nations;" the intention

of the editor was clear. Clipping in the George Jacobs Scrapbook. Articles in the New York *Times* and *Herald,* and in the Jewish periodicals, which were used as an index to national sentiment, refer to editors' and correspondents' comments on the Grant Order in newspapers in Chicago, Philadelphia, Cincinnati, St. Louis, Memphis, Springfield, and Clayton, Ill., Louisville, Newburg, Ind., Washington, and Boston. It was, indeed, a *cause célèbre,* and probably placed the Jews of America in a stronger limelight than ever before. The public discussion in 1863 was minor compared to that in 1868. There were many Jews who, like Adolph Moses of Quincy, regretted deeply the fact that "our people . . . should be so prominently paraded in this campaign;" *New York Times,* Nov. 30, 1868, quoting a letter written Sept. 3, 1868. The Order was even mentioned in the Rev. J. P. Neuman's eulogy of Grant at the grave! The Methodist pastor said that Grant had *not* written The Order, and that the deceased was not prejudiced against the Jews. *Phila. Press,* Aug. 5, 1885 (Lewis Mss.)

43. Simon Wolf, *The Presidents I Have Known,* pp. 65–6; *New York Herald,* June 23, 1868. The Rawlins letter was addressed to Lewis N. Dembitz of Louisville, Ky., who had voted for the nomination of Lincoln at the Republican National Convention in Chicago in 1860. Dembitz, the uncle of Louis Dembitz Brandeis, was a devoted and learned Jew, and the author of *Services in Synagogue and Home,* a guide to Jewish ritual. Markens, *op. cit.,* p. 141.

44. *New York Times,* Nov. 30, 1868.

45. *Boston Post* cited in Wolf, *op. cit.,* pp. 67–70; clippings in the George Jacobs Scrapbook. Ezekiel's letter was dated July 29, 1868, and the Union League warning, Aug. 24, 1868.

46. *Mess.,* quoted in *London Jewish Chronicle,* Sept. 6, 1872; *HL,* XII, No. 22, p. 4, Sept. 4, 1868; *Isr.,* XIV, No. 50, p. 4, June 19, 1868.

47. *HL,* XII, No. 21, p. 4, Aug. 28, 1868; *New York Times,* July 16, 1868; *Isr.,* XV, No. 5, p. 5, Aug. 7, 1868; unidentified clipping in the Moss Scrapbook. Reference to the last section of this chapter will give further justification for the attitude of the Tennessee Jews. Their right to urge Grant's defeat is unquestionable. Indeed, Jewish communities all over the country demonstrated a remarkable restraint in not throwing caution and party allegiances to the winds, and waging a campaign "as a bloc" against Grant. The faith in Grant's good will evinced by those who voted the Republican ticket was admirable; fortunately the General did not disappoint them.

48. *HL,* XII, No. 22, p. 4, Sept. 4, 1868. See *Isr.,* XV, No. 5, p. 5, Aug. 7, 1868, for the proposal that such a meeting be organized in Cincinnati—Wise opposed it.

49. *New York Times,* Oct. 13, and Nov. 30, 1868.

50. An undated clipping in Judge Cohen's Scrapbook.

51. *New York Herald,* Sept. 1, 1868; also *Chicago Tribune,* Aug. 29, 1868 (Lewis Mss.).

52. Wolf, *op. cit.,* 67–70. Emphasis added. Wolf was so fond of the General that his next son, born in 1869, was given the name of Adolph Grant. Wolf was not the only Republican Jew who turned the attack against his own co-religionists. Another, writing to the *Dayton* (Ohio) *Journal,* said, "There are men of

my faith who . . . deserve nothing better than Order No. 11." Clipping in the Moss Scrapbook.

53. Letter to the *Cincinnati Commercial*, reprinted in the *New York Herald*, Oct. 23, 1868.

54. Letter dated Oct. 15, 1868, one of a collection of Eckstein papers loaned to the writer by Mr. Edmond Uhry of N. Y., through the courtesy of Rabbi Louis I. Newman and Mr. Jeremy Newman. Eckstein and Geary had formed a cordial friendship before the war and maintained a desultory correspondence while Geary was in the Army and during his incumbency at Harrisburg. On May 6, 1868, Geary wrote Eckstein:

> . . . It is a matter of regret to find that there are any difficulties in your way which will prevent your giving your usual ardent support to the nominee of the Republican Party. I hope, however, that a satisfactory solution of this matter may be made prior to the election by the General himself.

> As for my own part I always found the class of citizens to which you refer, to be *my* ardent supporters, simply because I always give them even-handed justice . . .

In the Oct. 15 letter, the portion relating to The Order reads:

> I think you deserve the most exalted meed of praise for bringing about an amicable understanding between the Israelites and General Grant, and I sincerely hope it may result to your advantage. I think I deserve a small portion also, but of course this is confidential, but I cannot help feeling somewhat gratified with a long career, in which a spot cannot be pointed out where I have ever sanctioned the prosecution of any-one on account of his religious views—nor will I ever do so.

Geary evidently wanted Eckstein to understand that he, also, condemned Grant for issuing The Order, but that political considerations prevented his speaking out frankly.

On Aug. 19, 1869, Geary wrote Eckstein of his efforts to secure an office for him:

> . . . I have to state that I have done all in my power with the authorities at Washington, D. C., to have them do justice to you. What effects may be produced, I cannot at present inform you, but I will continue to interest myself in your behalf and keep you informed . . .

55. *Isr.*, IX, No. 30, p. 236, Jan. 30, 1863; XIV, No. 50, p. 4, June 19, 1868.

56. DuBois Papers.

57. *Ibid.*

58. *Ibid., Isr.*, IX, No. 25, p. 196, Dec. 26, 1862; *Chicago Tribune*, Dec. 18, 1862.

59. *Ibid.*

60. Quoted in *JR*, I, No. 21, p. 2, Jan. 30, 1863.

61. It is entirely possible that this was not written by Eckstein, but copied out by hand from a deposition which General Grant showed him when they had their conference in Covington, Ky. If Eckstein wrote it, why should he not have published it, rather than the vague story of satisfactory explanations which he received from Grant? Indeed if he had known the reason all along and believed Grant to be innocent of any intention to harm the Jews, why had he writ-

ten to Geary of his inability or reluctance to support Grant? A letter from Grant, dated Aug. 24, 1868, tells Eckstein, in part:

... Your determination relative to the publication, or rather nonpublication, of the substance of our conversation, suits me very well. Although I dislike to see what I say in conversation printed, yet, in this case, I could not have objected if you had deemed it advisable ...

Was Grant telling Eckstein to publish the "substance of our conversation," which he never did do? Or was he implying that reference to the spoken word was satisfactory, but that he would not permit him to publish any of the documents he had given him to read? These reservations cast a great deal of doubt on the nature of the paper found in Eckstein's files. If it were the only statement of its kind, it would not be very conclusive. But even without it, the *Cincinnati Commercial* correspondent and Rawlins offer sufficient evidence to clarify the episode.

62. *New York Herald*, June 23, 1868. It is typical of the defense of Grant that Rawlins should misrepresent an essential phase of The Order. Rawlins says very glibly, "... leaving all persons not justly amenable to its terms to be relieved on their individual application ...." But there was no such provision in The Order; to the contrary, it expressly forbade this: "No passes will be given these people to visit headquarters for the purpose of making personal application for trade permits." Eckstein, also, or rather the document found in his papers, glosses over this strict provision which made any appeal by a Jew impossible. When Silberman of Chicago tried to telegraph headquarters, he was arrested! This was, indeed, one of the most damning features of The Order: Jews were to be so circumscribed and hemmed in that they could *never* secure trading permits. There was to be *no* appeal.

63. Washburne Mss., Library of Congress. This letter is referred to in *Letters from Lloyd Lewis*, p. 24. That memorial volume, the tribute of his publishers to the eminent historian who had hoped to write a complete biography of Grant, led the present writer to request permission from Mrs. Lewis to examine her late husband's files on Grant and the Jews. Eager to have the fruits of her husband's research used by other students, she very generously forwarded all pertinent material. Such data drawn from the Lewis Mss. is gratefully acknowledged.

The elder Grant's testimony ought to serve as an effective rebuttal of another story of the origin of General Order No. 11, cited in the Lewis Mss. from a document in Mr. Lewis' possession which he referred to as "Cadwallader":

The exciting cause which led to its issuance was this:—While his headquarters were at Oxford, Miss. he was surprised by a sudden visit from his father then living at Covington or Newport, Ky. The general was glad to see him; showed him every possible attention; and enjoyed his society for a few days or two without unpleasant interruption. But several Cincinnati gentlemen of Hebrew persuasion soon appeared and notably Mr. Mack of the wealthy firm of Mack Bros. and posed as the personal friends of "Uncle Jesse." These the general also treated handsomely for his father's sake until he learned the real object of their visit to obtain special permits and privileges to buy and ship cotton. It seems that playing upon "Uncle Jesse's" cupidity, these men had entered into a partnership with him for that purpose, they agreeing to furnish all the capital needed, and he to obtain the trade permit from his son Gen. Grant. The impudence of these mercenaries was of course surprising, but the most astonishing feature of the whole transaction was that the father could have been so ignorant concerning his own son. The general's anger was bitter and malignant towards these men and greatly intensified by the mortification he felt at their having entrapped his old father into such an unworthy undertaking. The first train for the north bore them swiftly homeward, accompanied by "Uncle Jesse" with a stupendous flea in his ear. This was his last visit to the Army. The order expelling all "Jews" from his department was issued immediately . . .

From his own testimony, Jesse Grant did not return home until January 5, 1863, when The Order had already been revoked; he could not, then, have been so summarily dismissed from Oxford by his son. Nor, indeed, as we shall see, was this the first ruling regarding the Jews which General Grant issued—it could hardly be true, therefore, that this alleged "deal" with which the Cincinnati Jews enticed Jesse Grant was the major factor which induced the General to issue General Order No. 11. Indeed, it strikes one as being a typical barracks' story, passed on from one soldier to another as "the real, inside story." Despite the fact that his father's attempts to make fortunes for himself during the war were gossiped about from one end of the country to the other, the story does such violence to the General's integrity, and all other evidence is so strongly opposed to it, that we must perforce reject it out of hand as an unfounded rumor.

64. *The New York World*, Aug. 18, 1863, cited in Lewis Mss., and *Letters from Lloyd Lewis*, p. 21. The *World* reporter's reference to the smuggling Jews was of a piece with reams of such material written during this period. Rarely citing names or other evidence, it was easy to dramatize crimes with the "Jewish" label.

65. There was yet another witness, referred to in the Lewis Mss.—the Rev. J. P. Neuman, who preached the Grant eulogy. He said: "The order issued during the war excluding certain Jewish traders from a given military district, did not originate with him, but came from higher authority and was not against the religion of the Jews . . ." (*Philadelphia Press*, Aug. 5, 1885). Mr. Lewis, however, considered Neuman to be poor authority for anything: "But Neuman was untrustworthy. Sherman scoffed at his funeral sermon proving Grant a saint." *Letters from Lloyd Lewis*, p. 32.

66. After this was written, the present writer discovered that Lloyd Lewis had reached the same conclusion. Letter, July 8, 1946, Lewis to Eisenschiml, Lewis Mss; *Letters from Lloyd Lewis*, p. 25.

67. *WROR*, I, XVII, Pt. II, pp. 421-2. Emphasis added. Isaac M. Wise also believed that The Order originated in the War Dept., and argued that a coterie of cotton speculators around Stanton inspired Grant to take steps against Jewish traders who were their strongest competitors. *Isr.*, XV, No. 22, p. 4, Dec. 4, 1868.

68. *Ibid.*, p. 163. Emphasis added.

69. *Ibid.*, p. 337. Emphasis added.

70. *New York Times*, Nov. 30, 1868. The letter was written Sept. 14, 1868. Emphasis added.

In an interview which Grant gave to Rabbi E. B. M. Browne at Long Branch on August 27, 1875, he said:

> ... I think the Jew lives longer because he loves his life more. It is certain that the Jew takes no risk of life and limb, while even in the many railroad accidents Jews, though much more given to traveling, are rarely injured. And yet I have found Jewish soldiers among the bravest of the brave. The Jew risks his life only to show his patriotism and then he is fearless. The Jewish soldiers, as stated, I have found wonderfully courageous in our Army and in the Rebel lines as well. But there were army followers among us. It happened one day, that a number of complaints reached me and in each case it was a Jew and I gave the order excusing the Jewish traders. You know that during war times these nice distinctions were disregarded. We had no time to handle things with kid gloves. But it was no ill-feeling or a want of good-feeling towards the Jews. If such complaints would have been lodged against a dozen men each of whom wore a white cravat, a black broadcloth suit, beaver or gold spectacles, I should probably have issued a similar order against men so dressed ... I have intimate friends among the Jews. I have appointed more Jews than any of my predecessors. At my father's house in Covington you could find quite often in social intercourse Jews of Cincinnati. Cincinnati has really quite a number of very intelligent Jews. ...

71. Letter to the *Chicago Times*, quoted in *Isr.*, XIV, No. 49, June 12, 1868.

72. *In Memoriam: Jesse Seligman*, pp. 10, 20. See interview with Jesse Seligman on his friendship with Grant, *Philadelphia Press*, July 27, 1885. The Freund family of St. Louis preserves recollections of another Jew whom Grant liked, their ancestor, a baker in the St. Louis area, to whom Grant sold wood in his days as a farmer, and to whom he gave a contract for bread after the outbreak of war.

73. *UJE*, IX, p. 639; Simon Wolf, *The American Jew as Patriot, Soldier and Citizen*, pp. 164–70.

74. *DAB*, XVI, p. 572.

75. Simon Wolf, *The Presidents I Have Known*, pp. 63–98. One of the quaintest stories Wolf tells is this:

> One day I received a letter from a Jew in Jerusalem, who wrote me in jargon [Yiddish], which Henry Gersony, lately deceased, managed to decipher, and the request was that I should see the "King of the United States" and bring to his attention the fact that he, the Jew of Jerusalem, had a daughter whom he wished to be married, and he wanted to do the "King of the United States" the honor to have him contribute to her dowry. The request was so amusing that I stated it to the President, and he said, "Do you think this man is in earnest?" and I said, "None more so," and he promptly gave me a check for $25, which I forwarded to my correspondent. Subsequently I received a letter of thanks in Hebrew, also the portrait of General Grant in Hebrew letters, which I believe, will be found among the other Grant treasures on exhibition in the National Museum. (p. 94.)

76. *Ibid.*, p. 71.

77. Cyrus Adler and A. M. Margalith, *With Firmness in the Right: American Diplomatic Action Affecting Jews, 1840–1945*, pp. 100–11, 174–6.

78. *Ibid.*, pp. 100–1. Grant undoubtedly made this appointment out of a desire to placate Jewish opinion. Correspondence between Simon Wolf and Hamilton Fish, Grant's Secretary of State, indicates that Fish was extremely dubious about the propriety of the appointment. Wolf (not Peixotto) released the Grant letter quoted in the text to the press. Fish was so infuriated by its publication that he appears to have considered recalling Peixotto immediately. Wolf also disapproved—believing it to be "very wrong to ask our Government to aid and assist us as Jews. As American citizens we are entitled and of right can ask, but nothing incompatible with usage or International Law." Peixotto had apparently secured the backing of Joseph Seligman, Grant's close friend, and other prominent personages. The entire background of the Peixotto mission requires clarification. Letters in Fish Papers: Wolf to Peixotto, June 14, 1870; Wolf to Fish, Dec. 21, 1870; Peixotto to Seligman, Jan. 4, 1871; Fish to Wolf, Jan. 14, 1871.

The influence of internal political affairs on American foreign policy is well demonstrated by the letter which Eugene Schuyler, Chargé d'Affaires at Moscow, wrote to Fish on Sept. 29, 1872, accompanying the first of many consular reports on the Jewish status in Russia. Schuyler said to Fish that he was sending the report because "I have seen it stated that the Jews in the United States have shown some opposition to the reelection of President Grant, and I thought it might have some effect on them if the Government gave them another proof of the interest they voice in their welfare . . . I hope it will not arrive too late to be of service . . ." Schuyler's report is digested in Adler and Margalith, *op. cit.*, pp. 174–5.

79. *WROR*, III, II, p. 350.

80. *WROR*, I, XXIV, Pt. III, p. 119.

81. *WROR*, I, XVII, Pt. II, pp. 140–1. Emphasis added. See also *Home Letters of General Sherman*, pp. 229–30, 232, for further references to Jews as smugglers and profiteers.

82. *WROR*, III, II, p. 349.

83. *WROR*, III, II, p. 350.

84. *Home Letters of General Sherman*, p. 155. *Cf.* p. 136 for a letter which gives ample demonstration of the fact that he knew who Jews were and that he did not use the word as an epithet instead of a designative term.

On Nov. 17, 1862, Sherman wrote a letter to F. G. Pratt of Memphis, answering some of Pratt's suggestions about financial problems in the city. He concluded the letter, "Till then [when the Confederacy would have enough of war], let Union men feel confident in their real strength, and determination of our Government, and despise the street talk of Jews and secessionists." See *The American Hebrew*, Vol. 63, No. 7, p. 197, June 17, 1898, for Simon Wolf's belief that Sherman's reports prompted Grant to issue The Order.

The *Memphis Daily Bulletin* was far more fair-minded when it said, on Nov. 16, 1862, that "while we have many of this class of citizens [Jews] who are as loyal as our president himself, there are others who, for the sake of gain, will trade, and barter, and dicker with the enemies of the Government." The same words could well have characterized all of the citizens of Memphis.

85. Sam Shankman, *The Peres Family*, pp. 6–8.

86. *New York Journal of Commerce*, quoted in *Mess.*, XVIII, No. 12, p. 90, Sept. 20, 1865; *UJE*, VII, pp. 486–7.

87. For a good description of Irving Block, as well as of the type of military dishonesty which victimized Meyer, see S. McIlwaine, *Memphis Down in Dixie*, pp. 128–30.

88. Isaac A. Meyer, *My Life, Travels, and Adventures by Land and Sea*. The *Memphis Daily Bulletin*, Oct. 25, 26, 1862, tells the story of Isaac Levy who accused the Provost Marshall and an Army detective of arresting him for smuggling and then suggesting that he bribe them to obtain his liberty. The story was denied immediately, but such stories were current during the military occupation of Memphis.

89. Felsenthal reported to Einhorn that Tuska had denounced *all* the Northern Jews who came to Memphis, but after a long interchange of notes from Tuska and editorials by Einhorn, Tuska still insisted that he was not a secessionist, but had only referred to a few Jews who were guilty of illegal activities. *Sinai*, VII, pp. 199, 227, 257, 284; letter, Einhorn to Felsenthal, Sept. 3, 1862, American Jewish Archives.

90. Letter, Feb. 17, 1863, Leeser Collection.

91. *Occ.*, XX, No. 11, p. 487, Feb., 1863.

92. David Einhorn, *War with Amalek*, pp. 11–2.

93. This and other volumes cited are found in the *Records of the War Dept., Office of the Adjutant General*. Names are not cited because the War Department officials in charge of the records believed that embarrassment might result for descendants of the persons involved and refused to permit the writer to obtain photostatic copies of the pertinent pages. The persons themselves are unimportant; in this case, their religion was the important point. While the writer was turning pages in these aging records, he wondered how the Generals had been able to identify Jews so easily. Many of the names regarded as Jewish for the purposes of this study could just as well have been non-Jewish German names: Gunst, Brosman, Fisher, Buckhart, Schwartz, Finde, Brandenburg, Bloom, Kichen. The Loebs, Lazarus', Levys, and Wolffs were undoubtedly Jewish.

It is important to note that these and other records cited, with one exception, are localized in Memphis, which was not part of the Department of the Tennessee and was not included in the area covered by General Order No. Eleven. Court-martial records for the immediate area, Corinth, Oxford and Holly Springs, Miss., could not be discovered in the National Archives; they are probably irretrievably lost. But it is the author's conviction that the Memphis records are as dependable an index as the lost records would be, to Jewish malefaction in the area; they are intimately related, in addition, as background for the Sherman dispatches to Grant, which undoubtedly had a strong indirect influence on Grant's decision to issue The Order. For further light on Jewish business activities and law-breaking in Memphis, see James A. Wax, *The Jews of Memphis, 1860–1865*, pp. 18–41.

94. Pp. 13, 18, 21.

95. Unfortunately an exhaustive study of the corruption in cotton-buying and

smuggling in the Mississippi-Tennessee area has not yet been made. The results of such a study would be of great service in assisting us to determine the relative importance of the role of Jews. In 1863, however, a Military Court of Inquiry sat in St. Louis for five weeks, investigating the connivance of military officers in cotton-buying scandals. Evidence was uncovered which indicated that officers all the way up to the rank of colonel and general were implicated in the traffic, risking soldiers' lives to capture cotton stores, defrauding the Government of large sums of money obtained for confiscated cotton, and utilizing government transportation for the shipment of the merchandise. Among the hundreds of names of officers and civilians mentioned in the testimony (as reported in the columns of the *St. Louis Democrat*, Mar. 14–Apr. 23), none appears to be Jewish; two men whose names were not given, however, were referred to as Jews:

1) On the twelfth day of hearings, Apr. 2, 1863, Capt. William Finkler accused General Willis A. Gorman of complicity in cotton-trading, and referred to a Jew as his partner:

My moral belief is, that General Gorman was interested in some cotton operations. On the 11th of February last the steamer Carl went down the river to Friars' Point and Yazoo Pass, and was absent three days. The captain reported to me when he came back that he had on board twenty-eight bales and two sacks of cotton, taken by order of General Gorman. Upon the arrival of the cotton at Helena I seized it. The General (Gorman) wanted me to order this cotton ashore—that he knew the owner. I told him I would not do it; that I had told them before that the use of Government steamers for private purposes was wrong, and I could not consent to it. He told me he had an order from the Secretary of War. I asked him to send me the order. He sent me his Aid, ordering me verbally to deliver to a Jew, who came with the Aid, the cotton I seized. I refused and was arrested and released from duty by General Gorman. General Gorman sent the cotton to Memphis, where it was seized and sold for the benefit of the Government . . . (*St. Louis Democrat*, Apr. 3, 1863).

2) On the nineteenth day of testimony, Apr. 10, 1863, Capt. J. H. Burnham was giving the details of a military expedition sent out by Col. C. E. Hovey, for the express purpose of securing cotton:

Our company went down [on the 28th of July, 1862] in charge of Capt. Potter to Island 62 and brought up what was estimated at about 12 bales of cotton. It was taken from a man who passed for a Union man. He came up with us when we brought the cotton. He was a foreigner—a Jew, I think. I understood he had sent for us to come after the cotton . . . (*St. Louis Democrat*, Apr. 11, 1863).

It is interesting to note that in both cases high-ranking non-Jewish officers shared the guilt with Jews (if indeed the men in question were Jews).

The word "Jew" is mentioned no other time in the reams of testimony reported in the *St. Louis Democrat*, although two St. Louis Jews were called as witnesses to report on their transactions. One was M. Friede (testified on Apr. 10) who had gone to Helena and purchased cotton from civilians on permits obtained from Generals Curtis and Steele; Friede had no evidence to offer on illegal activities by military officers. The other Jew, Charles Taussig (testified on Apr. 14) reported that his firm, Taussig, Ansel and Co., had bought cotton in many places throughout the area on legal permits, and that he would submit to the court the names of persons he believed to be in possession of data about cotton-buying by army officers. Friede and Taussig were the only Jews called to the stand—were they too included in the "swarms of Jews" of whom Sherman complained? Friede was a St. Louis delegate to the Missouri state legislature, highly regarded by his fellow representatives (see reports of his speeches in *Isr.*, VII, No. 33, p. 202, Feb. 15, 1861; No. 36, p. 285, Mar. 8, 1861; *Sinai*, VI, No. 3, pp. 92–6, Apr., 1861). Taussig was a member of a very respectable family of German Jews in St. Louis, whose integrity and contribution to civic causes were unquestionable (see *The Reminiscences of Carl Schurz*, II, p. 40). Here, again, when specific persons are involved, rather than generalizations, the dishonesty of all Jews engaged in cotton-trading is not so certain as Grant and Sherman appear to have thought.

96. Pp. 34, 95.

97. P. 44.

98. Pp. 359–60.

99. P. 348.

100. Pp. 1, 26, 136–7.

101. *WROR*, I, XXXI, Pt. III, pp. 289–90. This order was first printed in the *Memphis Daily Bulletin* on Nov. 30, 1863, and appeared continuously until December 23. During this period, Loeb and Bros., one of the blacklisted firms, continued to advertise military clothing for sale, on the basis of "a special license from headquarters." *Ibid.*, Dec. 10, 18, 1863.

102. *Isr.*, X, No. 24, p. 188, Dec. 11, 1863.

103. A quite blatant example of the effect of prejudice is to be found in a dispatch from Brigadier General L. F. Ross to Major General John A. McClernand, from Bolivar, Tenn., July 25, 1862:

> The cotton speculators are quite clamorous for aid in getting their cotton away from Middlebury, Hickory Valley, &c., and offer to pay liberally for the service. I think I can bring it away with safety, and make it pay for the Government. As some of the Jew owners have as good as stolen the cotton from the planters, I have no conscientious scruples in making them pay liberally for getting it away. *WROR*, I, XVII, Pt. II, p. 120.

104. *Cincinnati Enquirer*, Jan. 5, 1863.

105. *Isr.*, IX, No. 26, p. 202, Jan. 2, 1863. See also Isr., XV, No. 5, p. 4, Aug. 7, 1868, for Wise's conviction that "The noise against the Jews at that time was a stratagem to cover the huge swindles practised on Uncle Sam's purse."

Notes to Chapter VII

1. See the excellent chapter on "Peter Stuyvesant Meets 'The Obstinate and Immovable Jews,'" pp. 43–57, in Anita L. Lebeson, *Jewish Pioneers in America*.

2. Abram V. Goodman, *American Overture: Jewish Rights in Colonial Times*, pp. 133–49.

3. *Ibid.*, pp. 111–2.

4. Leon Hühner, "The Struggle For Religious Liberty in North Carolina, with Special Reference to the Jews," pp. 37–71; E. Milton Altfeld, *The Jews' Struggle For Religious and Civil Liberty in Maryland.*

5. Philip S. Foner, *The Jews in American History, 1654–1865*, pp. 32–3.

6. *Ibid.*

7. *Tree of Liberty*, I, No. 5, p. 3, Sept. 13, 1800, quoted in Julia Miller, *Jews Connected with the History of Pittsburgh, 1749–1865*, pp. 26–30. See Schappes, "Anti-Semitism and Reaction, 1795–1800," pp. 109–37, for further illustrations.

8. Isaac Goldberg, *Major Noah*, pp. 111–2.

9. *Ibid.*, pp. 241–2.

10. *JE*, IV, pp. 354–5.

11. *UJE*, VII, pp. 17–8. No satisfactory biography has ever been written about this fascinating figure in American Jewish history. Many details of his Naval career require explication.

12. *Isr.*, VII, No. 20, p. 159, Nov. 16, 1860, quoting the *Florence* (Alabama) *Gazette*. The article concluded, "He said he had always hated the Jews ever since they crucified our Savior, Jesus Christ; and upon uttering these sentiments, he was applauded by his Douglas and Bell auditors."

13. *Isr.*, IX, No. 22, p. 172, Dec. 5, 1862, quoting an unidentified Dubuque paper; *Burlington Free Press*, Dec. 8, 1861; *Rochester Union and Advertiser*, cited in *Mess.*, XVII, No. 6, p. 42, Feb. 10, 1865. Even the Chicago Superintendent of Police adopted the habit; he listed Jews among the types of criminals captured by his officers. *JR*, I, No. 21, p. 2, Jan. 30, 1863.

14. Frank Moore (ed.), *Rebellion Record*, III, p. 114.

15. *New York Herald*, Jan. 10, 1864, cited in *Isr.*, X, No. 30, p. 237, Jan. 22, 1864.

16. Quoted from an unidentified Christian religious periodical in *Mess.*, XII, No. 24, p. 189, Dec. 19, 1862.

17. *Isr.*, VIII, No. 5, p. 36, Aug. 2, 1861.

18. *Mess.*, XV, No. 8, p. 67, Feb. 26, 1864.

19. *Isr.*, VII, No. 38, p. 301, Mar. 22, 1861.

20. *Isr.*, XI, No. 12, p. 92, Sept. 16, 1864.

21. *Isr.*, XI, No. 19, p. 148, Nov. 4, 1864.

22. Quoted in *Isr.*, VII, No. 30, p. 238, Jan. 25, 1861.

23. Quoted in *Mess.*, XIII, No. 16, p. 137, Apr. 24, 1863, and in *Isr.*, X, No. 7, p. 53, Aug. 14, 1863.

24. *Newburg Journal*, Aug. 31, 1864, quoted in *JR*, V, No. 1, p. 2, Sept. 23, 1864, and *Occ.*, XXII, No. 8, p. 369, Nov. 1864.

25. Quoted in *Isr.*, XI, No. 17, p. 132, Oct. 21, 1864.

26. Quoted in *Mess.*, XV, No. 24, p. 190, June 24, 1864.

27. Quoted in *The Hebrew*, I, No. 29, p. 4, July 1, 1864.

28. Although Belmont is never known to have been converted, he was, to all intents and purposes, a non-Jew. So far as can be discovered, he rarely displayed any interest in Jewish communal or religious life. In 1850, Wise was able to bring enough pressure on Belmont to extract a ten dollar contribution for his new synagogue in Albany, but he detected no real interest on Belmont's part: Wise, *Reminiscences*, p. 177. The editors were anxious to have Belmont's lack of Jewish affiliation clearly understood by the Republican press. *Isr.*, XI, No. 15, p. 116, Oct. 7, 1864; XIV, No. 35, p. 4, Mar. 6, 1868; *Mess.*, XVI, No. 17, p. 132, Nov. 4, 1864. See also, *Asm.*, XI, No. 18, p. 140, Feb. 16, 1855, for an anti-Jewish attack on Belmont when he was appointed Ambassador to the Netherlands.

29. *New York Herald*, quoted in *Mess.*, XVI, No. 17, p. 132, Nov. 4, 1864.

30. *Philadelphia Dispatch*, quoted in *HL*, VI, No. 22, p. 2, Aug. 18, 1865.

31. *Mess.*, XVIII, No. 16, p. 124, Oct. 27, 1865.

32. *Isr.*, IX, No. 37, p. 292, Mar. 20, 1863.

33. *Chicago Tribune*, Sept. 10, 1864, quoted in *Isr.*, XI, No. 13, p. 99, Sept. 23, 1864.

34. *Isr.*, XI, No. 46, p. 324, Apr. 17, 1865; *Mess.*, XVI, No. 17, p. 132, Nov. 4, 1864.

35. Lonn, *op. cit.*, pp. 266–7.

36. Quoted in *Isr.*, X, No. 44, p. 348, Apr. 29, 1864.

37. *JR*, II, No. 9, p. 2, May 8, 1863.

38. *Isr.*, X, No. 44, p. 248, Apr. 29, 1864.

39. Quoted in *Mess.*, XIII, No. 16, p. 137, Apr. 24, 1863.

40. Quoted in *Mess.*, XVI, No. 16, p. 124, Oct. 28, 1864.

41. Quoted in *Mess.*, XV, No. 5, p. 36, Feb. 5, 1864.

42. Quoted in *JR*, II, No. 1, p. 2, Mar. 13, 1863.

43. Quoted in *Mess.*, XV, No. 6, p. 44, Feb. 12, 1864.

44. Quoted in *Isr.*, IX, No. 35, p. 277, Mar. 6, 1863.

45. Quoted in *JR*, II, No. 2, p. 2, Mar. 20, 1863.

46. *JR*, II, No. 1, p. 2, Mar. 13, 1863.

47. *DAB*, XVI, p. 572.

48. Letter, July 29, 1863, in the possession of Mr. George S. Hellman of New York City.

49. Letter, July 3, 1861, in the Pennsylvania Historical Society.

50. *DAB*, II, pp. 169–70.

51. Quoted in *Isr.*, VIII, No. 5, p. 36, Aug. 2, 1861.

52. Quoted in *Isr.*, VIII, No. 7, pp. 52–3, Aug. 16, 1861.

53. *Ibid.*

54. Quoted in *Isr.*, IX, No. 33, p. 258, Feb. 20, 1863.

55. *Isr.*, IX, No. 41, p. 333, Apr. 24, 1863.

56. Quoted in *Isr.*, VIII, No. 11, p. 84, Sept. 13, 1861.

57. *New York Commercial Advertiser,* quoted in *Isr.*, IX, No. 22, p. 172, Dec. 5, 1862; *Mess.*, XII, No. 24, p. 188, Dec. 19, 1862.

58. *Cincinnati Commercial,* quoted in *Isr.*, VIII, No. 35, p. 276, Feb. 28, 1862; No. 36, p. 284, Mar. 7, 1862.

59. *New York Tribune,* quoted in *Mess.*, XII, No. 20, p. 157, Nov. 21, 1862.

60. *New York Herald,* quoted in *Mess.*, XIV, No. 3, p. 22, July 17, 1863.

61. *Hudson* (N.Y.) *Gazette,* quoted in *JR*, V, No. 7, p. 2, Nov. 11, 1864.

62. *New York Post,* quoted in *JR*, VI, No. 2, p. 2, Mar. 24, 1865.

63. Special Order No. 150, Headquarters Department of the Gulf, June 30, 1862, newspaper clipping in Phillips Papers in the Southern Historical Collection.

64. Quoted in *Mess.*, XV, No. 8, p. 60, Feb. 26, 1864; *Isr.*, X, No. 37, pp. 292-3, Mar. 11, 1864.

65. Simon Wolf, *The Presidents I Have Known,* pp. 8-9.

66. *Mess., op. cit.* See *Mess.*, XXXIV, No. 24, p. 4, Dec. 19, 1873, for evidence that Butler did not give up the idea.

67. *Autobiography and Personal Reminiscences of Major-General Benj. F. Butler,* p. 514.

68. Letters from Butler to Isaacs, Feb. 4, Feb. 13, Apr. 9, Aug. 3, 1864, in Board of Delegates correspondence files. Isaacs' later letters have not been preserved, but he apparently took advantage of his writing acquaintance with Butler to attempt to secure the release of a Mr. David or Davids (both spellings are used by Butler), who was captured by an Army Gunboat crew on suspicion of smuggling, his property confiscated and sold, and himself imprisoned. He was finally released, said Butler in his final communication to Isaacs, "not on account of any good in him, but because, not being able to prove anything more against him, than that he was a smuggler and Blockade Runner, and because of its being the custom of the Navy to release those caught running the blockade by water." One wonders what Isaacs had said in the man's defense to make Butler reply so vehemently. The portions of the Butler letters dealing with the David case were omitted by Isaacs in his *Messenger* articles, and by Max J. Kohler in his edition of this correspondence in *PAJHS*, No. 29 (1925), pp. 117-28.

69. Max J. Kohler, "The Board of Delegates of American Israelites, 1859-1878," pp. 121-128.

70. Wolf, *op. cit.* Wolf, on March 7, 1864, wrote the Rev. Dr. McMurdy (a friend of the General) that "my personal choice [for Republican presidential candidate in 1864] would be Gen. Butler, although he has not become acquainted with an honest, intelligent Jew. I trust the day may not be far distant when he will find a host, his admirers and adherents." *Private and Official Correspondence of Gen. Benjamin F. Butler . . . ,* III, p. 497.

71. Parton, pp. 317-19.

72. Butler, *op. cit.*, p. 510.

73. *Ibid.*, pp. 433-4.

74. *JR*, IV, No. 14, p. 2, July 18, 1864.

75. *JR*, V, No. 16, p. 2, Jan. 13, 1865.

76. Emanuel Hertz, *Abraham Lincoln: A New Portrait*, II, p. 957–8; Isaac Markens, "Lincoln and the Jews," p. 154.

77. See Sandburg, *op. cit.*, II, p. 70; III, p. 64; IV, p. 25, for references to the rumors about Butler's personal and familial profiteering. He is said to have admitted that his brother's fortune of some $200,000 was made in New Orleans. See Isachar Zacharie's report on a typical case in his letter to Lincoln, Jan. 14, 1863, in Appendix C.

78. The speech is reprinted in Herbert F. Eaton, *An Hour With the American Hebrew*.

79. See E. Merton Coulter's biography, *William G. Brownlow: Fighting Parson of the Southern Highlands*, for the fascinating details of Brownlow's erratic career.

80. Quoted in *Isr.*, VI, No. 36, p. 283, Mar. 9, 1860.

81. Another example is quoted in *Isr.*, VII, No. 29, pp. 229–30, Jan. 18, 1861.

82. Meade, *op. cit.*, p. 210.

83. Coulter, *op. cit.*, p. 386; *Mess.*, XI, No. 14, p. 111, Apr. 11, 1862.

84. *Parson Brownlow's Book*, p. 386.

85. Brownlow, *Portrait and Biography*, pp. 19–20, cited by Coulter, *op. cit.*, p. 201.

86. Quoted in *Isr.*, IX, No. 22, p. 172, Dec. 5, 1862; No. 23, p. 180, Dec. 12, 1862.

87. Speech at the Y.M.C.A. of New York City, May 19, 1862, quoted by Coulter, *op. cit.*, pp. 227–8.

88. *Cincinnati Daily Times*, Jan. 17, 1863, p. 2.

89. *Ibid.*, Jan. 21, 1863, p. 2.

90. Allan Nevins, *Ordeal of the Union*, II, p. 331.

91. Quoted in *Isr.*, VII, No. 38, p. 301, Mar. 22, 1861.

92. Quoted in *Isr.*, VIII, No. 35, p. 278, Feb. 28, 1862. Wilson's nomination as the Republican Vice-Presidential candidate in 1872 brought forth a protest similar to that aroused by Grant's nomination in 1868, albeit of less formidable proportions. Isaac M. Wise never forgot an anti-Jewish utterance. In 1872, he wrote that he would not vote for Wilson because "his conceptions of justice, equality and liberty are so narrow and ungenerous," and reminded his readers that Wilson had been a Know-Nothing. *Isr.*, XIX, No. 9, p. 8, Aug. 30, 1872. Wise, being a confirmed Democrat, would probably not have voted for Wilson even if he had been a great Judaeophile. The Republican rabbi of Chicago, the Rev. Bernhard Felsenthal, must have been confused about Wilson's attitude towards the Jews: in *Sinai*, VII, pp. 200–10, Aug., 1862, he wrote a tribute to Wilson as the Senator responsible for championing the revision of the chaplaincy laws in committee meetings.

93. C. F. Adams, *Charles Francis Adams. 1835–1915. An Autobiography*, pp. 94–5.

94. *Isr.*, XXIII, No. 1041 (New Series I, No. 10), p. 6, Aug. 28, 1874, quoting reports in *Nashville Republican Banner*.

95. See Sandburg, *op. cit.*, III, pp. 428–32, on Baker.

96. L. C. Baker, *History of the U. S. Secret Service*, p. 80.

97. *Ibid.*, p. 82.

98. Wolf, *op. cit.*, pp. 9–11.

99. Quoted in *Isr.*, IX, No. 33, p. 258, Feb. 20, 1863.

100. Henry Illoway, *Sefer Milchamot Elohim*, pp. 23–6. A similar episode occurred when General Dunstan, commanding Memphis in late 1864, cancelled "the usual drill and parade of the militia" on Yom Kippur, out of deference to the Jewish soldiers and "as a mark of respect to the occasion." *Memphis Bulletin*, Oct. 11, 1864, quoted in *Isr.*, XI, No. 17, p. 133, Oct. 24, 1864.

101. Quoted in *Mess.*, XI, No. 14, p. 111, Apr. 11, 1862.

102. Quoted in *Isr.*, XII, No. 9, p. 70, Sept. 1, 1865.

103. Quoted in *The Hebrew*, I, No. 29, p. 4, July 1, 1864.

104. Quoted *ibid.*, No. 27, p. 1, June 17, 1864.

105. Quoted *ibid.*, No. 26, p. 1, June 9, 1864.

106. Quoted *ibid.*, No. 28, p. 5, June 24, 1864.

107. Quoted in *Isr.*, XII, No. 12, p. 93, Sept. 22, 1865.

108. *Daily Illinois State Journal*, May 19, 1865.

109. Quoted in *Isr.*, VIII, No. 14, pp. 108–9, Oct. 4, 1861; No. 15, p. 117, Oct. 11, 1861.

110. Quoted in *Isr.*, VII, No. 34, p. 270, Feb. 22, 1861.

111. Quoted in *Mess.*, XV, No. 9, p. 68, Mar. 4, 1864.

112. *New York Times*, Feb. 28, 1864, p. 3.

113. *Mess.*, XVI, No. 4, p. 28, July 29, 1864.

114. *Isr.*, VII, No. 17, p. 132, Oct. 25, 1861.

115. The text of their resolution is printed in *Isr.*, VIII, No. 35, p. 278, Feb. 28, 1872.

116. Quoted in *Isr.*, X, No. 26, p. 204, Dec. 25, 1863.

117. *Isr.*, IX, No. 1, p. 5, July 4, 1862. See also *Mess.*, IX, No. 19, p. 148, May 17, 1861; No. 22, p. 172, June 7, where the editors volunteer to collect such statistics.

118. *Mess.*, XVII, No. 23, pp. 188–9, June 16, 1865; *Occ.*, XXIII, No. 4, p. 185, July, 1865; No. 7, pp. 324–5, Nov., 1865.

119. *North American Review*, Vol. 153, pp. 761–2, Dec., 1891. Rabbi Stephen S. Wise made one of his early appearances in print with an answer to Rogers' letter in the February 1892, issue of the *Review*, pp. 249–50. Isaac Mayer Wise was as despondent as ever. He blamed the editor of the *Review* for printing an article such as Rogers', but would not even attempt to answer the charge. "We could give hundreds of names of Jews who served in the Union army [and he could!] but of what use would it be? To prove the falsity of a lie never yet prevented its repetition." *Isr.*, XXXVIII, No. 23, p. 4, Dec. 3, 1891; No. 26, p. 6, Dec. 24, 1891.

There was a fascinating, but little known sequel to Rogers' challenge. A veteran of the Union army named Simon Gerstman, otherwise quite unknown, wrote to Rogers, objecting to his accusation against Jews and furnishing credentials which convinced Rogers that Gerstman had led a gallant career in the army. Rogers acknowledged his mistake and promised Gerstman that he would write a letter of retraction to the *Review*. Six months later Gerstman fell ill and mentioned the fact to Rogers in a letter (they had apparently established a regular correspondence). Rogers came to fetch him, and took him to his home in Niantic, Conn., and nursed him back to health. For once Wise had erred on the side of pessimism. In telling the story, he paid tribute to Rogers' change of heart. *Isr.*, XXXVIII, No. 25, p. 4, Dec. 17, 1891; No. 52, p. 4, June 23, 1892.

120. Simon Wolf, *The American Jew as Patriot, Soldier, and Citizen.*

121. *Isr.*, VIII, No. 36, p. 284, Mar. 7, 1862.

122. *Occ.*, XXII, No. 8, pp. 368–9, Nov. 1864.

123. Ella Lonn wrote her fascinating study, *Foreigners in the Confederacy*, to investigate and evaluate this legend. The evidence which she has marshalled from an exhaustive search of contemporary sources demonstrates that many thousands of foreigners were resident in the Confederacy, loyal to it, and active in its military campaigns.

Frank Moore cited an interesting example (in *The Rebellion Record*, VI, p. 412, reprinted from the *Richmond Enquirer* of July 15, 1863) of the Confederate belief that all traitors were foreigners:

Foreigners of every age and sex crowded the office of the provost-marshal, in Richmond, anxious to get passports to go North, by way of the blockade. The Jew, whose ample pockets were stuffed with confederate money; the Germans, with hands on pockets tightly pressed; Italians, with the silvery jargon; and the Irish woman, with "nine children and one at the breast," all beset the office and wanted passports to leave the country . . . It is not fair that those who have drained the very life-blood of our people, should be let off thus quietly, and not made to shed the first, at least, if not the last, drop of blood for the Government which protected them in the collection of their hoarded pelf.

An illustration of the general suspicion in which foreigners were held is a newspaper poem clipped by the Rev. George Jacobs and preserved in his scrapbook, entitled "Ho! Profundum," of which this is one verse:

Tis noon—yet scarcely is begun
Up in the treasury the run,
Where Dutch and Yankee, Jew and Hun,
Meet in stock jobbery.

124. R. E. Park, *Sketch of the Twelfth Alabama Infantry*, p. 10.

125. N. A. Davis, *The Campaign from Texas to Maryland with the Battle of Fredericksburg*, pp. 18–9.

126. See the authoritative biography by Meade, *op. cit.*, pp. 218, 280, etc. Although he never identified himself with Jewish causes or the Jewish communities of places in which he happened to reside, Benjamin always was pigeonholed as a Jew. When Sir William Howard Russell, the renowned British journalist, took a trip through the South at the outbreak of war, this was one of his comments about Louisiana:

It is a strange country indeed; one of the evils which afflicts the Louisianians, they say, is the preponderance and influence of South Carolina Jews, and Jews generally, such as Moise, Mordecai, Josephs, and Judah Benjamin, and others. The subtlety and keenness of the Caucasian [*sic.*] intellect give men a high place among a people who admire ability and dexterity, and are at the same time reckless of means and averse to labor. The Governor is supposed to be somewhat under the influence of the Hebrews . . .

W. H. Russell, *My Diary North and South,* entry for May 29, 1861. See Korn, "Judah P. Benjamin as a Jew," for details of Benjamin's lack of interest in the Jewish community.

127. J. B. Jones, *A Rebel War Clerk's Diary at the Confederate States Capital,* I, pp. 165-6.

128. *New York Tribune,* Mar. 7, 1865. The editor of the *Tribune,* in reprinting this communication from the Richmond paper, took occasion to object to all attempts in the North to amend the U. S. Constitution for the purpose of recognizing Christianity as the official religion of the nation. This gave rise to a lively correspondence on the subject.

129. *SHSP,* XXVIII, p. 290. See also Cobb's reference to Benjamin as "an eunuch" in letter to Mrs. Cobb, Jan. 15, 1862, in Thomas R. R. Cobb Collection, University of Georgia Library.

130. M. J. Kohler, "Judah P. Benjamin: Statesman and Jurist," p. 79.

131. *Richmond Sentinel,* January 25, 1864, clipping from the George Jacobs Scrapbook.

132. See Lonn, *op. cit.,* pp. 335-8, 390-5, for the evidence which led Miss Lonn to conclude that "Jewish merchants had largely acquired possession of the stores" in all the larger cities except New Orleans. Most of the accounts she quotes are highly colored by prejudice and anti-foreignism, but can nonetheless be interpreted as tributes to Jewish enterprise and ingenuity. It depends upon one's point of view. She quotes the story, for instance, of a German Jew who had pitched a tent on the "sandy waste between San Antonio and Brownsville," far from the nearest town, to sell crackers, cheese, and whisky, to the passing troops (p. 338). The anecdote had been directed as an attack against Jews by its original narrator, who finished by complaining that the Jew demanded Northern currency for the refreshments but accepted, under pressure, Confederate money. No word for the "rugged individualism" of that Jewish peddler?

When Frederick Law Olmsted wrote his *A Journey in the Seaboard Slave States* in 1856, he wrote, in the glib language of prejudice, that "a swarm of Jews, within the last ten years, has settled in nearly every southern town, many of them men of no character, opening cheap clothing and trinket shops; ruining, or driving out of business, many of the old retailers, and engaging in an unlawful trade with the simple negroes, which is found very profitable." (Quoted in Burton Rascoe, *An American Reader,* p. 226.)

133. *SHSP,* IX, p. 122. Foote feared Benjamin's influence on Davis so strongly that he said "he would never consent to the establishment of a supreme court of the Confederate States so long as Judah P. Benjamin shall continue to pollute

the ears of majesty Davis with his insidious counsels." *Richmond Daily Examiner,* Dec. 17, 1863.

134. *SHSP,* XI, p. 214; see also IX, p. 144 for another one of Foote's outbursts against Southern Jewry.

135. *SHSP,* X, pp. 8–9.

136. *SHSP,* X, p. 185.

137. *SHSP,* IX, pp. 122–3.

138. Jones, *op. cit.,* I, p. 213.

139. *Ibid.,* I, p. 221.

140. *Savannah Daily Morning News,* Sept. 16, 1862.

141. *Memoirs of Isidor Straus,* p. 16.

142. *Ibid.*

143. Letter from Huldah A. (Fain) Briant Papers, Apr. 14, 1863, Santa Lucah, Georgia, in the Flowers Mss. Collection, Duke University Library. A similar incident occurred in Milledgeville, Ga., according to a report in the *Memphis Daily Bulletin,* Apr. 28, 1863.

144. *The Burckmyer Letters, March 1863–June 1865,* p. 236.

145. Letter, Barnsley to Reid, March 26, 1863, in Barnsley Papers, University of Georgia Library.

146. See Coulter, *The Confederate States of America, 1861–1865,* pp. 223–229, for many such citations. The two preceding notes are derived from his references. Coulter, incidentally, is the first Civil War historian, dealing with either the North or the South, to give even passing attention to anti-Jewish prejudice as a social phenomenon of the war period. Coulter's entire picture of the inflationary process in the Confederacy offers ample evidence that the role of the Jews was minor at best, yet he himself appears not to understand fully the nature of anti-Jewish prejudice from a psychological point of view. The quotation itself is from Putnam, *Richmond During the War; Four Years of Personal Observation. By a Richmond Lady,* p. 271.

147. *Battle-Fields of the South, From Bull Run to Fredericksburgh, with Sketches of Confederate Commanders, and Gossip of the Camps. By an English Combatant,* p. 15. This paragraph demonstrates the true nature of prejudice. The "English Combatant" had undoubtedly been told this by someone who referred to Germans as "Dutchmen" and German Jews as "Dutch Jews." Knowing nothing of this Americanism, he solemnly libels Dutch and Dutch-Jewish immigrants, without realizing that there could only have been a handful of them in the Confederacy.

148. *Two Months in the Confederate States, Including a Visit to New Orleans under the Domination of General Butler. By an English Merchant,* p. 126, cited by Coulter, *op. cit.,* p. 227.

149. *Richmond Sentinel, loc. cit.*

150. *Savannah Daily Morning News,* Feb. 23, 1863.

151. *Richmond Sentinel, loc. cit.*

152. Quoted in *Occ.,* XXIV, No. 6, pp. 282–3, Sept., 1866. The Jews of the

North were also under the impression that anti-Jewish feelings were as strong in the Confederacy as in the Union. Isaac Leeser said that a reading of Southern papers gave one the impression that Jews and disaffected citizens were synonymous, that all smuggling was done by Jews, and that Judah P. Benjamin would never have been retained in office if the war had ended favorably for the Confederacy. *Occ.*, XXIII, No. 7, pp. 313–9, Oct. 1865.

153. The sermon was delivered on May 27, 1863, and reprinted in *JR*, II, No. 13, p. 1, June 5, 1863, as a curiosity.

154. See Professor J. G. Randall's first chapter, pp. 3–36, in *The Civil War and Reconstruction*, for a discussion of these problems.

155. See Professor Charles W. Ramsdell's excellent study of the economic problems of the Confederacy during the war, in *Behind the Lines in the Southern Confederacy*, pp. 14 ff. Professor Ramsdell comes to no conclusion as to the extent of unscrupulous practices (pp. 20–1); he does not even mention the accusations against Jews.

156. Cited in Coulter, *op. cit.*, p. 231. Even Southern clergymen were suspected of speculating! See the discussion on a bill to exempt ministers from conscription, Jan. 13, 1865, in *JCCS*, VII, p. 455.

157. Straus, *op. cit.*, pp. 15–7. Young Straus later went to Europe as an agent for a firm attempting to organize a systematic blockade-running fleet to supply the Confederacy with scarce goods. A large portion of the memoirs deals with his experiences in this regard.

In 1852, just before the elder Straus came to the United States, there were five Jewish families in Talbotton, but only eight men, not enough for a religious service. They had organized a Hebrew Benevolent Society and presented a silver ornament for a Torah-scroll to a N. Y. congregation, *Occ.*, X, No. 8, p. 414, Nov., 1852. All eight men were probably peddlers, operating in the surrounding country. That was the way Lazarus Straus reached Talbotton.

158. *Daily Richmond Examiner*, Jan. 7, 1864.

159. *JCCS*, VI, p. 598; *Daily Richmond Examiner*, Jan. 8, 1864. The same day the *Examiner* printed an unchallenged report that "very recently, two immensely wealthy Israelitish merchants on Broad Street, departed for the North leaving their wives and daughters to carry on the business of their stores."

160. *Daily Richmond Examiner*, Jan. 26, 1864.

161. *JCCS*, VII, pp. 454, 458, 465, 466, 490, 659.

162. Jones, *op. cit.*, II, p. 126.

163. *Ibid.*, I, pp. 304, 320.

164. *Ibid.*, II, p. 39.

165. *Ibid.*, I, p. 185.

166. *Ibid.*, II, p. 144.

167. It should be superfluous to comment that so unabashed a Judaeophobe as Jones ought not be regarded as a fair witness in any discussion of the role of Jews in the Confederacy. The editor of the 1935 edition of the Jones *Diary* felt that the Grant Order and the Jones comments were reliable evidence on the basis of the "where there's smoke, there's fire" theory of logic. "Certainly there is a strong presumption in the records of both sides," he states, "that fair-

minded men felt the general charge of profiteering could be made against the whole class of Jewish merchants." (I, p. 289.) Grant in later days admitted his Order was unfair; Jones cannot possibly be regarded as a "fair-minded witness." The above mentioned editor cites only one other witness, Colonel Fremantle, who asserted that Matamoros (a town on the Mexican-Texas border!) was "infested with numbers of Jews whose industry spoils the trade of established merchants." (Fremantle, *Three Months in the Southern States: April–June 1863*, p. 14). There is a great deal of difference between commercial success and profiteering! In fact, one might almost be inclined to suppose that the "established merchants" were the real profiteers whose extortionist practices were mitigated by the "industry" of the Jews.

168. *Savannah Daily Morning News*, Sept. 16, 1862. One item in the resolution, condemning "all newspapers giving currency to this slander and intolerance" and asking Jews to withhold their support from such newspapers, received a justifiable rebuke from the editor of the *News*. A newspaper which printed news about such events was, in his opinion, not necessarily guilty of sharing the opinions voiced. An editor could not be held responsible for the accuracy of his statements, let alone for sentiments expressed by others. He had performed a service to the Savannah Jews, he believed, by printing the report from Thomasville.

169. Ezekiel and Lichtenstein, *The History of the Jews of Richmond*, pp. 246–7. In 1865, the Rev. M. J. Michelbacher of Beth Ahabah was one of a number of distinguished Richmond citizens who signed a general appeal for an "adopt a soldier" plan in an effort to obtain more food for the military. Putnam, *op. cit.*, pp. 252–5.

170. See, for example, *Richmond Sentinel, loc. cit.*

171. *Isr.*, IX, No. 24, p. 188, Dec. 19, 1862. There is some doubt as to the authenticity of this report; the *Israelite* quoted no source. It might have been contained in a delayed message from the South or transmitted by a Jew coming North, but Col. Adler, so far as we know, was confined in a Richmond prison by Oct. 19, 1861, on charges of Northern sympathies, supposedly revealed by his bitter criticism of his superior officer's military talents. He attempted to commit suicide in Libby Prison, but was unsuccessful. Nine months later he escaped to the North. That would be about June 1862. He was, then, already in the North when the report appeared in the *Israelite*. Over a year later the same periodical was asking for information concerning Adler's whereabouts, since letters for him had been addressed to the editorial offices. The paper described him as "a Hungarian gentleman styling himself Colonel Adler, who was arrested in Cincinnati as an officer of the Confederate Army." Adler was indeed a soldier of fortune! William C. Harris, *Prison Life in the Tobacco Warehouse at Richmond*, p. 87, quoted in Lonn, *op. cit.*, pp. 177–8; *Frank Moore, Rebellion Record*, III, p. 51, citing the *Richmond Enquirer*, Oct. 19, 1861; *Isr.*, X, No. 8, p. 59, Aug. 21, 1863.

172. *Richmond Sentinel, loc. cit.*

173. *Savannah Daily Morning News*, Feb. 23, 1863, p. 1. This gentleman evidently prided himself upon his expert knowledge of Jewish religious practice. The bulk of his letter was an explanation that whole regiments of Jews could

be organized if the War Department would permit them to handle their own commissary problems! If they could obtain the animals for slaughter, and purchase their own utensils and keep them ritually clean, "professional butchers of their own—educated men," would handle the rest. He asked the Macon Jews to organize the "first Israelite Battalion of the Confederate army. Let them take for the battle flag—'*The Lion of the tribe of Judah*,' and the God of Moses, Abraham, Isaac, and Jacob will fight their battles for them, and tread our enemies beneath His feet." This suggestion will be a cause for levity among those who are familiar with the consternation aroused in American Jewish circles during the early years of World War II when pro-Zionists sought to organize a Jewish Army (it was finally done, as a Jewish Brigade of the British Army) whose personnel would be made up of Palestinian and refugee Jews.

174. Quoted in *Occ.*, XXIV, No. 6, pp. 282–3, Sept., 1866.

175. Quoted in *JR*, III, No. 23, p. 2, Feb. 26, 1864. The editor of the *Mobile Daily Advertiser and Register* (Nov. 5, 1863) had another answer: "If our fair friends will cease to patronize, instead of complain of the Jews, wear their old clothes, and give the money now spent in silks to thinly-clad and badly-shod soldiers, one source of speculation would soon dry up . . . Try it, and dry goods will fall to rational prices within six months."

176. Quoted in *Richmond Daily Whig*, Oct. 16, 1862.

177. *WROR*, I, XVII, pt. II, pp. 272–4.

178. Hopley, *Life in the South* . . . , II, pp. 41, 188.

Notes to Chapter VIII

1. *Isr.*, XI, No. 44, p. 350, Apr. 28, 1865; reprinted in Emanuel Hertz, *Abraham Lincoln, The Tribute of the Synagogue*, p. 98. Wise did not mention this conversation with Lincoln in his 1863 editorials on the Grant affair, but he did tell one of his colleagues, Rabbi Henry Vidaver of St. Louis, about it. Vidaver was the American Correspondent for the Hebrew monthly *HaMagid*, published in Germany. He wrote approximately the same version of the conversation that Wise referred to in his 1865 sermon, in his report on the Grant affair, which was printed in the Feb. 15, 1863, issue of *HaMagid*, p. 60. This would indicate that Wise had not deliberately delayed telling the story until Lincoln's passing. *The Jewish Record* was the only periodical which took note of Wise's remarks in 1865; it merely reprinted them under the title, "President Lincoln's Parentage," without comment, *JR*, VI, No. 7, p. 2, July 5, 1865. Wise's assertion has been known to writers for a long time, but since no other evidence has ever been discovered, it has not been given much weight in their writing about the mysteries of Lincoln's background. Wise may not have reported the conversation accurately, or may not have understood the meaning of the President's remarks. Perhaps Lincoln was joking about the descent of all men from Adam and Eve; again, Lincoln may have made some remarks about the universal character of the Bible, similar to those which he made to Abraham Kohn of Chicago, as we shall note later. It is almost incomprehensible that Lincoln should

have said the exact words quoted by Wise without having made similar statements to other acquaintances.

2. Letter, Lincoln to Jonas, Feb. 4, 1860, reprinted in Appendix B, where all of the extant correspondence between Lincoln and Jonas is collected, with notations of the source of each letter. All quotations in the section about Jonas are from those letters, unless otherwise cited in the notes. Data on Jonas' life, unless otherwise noted, is rather general knowledge and has been treated in Markens, *op. cit.*, pp. 123–8; Emanuel Hertz, *op. cit.*, pp. x–xi, and "An Intimate Friend of Lincoln"; Albert A. Woldman, "Lincoln's Jewish Friend."

3. *Occ.*, I, No. 11, p. 548, Feb. 1844—Joseph Jonas' narrative of his experiences on first coming to Cincinnati, and the gradual shift of his family from England to America.

4. W. A. Richardson, Jr., "Many Contests for the County Seat of Adams Co., Ill.," pp. 273–4.

5. Theodore C. Pease, *Illinois Election Returns 1818–1848*, p. 362.

6. *Ibid.*, p. 380.

7. Jonas was probably the first Jew in Quincy. It was not until 1852 that a sufficient number of co-religionists joined him to make possible the organization of a congregation. Their first step was to search for a Jewish ritual butcher. *Occ.*, X, No. 1, p. 57, Apr., 1852. There is no exact data on the earliest Jews in central Illinois. Rabbi Herman E. Snyder, in his *History of Temple Brith Sholom*, asserts that the earliest reliable evidence does not locate Jews in Springfield until 1855.

8. *Memoirs of Gustave Koerner*, I, pp. 479–80.

9. *The Diary of Orville Hickman Browning*, I, pp. 239, 256.

10. *Quincy Whig*, Oct. 7, 1858, cited in Edwin E. Sparks, *The Lincoln–Douglas Debates of 1858*, p. 389.

11. Letter in collection of the late Oliver R. Barrett, of Chicago. A photograph of the page from which these comments are quoted is printed on p. 288a of Hertz, *op. cit.* Hertz' assertion (p. xi) that this letter "establishes the interesting fact that Abraham Jonas was the first man to suggest Lincoln for the presidency, in a conference with Horace Greeley," is not supported by the letter itself. To the contrary, Asbury was the one who first mentioned Lincoln, and he was uncertain whether Jonas' support of the suggestion was based on friendship for him (Asbury) or genuine agreement with the proposal.

12. *The Diary of Orville Hickman Browning*, I, pp. 402, 425, 432. This diary records the dates of many other occasions when Jonas and Browning appeared together on the political platform: pp. 100, 158, 160, 321, 341, 567, 627. In another connection (I, p. 38) Browning refers to his friend as "Col. Jonas." The origin of this title has not been ascertained.

13. *Ibid.*, I, p. 440; Browning to Lincoln, Dec. 9, 1860, No. 4911 of the Robert Todd Lincoln Collection.

14. Sandburg, *op. cit.*, III, p. 485.

15. *The Diary of Orville Hickman Browning*, I, p. 671. Browning was, by this time, in the business of securing favors for his clients from the government, but this case must undoubtedly be differentiated from the others. The Jonas family

were friends, not clients. On Dec. 19, 1863, Browning records the fact that he went "to see Col Hoffman about Chas Jonas, a Prisoner at Johnsons Island," (I, p. 651). There are no further details; it is impossible therefore to tell whether this was at the prompting of the Jonas family or not, or whether it was to obtain his release or not. Jonas had been close to death during Aug. 1863, and Browning records the details of this illness (I, pp. 639–41).

16. Quoted from photograph in the Markens Collection. Markens is supposed to have found the document in the War Dept. Archives, Markens, *op. cit.*, p. 127.

17. *Ibid.*, p. 126.

18. *Diary of Orville Hickman Browning*, p. 672.

19. *New York World*, Sept. 24, 1864, editorial, "Mr. Lincoln's Unionism and Bunionism." All data and quotations in this section, except where noted, are taken from the Zacharie-Lincoln correspondence, printed in Appendix C.

20. *New York Herald*, Oct. 3, 1862, editorial, "The Head and Feet of the Nation"; Oct. 21, 1863, editorial, "More Important Negotiations for Peace." Professor Fred H. Harrington asserts that Zacharie had been a grocer and was also a book-pirate, citing his publication under his own name of *Surgical and Practical Observations on the Diseases of the Human Foot*, N. Y. 1860, the entire text of which was lifted from "John Eisenberg's book of the same title (London, 1845)." Harrington, *Fighting Politician: Major General N. P. Banks*, p. 247, n. 109. The writer must record his appreciation to Dr. Harringon for references in his volume which led the writer to the Banks Mss. in the Essex Institute, which in turn filled in many interesting details of the Zacharie-Lincoln-Banks story. Some of the letters cited below are printed in Dr. Harrington's article, "A Peace Mission of 1863."

21. A reproduction of this card is printed in Sandburg, *op. cit.*, II, p. 230.

22. *New York Herald*, Oct. 3, 1862.

23. The exact nature of Zacharie's position cannot be ascertained. According to a pay-receipt found among the Banks Mss., dated July 2, his salary for two months and 18 days service was $730.00, plus room and board for which bills were presented amounting to $342.00. His secretary was paid $365.00 for the same period of time. These payments were personally authorized by General Banks.

24. Harrington, *op. cit.*, pp. 126–7.

25. Letters, Zacharie to Banks, July 30, Oct. 16, Oct. 24, 1863, Banks Mss.

26. Letter, Banks to Col. Holabird, July 2, 1863, Banks Mss.

27. Letter, Banks to Seward, July 2, 1863, Banks Mss.

28. *Ibid.*

29. Letter, Zacharie to Banks, July 30, 1863, Banks Mss.

30. Letters, Zacharie to Banks, Sept. 8, 20, 1863; Letter, Chas. Johnson (Zacharie's secretary) to Banks, Sept. 24, 1863, Banks Mss.

31. Letter, Zacharie to Banks, Oct. 9, 1863, Banks Mss.

32. *Ibid.*

33. Letter, Zacharie to Banks, Oct. 16, 1863, Banks Mss.

34. *New York Herald*, Oct. 3, 1862.

35. Letter, Zacharie to Banks, Oct. 9, 1863, Banks Mss.

36. *Ibid.*

37. *Ibid.*

38. Letter, Zacharie to Banks, Oct. 24, 1863, Banks Mss.

39. *Ibid.*

40. *Mess.*, XV, No. 18, p. 141, May 13, 1864.

41. Goodman Mordecai's narrative of the episode appears in *New York Daily Tribune*, Feb. 13, 1901. Lewis and Zacharie were staunch political friends—the former guaranteeing in a letter to Lincoln that he would assure funds for any Jewish groups which would campaign for Lincoln—the letter (No. 37631 of the Robert Todd Lincoln Collection) inspired by a visit Dr. Zacharie paid to the President.

42. *Mess.*, XVI, No. 16, p. 124, Oct. 28, 1864.

43. *JR*, I, No. 7, p. 2, Oct. 24, 1862. Nevertheless, A. S. Cohen, its editor, was writing to Lincoln, on Sept. 1, 1863, that "a number of my subscribers had waited upon me and requested me to correspond with you relative to your nomination for the Presidentcy. A number of them desired me to state that they could use considerable influence by *money and votes* to secure your success. Especially through an organization known as the *Bnai Berith* which has branches in every town and City in the Union. They desired to know what your views were in regard to the Subject. The *Record* with its powerful influence with that class of people was to be obtained and your patronage asked for it and its Editor . . ." Cohen to Lincoln, Sept. 1, 1863, Nos. 11483–4, Robert Todd Lincoln Collection.

44. Letter, Hay to Isaacs, Nov. 1, 1864, in Board of Delegates correspondence files. See also another letter by Isaacs on the same subject, dated Oct. 26, 1864, and Hay's answer, dated Nov. 1, 1864, Nos. 37629–30 and 37796–7 of the Robert Todd Lincoln collection.

45. *New York World, loc. cit.*

46. *New York Herald*, Oct. 3, 1862. Compare this with George Denison's description: "His vest is of flowered velvet—his hair beautifully oiled—and his presence distills continual perfume sweeter than the winds that blow from Araby the blest." (*Diary and Correspondence of Salmon P. Chase*, p. 353.)

47. *New York World, loc. cit.*

48. Letter, Banks to Seward, July 2, 1863, Banks Mss. George S. Denison, Collector of Internal Revenue for Louisiana, was reporting on Zacharie's activities to Secretary Chase, meanwhile, in a most unfavorable manner. To him, Zacharie was just another one of the "host of speculators, Jews and camp-followers" who had swept into New Orleans to profit by the Union military occupation. He wondered how the President could "send here as his private correspondent a vulgar little scoundrel like Dr. Zachary—who takes bribes, and whose only object is to make money . . ." He accused Zacharie of profiting from the business dealings of Jews whom he sent into Confederate territory to spy out the land for him. This latter may or may not have been true, although Banks' instructions to Zacharie requested that he send trustworthy spies into Mississippi to ascertain

information about the enemy's military strength and strategy. (See letter, Banks to Zacharie, Jan. 1, 1863, Banks Mss.) The Denison reports are to be found in *Diary and Correspondence of Salmon P. Chase*, pp. 353, 355–6, 375. General G. F. Shepley, writing to Butler about Zacharie's attempts to track down data which would reflect unfavorably upon Butler's previous administration of the Department of the Gulf, finished his letter by saying that "the Christ killers, as Andrew calls them, have it all their own way." (*Private and Official Correspondence of Gen. Benjamin F. Butler During the Period of the Civil War*, III, p. 14.)

49. Albert A. Woldman, "Lincoln's Jewish Doctor," p. 189. See also Whitelaw Reid to Zacharie, May 13, 1872, Banks Mss, for indications of Zacharie's activities as a Liberal Republican in the 1872 campaign.

50. Richard S. Lambert, *For the Time is at Hand*, p. 82. Lambert, apparently, quoted this from Monk's letter to a friend, describing his interview with Lincoln. No reference is given for the quotation.

51. Hammerslough, according to Markens, *op. cit.*, pp. 128–9, had frequent personal dealings with Lincoln during his Springfield years, attended the first Inauguration, called on Lincoln whenever he was in Washington, and once escorted Mrs. Lincoln's sister from Springfield to Washington. Unfortunately he never recorded his recollections of his relations with the President.

52. Markens, *op. cit.*, pp. 129–30. Rice lived in Jacksonville, Ill., from 1853 to 1861. He apparently was one of thousands upon thousands of Illinoisans whom Lincoln ran into from time to time and knew by name. Rice said he offered to present a suit to the President-Elect to wear at the first Inauguration, but that a Springfield firm's gift for that purpose had already been accepted. He had Lincoln's help in an effort to secure an oppointment as military store-keeper for southern Illinois, but the office had already been given to someone else by Cameron before Rice consulted Lincoln. See *Lincoln Lore*, No. 1049 (May 16,1949), for data on yet another of Lincoln's Jewish friends, Lewis Rosenthal.

53. Markens, *op. cit.*, pp. 133–4.

54. *Ibid.*, pp. 137–8.

55. *Ibid.*, pp. 138–9; A. J. Dittenhoefer, *How We Elected Lincoln*.

56. *Ibid.*, pp. 139–40.

57. Wolf, *The Presidents I Have Known*, pp. 4–49.

58. Markens, *op. cit.*, pp. 134–6.

59. *Ibid.*, p. 161; manuscript biography in American Jewish Archives; Louis A. Warren, "The War Headquarters of Lincoln," in *Lincoln Lore*, No. 998, May 24, 1948.

60. Myers' memorandum about his conference with Lincoln, in company with Judge Campbell, on April 5, 1865, concerning peace terms with the Confederacy, in Virginia Historical Society, Richmond.

61. Sandburg, *op. cit.*, III, p. 232.

62. Markens, *op. cit.*, pp. 134–5. Raphall wrote to Lincoln on March 17, 1864, to thank him for a favor to his son-in-law, Capt. C. M. Levy. There is no indication of the nature of the favor; a C. M. Levy (the same or another) was dismissed from the military service by Court Martial on Oct. 9, 1863, and "for-

ever disqualified to hold any office of trust or profit in the United States," according to a letter from Assistant Adjutant General S. F. Chalfin, dated July 16, 1864, found in the Robert Todd Lincoln Papers, No. 34507. In his letter, No. 31163 of that same collection, Raphall mentioned that he was sending Lincoln several photographs of himself "with sincerest prayers for your continued health and prosperity."

63. Markens, *op. cit.*, pp. 131–2. See also the very interesting description of Kohn's 70th birthday on May 7, 1863, in *Isr.*, IX, No. 46, p. 362, May 22, 1863. Kohn's daughter, who had married Rabbi Liebman Adler's son, endeavored to find the painting in the White House during the McKinley administration, but was unsuccessful in her search.

64. *JR*, I, No. 13, p. 2, Dec. 5, 1862. The letter itself is, to the writer's knowledge, not extant. The incident was brought to the attention of Admiral George Preble, who referred to it in his *History of the Flag of the United States*, N. Y. 1894, and of (then) Governor McKinley who spoke of it in a speech at Ottawa, Kansas, June 20, 1895. McKinley spoke as though it were a silk flag, rather than a painting. H. L. Meites, in his *History of the Jews of Chicago* (p. 84) had the bright idea of reproducing the flag, implying that he had a copy of the original. The confusion about the nature of Kohn's gift, and its disappearance, have led many to believe that the entire episode was legendary. The discovery of Hay's detailed letter to A. S. Cohen in the columns of the *Record* is convincing proof of the historicity of Kohn's painting. It should certainly not, however, be called a "Jewish flag," as some writers have done.

65. Letter, Lincoln to Speed, Aug. 24, 1855, Massachusetts Historical Society.

66. Letter, Lincoln to Canisius, May 17, 1859, Chicago Historical Society.

67. *Isr.*, XI, No. 44, pp. 349–50, Apr. 28, 1865. Many Protestant preachers condemned Lincoln for having witnessed "immoral" theatrical performances. Some of them almost felt that the assassination was divine punishment for his sin. See quotations from such sermons in Sandburg, *op. cit.*, IV, pp. 357–9. It is interesting to compare Julius Eckman's attack on wealthy San Francisco Jews who insisted on frequenting the theater on Friday nights, reprinted from the *Gleaner* in *Mess.*, XV, No. 9, p. 66, Mar. 4, 1864. It was said, in New York, that if Lincoln had been a Catholic or a Jew, he would not have been at the theater that night, but in the church or synagogue. (F. N. Wolff, *Four Generations*, p. 20.)

68. *JR*, VI, No. 5, p. 1, Apr. 21, 1865; *Isr.*, XI, No. 43, same date.

69. *Ibid.*

70. *Occ.*, XXIII, No. 2, p. 84, May, 1865; No. 3, p. 115, June.

71. San Francisco *Daily Alta California*, Apr. 16, 1865, reprinted in Hertz, *op. cit.*, pp. 138–9.

72. St. Louis *Daily Missouri Republican*, Apr. 19, 1865.

73. *JR*, VI, No. 5, p. 3, Apr. 28, 1865.

74. *Ibid.*

75. *Board Minutes of Temple Beth Israel, 1862–1868*, pp. 50–1. Similar resolutions were adopted by most of the congregations throughout the North, recorded in their minutes, and published in the local press. The reaction of

Southern congregations is, for the most part, unrecorded, because congregational life was so disrupted that no minutes were kept at the end of the war. Three Charleston Jews, however, participated in civic exercises (Markens, *op. cit.*, p. 149); the Temimi Derech congregation of New Orleans passed resolutions which were published in *Mess.*, XVII, No. 17, p. 141, May 5, 1865, and had a memorial service at which an address was given by Col. P. J. Joachimsen of the Union Army (text in Hertz, *op. cit.*, pp. 29–38); Rabbi Bernard Illowy gave a memorial sermon in his New Orleans synagogue, Shaarey Chesed (text *ibid*, pp. 160–3). The writer has not been able to verify Markens' statement that Michelbacher gave a memorial address at Richmond (*op. cit.*, p. 149).

76. *Isr.*, XI, No. 43, p. 339, Apr. 21, 1865.

77. *JR*, VI, No. 5, p. 2, Apr. 21, 1865.

78. Most of the sermons preached in Lincoln's memory are reprinted in Hertz, *op. cit.* Those which Hertz did not uncover in his research and which have been located by the writer are as follows:

(1) *Samuel Adler*, Apr. 19, 1865, longer excerpt than Hertz (*JR*, VI, No. 5, p. 3, Apr. 21, 1865).

   Samuel Adler, June 1, 1865 (*JR*, VI, No. 12, p. 1, June 9, 1865; *Mess.*, XVII, No. 22, p. 181, June 9, 1865).

(2) *Samuel M. Isaacs*, Apr. 15, 1865 (*JR*, VI, No. 5, p. 1, Apr. 21, 1865). June 1, 1865 (*Mess.*, XVII, No. 22, p. 181, June 9, 1865).

(3) *Isaac Leeser*, Apr. 19, 1865 (*Occ.*, XXIII, No. 2, pp. 84–6, May 1865). Apr. 22, 1865 (*Occ.*, XXIII, No. 4, pp. 154–65, July 1865).

(4) *M. H. Myers*, Apr. 17, 1865 (*JR*, VI, No. 5, p. 2, Apr. 21, 1865).

(5) *Isaac Noot*, Apr. 19, 1865 (*JR*, VI, No. 5, p. 2, Apr. 21, 1865). June 1, 1865 (*JR*, VI, No. 12, p. 2, June 9, 1865).

(6) *Morris J. Raphall*, Apr. 19, 1865, prayer not given in Hertz' text (*JR*, VI, No. 5, p. 3, Apr. 21, 1865). June 1, 1865 (*JR*, VI, No. 2, p. 1, June 9, 1865; *Mess.*, XVII, No. 22, p. 181, June 9, 1865).

(7) *Leon Sternberger*, Apr. 19, 1865 (*JR*, VI, No. 5, pp. 2–3, Apr. 21, 1865).

These sermons were reported in part or entirety, but the periodicals recorded dozens more in brief summaries or passing mention. There was probably no synagogue in the entire North which did not conduct services, and no rabbi or cantor who did not deliver a sermon on Lincoln's death.

The *Record* was the only periodical which attempted to publish the complete texts, or at least summaries, of all the memorial sermons which were preached in a single city—New York in this case. It also printed reports from Philadelphia and other cities. The *Messenger, Israelite,* and *Occident* complained that they had not the space to print everything sent to them, but the *Occident* suggested that a special volume be published in memory of Lincoln by some Jewish organization, preserving all of the sermons. *Isr.*, XI, No. 45, p. 357, May 5, 1865; No. 46, p. 365, May 12; *Mess.*, XVII, No. 18, p. 148, May 12; *Occ.*, XXIII, No. 6, p. 286, Sept.

An interesting problem was posed for Jews by President Johnson's designation of June 1 as the National Day of Mourning for Lincoln, because that was the second day of the Shavuot Festival. It had previously been set for May 25, but when it was discovered that that date was a minor Christian holy day, it was postponed. The Jews felt aggrieved that their festival was ignored (*Mess.*, XVII, No. 17, pp. 139–41, May 5, 1865; *JR*, VI, No. 7, p. 2, June 5, 1865). Most of the Orthodox and Conservative rabbis alluded to the fact that Jewish tradition prohibits mourning or sorrow on a feast-day, and said, therefore, that they were reluctant to mention Lincoln's assassination.

Judaism was rarely taken into consideration in matters of state. Lincoln's reference to Christianity, it will be remembered, in his first Inaugural, was attacked by Wise. Another such instance was a message which he addressed to the armed forces, commending the observance of Sunday rest and worship (Sandburg, *op. cit.*, III, p. 374, with evidence that the order was written by Stanton). The *Messenger* asked that equal opportunity be given to Jews to observe their Sabbath:

> ... We trust measures will be taken to afford Jewish soldiers immunity from guard duty on their Sabbath, and to exempt them on that day from all labor that is not strictly necessary. Arrangements could readily be made to exclude them from the provisions of the "Sunday" order, so that for six days in the week they should discharge the duties of soldiers, and be permitted to rest on their Sabbath. If the President should deem the Jewish soldiers—inasmuch as they have no distinctive regimental organization—too insignificant to consider their claims in a "general order," it might at least be made the subject of a recommendation to commanding officers, so that soldiers of whatever religious faith may be treated on an equal footing ... (*Mess.*, XII, No. 20, p. 157, Nov. 21, 1862)

B. Behrend of Narrowsburg, N. Y., wrote to Lincoln along similar lines and sent a copy of his letter to Leeser. See also *JR*, I, No. 6, p. 2, Oct. 15, 1862, for an editorial condemning McClellan's message to his army on the Emancipation Proclamation for its references to Christianity.

79. Hertz, *op. cit.*, p. 13.

80. *Ibid.*, p. 92.

81. *Ibid.*, p. 71.

82. *Ibid.*, p. 48.

83. *Ibid.*, p. 160.

84. *Ibid.*, p. 106.

85. *Ibid.*, p. 101.

86. *Ibid.*, p. 135.

87. *Ibid.*, p. 31.

88. *Ibid.*, p. 154.

89. *Ibid.*, pp. 96–7.

90. *Ibid.*, pp. 9–10.

91. *Ibid.*, pp. 111–12.

92. *JR*, VI, No. 5, p. 3, Apr. 21, 1865.

93. Hertz, *op. cit.*, pp. 161–2.

94. *Ibid.*, p. 74.

95. *Ibid.*, p. 118.

96. *Ibid.*, p. 162.

97. *Ibid.*, p. 94.

98. *Ibid.*, p. 49.

99. *Ibid.*, p. 4.

100. *Ibid.*, pp. 117–8.

101. *Ibid.*, p. 139.

102. *Ibid.*, p. 11.

103. Markens, *op. cit.*, p. 149.

104. M. H. Newmark, *Sixty Years in California, 1853–1913, Containing the Reminiscences of Harris Newmark*, pp. 338–9.

105. Markens, *op. cit.*, p. 147.

106. *Ibid.*, p. 144.

107. Clippings from unidentified Pittsburgh papers in Judge Cohen's Scrapbook.

108. Markens, *op. cit.*, pp. 132–3.

109. *Ibid.*, p. 128.

110. *JR*, IV, No. 5, p. 2, Apr. 28, 1865.

111. *Occ.*, XXIII, No. 4, pp. 172–4, July, 1865. The original of this letter is not among the papers of the Leeser Collection, so the author cannot be identified with any positive assurance. A letter to Leeser, however, from one David Haas (or Maas) of Trenton, dated May 27, 1865, referring to the attitude of some Northern Jews towards the South, may be a clue to the identity of the author of the letter which Leeser published. The pertinent passage of the Trenton letter is as follows:

> Your favor of yesterday is at hand and I am happy to find that our sentiments on the subject referred to in mine of a previous date are generally in accordance.—I supposed that I would be too late for the next month's Occident with the communication I took the liberty of sending you, but it will do as well for the next month, and perhaps as you say it will be better at that time when the furor which seems to have maddened some of our people will have passed over.—The intolerance betrayed by many persons, in whom a better state of feeling might have been expected, during the recent sectional struggle is most extraordinary, and very inconsistent in such of them as profess Judaism, and have suffered so much from the intolerance of others. The only excuse for them is, that they were afflicted with a species of insanity which deprived them momentarily of their reason. The fit will pass over, and they will be astonished at their own folly.—

112. *Occ.*, XXIII, No. 44, pp. 162–3, July 1865.

113. Paul M. Angle, "The Building of the Lincoln Monument," in *Lincoln Centennial Association Papers*, p. 29.

114. H. E. Snyder, *A Brief History of the Jews in Springfield, Ill., and of Temple B'rith Sholom; Isr.*, XI, No. 50, p. 397, June 9, 1865.

115. *Isr.*, XII, No. 1, p. 5, July 7, 1865.

116. From duplicate receipts in the Illinois State Historical Library, numbered

as follows: 13½, 113, 246, 371, 465, 555, 667, 962, 1042, 3571, 4644, 4808. This data was secured through the good offices and diligence of Mr. Morton A. Barker of Springfield, Ill.

117. Copy of his letter in Morais Collection.

118. Hertz, *op. cit.*, p. 168.

119. *Mess.*, XVII, No. 19, p. 155, May 19, 1865; No. 21, June 2.

BIBLIOGRAPHY

(This is a selective bibliography to the extent that newspapers quoted in other newspapers and single manuscript pages or letters are not listed here, but in the pertinent notes.)

PRIMARY SOURCES

Ia. GENERAL MANUSCRIPT MATERIAL

Nathaniel P. Banks Papers, Essex Institute.
Orville H. Browning Papers, Illinois State Historical Library.
DuBois Papers, Chicago Historical Society.
Hamilton Fish Papers, Library of Congress.
Robert Todd Lincoln Collection of Abraham Lincoln Papers, Library of Congress.
Lyman Trumbull Papers, Library of Congress.
Gerrit Smith Papers, Syracuse University Library.
Records of the War Department, Office of the Adjutant General, National Archives.
Records of the Veterans Administration, National Archives.

Ib. JEWISH MANUSCRIPT MATERIAL

Michael M. Allen Diary and Papers, Mrs. Clarence M. Allen, N. Y. (Photostats in American Jewish Archives.)
Anshi Chesed Board of Trustees Minutes, 1856–1866, Temple Emanu-El, N. Y.
Board of Delegates of American Israelites Executive Committee Minute Book, and *Correspondence Files*, American Jewish Historical Society Library.
Memoirs of Henry Beck, 1864–5, Marcus Collection.
Cohen Papers, Dropsie College Library.
Eckstein Papers, Mr. Edmond Uhry, N. Y. (Photostats in American Jewish Archives.)
Einhorn Papers, Marcus Collection.
Einhorn Papers, American Jewish Historical Society Library.
Emanuel Letters, Marcus Collection.
Felsenthal Letters, Miss Julia Felsenthal. (Photostats in American Jewish Archives.)
Fischel Papers, in *Board of Delegates of American Israelites Correspondence Files*, American Jewish Historical Society Library.
Gutheim Papers, American Jewish Archives.
Major Alexander Hart Diary, American Jewish Archives.
Indianapolis Hebrew Congregation Trustees Minute Book, Indianapolis, Ind.
Isaacs Papers, in *Board of Delegates of American Israelites Correspondence Files*, American Jewish Historical Society Library.
Kahl Montgomery Minutes, Montgomery, Ala. (Photostats in American Jewish Archives.)
Leeser Collection, Dropsie College Library.
Lloyd Lewis Mss., Files bearing upon Grant's General Order Number Eleven.
Isaac A. Meyer, *My Life, Travels, and Adventures by Land and Sea*, Marcus Collection.

Mikveh Israel Adjunta Minutes, Philadelphia. (Photostats in American Jewish Archives.)

Morais Collection, Dropsie College Library.

Moses Papers, Marcus Collection.

Minutes of the Philadelphia Society for the Visitation of the Sick and Mutual Assistance, Mikveh Israel Archives, Philadelphia.

Phillips Papers, Library of Congress.

Phillips Papers, Southern Historical Collection, University of North Carolina Library.

Sarner Papers, Mrs. Martha Sarner Levy, Bradford, Pa.

Shearith Israel Trustees Minutes, N. Y.

Memoirs of Isidor Straus, American Jewish Historical Society Library.

Temple Beth Israel Board of Trustees Minutes, Jackson, Mich., American Jewish Archives.

Temple Emanu-El Board of Directors Minutes, N. Y.

IIa. GENERAL PERIODICALS

Baltimore Sunday Herald.
Chicago Daily Tribune.
Cincinnati Commercial.
Cincinnati Daily Times.
Cincinnati Daily Enquirer.
Cincinnati Daily Gazette.
Cleveland Leader.
Congressional Globe, Washington.
Memphis Daily Appeal.
Memphis Daily Avalanche.
Memphis Daily Bulletin.
Mobile Advertiser and Register.
New Orleans Daily Picayune.
New York Herald.
New York Times.
New York Tribune.
New York World.
North American Review.
Philadelphia Enquirer.
Philadelphia Sunday Dispatch.
Richmond Daily Dispatch.
Richmond Daily Examiner.
Savannah Daily Morning News.
St. Louis Democrat.

IIb. JEWISH PERIODICALS

The Asmonean, N. Y.
Archives Israelites, Paris.
The Hebrew, San Francisco.
The Hebrew Leader, N. Y.
The Israelite, Cincinnati.
The Jewish Exponent, Philadelphia.
The Jewish Messenger, N. Y.
The Jewish Record, N. Y.
The Occident, and American Jewish Advocate, Philadelphia.
Sinai, Baltimore and Philadelphia.
The Weekly Gleaner, San Francisco.

BIBLIOGRAPHY

III. JEWISH SCRAPBOOKS, CLIPPING COLLECTIONS, MISCELLANEOUS PAPERS, PICTURE COLLECTIONS.

Josiah Cohen Scrapbook, Marcus Collection.
Jacob Frankel Clippings and Pictures, Mr. Joseph Frankel, N. Y., and Mrs. Pearl E. Whitely, Philadelphia.
Nathan Grossmayer Clippings and Papers, Mr. Max Grossmayer, Long Beach, Calif.
George Jacobs Scrapbook, Miss Rebecca Jacobs, Philadelphia.
Isaac Markens Picture Collection, American Jewish Historical Society Library.
Moss Scrapbook, American Jewish Historical Society Library.
I. Solomon Scrapbook, Duke University Library.

IVa. GENERAL BOOKS AND PAMPHLETS.

A Record of the Commissioned Officers, Non-Commissioned Officers and Privates of the Regiments which were Organized in the State of New York . . . to Assist in Suppressing the Rebellion . . . 2 vols., Albany, 1864.
"An English Combatant," *Battle-Fields of the South, from Bull Run to Fredericksburgh, with Sketches of Confederate Commanders, and Gossip of the Camps*, New York, 1864.
Charles Francis Adams, 1835–1915, An Autobiography, Boston, 1916.
Angle, Paul M., *New Letters and Papers of Lincoln*, New York, 1930.
Annual Report of the American and Foreign Anti-Slavery Society, New York, 1853.
Baker, Lafayette C., *History of the U. S. Secret Service*, New York, 1867.
Beale, Howard K. (ed.), *The Diary of Edward Bates, 1859–1866*, Washington, 1933.
Blake, Henry N., *Three Years in the Army of the Potomac*, Boston, 1865.
Brownlow, William G., *Sketches of the Rise, Progress, and Decline of Secession; with a Narrative of Personal Adventures among the Rebels*, Philadelphia, 1862.
Autobiography and Personal Reminiscences of Major-General Benj. F. Butler, Boston, 1892.
Chesnut, Mary Boykind, *A Diary From Dixie*, New York, 1929.
Cobb, Thomas R. R., "Extracts from Letters of . . . to his Wife, February 3, 1861–December 10, 1862," *Southern Historical Society Papers*, XXVIII (1900), pp. 280–301.
Dana, Charles A., *Recollections of the Civil War With the Leaders at Washington and in the Field in the Sixties*, New York, 1898.
Davis, N. A., *The Campaign From Texas to Maryland with the Battle of Fredericksburg*, Richmond, 1863.
Diary and Correspondence of Salmon P. Chase, Washington, 1903.
Dittenhoefer, A. J., *How We Elected Lincoln*, New York, 1916.
Fremantle, Lt. Col. Arthur J. L., *Three Months in the Southern States: April–June 1863*, New York, 1864.
Hopley, Catherine C. [Sarah E. Jones, pseud.], *Life in the South; from The Commencement of the War. By a Blockaded British Subject. Being a Social History of Those who took part in the Battles, from a Personal Acquaintance with Them in Their Homes. From the Spring of 1860 to August 1862*, 2 Vols., London, 1863.
Howe, M. A. De Wolfe (ed.), *Home Letters of General Sherman*, New York, 1909.
Jones, John Beauchamp, *A Rebel War Clerk's Diary at the Confederate States Capital*, 2 vols., New York, 1935.
Journal of the Congress of the Confederate States of America, 1861–1865, 7 vols., Washington, 1904–5.
Memoirs of Gustave Koerner, 2 vols., Cedar Rapids, 1909.
Moore, Frank (ed.), *The Rebellion Record: A Diary of American Events, with Documents, Narratives, Illustrative Incidents, Poetry, etc. . . .* 12 vols., New York, 1861–8.

Park, R. E., *Sketch of the Twelfth Alabama Infantry*, Richmond, 1906.

Parton, James, *History of the Administration of the Department of the Gulf in the Year 1862*, New York, 1864.

Pease, T. C., and James G. Randall (eds.), *The Diary of Orville Hickman Browning*, 2 vols. Springfield, 1925, 1933.

Private and Official Correspondence of Gen. Benjamin F. Butler During the Period of the Civil War, 5 vols., Norwood, 1917.

Proceedings of the First Confederate Congress, Southern Historical Society Papers, Richmond, 1923–1943.

[Putnam, Sallie A.], *Richmond During the War; Four Years of Personal Observation. By a Richmond Lady*, New York, 1867.

Reminiscences of Carl Schurz, 3 vols., New York, 1908.

Russell, William Howard, *My Diary North and South*, New York, 1863.

War of the Rebellion: . . . Official Records of the Union and Confederate Armies, 128 vols., Washington, 1880–1901.

IVb. JEWISH BOOKS AND PAMPHLETS.

Adler, Cyrus, *Lectures, Selected Papers, Addresses*, Philadelphia, 1933.

Aunt Sister's Book, New York, 1929.

Benjamin, J. J., *Drei Jahre in Amerika*, Hanover, 1862.

Bond, H. L., "Dr. Szold and Timbuctoo," *American Jews' Annual 5650*, Cincinnati, 1889.

Bondi, August, *Autobiography of August Bondi, 1833–1907*, Galesburg, 1910.

Eaton, Herbert F., *An Hour with the American Hebrew*, New York, 1879.

Einhorn, David, *War With Amalek*, Philadelphia, 1864.

Gottheil, Gustav, *Moses Versus Slavery: Being Two Discourses on the Slave Question*, Manchester, 1861.

Hertz, Emanuel, *Abraham Lincoln, The Tribute of the Synagogue*, New York, 1927.

Illoway, Henry, *Sefer Milchamot Elohim: Being the Controversial Letters and the Casuistic Decisions of the Late Rabbi Bernard Illowy, Ph.D. With a Short History of His Life and Activities*, Berlin, 1914.

In Memoriam: Jesse Seligman, New York, 1894.

Kohut, Rebekah, *My Portion*, New York, 1925.

Kuhn, Arthur K., *Herman Kuhn*, n.p., n.d.

Leon, L., *Diary of a Tar Heel Confederate Soldier*, Charlotte, 1913.

Morais, Henry Samuel, *The Jews of Philadelphia*, Philadelphia, 1894.

Newmark, M. H., *Sixty Years in California, 1854–1913, Containing the Reminiscences of Harris Newmark*, New York, 1930.

Raphall, Morris J., *The Bible View of Slavery*, New York, 1861.

Report of the Proceedings of the Thirteenth Annual Meeting of District Grand Lodge No. 2, Independent Order of B'nai B'rith, Held in Cincinnati Ohio, on July 9, 1865, and Following Days, Cincinnati, 1865.

Wolf, Simon, *The Presidents I Have Known From 1860 to 1918*, Washington, 1918.

Wolff, Frances N., *Four Generations*, New York, 1939.

SECONDARY SOURCES

A. GENERAL

Angle, Paul M., "The Building of the Lincoln Monument," *Lincoln Centennial Association Papers*, III (1926), pp. 17–62.

Barbee, David R., "President Lincoln and Doctor Gurley," *Abraham Lincoln Quarterly*, V (1948), pp. 3–24.

Billington, Ray A., *The Protestant Crusade, 1800–1860*, New York, 1938.

Cole, Arthur C., *The Irrepressible Conflict*, New York, 1934.

Coulter, E. Merton, "Commercial Intercourse with the Confederacy in the Mississippi Valley, 1861–1865," *Mississippi Valley Historical Review*, V (1919), pp. 377–95.

———, *William G. Brownlow: Fighting Parson of the Southern Highlands*, Chapel Hill, 1937.

———, *The Confederate States of America 1861–1865*, Baton Rouge, 1950.

Dabney, T. E., *One Hundred Years*, Baton Rouge, 1944.

Dictionary of American Biography, 22 vols., New York, 1946.

Harrington, F. H., "A Peace Mission of 1863," *American Historical Review* XLVI (1940), pp. 76–86.

———, *Fighting Politician, Major General N. P. Banks*, Philadelphia, 1948.

Heartman, Charles F., *Americana Catalogue*, Biloxi, 1947.

Hertz, Emanuel, *Abraham Lincoln: A New Portrait*, 2 vols., New York, 1931.

Hesseltine, William B., *Ulysses S. Grant: Politician*, New York, 1935.

Letters from Lloyd Lewis, Boston, 1950.

Lonn, Ella, *Foreigners in the Confederacy*, Chapel Hill, 1940.

Meade, Robert D., *Judah P. Benjamin, Confederate Statesman*, New York, 1943.

McIlwaine, Shields, *Memphis Down in Dixie*, New York, 1948.

Nevins, Allan, *Ordeal of the Union*, 2 vols., New York, 1947.

Parks, Joseph H., "A Confederate Trade Center Under Federal Occupation: Memphis, 1862 to 1865," *Journal of Southern History*, VII (1941), pp. 289–314.

Pease, Theodore C., *Illinois Election Returns, 1818–1848*. (*Collections of the Illinois State Historical Library* XVIII, Statistical Series I), Springfield, 1923.

Ramsdell, Charles W., *Behind the Lines in the Southern Confederacy*, Baton Rouge, 1944.

Randall, James G., *The Civil War and Reconstruction*, New York, 1937.

Rascoe, Burton, *An American Reader*, New York, 1939.

Richardson, W. A., Jr., "Many Contests for the County Seat of Adams Co., Ill." *Journal of the Illinois State Historical Society*, XVII (1924–5), pp. 369–80.

Sandburg, Carl, *Abraham Lincoln, The War Years*, 4 vols., New York, 1939.

Schuricht, Hermann, *History of the German Element in Virginia*, 2 vols., Baltimore, 1900.

Sparks, Edwin E., *The Lincoln-Douglas Debates of 1858* (*Collections of the Illinois State Historical Library*, III, Lincoln Series I), Springfield, 1908.

Staiger, C. Bruce, "Abolitionism and the Presbyterian Schism of 1837–1838," *Mississippi Valley Historical Review*, XXXVI (1949), pp. 391–414.

Sweet, W. W., *The Story of Religions in America*, New York, 1930.

The United States Army Chaplaincy (War Department Pamphlet 16–1), Washington, 1946.

Tyler, L. G. (ed.), *Encyclopedia of Virginia Biography*, New York, 1915.

Warren, Louis A., "The War Headquarters of Lincoln," *Lincoln Lore* No. 998, May 24, 1948.

Zucker, A. E. (ed.), *The Forty-Eighters*, New York, 1950.

B. Jewish

Adler, Cyrus, and A. M. Margalith, *With Firmness in the Right: American Diplomatic Action Affecting Jews, 1840–1945*, New York, 1946.

Adler, Selig, "Zebulon B. Vance and the 'Scattered Nation,' " in *Journal of Southern History*, VII (1941), pp. 357–77.

Altfeld, E. Milton, *The Jews' Struggle for Religious and Civil Liberty in Maryland*, Baltimore, 1924.

Annals of Ramah Lodge No. 33, Independent Order of B'nai B'rith, Chicago, 1929.

Baron, Salo W., and Jeanette, M., *Palestinian Messengers in America, 1849–79,* (reprinted from *Jewish Social Studies,* V, pp. 115–62, 225–92), New York, 1943.

Brickner, Barnett R., *The Jews of Cincinnati* (unpublished doctoral thesis), Cincinnati, 1938.

David Einhorn Memorial Volume, New York, 1911.

Davis, Edward, *The History of Rodeph Shalom Congregation, Philadelphia, 1802–1926,* Philadelphia, 1926.

Elzas, Barnett A., *The Jews of South Carolina,* Philadelphia, 1905.

Engelman, U. Z., "Jewish Statistics in the U. S. Census of Religious Bodies (1850–1936), *Jewish Social Studies* IX (1947), pp. 127–74.

Ezekiel, H. T., and Gaston Lichtenstein, *The History of the Jews of Richmond From 1769 to 1917,* Richmond, 1917.

Felsenthal, Emma, *Bernhard Felsenthal, Teacher in Israel,* New York, 1924.

Foner, Philip S., *The Jews in American History, 1654–1865,* New York, 1945.

Frankland, A. E., "Fragments of History," *American Jews' Annual 5651,* Cincinnati, 1890.

Friedenberg, Albert M., "Calendar of American Jewish Cases," *Publications of the American Jewish Historical Society,* No. 12 (1904), pp. 87–99.

Friedman, Lee M., *Jewish Pioneers and Patriots,* Philadelphia, 1942.

Goldberg, Isaac, *Major Noah, American Jewish Pioneer,* Philadelphia, 1936.

Goldstein, Israel, *A Century of Judaism in New York,* New York, 1930.

Goodman, Abram V., *American Overture,* Philadelphia, 1947.

Grinstein, Hyman B., *The Rise of the Jewish Community of New York, 1654–1860,* Philadelphia, 1945.

Heller, James G., *As Yesterday When It Is Past,* Cincinnati, 1942.

Heller, Max, *Jubilee Souvenir of Temple Sinai, 1872–1922,* New Orleans, 1922.

Hennig, Helen Kohn, *The Tree of Life, Fifty Years of Congregational Life at the Tree of Life Synagogue,* Columbia, 1945.

Hertz, Emanuel, "An Intimate Friend of Lincoln," *American Hebrew,* July 8, 1927.

Hertz, Richard C., *The Rabbi Yesterday and Today,* Glencoe, 1943.

Hühner, Leon, *Judah Touro,* Philadelphia, 1946.

———, "The Struggle for Religious Liberty in North Carolina, with Special Reference to the Jews," *Publications of the American Jewish Historical Society,* No. 16 (1907), pp. 37–71.

Isaacs, Myer S., "A Jewish Army Chaplain," *Publications of the American Jewish Historical Society,* No. 12 (1904), pp. 127–37.

The Jewish Encyclopedia, 12 vols., New York, 1901–5.

Keneseth Israel 90th Anniversary Booklet, Philadelphia, 1937.

Kohler, Max J., "Judah P. Benjamin: Statesman and Jurist," *Publications of the American Jewish Historical Society,* No. 12 (1904), pp. 63–85.

———, "The Board of Delegates of American Israelites 1859–1878," *Publications of the American Jewish Historical Society,* No. 29 (1925), pp. 75–135.

———, "The Jews and the American Anti-Slavery Movement," *Publications of the American Jewish Historical Society,* No. 5 (1897), pp. 137–55.

Korn, Bertram W., "Isaac Mayer Wise on The Civil War," *Hebrew Union College Annual,* XX (1947), pp. 635–58.

———, "Judah P. Benjamin as a Jew," *Publications of the American Jewish Historical Society,* No. 38 (1949), pp. 153–71.

Lebeson, Anita, L., *Jewish Pioneers in America,* New York, 1931.

Leigh, Mrs. T. R., "The Jews in the Confederacy," *Southern Historical Society Papers,* XXXIX (1914), pp. 177–80.

Lilienthal, Sophia, *The Lilienthal Family Record,* San Francisco, 1930.

Linfield, A. S., "Statistics of Jews and Jewish Organizations in the United States," *American Jewish Year Book,* XL (1938–9), pp. 61–82.

BIBLIOGRAPHY

Marcovitch, Anne, "A History of Temple Beth El," in *Temple Beth El 80th Anniversary Booklet*, Knoxville, 1947.

Marcus, Jacob R., *The Americanization of Isaac Mayer Wise*, Cincinnati, 1931.

———, "Light on Early Connecticut Jewry," *American Jewish Archives*, Vol. I, No. 2 (1949), pp. 3–37.

Markens, Isaac, "Lincoln and the Jews," *Publications of the American Jewish Historical Society*, No. 17 (1909), pp. 109–65.

May, Max B., *Isaac Mayer Wise*, New York, 1916.

Meites, Hyman L. (ed.), *History of the Jews of Chicago*, Chicago, 1924.

Mielziner, E. M. F., *Moses Mielziner, 1823–1903*, New York, 1931.

Miller, Julia, *Jews Connected with the History of Pittsburgh, 1749–1865* (unpublished master's thesis), Pittsburgh, 1930.

Moise, L. C., *Biography of Isaac Harby*, Columbia, 1931.

Philipson, David, and Louis Grossman, *Isaac Mayer Wise, Life and Selected Writings*, Cincinnati, 1900.

Philipson, David, *The Reform Movement in Judaism*, New York, 1931.

Pollak, Gustav, *Michael Heilprin and His Sons*, New York, 1912.

Rabinowitz, Benjamin, "The Young Men's Hebrew Associations (1854–1913)," *Publications of the American Jewish Historical Society*, No. 37 (1947), pp. 221–326.

Rubenstein, Charles A., *History of Har Sinai Congregation of the City of Baltimore*, Baltimore, 1918.

Schappes, Morris U., "Anti-Semitism and Reaction, 1795–1800," *Publications of the American Jewish Historical Society*, No. 38 (1948), Pt. 2, pp. 109–37.

———, *A Documentary History of the Jews in the United States*, New York, 1950.

Shankman, Sam, *The Peres Family*, Kingsport, 1938.

Snyder, Herman E., *History of Temple Brith Sholom*, Springfield, 1935.

Stern, Myer, *The Rise and Progress of Reform Judaism Embracing a History Made From the Official Records of Temple Emanu-El of New York*, New York, 1895.

Tarshish, Allan, *The Rise of American Judaism* (unpublished doctoral thesis), Cincinnati, 1938.

Trachtenberg, Joshua, *Consider the Days*, Easton, 1944.

The Universal Jewish Encyclopedia, 10 vols., New York, 1939–43.

Vaxer, M., "Haym M. Solomon Frees His Slave," *Publications of the American Jewish Historical Society*, No. 37 (1947), pp. 447–8.

Wax, James A., *History of the United Hebrew Congregation, St. Louis* (unpublished manuscript), St. Louis, 1942.

———, "Isidor Bush, American Patriot and Abolitionist," *Historia Judaica*, V (1943), pp. 183–203.

———, *The Jews of Memphis, 1860–1865*. (Reprinted from *The West Tennessee Historical Society Papers*, No. III), Memphis, 1949.

Wise, Isaac M., *Reminiscences*, Cincinnati, 1901.

Woldman, Albert A., "Lincoln's Jewish Friend," *B'nai B'rith National Jewish Monthly*, February, 1937.

Wolf, Simon, *The American Jew as Patriot, Soldier and Citizen*, Philadelphia, 1895.

ACKNOWLEDGMENTS

To PROFESSOR JACOB R. MARCUS, teacher and friend, who spent almost as much time with *American Jewry and the Civil War* as the writer did; whose understanding and instinct were of constant help in ferreting out facts and obscure sources; whose own rich collection of unique documents and manuscripts, assembled over a long period of years, was full of surprises and interesting verifications; whose patience was taxed many times and whose hours were frequently occupied by long discussions far into the night. Dr. Marcus was in many ways the reason for the writing of this study originally as a doctoral dissertation at Hebrew Union College. To him goes my profound and affectionate gratitude.

To the librarians and library staffs of the Hebrew Union College, Jewish Theological Seminary, Dropsie College, and the University of Cincinnati; to Dr. Joshua Bloch of the Jewish Division of the N.Y. Public Library, and Messrs. Solon Buck and St. George L. Sioussat of the Manuscript Division of the Library of Congress; and the officers and directors of many libraries and historical societies throughout the country, who answered my inquiries and requests promptly and efficiently. To Miss Elizabeth B. Drewry of the War Records Division of the National Archives, Rabbi Isidore S. Meyer, Librarian of the American Jewish Historical Society, Dr. Roy P. Basler and Mrs. Marian Bonzi of the Abraham Lincoln Association, and Dr. J. Monaghan of the Illinois State Historical Library, for many courtesies beyond the line of duty.

To hundreds of persons all over America who took the time to answer letters and the risk of lending material for copying, or who acted as detective agents in hunting out descendants of those who figure in this story. Especially to the following:

Rabbi Morris M. Feuerlicht of Indianapolis for material on his congregation and local persons; Mr. and Mrs. George Jacobs of Cincinnati and the Misses Jacobs of Philadelphia for the "find" of the Rev. George Jacobs scrapbook; the Rev. D. A. Jessurun Cardozo of Philadelphia for permission to search through the minute-books and correspondence files of his congregation, Mikveh Israel; Dr. Abraham A. Neuman for stories and suggestions; Dr. Julian B. Feibelman, Mr. Leonard Levy, and the Board of Trustees of Temple Sinai, New Orleans, for the opportunity to search through the Gutheim papers; Mr. Henry Jacobs and Miss Miriam Goldsmith of New Orleans for material on Mrs. Gutheim; Mrs. Clarence M. Allen and Mrs. Charles A. May of New York, and Miss Alice de Ford of Philadelphia, for data on Michael M. Allen; Mr. Edward Grusd, Editor of the *B'nai B'rith National Jewish Monthly* for many favors and especially for assistance, through the co-operation of Rabbi Herbert Hendel, in locating Mrs. Martha Sarner Levy of Bradford, Pa., who provided material on Chaplain Ferdinand Sarner; to Mrs. Bernard N. Block, Mrs. Norton L. Goldsmith, and Dr. Joseph Rauch, all of Louisville, Rabbi Stanley Brav (now of Cincinnati) and Mr. Harold G. Gotthelf of Vicksburg, Miss., for data on Chaplain Bernhard Gotthelf; to Rabbi David H. Wice, Rabbi Louis Wolsey, Mr. Arthur A. Fleisher, the Rev. Leon H. Elmaleh, all of Philadelphia, Rabbi Samuel Volkman and Mr. E. J. Goodman of Scranton, and Mrs. Oscar Rosenblum of N.Y. for help in locating Miss Frances V. Franklin, Mr. Joseph C. Frankel of N.Y., and Mrs. Pearl E. Whitely of Philadelphia, descendants of Chaplain Jacob Frankel; Mrs. William H. Fineshriber of Philadelphia for a story of Paducah days; Mr. Jeremy Newman, Rabbi Louis I. Newman, and Mr. Edmond Uhry for the Eckstein papers; Dr. Jacob Lestchinsky and Dr. H.S. Linfield for data on Jewish population statistics; to Mr. Morris U. Schappes of N.Y. for advice on many matters; Rabbi James A. Wax of Memphis for helpful items from the Memphis papers and much interest; to Mrs. David Lefkowitz, Jr., of Shreveport for valuable suggestions; Messrs. Ray A. Billington, Otto Eisenschiml, Ralph G. Newman, Alexander J. Isaacs, Joseph Eisendrath, Jr., Paul M. Angle, Harry Hershenson, and the late, great Lloyd Lewis, all of Chicago, for courteous answers to inquiries and helpful suggestions; Mrs. Lloyd Lewis for the file on the Grant affair assembled by her husband before his passing; Professor Ella Lonn of Goucher College for sound advice; Dr. Lee M. Friedman of Boston, President of the American Jewish Historical Society, for many suggestions and more than a few important items; Dr. Benjamin P. Thomas, of Springfield, Professor Selig Adler of the University of Buffalo, Dr. David R. Barbee of Washington, and Mr. Albert A. Woldman of Cleveland, for clarification of, and advice on, certain aspects of this study; Miss Julia I. Felsenthal of Chicago for active support in hunting down obscure material; Mr. Louis Broido and Mr. Frank L. Weil of N.Y. for a very special favor; Mr. Leon J. Obermayer of Philadelphia for another very helpful favor; Mr. Benjamin Barondess of N.Y. for an exciting discussion on Wise and Lincoln; Mr. Max Grossmayer of Long Beach, Calif., for the interesting data on his father's patriotic activities; Mrs. Marx M. Levy of Shreveport for helpful data about her grandfather, the Rev. M. Wurzel; Dr. David de Sola Pool of N.Y. for answers to many inquiries; Mr. Morton A. Barker of Springfield, Ill., for help in connection with the records of the National Lincoln Monument Association; Rabbis Milton Greenwald of Evansville, Herman E. Snyder of Springfield, Julius Mark of N.Y., and Joseph I. Weiss of Columbus, and many other colleagues for time and effort; Mr. Albert Friedlander and other students at Hebrew Union College who, in and out of class, offered their services and assistance in various ways.

To Mildred and Abel Fagen of Glencoe who offered the hospitality of "Dream Farm" for the writing of this book; to Mrs. Sylvia Dunsker, Mrs. Martha Beerman, Mrs. Martha Blackman, Miss Ethel Silverstein, Miss Eleanor R. Schwartz, and Mr. Ted Levy for technical assistance. To Miss Rita E. Rosenfeld and Dr. Maurice Jacobs for invaluable help with proofreading; to Dr. Solomon Grayzel and Mr. Lesser Zussman of The Jewish Publication Society for help in varied problems of publication; and to Mrs. Margaret Bailey Tinkcom, a superb indexer.

And, finally, to the Hebrew Union College and the late Rev. Dr. David Philipson, for enabling me to engage in historical research for two years as the first Ella H. Philipson Fellow in American Jewish History.

INDEX

Abolitionists: anti-Semitism among, 249 *n* 48, 250 *n* 66; criticized by "Judaeus," 249 *n* 50; held responsible for Civil War, 25, 26; Jewish, 16, 20, 22; Lyon criticizes, 251 *n* 76; Morais on, 35; opposed by Raphall, 17

Abrahams, Simon, 114

Acculturation, 218

Adams, Charles Francis, 169

Adath Israel Congregation, Louisville, 82

Adjunta, Mikveh Israel, 38

Adler, Adolphus H., 185, 293 *n* 171

Adler, Liebman, 35, 299 *n* 63

Adler, Samuel, 73, 207, 211

Adler, Selig, 273 *n* 23

Affelder, Jacob, 102

Ahavas Chesed Congregation, New York, 241

"Alert," Philadelphia, 103

Aliens: Confederacy suspicious of, 176, 289 *n* 123; Massachusetts restricts privileges of, 206

Allemania Club, Cincinnati, 103, 269 *n* 95

Allen, Michael, chaplain, 5th Pa. Cavalry, 58–62, 65, 262 *n* 73

Alton, Ill., 215

American Jewish Publication Society, 6

American Society for Ameliorating the Conditions of the Jews, 246 *ns* 14 and 27

American Society for Promoting National Unity, 247 *n* 19

Americanization, 4–5; Civil War accelerates, 217

Anderath El Congregation, New York, 241

Anderson, Major Robert, 34

Anshe Chesed Congregation, Cleveland, 86, 87

Anshe Chesed Congregation, Vicksburg, 82

Anshi Chesed Congregation, New York, 241; and Board of Delegates, 260 *n* 62; Mielziner rabbi of, 19; Sarner and, 85; war relief contributions of, 103

Anti-Semitism: in abolitionist press, 249 *n* 48; in army, 153–55; during Civil War, 156–88, 218–19; in colonial era, 156; in Confederacy, 175–87; 290 *n* 132; fear of, 13, 81; among Federalists, 156–57; Jewish press fights, 173–75; in newspapers, 159–63, 171, 173, 174, 183–84, 185; Sherman guilty of, 147–50; in Union, 158–75; was Grant guilty of, 143–46. *See also* Prejudice.

Archives Israelites, on Sarner, 85

Army, Confederate: anti-Semitism in, 176–77; chaplains in, 57, 256 *n* 3; German Artillery of Macon, Ga., 109; Jewish companies in, 119; Jewish regiments proposed, 293–94 *n* 173

Army, U. S.: Jewish companies in, 116–19, 269 *n* 95; number of Jews in, 56, 119, 271 *n* 12; sketches of military life, 88. *See also under* names of regiments.

Asbury, Henry, 190, 192, 193, 295 *n* 11

Asheim, W., 240

Asmonean, the, 246 *n* 14, 251 *n* 76

Auerbach, Henry M., 88

Badeau, Adam, 133

Baer, M., 52

Baker, Lafayette C., 169–70

Ballin, J., 240

Baltimore, Md.: Har Sinai Congregation, 8, 22; Jewish community in, 1860, 1; Reform in, 11; secessionist riots in, 21–22

Baltimore Association for the Educational and Moral Improvement of the Colored People, 251 *n* 71

Bancroft, George, 242

Bangor, Maine, 66

Banks, Nathaniel P., 195; advocates negotiated peace with Confederacy, 196–98, 234; Illowy and, 170–71; relations with Zacharie, 195–202; Zacharie on, 229–31, 233

Baptist College Hospital, Washington, 96

Barnhart, Lazarus, 159

INDEX

Bushnell, Mr., 192
Butler, Benjamin F., 159; anti-Semitism of, 102, 164–66; attacks Benjamin, 159; governor of New Orleans, 196, 229, 230; and Myer S. Isaacs, 164, 172, 173, 286 *n* 68; for President, 286 *n* 70; profiteer, 287 *n* 77; and Wolf, 165, 173

California, newspapers condemn bigotry, 171-72
Cameron, Simon, rejects Fischel's application for commission as chaplain, 62, 67
Cameron's Dragoons. *See* Cavalry, 5th Pennsylvania.
Carlin, W. H., 224
Catholics: chaplains with Union Army, 56; propaganda against, 157
Cavalry, 5th Pennsylvania, 64; Michael Allen chaplain of, 58–62, 65
Central Conference of American Rabbis, 7
Ceres Union, 214, 241
Chalfin, S. F., 299 *n* 62
Chaplains: character of, 60–61; civilian, in Potomac area, 68, 74–75; Confederate, 57, 256 *n* 3; controversy over Jewish, 56–97, 203, 218; duties described, 60; first commissioned, 56; Fischel's advice to Jewish, 75; hospital and regimental, 77, 78–80; of minority faiths, 256–57 *n* 7; non-clergymen serve as, 60–61; Russell on Jewish, 258 *n* 34
Charitable associations, war work of, 107–8
Charities: contributions to, 266 *n* 29; federation of, 4; foster homes organized, 4; societies organized for, 3–4. *See also* Beneficial Associations; Hospitals; Sanitary Commission.
Charleston, S. C.: Congregation Beth Elohim, 45–46, 52, 53, 252 *n* 77, 256 *n* 93; Congregation Shearith Israel, 52, 53; congregations in, 3; Englishman on Jews in, 180; "Free Market," 99; Jewish community asks aid, 112; Lincoln memorial services, 300 *n* 75; Reform in, 11
Chase, Salmon P., 162, 197
Chebra Anshe Emuno, 241
Chicago, Ill.: B'nai Sholem Congregation, 215; Jewish company raised in, 118–19; Jews in, 1860, 1; KAM Congregation, 204, 215; Lincoln memorial services in, 214; Sinai Temple, 23; Zion Congregation, 23
Children, foster homes for, 4

Chilton, Congressman, 178
Cincinnati, Ohio: Jewish community in, 1860, 1; Jewish hospital in, 4; Sanitary Fair in, 103; Talmud Yelodim Institute, 42; trade with Confederacy, 162; war relief work in, 108
Cincinnati Relief Union, 99
Civil rights: American Jewry fights for, 14; chaplaincy controversy, 56, 63–64, 68, 72, 218; denied traders in Memphis, 1862, 151; Lincoln administration and, 128; minorities and, 19, 21, 27
Clark, Senator, 127
Clay, Henry, 194, 230
Clergymen, Lincoln on, 250 *n* 56
Cleveland, Ohio: Anshe Chesed Congregation, 86, 87; Jews in, 1860, 1; rabbinical conference in, 9
Cobb, Sylvanus, 252 *n* 76
Cobb, Thomas R. R., 177, 290 *n* 129
Cohen, A. S., 205
Cohen, G. M., 87
Cohen, Mrs. Henry M., 101, 102
Cohen, Jacob A., 28
Cohen, Jacob C., 271 *n* 12
Cohen, Jacob S., 199
Cohen, Josiah, 102, 214; and anti-Jewish prejudice, 173–74; supports Republican Party, 1868, 136
Cohen, LeRoy R., 264 *n* 112
Cohen, S., 112
Cohn, Elkan, 207, 213
Columbia, S. C.: burning of, 53; Jewish community asks aid, 112; Tree of Life Synagogue, 53
Columbus, Ga., B'nai Israel Congregation, 49
Columbus, Iowa, 66
Concordia Club, Chicago, helps raise Jewish company, 118
Concordia Guards, 118–19
Confederacy, the: anti-Semitism in, 159, 175–87, 290 *n* 132; economy of, 181–82; Gutheim supports, 47–50; hostility to aliens, 176, 289 *n* 123; illegal trade with, 121–22, 147, 155; Jacobs supports, 52–55; Northern Jews accused of supporting, 159–60, 162–63; loans to, 160; proposal for negotiating peace with, 196–98; rabbinical support for, 29, 47–51, 52–55; Wise defends, 26, 40. *See also* South, the.
Confirmation ceremony, 11
Congregation Brith Kodesh, Rochester, war relief work done by, 104

317

INDEX

Jonas, Charles H., 194, 296 *n* 15

Jonas, Joseph, 189

Jones, Alfred T.: on Allen, 60; eulogizes Lincoln, 207, 210

Jones, John Beauchamp, anti-Semitism of, 178–79, 184, 292–93 *n* 167

Josephi, Henry, 241

Josephs, Mr., 290 *n* 126

"Joshua," 116

Judaeophobia. *See* Anti-Semitism.

"Judaeus," 249 *n* 50

Judaism: adaptability of, 87–88; denial of, by soldiers, 96; development of American, 8; in matters of state, 301 *n* 78

Kahl Montgomery Congregation, Montgomery, invites Gutheim to pulpit, 49, 50

Kakeles, Seligman, 16

Kalisch, Isidore, 169, 262 *n* 80; applies for chaplain's commission, 81–82

KAM Congregation, Chicago, 204, 215

Kaufmann, Sigismund, 203

Kayton, Barney, 93

Kaskel, Cesar, protests General Order No. 11, 124–25, 128, 142, 144

Kaskel, J. W., 124

Kellogg, William, 270 *n* 6

Keneseth Israel, Philadelphia: contributes to Lincoln memorial, 215; Einhorn invited to, 22; Gotthelf in, 82

Kind, Leopold, 66

Kleinfeld, S. H., 263 *n* 101

Know-Nothing Party, 118, 157; aids Wilson, 168; Brownlow aids, 166; Jews and, 274 *n* 41; Lincoln and, 192, 205–6, 226–27

Knoxville, Tenn., Hebrew Benevolent Association, 109

Koch, Mr., 240

Kohn, Abraham, 118, 214, 299 *ns* 63 and 64; Lincoln and, 204–5, 294 *n* 1

Körner, Gustav, 190, 193

Kramer, Mr., 241

Kriegshaber, William, 83

Kuhn, George, 109

Kuhn, Herman, 265 *n* 116

Kursheedt, Edwin, 90

Ladies' Confederate Memorial Association, New Orleans, 50

Ladies' Hebrew Association for the Relief of Sick and Wounded Soldiers, Philadelphia, 100–2

LaPorte, Ind., 215

Lazrus, Moses, 104

Leary, C. L., 66

Lee, Robert E., 264 *n* 112; letter to Michelbacher, 94, 95

Leeser, Isaac, 55; aids Fischel, 68; Allen pupil of, 58; answers American Society's propaganda, 246 *n* 27; asks aid for Southern Jewry, 112; attacked as secessionist, 46–47; calls for congregational union, 9, 12, 219; chaplaincy controversy, 63; commends Frankel's work, 78; comments on anti-Semitism in South, 292 *n* 152; defends Board of Delegates, 259 *n* 55; on denial of Judaism by soldiers, 96; denounces Jewish smugglers, 152; on General Order No. 11, 132; on Gutheim's exile, 48, 50; hostility to Wise, 10; on Jews in politics, 24, 44, 274 *n* 41; on lack of support for Fischel, 260 *n* 63; Lincoln memorial sermon, 207, 210, 215; maintains neutrality toward war, 44–45; notes fear of anti-Semitism, 81; *Philadelphia Enquirer* and, 129; protests prejudice, 175; Raphall and, 249 *n* 53; resolutions on, Congregation Beth Elohim, 45–46; reviews *The Rebecca*, 86; secretary, Board of Ministers, 77; speaks for Traditionalism, 9, 11; urges appointment of hospital chaplains, 80; visits postwar Richmond, 112; work of, 6

Leon, L., 264–65 *n* 112

Lestchinsky, Jacob, 245 *n* 1

Levi, Jacob, edits *The Rebecca*, 86

Levin, Lewis C., 274 *n* 41

Levy, Mrs. Comodore, 266 *n* 11

Levy, Isaac, 281 *n* 88

Levy, C. M., 108, 298–90 *n* 62

Levy, Isaac J., 92

Levy, Leonard, 255 *n* 69

Levy, Mrs. Martha Sarner, 84

Levy, Miriam E., 264 *n* 110

Levy, Myer, 93

Levy, Uriah P., 158

Lewin, Julius, 256 *n* 3

Lewis, Lloyd, 278 *n* 65

Lewis, Mrs. Lloyd, 277 *n* 63

Lewis, Samuel A., 199, 297 *n* 41

Libraries, German language, for hospitals, 83

Lieber, Francis, 19

Lieberman, L. J., 38

Light, S., 117

Light Infantry Blues, Richmond, 119

Lilienthal, Max: Allen pupil of, 58; attitude toward South, 213; on Booth, 212; favors Union cause, 35; and General

INDEX

Smugglers: in Dept. of Tennessee, 152–53, 282–83 *n* 95; Jews numbered among, 168; Navy policy on, 286 *n* 68; newspapers on, 162–63; Sherman on, 187

Society of Concord Congregation, Syracuse, 86; volunteer to recruit a company, 117

Solomon, Edward S., 118, 145

Solomons, Adolphus S., 124, 203

South, the: attitude of Jews toward, 302 *n* 111; Leeser visits postwar, 45; Lincoln memorial services in, 300 *n* 75; Morais' attitude toward, 35, 36; rabbis on, 212–213. *See also* Confederacy.

Southern Historical Society, 50

Speculation: in cotton, 121–22, 147, 155, 282–83 *n* 95; in gold, 161; Zacharie charged with, 231

Speculators: in cotton, 270 *n* 8, 271 *n* 12; Jews attacked as, 179–80, 181, 186, 294 *n* 175; Ross on, 283 *n* 103

Speeches, on Civil War, list of printed, 220–21

Spiegel, Marcus M., 271 *n* 12

Springfield, Ill.: Jews in, 295 *n* 7; press defends Jews, 172

Stanton, Edwin M., 170, 194, 270 *n* 8, 278 *n* 67

Starbuck, C. W., 99

Stark, James, 191, 224

Steele, Frederick, 282 *n* 95

Stettheimer, S., 104

Stoddard, W. O., 61

Straus, Isidor, 183

Straus, Lazarus, 183, 292 *n* 157

Strauss, Moses, 126

Stuyvesant, Peter, 1, 156

Sullivan, Mr., 223

Sulzberger, J., 240

Sumner, Senator, 127

Sunday schools, 5

Synagogues: educational functions of, 3, 5; perpetuate local traditions, 12; place of, 3; special services in, 34

Syracuse, N. Y., 32; Jewish company raised in, 117–18; Society of Concord Congregation, 86

Szold, Benjamin, 94; and Baltimore Association, 251 *n* 71; and execution of Kuhn, 109

Talbotton, Ga., merchants denounced in, 179, 183, 292 *n* 157

Talmud Yelodim Institute, Cincinnati, 42

Tarshish, Allan, 245 *n* 1

Taussig, Charles, 283 *n* 95

Taussig, Ansel and Co., 283 *n* 95

Taylor, Zachary, 190

Temimi Derech Congregation, New Orleans, 210

Temple Emanu-El, New York City, 11; Major Anderson attends, 34; contributions to Jews' Hospital, 106; Gottheil rabbi of, 19; Gutheim rabbi of, 50; war relief contributions of, 103

Temple Sinai, New Orleans, Gutheim rabbi of, 50

Tennessee: anti-Confederate forces in, 167; and Grant's election, 1868, 275 *n* 47

Tennessee, Dept. of, expulsion of Jews from, 1862, 122–55; illegal trade in, 282–83 *n* 95

Textbooks, 5

Thirteenth Ohio Volunteers, 88

Thirty-Ninth Illinois Volunteers, 92

Thomasville, Ga., merchants denounced in, 179

Thoroughman, Mr., 193

Tickner & Co., 154

Ticknor, Dr. and Mrs. F. O., 99–100

Touro, Judah, 5; frees slaves, 16; gift to Jews' Hospital, 105

Trade: with Confederacy, 121–22, 147, 155; in New Orleans, 1863, 231, 233

Traditionalism, in American Jewry, 9, 10, 11–12

Treasury, U. S., agents engage in illegal trade, 122

Tree of Life Congregation, Columbia, S. C., 53

Turlu, Charles H., 139

Tuska, Simon, 18, 152, 214, 281 *n* 89

Twenty-third Ohio Volunteers, 90

Tyler, Daniel, 94

Tyng, Rev. Dr., 242

Uhry, Edmond, 276 *n* 54

Uniforms, *New York Times* on quality of, 106

Union, the, rabbis support, 35–39, 51. *See also* North, the.

Union of American Hebrew Congregations, 7, 219

Union League, Philadelphia, Morais and, 38, 253 *n* 26

Union League Association, Richmond, 134

United Hebrew Beneficial Society, 59